Archeology of the Mammoth Cave Area

STUDIES IN ARCHEOLOGY

Consulting Editor: Stuart Struever

Department of Anthropology
Northwestern University
Evanston, Illinois

Charles R. McGimsey III. **Public Archeology**

Lewis R. Binford. **An Archaeological Perspective**

Muriel Porter Weaver. **The Aztecs, Maya, and Their Predecessors:
Archaeology of Mesoamerica**

Joseph W. Michels. **Dating Methods in Archaeology**

G. Garth Sampson. **The Stone Age Archaeology of Southern Africa**

Fred T. Plog. **The Study of Prehistoric Change**

Patty Jo Watson. **Archeology of the Mammoth Cave Area**

Archeology of the Mammoth Cave Area

Edited by PATTY JO WATSON

Department of Anthropology
Washington University
St. Louis, Missouri

ACADEMIC PRESS   New York and London
A Subsidiary of Harcourt Brace Jovanovich, Publishers

ACADEMIC PRESS, INC.
111 Fifth Avenue, New York, New York 10003

United Kingdom Edition published by
ACADEMIC PRESS, INC. (LONDON) LTD.
24/28 Oval Road, London NW1

Library of Congress Cataloging in Publication Data

Watson, Patty Jo, Date
    Archeology of the Mammoth Cave area.

    (Studies in archeology)
    Continues the editor's The prehistory of Salts Cave,
Kentucky.
    Bibliography: p.
    1.   Salts Cave, Ky.   2.   Indians of North America—
Kentucky—Antiquities.   3.   Mammoth Cave National Park
—Antiquities.   4.   Kentucky—Antiquities.   I.   Title.
E78.K3W37   917.69′754′034   73-19967
ISBN 0—12—785927—6

In Memoriam

LOUISE W. STORTS

Member, Cave Research Foundation
and
enthusiastic participant in
the Salts Cave Archeological Project

JOSEPH R. CALDWELL

Colleague and friend,
whose generous advice and support
were crucial to the initiation of
the work described in this book

Contents

List of Contributors

VAUGHN M. BRYANT, Jr., Department of Sociology and Anthropology, Texas A & M University, College Station, Texas

LATHEL F. DUFFIELD, Department of Anthropology, University of Kentucky, Lexington, Kentucky

ELIZABETH M. DUSSEAU, Department of Epidemiology, School of Public Health, University of Michigan, Ann Arbor, Michigan

GARY F. FRY, Department of Sociology and Anthropology, Youngstown State University, Youngstown, Ohio

MARY ELIZABETH KING, The Museum, Texas Tech University, Lubbock, Texas

WILLIAM H. MARQUARDT, Department of Anthropology, Washington University, St. Louis, Missouri

STEPHEN MOLNAR, Department of Anthropology, Washington University, St. Louis, Missouri

RICHARD J. PORTER, Department of Epidemiology, School of Public Health, University of Michigan, Ann Arbor, Michigan

LOUISE M. ROBBINS, Department of Anthropology, Mississippi State University, State College, Mississippi

JAMES SCHOENWETTER, Department of Anthropology, Arizona State University, Tempe, Arizona

DAVID H. STANSBERY, Director, Museum of Zoology, Ohio State University, Columbus, Ohio

ROBERT B. STEWART, Department of Anthropology, Sam Houston State University, Huntsville, Texas

STEVEN WARD, Department of Anthropology, Washington University, St. Louis, Missouri

PATTY JO WATSON, Department of Anthropology, Washington University, St. Louis, Missouri

RICHARD A. YARNELL, Department of Anthropology, University of North Carolina, Chapel Hill, North Carolina

Photo Credits

Preface

Since August 1963, the Cave Research Foundation has sponsored archeological work in some of the large caves in the Flint Mammoth Cave system within Mammoth Cave National Park, Kentucky (see Figure 1), particularly in Salts Cave (Watson *et al.* 1969) and—more recently—in Mammoth Cave, Lee Cave, and Bluff Cave (see Figure 2). The initial work in Salts Cave was described in 1969; the present volume is an account of the investigations and analyses carried out since then, many of which have been financed by National Geographic Society Research Grants. This book is thus a sequel to the earlier account of *The Prehistory of Salts Cave, Kentucky*, and as such does not repeat the general background information presented there (Watson *et al.* 1969: 1–5).

Our work in the caves has two major purposes. One of these is highly specialized: We want to describe and to explain the aboriginal utilization of portions of the world's largest cave system[1] (Figures 3.1, 10.1, and 23.1). The prehistoric use of these great caves—an unusual if not unique culture historical phenomenon—is of considerable intrinsic interest.

The second aim is somewhat more general: We will use the well-preserved material from the cave interiors (especially the abundant remains of desiccated human paleofecal matter) to document prehistoric diet in this place and time. Details of prehistoric subsistence patterns are usually considered significant by archeologists, and the chronological period represented by the remains in the Flint Mammoth Cave system is an especially important one in the regional sequence. The time span in question—the last two millenia B.C.—is that when plant cultivation was beginning in this part of the New World, and the botanical material from the caves reflects this transitional economic phase. Hence much of the analysis reported in this book is botanical, or more precisely, paleoethnobotanical. By means of these analyses, we hope to gather data bearing on the development of horticulture in this region that may help answer some of the important questions anthropologists and historians pose about the origin of food production and its role in cultural evolution. More specifically, we want to know what sort of local economy gave rise to horticulture and whether it developed essentially indigenously or was a result of ideas (and seeds) ultimately derived from Mesoamerica. Fuller discussion of these matters is provided in Part VI.

---

[1] In September, 1972, Cave Research Foundation mapping and exploring parties succeeded in connecting remote passages of Floyd Collins Crystal Cave (which joins Salts Cave in the Flint Ridge Cave System) with those of Mammoth Cave, thus integrating the two large cave systems into one—the Flint Mammoth Cave System—with a total of more than 145 mapped miles of passage. So far as we now know, the low-lying, tortuous passages joining the two ridges were never entered by prehistoric people.

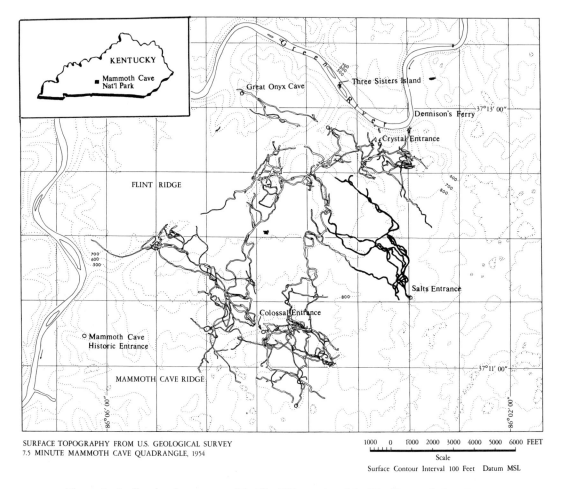

SURFACE TOPOGRAPHY FROM U.S. GEOLOGICAL SURVEY
7.5 MINUTE MAMMOTH CAVE QUADRANGLE, 1954

1000   0   1000   2000   3000   4000   5000   6000 FEET

Scale

Surface Contour Interval 100 Feet   Datum MSL

Figure 1   Small-scale reference map of the Flint Ridge section of the Flint Mammoth Cave System.

Aboriginal use patterns in the caves consist predominantly of evidence for mining of large quantities of sulfate minerals from the cavern walls and ceiling. These minerals are gypsum ($CaSO_4 \cdot 2H_2O$) and mirabilite ($Na_2SO_4 \cdot 10H_2O$) for the most part, although some epsomite ($MgSO_4 \cdot 7H_2O$) is also present at least in Lower Salts Cave. Gypsum may have been made into paint or plaster; it is also possible that the crystals and powder were thought to possess supernatural qualities. In any case, so much gypsum was removed from Salts and Mammoth Caves that it was probably traded beyond the immediate vicinity. Mirabilite and epsomite are both cathartic salts. In addition, mirabilite tastes salty and can be used—in moderation—as a seasoning (Watson *et al.* 1969: 57–58).

The aborigines also explored the deep cave interiors, probably in search of further mineral deposits but perhaps partially for amusement or sport.

Illumination, and, hence, activity within the

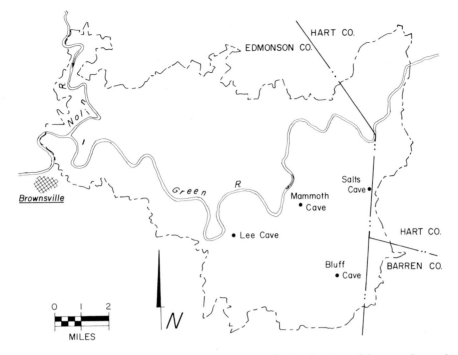

Figure 2 Mammoth Cave National Park, Kentucky. Map showing locations of the caves discussed in this volume.

caves, was made possible by the use of cane and weed stalk torches; charred and broken remains of these torches litter floors everywhere throughout the main passageways. In both Salts and Mammoth Caves, a few Indians penetrated remote, narrow, twisting complexes of canyons and crawlways more than a mile from the entrance and at levels 200 or more feet below the upper passages.

Two aboriginal bodies ("mummies") have been found in Salts and Mammoth Caves, respectively. Both finds were made long before the present project began (see Meloy 1971, and Meloy and Watson in Watson *et al.* 1969: 65–69), but analysis of the Salts Cave mummy was made under the project auspices and both desiccated cadavers have been described in print (Neumann

1938, Robbins 1971, and see pages 137–161 of this volume).

Our initial investigations in Mammoth Cave National Park were confined wholly to the interior of Salts Cave in Flint Ridge where observation, recording, and collection of aboriginal cultural debris as well as some limited excavations were carried out.

Beginning in April, 1969, field work was expanded to include excavation in Salts Cave Vestibule, a search for and testing of possible surface sites near Salts Sink, and recording of prehistoric remains in other caves within the Park (Mammoth Cave in Mammoth Cave Ridge, Lee Cave and Bluff Cave in Joppa Ridge). Two trips into Wyandotte Cave in southern Indiana were made to compare possible aboriginal materials there with those in Mammoth Cave National Park and to collect radiocarbon samples. Finally, visits were made to three museums that house material from Mammoth Cave National Park.

Other research outside Mammoth Cave National Park included quantitative analysis of a series of human paleofecal specimens from Mammoth Cave and Upper Salts Cave, pollen and parasitological analyses of several paleofecal specimens, analysis of charred plant material recovered by flotation of sediments excavated in Salts Vestibule, study of textile fragments recovered from Upper Salts Cave, and some further research into the recent history of Salts Cave.

Acknowledgments

A long-term study such as the one described in this book necessarily owes a great deal to the good will and cooperation of many people. Since 1969, much of our work has been subsidized by National Geographic Society research grants, for which we heartily thank Leonard Carmichael and the Committee for Research and Exploration.

We are deeply grateful to Cave Research Foundation President Joseph K. Davidson, (recently succeeded by Stanley D. Sides), and to the Directors, Members, and Joint Venturers of the Cave Research Foundation, whose physical facilities, cartographic services, advice, and assistance in the cave were vital to the success of our work. In addition, the Foundation kindly granted us permission to reproduce a number of their maps in this volume.

We owe a large debt of gratitude to the officials and cave guides of the National Park Service at Mammoth Cave National Park who have graciously cooperated in all phases of our investigations, particularly those in Mammoth Cave itself. Successive Superintendents Robert Bendt and Joseph Kulesza have been more than kind. We would like to thank them and Chief Naturalists Edwin Rothfuss and Leonard W. McKenzie for expediting numerous aspects of the research. We are grateful to Mr. Rothfuss for enabling us to photograph and make observations on Lost John, the Mammoth Cave mummy, and to Superintendent Kulesza for giving us permission to reproduce the 1908 Kaemper map of Mammoth Cave.

So many of the nearly 300 Joint Venturers and Members of the Cave Research Foundation have helped us over the past three years that it is not possible to name them all. Gordon L. and Judith E. Smith, managers and suppliers of the CRF base camp on Flint Ridge, were unfailing sources of help on all sorts of local matters on the surface and in the cave; Roger W. Brucker, together with Burnell F. Ehman and Thomas A. Brucker, planned and carried out the successful search for the aboriginal route to Lower Salts; Stanley D. Sides' aid in working out the recent history of Salts Cave was invaluable, as was the generous assistance of Harold Meloy in both Mammoth Cave and Wyandotte; Gary Eller, Research Coordinator, John P. Freeman, Personnel Director, and a long series of individual expedition leaders were unfailingly helpful in making sure we got to and from those cave areas we wished to see; William B. White, Chief Scientist, helped with geological and mineralogical matters; John L. Bassett, Arthur N. Palmer, Margaret V. Palmer, and Steve G. Wells consulted with us concerning the Salts Cave Vestibule sediments; Log Keeper Greer Price was enthusiastic in his support of the archeological field parties in the cave, and also obtained the identifications of raw material for many of the artifacts from Salts Cave Vestibule; John Bridge kindly provided us with his copy of the text on the Mumy Hall rock inscribed 100 years ago by J. M. Smith; Kim Dale found the Cutliff and Lee inscribed mummy rock and was a faithful and skilled excavator in Salts Vestibule, as was Theodore V. Lotz.

The CRF cartographic staff under Denver P. Burns, John P. Wilcox, and Patricia and William Crowther has been exceedingly helpful throughout the period of our work, expeditiously furnishing us maps and information for every part of the cave system of concern to us. The fine series of maps in this volume was produced by Patricia Crowther, whose patience, cheerful competence, and drafting skills are deeply appreciated.

Jacqueline F. Austin, CRF Treasurer during most of the time covered by this report, did a masterful job of husbanding our finances and keeping careful account of expenditures. (Moreover, her management of the Flint Ridge kitchen facilities, and the meals she produced there during spring break week in April, 1969, will not be forgotten by the archeological crew fortunate enough to be in residence at that time.) Dennis E. Drum, the present CRF Comptroller, is now capably keeping our books.

William R. Curtsinger, an outstanding photographer, generously lent his expertise on many occasions throughout the span of the archeological project. During the spring, 1969, field season he was joined by another skilled photographer, Robert P. Lindsley, who—in addition to other CRF Joint Venturer photographers gave us his services.

We are grateful to the late Dr. E. Robert Pohl of Horse Cave, Kentucky, and to Philip M. Smith, first president of the Cave Research Foundation, for continuing to support and advise us as they have done since the inception of the project in 1963.

Our surface work around Salts Cave was greatly facilitated by Mr. and Mrs. Marvin Sell, who at that time lived on their farm adjacent to the Park boundary and very near Salts Sink. They hospitably allowed us to use their property as a staging area when preparing to enter the cave, permitted us to excavate test pits in their fields, and freely gave us advice and help on innumerable occasions.

Dr. William R. Halliday of Seattle, Washington, generously furnished copies of manuscript material and photos pertaining to Russell Neville and his 1927 expedition into Salts Cave; Mr. Ellis Jones of Cave City, Kentucky, kindly made available to us his collection of historical materials on Mammoth Cave.

I owe special thanks to a succession of eager Washington University undergraduate and graduate students who raked large areas of forest floor around Salts Sink, aided in the documentation of aboriginal remains in Lower Salts and Lower Mammoth Caves, and complainingly but stalwartly carried a total of nearly a ton of cave sediment up the steep slopes out of the Vestibule and Salts Sink to the flotation area.

David L. Webster made the plot of Salts Vestibule and supervised excavation of the first trench there. Charles L. Redman supervised much of the excavation of Test E and initiated many insights into the nature of the Vestibule stratigraphy. Steven A. LeBlanc worked out some of the preliminary statistical manipulations for the Salts Cave paleofecal contents. We are grateful to the Computing Facility of Washington University for providing the necessary computer time for his analyses, and for the detailed study of Mammoth Cave paleofecal constituents by William H. Marquardt.

Michael E. Emrick made the final inked drawing of the Vestibule plan and section and also prepared preliminary drawings of many of the Vestibule trench profiles. Final drawings of those profiles, of the Test E plans, and of several other figures were skillfully executed by William H. Marquardt and Fred W. Fischer.

James B. Griffin and the University of Michigan Radiocarbon Laboratory very generously donated to the project—in addition to 11 determinations provided earlier—the two dates on internal tissue from Little Al(ice), the Salts Cave mummy.

We should like to thank Vorsila L. Bohrer for commenting on an earlier version of Yarnell's "Plant Food and Cultivation of the Salts Cavers." We are grateful to Elizabeth Pillaert, Curator, and William G. Reeder, Director of the Osteology Laboratory of the Zoological Museum at the University of Wisconsin, for providing work space and access to the faunal collections there.

Earle E. Latham, Soil Scientist with the Soil Conservation Service in Glasgow, Kentucky, kindly took the time to examine and discuss with us soil profiles in and around Salts Sink.

We are indebted to George F. Jackson, formerly on the staff at Wyandotte Cave, who generously gave us information and advice about it and about the 1927 Neville expedition to Salts Cave. At Wyandotte itself—now operated by the State of Indiana—we were hospitably received by the present manager, Mr. Herdis H. Conder, and ably assisted in the cave by Guides James Pease and Thomas Crecelius. Geologist Richard Powell very kindly provided us with a copy of the 1966 Wyandotte Cave map, which he was instrumental in preparing, and with geological information about the cave.

At the museums visited in search of Mammoth Cave area materials, every courtesy was extended by those in charge of the collections: J. Lawrence Angel, Clifford Evans, Lucile E. St. Hoyme, and George Metcalf in the Department of Anthropology, U.S. National Museum of Natural History, Smithsonian Institution, in Washington, D.C.; Stanley A. Freed and Richard A. Gould at the American Museum of Natural History in New York; Frederick J. Dockstader and U. Vincent Wilson at the Museum of the American Indian, Heye Foundation, in New York; Stephen Williams and Mrs. P. Shaplin at the Peabody Museum of Archaeology and Ethnology, Harvard University. At the St. Louis Museum of Science and Natural History, James Houser and Leonard Blake were very helpful.

Richard A. Watson, as always, was liberal with editorial assistance.

Finally, I want to thank Washington University Poet in Residence, Donald Finkel, for giving us a completely new perspective on Salts Cave with his poem, *Answer Back*.

Part I

SURFACE WORK IN MAMMOTH CAVE NATIONAL PARK

Chapter 1

Survey and Excavation in the Vicinity of Salts Cave

PATTY JO WATSON

Washington University

Surface work began in April, 1969, when Salts Sink[1] and the area immediately adjacent to it were searched for open-air occupation sites possibly contemporaneous with the prehistoric use of the cave (Figures 1.1 and 1.2). Between April 5 and April 11, 1969, the level and nearly level places inside the Sink were raked clear, especially around the spring at the south end where local people reported having found flint fragments and arrowheads in the past. However, nothing at all

[1]In the numbering system used by Schwartz and Sloan (1960) on their archeological base map, Salts Cave is MC 8, the area to the west of the Sink is MC 9, and a third area just to the north of the Sink is MC 10. Area MC 9 certainly corresponds to the relatively abundant chipped stone strewn about the west edge of the Sink as described in this section, while MC 10 may well be the amorphous site we noted to the northeast of the Sink (page 7).

Salts Sink is described in Watson *et al.* (1969, page 2, Plate 1); it and the other landmarks referred to in this section can be found on USGS topographic map of the Mammoth Cave Quadrangle, 7.5 minute series, 1954. Another excellent reference is the Topographic Map of the Proposed Mammoth Cave National Park, USGS, 1933 edition.

was found inside the Sink, and we concluded that whatever material might once have been there must have been removed by local farmers, or covered by thick slope wash.

Outside the Sink, four transects were laid out running north, south, east, and west from the Sink (Figures 1.3 and 1.5). Each transect was 1 m wide and 40–60 m long. The surface of the ground was laid bare in each of these strips by clearing away the leaves and sticks with rakes, hoes, and small-bladed shovels (Figure 1.4).

Only the west transect contained any chipped stone. Further examination of the surface on the west side of the Sink revealed a scatter of chipped stone there, so a rough grid[2] was laid out on the west slope and the entire area was cleared of leaves and sticks. After the initial survey that indicated the presence of chipped stone in this

[2]Much of this work as well as the tabulation of artifactual material found in the northwest and southwest quadrants of the Salts Sink surface survey was done under the immediate supervision of University of Kentucky student archeologists, David Smith and Wesley Cowan.

TABLE 1.1   Salts Sink Surface Survey—Material Collected April 1969

Southwest Quadrant		Chunks	Cores	Unutilized flakes	Utilized flakes	Knife fragments	Scrapers	spokeshave scrapers	flake scrapers
A	1	4	1	6	5	1			
	2								
A A–B	3	2			1				
	4	2		6	5				
	5								
	6								
	7			2					
	8								
	9	1		1	1		1		
	9–10	1		6	1				
	10	3	4	7	2				
	11	3	4	7	2				
	12	4	4	5	8				
	13	2	1	3		1			
Totals		*22*	*14*	*43*	*25*	*2*	*1*	*0*	*0*
B		21	5	47	23		1		1
	1	1	2	2	1			1	
	2	2		2	2			2	
(see A 3)	3								
	4	5		7	4			1	1
	5	5		2	1				
	6	2				1			
	7	1	1					2	
	7–8	1							
	8	5		1	2	1			
	9	9	1	3	2	1			2
	10								
B–C overlap	9–9								
B–C overlap	10–10	21	8	29	5	1			
B	11	40	3	23	9				3
	12	5	4	9	3				
	13	2		1				1	
Totals		*120*	*24*	*126*	*52*	*4*	*1*	*7*	*7*
C	1								
	2								
	3								
	4								
	5								
	6			5	2				
	7								
	8								
	9	12	1	2		1		1	
(see B)	9–10								
	11	1	1		1				
	12	1		1	1				
	13								
Totals		*14*	*2*	*8*	*4*	*1*	*0*	*1*	*0*

4

end scrapers	chunk scrapers	Projectile point fragments	Projectile point tips	bases	Awls	Gravers	Flake knife	Gorget	Totals
									17
									0
									3
									13
									0
									0
									2
									0
									4
									8
									16
									16
		1							22
	1								8
0	1	1	0	0	0	0	0	0	109
1		1	1	2					103
									7
									8
									0
									18
				1					9
									3
									4
							1		2
									9
				1	1				20
									0
								1	1
1		2	1	1		2			71
		3				1			82
			1						22
									4
2	0	6	3	5	1	3	1	1	363
									0
									0
									0
									0
									0
						1			8
									0
									0
									17
									0
									3
									3
									0
0		0	0	0	0	1	0	0	31

TABLE 1.1—(cont.)

		Chunks	Cores	Unutilized flakes	Utilized flakes	Knife fragments	Scrapers	spokeshave scrapers	flake scrapers
Southwest Quadrant									
D	1								
	2								
	3								
	4								
	5								
	6	1							
	7	1							
	8								
	9						1		
	10								
	11								
	12								
	13								
Southwest Quadrant									
hilltop to west		5							
Totals		*7*	*0*	*0*	*0*	*0*	*1*	*0*	*0*
Northwest Quadrant									
Z		7							
	1	2		24	11				
	1–2	4	6						
	2	2		7	3				
A	1	9	5	8		1			2
	2	7	4		1		1		1
	3	2							
	4				1				
	5								
B	1	20	2	16			1		
	2	9	2	14	4			1	
	3	5	2	7	1		1		
	4	4	2	9					
	5	6		2					
C	3			1	3				
West Transect		43	10	58	11				1
Totals		*120*	*33*	*146*	*40*	*1*	*3*	*1*	*4*

area, we kept all items found in separate bags for each grid unit and the material was later tabulated at the University of Kentucky according to these units (Figure 1.3, Table 1.1.). Test pits (Figure 1.5.) revealed more chipped stone like that collected from the surface but no other signs of occupation debris were found, even in the areas of densest scatter. One possible explanation is that this area around the Sink was never occupied intensively but was only visited or camped on by small, transient groups. Another possible explanation of the situation we found (which could be combined with the first explanation) is that recent cultivation (up to about 1935 when the land became part of the proposed Mammoth Cave National Park) and consequent increased erosion of the

TABLE 1.1—(cont.)

end scrapers	chunk scrapers	Projectile point fragments	Projectile tips	point bases	Awls	Gravers	Flake knife	gorget	*Totals*
									0
									0
									0
									0
									0
									1
									1
									0
									1
									0
									0
									0
									0
	1								*6*
0	*1*	*0*	*0*	*0*	*0*	*0*	*0*	*0*	*9*
									7
		1							*38*
									10
									12
									25
		1		1					*16*
									2
									1
									0
		1							*45*
									30
		2							*18*
									15
									8
		1							*5*
		3							*126*
0	*0*	*9*	*0*	*1*	*0*	*0*	*0*	*0*	*358*

western slope into the Sink may have destroyed any archeological deposits once present.

In the southeastern and northeastern quadrants, strips 20 m long and 1 m wide were cleared every 10 m but finds were so sparse that no further work was undertaken in these areas.

Several hundred yards northeast of the Sink near a small spring we found chert flakes, two cores, and a scraper. The area of scatter was poorly defined and the quantity was very low, so no test trenching was undertaken here.

Rimming the Sink on the east and southeast is a low ridge. A few flakes were found on its surface, so it was tested by digging the small pits I and II (see Figure 1.5). Chipped stone material was scant (Tables 1.2 and 1.3) and no other cultural debris

Figure 1.1 General view of Salts Sink.

Figure 1.2 At the bottom of Salts Sink; the grated opening is the entrance to the cave.

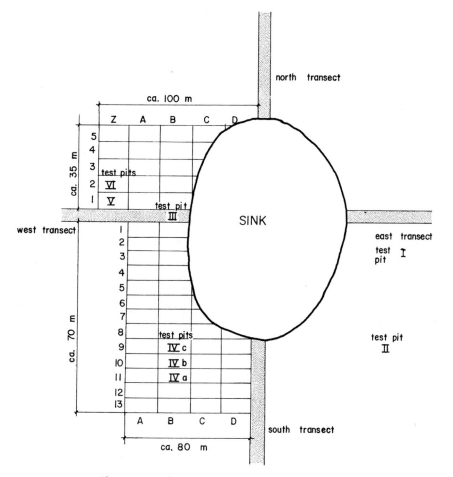

Figure 1.3 Salts Sink. Sketch map of surface survey grid.

was found. In pit I, the gray-black topsoil shaded into yellow, sandy clay at about 20 cm below the surface. The clay was excavated to a total depth of 60 cm and was found to contain no prehistoric cultural remains.

Pit II was laid out as a 1 × 2 m trench cutting into the slope of the ridge. Topsoil was apparent only in the upper end to a depth of some 10 cm. Below that (and beginning at the surface in the downhill half of the trench) was yellow-orange sandy clay.

Pit III was a 2 × 2 m test square in the west transect dug into yellow sandy clay (surmounted by only 1–2 cm of humus) that yielded very few artifacts.

Surface Work on the Marvin Sell Farm Near Salts Sink

The Sell house lies just across the road from the Park boundary about one-third of a mile southeast of Salts Sink. The Sells told us of two places on their property where they often found chipped stone implements. These two areas were designated MC–01 and MC–02 by David Smith.

Area MC–01

This area is located about 320 m north of the Sell house in an old tobacco field. Surface collection of the area yielded several pieces of chipped

Figure 1.4   Salts Sink. Clearing the West Transect.

stone including one corner-notched projectile point and one scraper. The Sells have a number of projectile points found here at various times in the past. A 2 × 2 m test pit revealed a few flakes in the plow zone but nothing below that.

Area MC—02

This area is located about 640 m north-northeast of the Sell house, also in a cultivated field. The field is at the junction of an east—west-running gravel road and a north—south-running gravel road. The findings here were similar to those at MC—01. Chipped stone was found on the surface, but in three 1 × 1 m test pits, chert occurred only very sparsely in the plow zone and none was found below it.

Discussion of the Prehistoric Surface Materials in the Vicinity of Salts Sink

The aboriginal remains found around Salts Sink are somewhat enigmatic. The preponderance of cores, fragments of raw material (chert), and of utilized and unutilized flakes might indicate a workshop or knapping situation.

Mr. Marvin Sell, long-time resident in the vicinity of Salts Cave, told us of a nearby spring where there was an outcrop that used to produce fragments of good quality chert. On a visit to the spring in April, 1969, we found only very poor pieces that were quite unworkable. The source as Mr. Sell knew it years ago has apparently been exhausted.

There is good chert in Mammoth Cave (especially in Flint Alley, see pages 180—188), but the little we have found in Salts is of rather poor quality except for a small outcropping in the T survey passage that runs from Wilson's Accident to Dismal Valley (Figure 10.1). It seems somewhat unlikely, but is not impossible, that the raw material for the chert items found around the Sink came originally from somewhere inside the cave.

The most distinctive categories of tools in the Salts Sink collection are the projectile points, the spokeshave scrapers, and the knives. As is true

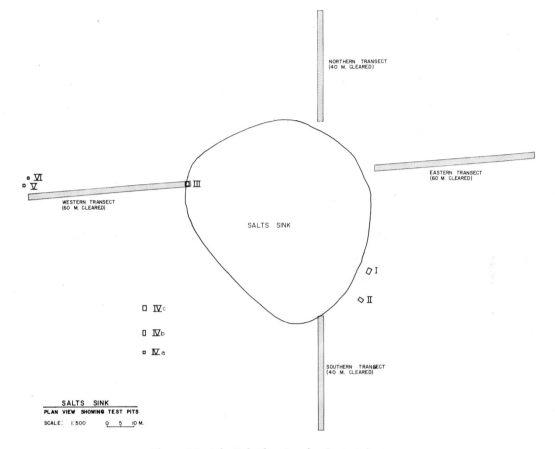

Figure 1.5   Salts Sink. Plan view showing test pits.

of the projectile points found in Salts Vestibule excavations, the points from the surface around the Sink are generally large and more or less lanceolate in form, often with a triangular ("turkeytail") or fan-shaped tang (Figure 1.6): "Type specimen: crude, long, parallel blades, corner notched with fairly strong shoulders and convex bases often pointed or dove tailed. They seldom show very elaborate secondary chipping... [Smith n.d.]." Among the ten projectile points complete enough for analysis, the shapes of seven conformed to the type as described, whereas three differed from it in various ways.

The knives, Smith states, are quite well made in comparison to the projectile points: "Contrary to an eastern Kentucky Early Woodland rule of gene-

rally thick ovate knives with blunt tips, those of Salts Cave are reminiscent of a much later period. The knives are thin and parallel-sided with pointed tips and exhibit more secondary chipping and higher quality workmanship than most Early Woodland knives [Smith n.d.]." Of the 12 most complete specimens, the shapes of only 2 differ significantly from the type description; they are too thick.

With respect to the spokeshave scrapers, Smith notes that their presence in considerable numbers in the Salts Sink collections tends to strengthen the suggestion that the complex is no earlier than Early Woodland.

University of Kentucky student archeologist, Wesley Cowan, undertook a study of the cores and

TABLE 1.2 Salts Sink Surface—Test Pits

Pit and level	Cores	Core fragments	Raw material	Slightly utilized flakes	Utilized flakes	Waste flakes	Scrapers	Projectile points	Retouched flakes	Knives	Miscellaneous	Totals
I Surface							1					1
0–10 cm		1	1		3	39	2	1 fragment	2			49
10–20 cm		1	1	2	3	24						31
I extension												
0–10 cm					2	16	1		1		1 fragment china saucer	21
10–20 cm				1						1		2
II 0–10 cm		1			4	38	1				1 large quartz pebble	45
10–20 cm					3	28			1			32
III 0–10 cm	2			5	2	38			1			48
10–20 cm			1			9	1					11
Totals	*0*	*4*	*4*	*8*	*17*	*192*	*6*	*1*	*6*	*1*	*2*	*240*

12

TABLE 1.3   Salts Sink Surface—Test Pits

Pit and Level		Cores	Percussion flakes	Billet flakes	Nondescript flakes	Recognizable tools	*Totals*
IVa	Plowzone		1	2	2		*5*
IVb	Plowzone						
	to 30 cm	4	5	5	29	4	*47*
	30—40 cm						*0*
	40—50 cm						*0*
IVc	Plowzone						
	to 30 cm		5		26	2	*33*
V	Plowzone						
	to 20 cm		14	8	51		*73*
	20—30 cm						*0*
	30—40 cm						*0*
VI	Plowzone						
	to 20 cm		11	4	27		*42*
Totals		*4*	*36*	*19*	*135*	*6*	*200*

flakes in this Salts Sink material in order to investigate techniques of manufacture (Cowan n.d.). He divided the flakes into two groups: percussion flakes and billet flakes. He also looked for bipolar and blade flakes, but found none. Percussion flakes are usually short and thick—more wide than long—and display clear-cut bulbs of percussion. The striking platform is usually an unprepared one. These flakes are presumed to have been removed by direct percussion with some object, such as a hammerstone, harder than the chert itself.

Billet flakes have poorly defined bulbs of percussion and are characterized by prepared striking platforms. They are usually longer than they are wide, and have a peculiar lip at the end of initial impact. It is thought that these flakes were formed by striking the core with an object softer than the chert, such as a wood, bone, or antler billet hammer.

Bipolar flakes are produced by holding the core against another rock and hitting it with a hammerstone. If a single flake results, it will have two bulbs of percussion. This kind of flake is rare in general, and does not occur at all in the Salts Sink chipped stone examined by Cowan.

Blade flakes (synonomous with "blades" in the usual Old World terminology) are thought to have

been punched off a rather special kind of core by means of indirect percussion. None occurs at Salts Sink.

A core is defined as any piece of chert exhibiting a number of flake scars.

Cowan worked with 857 cores and flakes from the Salts Sink surface collection and test pits. He sorted them into the categories just described with the following results:

120	percussion flakes	(14%)
53	billet flakes	(6%)
0	bipolar flakes	
0	blade flakes	
61	cores	(7%)
623	nondescript flakes (i.e., neither percussion, billet, bipolar, nor blade)	
		(73%)

Thus it appears that the Salts Sink industry is technologically somewhat amorphous, but, insofar as distinctions can be made, is predominantly the result of direct percussion technique, involving the use of hammerstones. The fact that no hammerstones were found is a strong argument against the interpretation of this agglomeration of chipped stone as representing a workshop area.

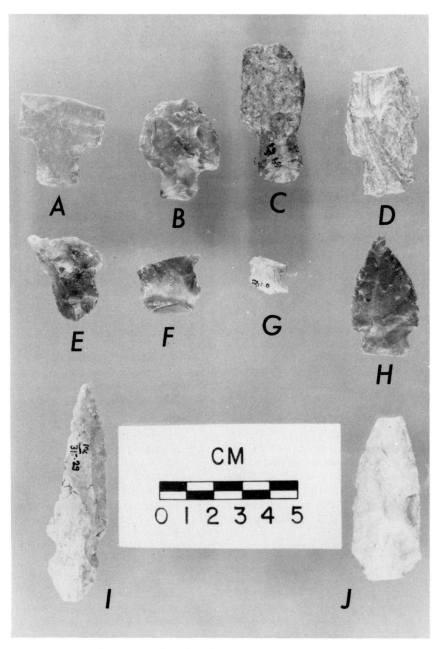

Figure 1.6   Salts Sink surface collections: Projectile points.

Preliminary Investigation of Soils at Salts Sink

To obtain more information about the history of the Salts Sink area, we contacted the County Soil Conservation Office in Glasgow, Kentucky. Mr. Earle Latham, Soil Scientist of the U.S. Department of Agriculture, visited Salts Sink on April 10, 1970, and explored the soil profiles in four different places with a 1-inch diameter soil auger. On the southwest slope above the Sink, he found a more or less normal sequence of A, B, and C horizons: several centimeters (varying from 5 to 12 cm) of loam or silty loam overlying sandy loam, below which is the sandstone bedrock at 75 cm below the surface. In another sample area in the west transect near the edge of the Sink, the sequence is similar except that the C horizon is more clayey and the bedrock is below the maximum depth the auger can reach (130 cm).

The third sample area was at the south side of the Sink, on the low earth mound that rims the eastern edge of the Sink. Here again there is a normal soil profile (silt loam and silty clay loam becoming sandier downward to bedrock at 105 cm), although the A, or topsoil, zone is quite thin. Thus the mound is probably a natural surface feature.

The final sample spot was at the bottom of the Sink some 6 m south of the cave gate. Here, as might be expected, the soil auger revealed a lack of soil formation. There is an upper layer about 5 cm thick of very dark brown, almost black, humus beneath which is fine sandy loam to the maximum depth the soil auger was able to penetrate (between 105 and 130 cm). At the bottom of the profile small bits of charcoal are present in the loam. The profile here obviously represents fairly recent slope wash with even more recent decaying organic debris on top. The charcoal could be from a brush fire at or near the Sink.

Surface Work Elsewhere within the Park

On November 27 and 29, 1969, survey parties walked along both sides of the Green River from Dennison's Ferry to Three Sisters Island. We were particularly interested in the flats just back from the river and in rock shelters. Although several shelters were found, all were quite shallow and barren of cultural debris.

A small cave opening high in the bluff above the river (south side)—Cathedral Cave—would have made a likely dwelling place or camp, but has been so trampled and altered by recent traffic that prehistoric material if ever present must have been removed or destroyed. We found only one small chert flake on the slope below the cave mouth.

The only other archeological remains found were scattered chert flakes near a sink on the north bank of the river just upstream of Three Sisters Island. Schwartz and Sloan (1960) noted a site—MC–18—in this general area but down on the river flat where we were unable to find anything.

One of the survey parties dug a 1-m-deep hole in the alluvium on the south side of the river between Great Onyx Cave and Three Sisters Hollow. Homogeneous alluvium continues from top to bottom, and is probably much deeper than a meter everywhere within the present floodzone where spring floods sometimes raise the river level 6–10 m or even more. Hence, any sites that once may have existed along the river have long since been washed away or buried.

Schwartz and Sloan (1960) report another possible village site—MC–19—on the left bank of the Green River about 400 m northwest of the entrance to Great Onyx Cave. On May 29, 1969, two crew members were sent to relocate this site. They found the spot indicated on the map and raked the surface, but did not recover any chipped stone; hence the status of the site is unclear.

Chert flakes and fragments of projectile points and drills were found in April, 1970, by other project personnel on the surface in and near the Daniels cemetery half a mile southeast of Crystal Cave (see Table 1.4). In April, 1971, more chert was collected from this area and from an area along the western edge of the road leading to Floyd Collins' Crystal Cave at a point called the S-curve, about 1200 m south of the cave entrance. The items found in the scatters at these two locations are comparable to those found around

TABLE 1.4 Flint Ridge Surface Collections: S Curve, Daniels Cemetery

Locality	Cores	Core fragments	Raw material	Hammer stones	Utilized flakes	Waste flakes	Retouched flakes	Projectile points	Scrapers	"Drills" fragments	Knife fragments	Miscellaneous	Totals (excluding Misc.)
S curve Daniels	1				3[a]	168	4	6[b]	2[d]		3	Clam shell	187
Cemetery	12		4	2	51[a]	261	3	8[c]	3[d]	3[e]	6	chipped celt fragment	353
Totals	*13*	*0*	*4*	*2*	*54*	*429*	*7*	*14*	*5*	*3*	*9*		*540*

[a]S curve: seven moderately to heavily utilized, the rest showing only slight wear. Daniels Cemetery: ten moderate to heavy, the rest slight.

[b]One complete side notched point, 45 × 20 mm maximum dimensions; five basal fragments.

[c]Two complete points, 25 × 21 mm and 45 × 24 mm, the smaller with a short, wide tang, the larger sidenotched. The fragments comprise three tip ends and three basal ends.

[d]One tanged, transverse ended scraper from each locality; the rest are scrapers on flakes.

[e]Although these items are shaped like those usually referred to as drills, they show no indication of circular wear patterns at the tips when viewed under magnification.

16

Figure 1.7 Salts Sink surface collections: A–D, Knives; E. Gorget fragment; F, G. Spokeshaves.

the west edge of Salts Sink (Table 1.1). Thus, it is possible that the Salts Sink scatter is simply one of several in the general vicinity of Flint Ridge and has no particular relevance to the cave opening out of the Sink.

Several years ago, a surface survey of various areas in Mammoth Cave National Park was carried out by Schwartz and Sloan (1960). They list a total of approximately 29 sites (the status of some sites is ambiguous), the descriptions of most of which are like those of the sites we found. Insofar as indicated by distinctive tool types (projectile points and drills for the most part), the sites seem to range from late Archaic to Early Woodland.

In the collections of the Peabody Museum of Archeology and Ethnology is a series of stone tools from Indian Hill, a high bluff overlooking Green River just inside the western boundary of the Park near Brownsville (about one and one-quarter miles northeast of the town). Many of the chipped stone and ground stone artifacts from Indian Hill are similar to items collected in Mammoth Cave National Park from the surface and from our Salts Cave Vestibule excavations. The Peabody Museum objects are enumerated below; all were collected by F. W. Putnam in 1881.

81-34/24858—Bell pestle, bottom is ground smooth but not battered.

81-34/24859—Conical pestle, but with no signs of battering on the base.

81-34/24862—Large oval chert flake.

81-34/24863—Greenstone celt with a polished bit (75 × 57 × 25 mm).

81-34/24865—Lanceolate, bifacially pressure-flaked knife with part of one edge steeply retouched; 125 × 5 × 7 mm.

81-34/24866—Large oval chert flake, somewhat better made than 24862.

81-34/24867—Two projectile points; one contracting stemmed (65 × 32 mm) and one side notched (65 × 30 mm).

81-34/24868—Two projectile points; one expanding stemmed (46 × 25 mm), the other indeterminate (40 × 20 mm).

81-34/24869—Projectile point, parallel stemmed (49 × 28 mm).

81-34/24870—Three projectile points; all three have more or less pointed tangs, the two larger have the tips broken off (70 × 35 mm and 62 × 37 mm, both incomplete), the third is complete and much like a small-size version of the turkeytail points found at Salts Sink and in Salts Vestibule (the dimensions are 52 × 25 mm).

81-34/24871—Winged drill, 50 × 25 mm.

81-34/24872—Fragment of a scraper.

According to the Peabody catalog (Vol. 6), all these items are from a plowed field on top of Indian Hill.

There are surface collections from "Salts Cave Fields" and from Eaton Valley (or Eaton Hollow) now in storage at the American Museum of Natural History. These collections were apparently made by N. C. Nelson in 1916, although a manuscript by Nelson that describes the Eaton Valley finds is dated 1923, and the acquisition numbers begin with "1923."

The Salts Cave Fields material comprises a box (20.1/213) of chipped stone flakes and projectile points. There are 40 pieces in all and about 16 are fragments of projectile points; one is a complete, small, stemmed point (33 × 12 mm maximum). Most of the fragments are tip ends, but five are basal pieces and all are tanged, one having a turkeytail tang like those from Salts Vestibule and our collections at Salts Sink.

The Eaton Valley collections are in drawers No. 588 and 589, and come from six different sites in Eaton Valley (a sketch map accompanying the 1923 manuscript shows the relative locations of these sites). Apparently no detailed analyses of this material were ever undertaken by Nelson, but he refers to the sites as workshops, and much of the cataloged chert consists of nodule fragments, core fragments, and large trimming flakes.

Part
II   **SALTS CAVE**

Recent History of Salts Cave

PATTY JO WATSON

Washington University

Further research into the recent history of Salts Cave has confirmed most of the tentative outline published earlier (Watson *et al.* 1969: 10–11). It has also provided more details about some of the events listed there. The abbreviated outline that follows incorporates all the information of which I am presently aware and owes much to the researches of Stanley D. Sides, President of the Cave Research Foundation, and Harold Meloy, Member of the Cave Research Foundation.

Chronological Outline of Salts Cave Recent History

1794—	Land over Salts Cave patented by William West, according to Col. Bennett Young (Young 1910: 299).
1802—	William West claims a 109-acre tract of land that includes the sink and the entrance to what is now known as Salts Cave.
1804—	The Salts Cave tract is surveyed on March 18 (Warren County Surveyor's Book, p. 121).
1809—	On June 15, John West, presumably a relative of William West, scratches his name on a rock near the northern end of the cave now known as Salts Cave.
1812–1813—	Salts Cave is prospected for saltpeter (Hovey 1897: 291).
1826—	Grant of conveyance is made to William West for the 109-acre tract containing "West's Cave," later (beginning about 1840) known as Salts Cave.
1848—	June 6. Dr. John Croghan buys Salts Sink, the cave, and the surrounding land for $268.38 at a Hart County Commissioners' sale.

1849 —   Croghan dies; Salts Sink and the natural entrance to the cave become a part of Croghan's Mammoth Cave Estate.

1870s —   Louis Vial owns the northern entrance to Salts Cave which he and his friends explore, according to an article written by Vial's daughter and entitled "Reminiscences of Mammoth Cave" (*Glasgow Times*, n.d.; copies of this clipping were obtained from Ellis Jones, Cave City, Kentucky; and Gordon L. Smith, Louisville, Kentucky).

1875 —   March 8. T. E. Lee, J. L. Lee, and W. D. Cutliff discover the Salts Cave mummy (named "Little Alice" nearly 50 years later by Miss Betty Breaden; Gordon L. Smith, personal communication). Little Alice is sold to Larkin J. Proctor, owner of nearby Proctor's Cave. (For the further travels of Little Alice, see Meloy 1971: 9–13; Robbins 1971, and pages 140–141 of this volume.)

ca. 1882–1883 —   Cutliff collects aboriginal materials in Salts Cave and sells them to Putnam of the Peabody Museum, Harvard University.

1893 —   Theodore Hazen, whose wife then owned property near Salts Cave (Sides 1971: 63), opens a "new entrance" into Salts Cave (Young 1910: 300), apparently that now known as the Chapman Entrance, the same opening reportedly used 20 years earlier by Vial and his friends.

1897 —   July. Pike Chapman, Hazen's nephew, is killed during an attempt to enlarge the northern entrance to Salts Cave. The enlargement is part of a commercialization project by Hazen in competition with the Louisville and Nashville Railway's commercialization of nearby Colossal Cave. Trails are built into the north end of Upper Salts from the Chapman Entrance, but before Hazen can benefit from this work the Louisville and Nashville Railway Company brings suit against him, and takes over much of his property including that above the Chapman Entrance (Sides 1971: 67).

ca. 1895–1910 —   Col. Bennett Young pays for collections of artifacts from Salts Cave, and notes that although he went into Salts Cave in 1894 (and apparently also in 1897, Sides 1971: 67) via the "Hazen Entrance" (i.e., the Chapman Entrance), it has now (1910) fallen shut. An article published by Col. Young on August 15, 1897, in the *Louisville Courier-Journal* (Vol. XXCIX, new series) includes pictures of Mr. and Mrs. Hazen, Pike Chapman, and Little Alice, as well as pictures of artifacts and a gourd from the cave.

1903 —   First known map of Salts Cave is published by French speleologist, Max de la Forest. Unknown Cave is shown as an entrace to Salts, although a connection between the two caves is not found until 1960.

1912 —   Edmund Turner and Floyd Collins explore extensively in Salts Cave.

1916 —   N. C. Nelson visits Salts Cave and notes the remnants of prehistoric middens in the Vestibule (Nelson 1917: 30). This midden debris is referred to earlier by Col. Young (1910: 305).

1917—	August 16. After the accidental burning of the unrecorded original deed, a local resident, Lark Burnett(e) (d. 1937), obtains an imperfect title to the natural entrance to Salts Cave for $25.00 (see Watson *et al.* 1969: 11). Burnett(e) attempts to commercialize Salts Cave and even has hand bills printed listing its attractions. (One of these is on file at the Visitor Center, Mammoth Cave National Park.) Mammoth Cave National Park acquires rights to the natural entrance in Salts Sink from Burnett(e)'s widow in 1937.
pre-1920—	The natural entrance to Salts Cave via Salts Sink is reported to be closed (Fowke 1922: 116).
1921—	May. The Colossal Cavern Company leases surface rights on 300 acres near the Chapman Entrance of Salts Cave to A. J. Musselman of Chicago. Musselman has a golf course built there as well as 21 log huts and a large dining and recreation hall, all completed by the spring of 1922. This establishment is known as the Blue Grass Country Club. According to local stories, the big city golfers entered the cave via the Chapman Entrance and stored illegal gallon jugs of whiskey there, many of which were appropriated by local cavers sneaking in from Salts Sink.
1926—	The President of the United States signs an Act of Congress providing for the acquisition of land for the proposed Mammoth Cave National Park.
1927—	July 11–13. A group of cave explorers organized by Russell T. Neville spends two days inside Salts Cave (Watson *et al.* 1969: 11; Jackson 1969; Neville n.d.).
1928—	The Blue Grass Country Club is closed.
1933—	May 23. The Country Club buildings are occupied by Company 510 of the Civilian Conservation Corps.
1935–1940—	January 23, 1935. Colossal Cavern Company holdings (including the northern end of Salts Cave) are transferred to the National Parks Association. In April 25, 1940, the Louisville and Nashville Railway Company makes over the rest of its holdings to Mammoth Cave National Park.
1953—	Lower Salts Cave including Indian Avenue with its undisturbed prehistoric debris is discovered by cavers from Louisville, Kentucky.
1964—	A large Job Corps camp is established in the old Blue Grass Country Club—CCC area. The former dining and recreation hall is used as a storage place for heavy tools and equipment until it burns down.

Chapter 3

Observation and Recording in Salts Cave

PATTY JO WATSON

Washington University

Upper Salts: The Salts Cave Mummy

In conjuction with her work on the desiccated cadaver from Salts Cave (Robbins 1971), Louise Robbins wished to examine the place in the cave where—according to tradition—the body had been found in 1875 by local Kentuckian spelunkers. Consequently, on April 9, 1969, a party was sent to the traditional find spot in a passage ("Mumy Hall" according to a pencilled note on the wall) running west from the bottom of Mummy Valley (see Figure 3.1) Within a few minutes of beginning the search, Kim Dale, one of the Cave Research Foundation volunteers, found on a ledge a limestone rock bearing the following inscription (see Figures 3.2a, b):

> *Sir*
> *I have found one of the Grat wonders of the*
> *world in this cave, whitch is a muma*
> *Can all seed hereafter*
> *found March the 8 1875*
> *T. E. lee J. L. lee*
>   *an W. d. Cutliff*
>   *dicuvers*

The words are partly written, partly incised onto the soft limestone rock with a very blunt pencil so that much of the inscription is more like engraving than actual writing.

There is some chance that the stone is a forgery because Upper Salts was commercialized, in a feeble way, during the 1920s (see page 23), and the exploiters of commercial caves in those days were notoriously adept at faking tourist attractions. However, it is equally likely that the inscription is genuine, and actually records the discovery of the Salts Cave aboriginal body by Cutliff and the Lees 100 years ago.

More recently, Cave Research Foundation parties, recording old names and dates in Upper Salts, found another inscribed rock in Mumy Hall, lying on a shelf at floor level against the west wall opposite the mummy ledge:

> *How are you grave robbers. What is it you*
> *would not do. They is nothing too mean for*
> *you to do. You low down scoundrls. What is*
> *it you wouldn't do. Just think for a sec of*
> *men to steal the dead. . . . [illegible, perhaps*

25

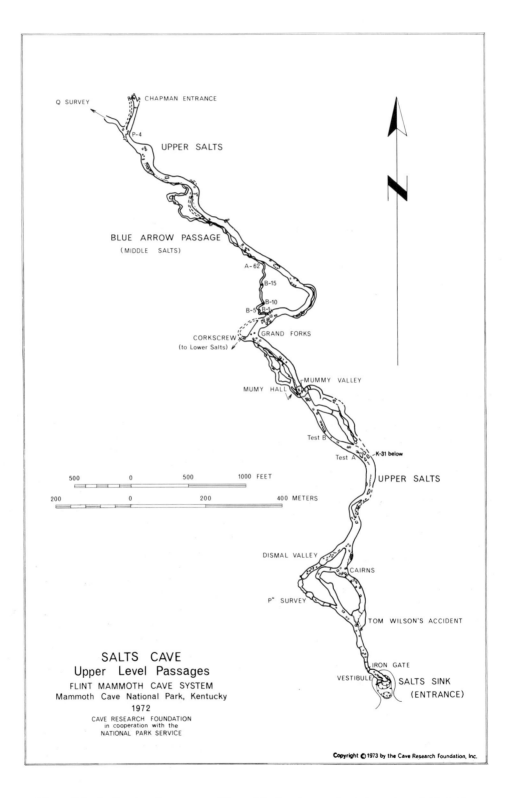

Figure 3.1 Small-scale reference map of Upper Salts Cave (a more detailed map is available in Watson *et al.* 1969: Figure 3).

Figure 3.2 Inscribed rock found in Mumy Hall, Upper Salts Cave. (a) View showing the rock *in situ*. (b) Close up showing writing.

"Just speculate on it"]. *Sir you are worse
than a murderer. Are you not afraid it will
follow you in your paths of a day and your bed
at night. You low down dirty damed thief of
hell yours most . . .* [illegible: *"respect-
fully"?*]   *J M Smith
P. S. Call again you honest fellows when you
get hard up for a few dimes or call at some
other grave yard.*

This second inscription is also written on a soft,
chalky piece of limestone with a pencil. J. M.
Smith is a name frequently seen in Upper Salts,
often with dates in the 1870s. Hence, he was a contemporary of Cutliff and the Lees, and possibly a
rival explorer.

Other Work in Upper Salts

Other observation and recording in Upper Salts
was very limited because so much of our earlier
work in the cave had been in these passageways
(Watson *et al.* 1969: 12–25). On November 28,
1969, an attempt was made to carry out a systematized surveying procedure in Upper Salts. The
main cave passage between the foot of Wilson's
Accident and Mummy Valley was divided into 50-
m lengths, and each 50-m length into five 10-m
lengths. Numbers from 1 to 5 were written on
separate pieces of paper, then at each survey point
that marked the beginning of one of the 50-m
lengths of passage, one of the numbers was randomly chosen. All the prehistoric debris within
the 10-m length of passage designated by that
number was then recorded on mimeographed
forms, and the party continued to the next 50-m
strip.

At the completion of this endeavor, it was apparent that the sampling procedure was satisfactory, but that recording was still an unreal-
istically time-consuming process, and that it is
virtually impossible to define all of the features
(in particular, the nature and degree of mining
activity, and the extent and intensity of smoke
blackening) in a way that enables them to be
meaningfully quantified. In other words, the

survey procedure produced negative results because it did not enable us to arrive at a quantified summary of aboriginal debris in the sampled
area in a way that is not so laborious and tedious
as to be impractical. Hence, we continued our
original technique of recording qualitatively the
nature and relative density of material as we
moved from one survey station to the next. We
obtained several kinds of information by this
technique.

First, we traced the aborigines through the cave
system and plotted on the cave maps those portions of the system with which they were familiar
and the specific passages they entered.

Second, we noted whether the prehistoric cavers
were working (mining) in the particular passage or
complex of passages, or whether they simply
moved through, probably exploring.

Third, we were able to judge by the quantity of
debris relative to that in Upper and Middle Salts
(dense) versus that in Indian Avenue of Lower
Salts (sparse), how heavy the traffic was in the passage in question.

In short, our recording was designed to enable us
to classify passages or passage complexes as to
presence or absence of aboriginal activity, and, if
present, the nature and intensity of that activity.
We decided that quantification by counting fragments of charcoal, cane and weed stalks, and torch
smudges on the passage walls and ceilings—
although theoretically feasible—would have been
much too time consuming and open to error to be a
desirable recording procedure. Even more important is the fact that only in a few passages can
we be certain that these materials are strictly *in
situ*.

With a little experience, we found it quite possible to make efficient, qualitative assessments
of the prehistoric remains that would enable us to
gather the kinds of information we wanted. The
materials present in every passage entered by the
Indians are charcoal, and torch and campfire fuels.
The fuel consists of pieces of cane, dried weed
stalks, and woody twigs and branches. Besides
these items lying on the cave floor or on ledges,
there are charcoal smudges on the walls and ceiling and on breakdown blocks where torches accidentally brushed the rock, or were deliberately

struck against it to knock off excess charcoal. Sometimes occurring with these ubiquitous traces are paleofecal deposits, pieces of squash and gourd shell, fragments of grass or bark torch ties, fragments of clam shell spoons or scoops, and places where the gypsum crust on wall or ceiling has been battered and partially removed. For our present purposes we recorded simply presence or absence and density (relative to Upper Salts and Middle Salts vis-à-vis Indian Avenue in Lower Salts) of the torch/campfire fuels and smudges. However counts and measurements were made of the less common items, and—where the traces were clear enough to make this possible—the amount of mining is indicated by estimating dimensions of wall areas denuded of mineral or battered by mining tools.

Our density standards (Upper Salts and Indian Avenue of Lower Salts, respectively) are defined in Watson *et al.* (1969: 12—31).

Other observations in Upper Salts were made on a trip to the area beyond the Chapman Entrance (a Q survey that runs northwest from P4) to determine the extent of the prehistoric material there. There is some question as to the status of the Chapman Entrance in prehistoric times: Was it open to aboriginal traffic or not? Because of the constructional activity carried out here by Hazen (page 22), it is very difficult to arrive at an assessment of the prehistoric material that was once present. However, the quantity of material gives no indication that the Indians used the Chapman Entrance. There is certainly cultural debris present near this entrance, and in the Q survey there are gourd fragments, paleofecal fragments, a worked clam shell, and battering on the walls, as well as torch debris; the latter extends north to Q51, not far from the terminal breakdown that ends the passage. But the quantity of these remains is not high. The simplest interpretation on present evidence is that the Indians used only Salts Sink entrance and reached the Chapman and Q survey area by traversing all of Upper Salts, a trip that now takes about an hour.

Only paleofecal material from the cave interior was collected from Upper Salts. These specimens were used for dietary, parasitological, and pollen analyses. The following were collected from the Vestibule area:

- Two chert fragments, one from near the top of the entrance slope at the south end of the Vestibule and one from near the Iron Gate at the north end of the Vestibule.

- Bone fragments from the rock slope below the Iron Gate (see page 156).

- One fragment of mussel shell with a small perforation (1 mm in diameter) at one end. The shell had been smoothed and polished all over; the rough outer coat is completely gone.

Two photos taken by Russell Neville of artifactual materials he found in Salts Cave were made available to us by Dr. William Halliday of Seattle, Washington. One photo shows several fragments and bundles of textile and vegetal fiber. One is a fair-sized piece (there is no scale in the picture) of open-twined textile, five or six small fragments of slippers, four small lots of fiber or raw material, and one unidentified vegetative item (a dried leaf perhaps). The other photo shows a number of stone artifacts including a full-ground celt and nine projectile points. Again, there is no scale, but two of the points are clearly quite large, comparable to the presumed dart points found at Salts Sink and Salts Cave Vestibule (Figures 1.6 and 12.1, pages 11 and 88). A third, long and slender, might be a turkeytail point. The stone implements—if indeed they are from inside the cave—must have come from Salts Vestibule, whereas the textile material presumably was found in Upper Salts.

The Salts Cave Textiles: A Preliminary Account

MARY ELIZABETH KING

The Museum of Texas Tech University

For at least 150 years, Salts Cave has been the discovery site for prehistoric textiles in a variety of forms. Young (1910) illustrates "moccasins," bags, what appears to be a tumpline, a band or belt, baskets or "headdresses," and possible mats or blankets as well as cordage and fiber bundles. Nearby Mammoth Cave has produced some similar items (Figure 21.1), including a loincloth still wrapped around the body of the prehistoric gypsum miner, "Lost John," who is now on display inside the cave.

The commonest items are the "moccasins," also called "sandals" and "slippers." These were apparently often discarded in Salts and other caves by their owners. "Sandal" is an inappropriate term for these specimens, for they are distinctly shoelike with sides and closed toes and heels. Since the word "moccasins" brings to mind footgear made of skin and having a general shape in common, "slipper," or even "shoe," are perhaps more suitable terms for these articles of clothing. Early reports (Holmes 1885: 417; Putnam 1876: 49; Young 1910) refer to the slippers as being "braided" or "plaited," but by 1920, Orchard had correctly identified them as twined.

Many of the textile items collected before 1920 were virtually intact, presenting few problems in identification. The Salts Cave specimens reported here are all fragmentary (although two slippers were relatively complete when found; Watson *et al.* 1969: Plate 5 upper and Plate 9 upper), and identification of the items represented by fragments is, in some cases, highly arbitrary. It is likely that the bulk of the fragments worked in close twining came from slippers. The spaced (open) twining fragments could have come from bags, blankets, or loincloths, since all of these garments have been reported to have been fashioned in this technique. They might also have come from slippers as well, for Watson (page 176 of this volume) reports having seen one slipper worked in spaced twining, and this was the usual technique used to manufacture slippers found by Funkhouser and Webb in the dry rock shelters of Lee County, Kentucky (Funkhouser and Webb 1929).

Three basic techniques—twining, braiding, and weaving—are represented in the present collection (Table 4.1), and, with one addition, these seem to comprise the technical repertoire of the local textile artisans. Within the basic categories,

TABLE 4.1 Salts Cave Textile Remains in the Illinois State Museum Collection, Summary of Technical Data for Individual Specimens

Specimen Number	No. of Fragments	Warp					Weft					Techniques present			
		Fiber	Spin/Ply	Diameter (mm)	Count per cm	Length (cm)[a]	Fiber	Spin/Ply	Diameter (mm)	Count per cm	Length (cm)[a]	Plain weave	Plain twining	Countered twining	Spaced twining
SCU 4	8+	RM?[b]	Z–S	4–5	2	13.5	RM?[b]	Z	3.5–5	2	6	X		X	
SCU 5	1	RM?	Z–S	3–3.5	2½	7	RM?	Z	3–3.5	3	5			X	
SCU 12	1	RM?	Z–S	3.5	2–3	3	RM?	Z	3	3	4			X	
SCU 24	4	RM?	Z	6	2	11.3	RM?	Z	4–6	2	3.5	X		X	
SCU 36	3	RM?	Z–S	4	2	13	RM?	Z	4–5	2	4.5	X			
SCU 44	?	?	?	?	?	?	?	?	?	?	?				X
SCU 48	1	?	Z–S	4	3	7.5	?	Z–S	3		2.6				X
SCU 99[c]	6+	RM?	Z–S	2	2	2.8	RM?	Z	3–5	3	6			X	
SCU 100[c]	6	RM?	Z–S	2.5	2	5.6	RM?	Z	3.5–5	3	6.5			X	
SCU 111	1?	?	?	?	?	?	?	?	?	?	?				
SCU 117	7	RM?	Z–S	2.5	2	8	RM?	Z	2.5	2½	5.5	X	X	X	
SCU 137	1	RM?	Z	4	1½	3	RM?	Z	5	2	5	X		X	
SCU 164	3+	?	Z–S	2.5	3	2	?	Z–S	2.5	1	5				X

TABLE 4.1—(cont.)

	Twining direction		Weft selvage		Object			Other associated techniques			Provenience	Remarks
	Down to Right (S)	Down to Left (Z)	Plain	Two-level	Slipper	Fabric	Cordage	Braid	Knots	Sewing		
SCU 4	×	×		×	×					× ?	P59	
SCU 5	×	×		×	×						P54	
SCU 12	×	×		?	×		×				P50	
SCU 24	×	×		×	×						P59	
SCU 36				×	×						P53	
SCU 44						×					B1	Missing
SCU 48		×	×			×			?		P53–54	
SCU 99[c]	×	×		×	×						Test A, 40–50 cm	
SCU 100	×	×		×	×						Test A, 40–50 cm	
SCU 111					× ?						P54–55	No structure left
SCU 117	×	×		×	×			×		× ?	P62–63	
SCU 137	×	×			×						Test A, disturbed	
SCU 164	×	×	×			×	×		×		Test B, 0–10 cm	

[a] Dimensions are given for largest fragment.

[b] RM = "rattlesnake master," *Eryngium yuccafolium.*

[c] SCU 99 and 100 are apparently from the same slipper.

only one type of weaving, plain weave (over-one, under-one), has been found. There is only one type of braid, three-strand flat braid, in this collection of textile materials. However, Orchard (1920:7) reports "braided material, sometimes of six or eight strands" from Salts, and Young (1910: 308) found braids of "three, four, and five threads, varying in shape from flat to slightly oval and box-shaped." I have not yet examined the cordage in the Illinois State Museum collection, and it is possible that other braiding techniques might be found. Twining, however, seems to be commonly found in three forms: simple, two-strand, close or compact weft twining, in which the twining twist is the same in each row and the rows are adjacent to one another; spaced or open twining, in which the rows are separated, leaving varying amounts of uncovered warps between rows, but otherwise like close twining; and compact, countered twining (also called chevron twining; Orchard 1920; Watson 1969), in which the twining twist changes in successive rows producing a herringbone effect. All of these are forms of simple weft twining.

Twining is one of the earliest known textile techniques. It requires only that the warp elements be secured at one end; heddles and shuttles are not used, the interworking of the warp and weft being performed with the fingers. Weaving, which clearly follows twining chronologically wherever such a sequence can be dated, is usually done on some sort of loom, often one equipped with heddles and utilizing shuttles. It is doubtful, nonetheless, that the weaving found in Salts Cave necessitated any such equipment, for it is often found combined with twining in a single slipper.

It should be noted that it is sometimes difficult to distinguish weft-faced plain weave from simple compact weft twining. This may complicate the interpretation of some reports. Schwartz (1958c) notes the presence of "simple," or plain, weave and of twining, but he does not break down the twining into plain, spaced, or countered. Thus one cannot be sure that he recognized plain, compact twining. Orchard (1920) does refer to "close" twining and "chevron" twining, and he records the presence of some "checker weave" (that is, plain weave) sandals crudely made of "coarse, fibrous material" (Orchard 1920: 8). He may have missed plain weave done in the same fiber as the close and countered twining. Only one example of two or more of these techniques combined in a single specimen seems to have been previously recorded (Watson 1969).

Another technique known to the users of Salts Cave was twilled basketry. No examples occur in the 1963 Illinois State Museum collection, but Young (1910:311) illustrates a basket or headdress worked in what appears to be 3/2 (over-three, under-two) twill. Two of these were found in Salts. He describes them as being made of split strips from "the outer surface of the cane," very regular, and "little more than one eighth of an inch in width" (Young 1910: 321). These baskets, now in the reference collections of the Museum of the American Indian, are approximately 21.5 and 14.5 cm in diameter with incomplete heights of about 5.5 and 7.5 cm (Lynette Miller, personal communication, January 24, 1973; cf. page 172 of this volume, item 5/2269). They are bowl-shaped with straight sides. Although they would be perfectly usable as small baskets, it is also possible that they served as hats, as some early observers insisted. The presumably aboriginal basket recently found in Mammoth Cave is reportedly larger than the basketry objects from Salts Cave just discussed, and was probably a container (page 188, Figures 22.1 and 22.2 this volume).

Although all of the specimens in the present collection are natural tan color with little or no variation, Young (1910: 308) reports a cloth with black (dyed) stripes and another with white (bleached) stripes. His illustration of the latter piece, however, appears to be simply a case of using slightly different shades of fiber for warp and weft in spaced twining (Young 1910:303). Orchard (1920: 19) also notes that the edge finish of a bag appeared to have been dyed.

The only other ornamentation that has been observed is the use of turkey and eagle feathers. Young (1910: 316) notes the occurrence of feathers with pierced quills in Salts Cave, and feathers collected from Salts Cave by F. W. Putnam are present in the Peabody Museum (page 177 of this volume, item 75–2/8220). Schwartz (1960: 133) refers to "feather blankets and fans of turkey-tail feathers" reported by nineteenth-century archeologists (see

Meriam 1844, reprinted in Meloy 1971; further comparative material is provided by Meloy and Watson 1969: 68). Schwartz infers—perhaps from Young's account of pierced feathers in combination with Meriam's description of feather headdresses accompanying a prehistoric, desiccated burial from Short Cave (this burial is known as Fawn Hoof; see pages 144–145 of this volume)—that the feather blankets were made by drilling holes in the feather shafts and suspending them from the twining. This was not the method used by the prehistoric Southwestern Indians for twined feather blankets; there feathers were fastened to the yarns used for the warps by wrapping the quill around the element. Nor is it like the technique reported for the Cherokee (Lewis and Kneberg 1958: 162–163), who sewed turkey feathers between narrow strips of bark, which in turn were sewed together so that the feathers overlapped. Both mantles and skirts were constructed in this manner. However, since apparently no examples of Kentucky featherwork remain intact, the question is academic.

The studies on Salts Cave fibers by Volney Jones are not complete (page 38), but previous work by Jones (1936) on Kentucky material suggests that certain fibers are more likely to occur than others: the inner bark of pawpaw (*Asimina trilobata*), *Apocynum* (sometimes called Indian hemp), cattail (*Typha*) and rush, the inner bark of leatherwood (*Dirca palustris*) and linden (*Tilia*), canary grass (*Phalaris caroliniana*), and rattlesnake master (*Eryngium yuccafolium*). Young (1910: 306) also found pawpaw, cattail, *Apocynum*, and grass in his Salts Cave collections. Other comparative material is summarized in Watson 1969.

From the existing Salts Cave textiles, as well as those described from Mammoth Cave, a reasonably clear picture emerges. Techniques utilized were not unlike those known to a wide variety of American Indians: weft twining, plain weave, braiding, and twill. Ornamentation was probably restricted to simple dyed stripes in earth colors and to the occasional use of feathers. Tassels may also have served as decoration, and some textiles have braided edges that represent a very simple form of ornamental border. It was not an elaborate textile industry, although its practitioners were

obviously quite competent. Garments seem to have been relatively limited in number and mainly of simple rectangular form: blankets, loincloths, caps, bags, and, one would expect, some sort of skirtlike garment for women. The slipper represents the most innovative article of clothing. Its shape seems to be unique in North American footgear; its nearest match being a rare type of Precolumbian Peruvian leather slipper. It is a far cry from the usual flat, simply shaped sandals found in most Southwestern sites, and even represents a more ambitious undertaking than the cut and sewn leather Plains moccasin.

The Illinois State Museum's 1963 Collection from Salts Cave

The textile fragments described here were obtained during the initial field work in Salts Cave in 1963 (see Watson *et al.* 1969). The work was sponsored by the Illinois State Museum Society and, together with the other materials recovered at the that time, these textile remains are a part of the Museum's collections.

The Salts Cave series contains 13 textile specimens, some with possibly more than one item represented. One specimen (SCU 44) could not be located, so descriptions are limited for this piece. Except for fragments associated with textiles, I did not examine any of the cordage found. All pieces were fragmentary. Owing to circumstance and pressures of time, it was not possible for me to examine any of the whole slippers or other textiles in the more extensive collections of other museums (see pages 168–178 of this volume). This situation, combined with the fact that the fiber analysis is not completed, makes it necessary to view this as a preliminary report, subject to change when more information is available.

Slipper Fragments

The 1963 collection contains eight to ten specimens (one supposed slipper fragment is now reduced to unidentifiable fiber bits; and SCU 99 and 100 may be from the same specimen) with a total of about 44 fragments that probably came from slippers. None is now intact enough to establish size or specific details of manufacture, although two examples (SCU 99—100 and SCU 117) were nearly complete when found. Brief descriptions of the slipper fragments are given in Watson 1969.

The technical data for specific specimens can be found in Table 4.1. Certain generalizations can, however, be made. The slippers were apparently all made in approximately the same way, achieving a more-or-less standard shape. Two basic techniques, plain weave and twining, were used, and braiding was used as a finishing technique. All of the twining variations reported from Kentucky caves and rock shelters can be found in the Salts Cave slippers, although plain spaced twining is reported for only one slipper (in the collection of the Peabody Museum, item /8233; see page 176). In the Illinois State Museum collection, four specimens are countered twining; three specimens show a combination of plain weave and countered twining; in one specimen plain weave, plain twining, and countered twining are combined; and one is plain weave. As noted by Watson (page 179), the preference for countered twining runs through all known collections of slippers from Salts and Mammoth Caves. In the Illinois State Museum collection of fragments, the only plain twining slants down to the right, or has a twining twist of S. Countered twining obviously slants alternately left and right, or twists S and Z. In all of the slippers the wefts are single-ply yarns, Z-spun. In all but two cases (SCU 24 and 137) the warps are two-ply, Z-spun, S-plied; the exceptions are single-ply, Z-spun.

The slippers were manufactured in a rather unusual way. It now appears, however, that it is not quite what has been previously reported. Orchard (1920: 11ff) suggests that the slippers were made on a warp-weighted loom with the warps attached to the loom bar in such a way that the loops form concentric half-circles above the beam (Orchard 1920: 16). Then:

> The weave was commenced near the looped warp and carried along to the length required, when the edges were turned up to make the sides of the sandal. The operation would have left the looped warp strands out of line with the curvature of the

heel. To overcome such defects the warp-elements above the tread could have been drawn through the weave, much like a draw-string, toward the toe of the sandal, until the slack was taken up sufficiently to give shape to the heel.

None of the specimens examined show that the ends of the weave were brought together to make a seam at the heal, which accounts for the presence of those uncovered strands at that part of the sandal. At the completion of the desired length of weave, the corners were turned over and the edges brought together, where the ends of the warp-strands were braided, making a seam from the point of the toe to the instep. The upper warp elements were evidently drawn tight to make the sides of the sandal fit snugly to the foot. A finishing edge around the opening has been made by coil-stitching a strand of the same material as that used in making the sandal. The ends of this finishing edge were turned back over the instep and looped into the upper edge of the sandal, just back of the instep, forming a lacing, in all probability to keep the sandal firmly in position while being worn (Orchard 1920: 13—14).

I have been bothered by nagging doubts about the validity of Orchard's "loom" setup for the construction of the slippers. My general feeling is that such a warp arrangement would produce an area at the heel with far longer loops than in fact exist in illustrated specimens and that it would be difficult to draw warps through the slipper once completed. A far simpler warping arrangement that would not produce this situation would be simply to double the warps over a suspended cord or stick. This arrangement would also tend to produce the sharp point at the base of the heel which Orchard cites (Orchard 1920: 12) as proof that the slipper was not shaped during construction, and the uncovered warps would correspond to the portion that passed over the suspension string or stick. Furthermore, the warps need not be weighted, although it might be easier to work if they were. Lynette Miller of the Museum of the American Indian tells me (personal communication, January 24, 1973) that she has experimented with the work held in the hand. I agree that this should be possible, but suspect that it would be simpler if the warps were suspended. When working in this fashion, there is then no need to "turn up the edges to make the sides" (Orchard 1920: 13), because

Figure 4.1 Plain weave fragment (SCU 4) showing weft selvage. Dimensions of fragment are 12.5 by 6 cm.

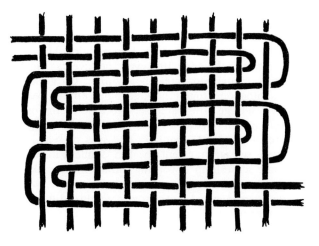

Figure 4.2 Diagram of plain weave weft selvage construction.

Figure 4.3 Countered twining fragment (SCU 5) showing weft selvage. Dimensions of fragment are 7 × 4.8 cm.

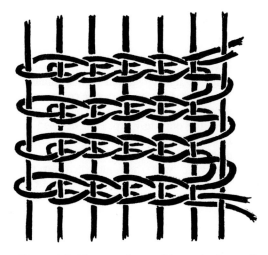

Figure 4.4 Diagram of a possible construction method for a weft selvage in countered twining.

the heel and sides are automatically created in the twining process. All that would be required would be to fold in and fasten the toe seam as suggested by Orchard. He is quite right that no shaping was necessary. If one experiments with folding a rectangle in the manner described, with the heel edge fastened together, the typical Kentucky slipper shape emerges.

The finishing cord noted by Orchard (1920: 14) is probably just the outer warp. At first I also assumed that the slippers had an additional cord, overcast to the edge. However, the "overcasting" yarns seemed to enter the twining. On closer examination, I found the edge to be a kind of two-level selvage. This same selvage type occurs on both woven (Figures 4.1 and 4.2) and twined (Figures 4.3 and 4.4) examples and was present in every selvage fragment checked. While it makes some sense from a working standpoint to make this kind of selvage in weft twining where two yarns are involved in each row, it would ordinarily make none at all for plain weave. For plain weave, it would be necessary to carry two wefts simultaneously, making this what has been described as "two-bobbin weaving" (O'Neale 1948: 127). A similar, but by no means identical, kind of woven selvage occurs in some ancient Peruvian textiles and in many prehistoric Chihuahua textiles. In these, all the weft loops pass around the outer warp. The only explanation I have for these curious selvages is that when twining and plain weave were used together in a single slipper, it was necessary to carry two wefts simultaneously in the woven areas in order to have them available for twining. To achieve similar weft selvages, the slipper maker was forced to devise constructions in which only one of the wefts in each twining pair passed over the outside warp. Had he used both twining wefts, the resulting selvage would have been impossible to duplicate in weaving. This twining selvage was then modified for plain weave to avoid having both wefts of the pair turn over the outside warp. It would be unnecessary to use this form of selvage for slippers woven entirely in plain weave. If such slippers exist and have this selvage, it merely reflects an habitual approach to selvage construction.

Since I have not seen any complete slippers, I cannot dispute Orchard's statement that the ends of the outer warp are run back into the edge and serve as lacings for the slippers. It is possible that these are unused warp ends, or that the unusual selvage was in fact designed to permit the outer warp to be pulled tighter, and the extra warp length was then available for lacings.

Aside from selvages, two slipper fragments have bits of what appears to be sewing. One (SCU 4) has an extra element just below the edge which seems to pass under some, but not all, warps (Figure 4.5). The other (SCU 117) has two stitches (?) (Figure 4.6) across the wefts on the third and fourth warps from the edge. They are roughly parallel to the warps and almost appear to be a warp splice. Such a splice, however, would only make sense if the slippers were constructed on a circular warp. Hence, I can only assume that they were stitches which served some unknown function.

Several photographs of whole slippers show a braid at the center toe, as described by Orchard. A fragment in this collection (SCU 117) also has a three-strand flat braid in this area that utilizes warp yarns (Figure 4.7). In this fragment it is not clear whether all or only some of the warp ends go into the braid, but the latter seems more likely. It is impossible to tell what might have happened to any warps not used in the braid. Other photographs, including one of Orchard's illustrations (Orchard 1920: Plate 3), show no braid at all, but only an overcast seam down the toe. There is no indication of what happens to the unwoven warp ends. They could be run back into the construction, or perhaps they were used for the toe stuffing mentioned by Orchard (1920: 15). Without examining an intact slipper, I cannot be definite about the way in which the toe seam is finished, but it appears that, in at least some cases, a braid is employed in some manner to engage the unwoven warps.

According to a personal communication from Richard Ford (January 17, 1973), Volney Jones's initial work on this collection indicates that the fiber used for most, if not all, of the slippers was *Eryngium yuccafolium* (rattlesnake master), a yucca-like member of the umbelliferae (parsley) family.

Figure 4.5

Figure 4.7 The center toe fragment of SCU 117 showing the three-strand flat braid made from warp ends. Dimensions of the fragment, excluding the braid, are 5.7 × 4.7 cm.

Spaced Twining

This category is easier to deal with. There were only three examples in the collection, and one of these cannot be located. The two I have examined (SCU 48 and 164) are similar in nature—both have plied warps and wefts, both are twined down to the left (a Z twist in the twining wefts). Wefts are spaced about 1 cm apart on one example and 2 cm apart in the other. The selvages are simple; wefts are simply carried from row to row at alternate edges (Figures 4.8 and 4.9).

As to fiber, I would guess that it might be different from that used in the slippers, perhaps *Apocynum*, but a determination will have to await completion of the fiber studies.

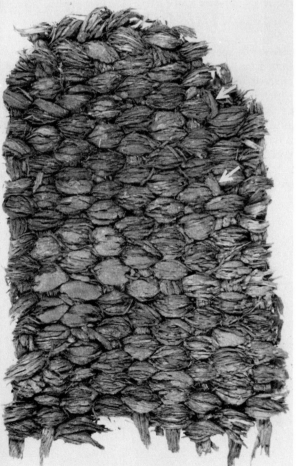

Figure 4.6

Figure 4.5 Fragment (SCU 4) with an extra thread run alongside the weft selvage. Dimensions are 3.2 × 1.2 cm.

Figure 4.6 Arrows point to "stitches" or splices in a fragment of SCU 117. Note the two rows of countered twining at the top; otherwise the fragment is woven in plain weave. Dimensions of the fragment are 8 × 4.8 cm.

Figure 4.8 A fragment of spaced twining (SCU 164). Dimensions are 3.2 by 2.2 cm.

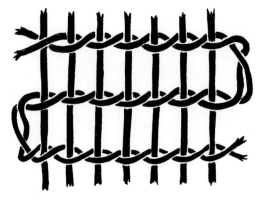

Figure 4.9 Diagram of weft selvages in spaced twining.

Other Fragments

The fragments are too small (one is 7.5 × 2.6 cm; the largest of the pieces of the other is 4 × 2 cm) to tell what they might have come from. Previous publications indicate that bags in this technique were not uncommon, and it was also used for blankets and loincloths. In the absence of clothed mummies in Salts Cave, I suspect bags are the most likely source for our fragments.

Several specimens have associated cordage, sometimes knotted. One, SCU 12, has several associated bits of yarn about 2–3 cm long, one of which has an overhand knot. It might be a slipper tie. Another, SCU 164, has a bit of cordage 4.5 cm long made of split leaf with only a slight Z twist. It has what appears to be a granny knot at one end. Specimen SCU 5 also has a bit of cordage, but without knots. Many of these fragments could be broken off warps or bits of slipper ties.

Chapter 5

Identification and Quantification of Components in Salts Cave Paleofeces, 1970–1972

ROBERT B. STEWART

Sam Houston State University

Beginning in the spring of 1970, Robert B. Stewart conducted a series of quantitative, wet analyses of constituents in paleofecal specimens from Salts Cave and Mammoth Cave. Stewart's results for specimens from Salts Cave are reported here; the Mammoth Cave data are included in Marquardt's chapter in Part III.

TABLE 5.1 Weight of Components in Fecal Specimens from Upper Salts Cave[a]

Sample number and provenience	Components	Weight (gm)
1A—P81, Iron Gate	Chenopod	0.20
	Rubus	0.05
	Maygrass	0.01
	Unidentified	0.08
2A1—Cairns	Chenopod	0.02
	Hickory	0.10
	Unidentified	0.05
	Unidentified skin	0.16
2A2—Cairns	Chenopod	0.01
	Hickory	0.08
	Unidentified	0.03
	Unidentified skin	0.20

TABLE 5.1—(cont.)

Sample number and provenience	Components	Weight (gm)
2A3—Cairns	Sunflower	0.09
	Strawberry	Trace
	Unidentified	0.11
	Unidentified skin	0.10
	Fish scale	—
2A4—Cairns	Chenopod	0.08
	Hickory	0.02
	Unidentified	0.09
2A5—Cairns	Chenopod	Trace
	Sunflower	Trace
	Hickory	0.10
	Strawberry	Trace
	Unidentified	0.11
	Unidentified skin	0.04
3A—P60	Sunflower	0.01
	Hickory	0.01
	Unidentified	0.05
	Fruit skin	0.24
	Sand	0.02
4A—P62	Chenopod	0.16
	Sunflower	0.08
	Hickory	0.02
	Unidentified	0.05
	Charcoal	Trace
6A—P62	Chenopod	0.23
	Sunflower	0.03
	Hickory	0.10
	Unidentified	0.08
7A—P60	Chenopod	0.21
	Sunflower	0.04
	Hickory	0.07
	Unidentified	0.09
	Grape	0.04
8A—P50, Mummy Valley	Chenopod	0.01
	Sunflower	0.24
	Hickory	0.10
	Maygrass	0.03
	Strawberry	0.01

[a] The samples for analysis were prepared by taking at random .5 gram (dry weight) of each specimen, soaking it in water, and picking it apart. The unidentified category is largely chenopod seeds and plant parts. The weights of the various components are dry weights. A trace is less than .01 gram.

TABLE 5.2 Weight of Components of Fecal Specimens from Upper Salts Cave, Survey Station K31[a]

Sample no.[b]	Chenopod	Sunflower	Iva	Hickory	Rubus	Maygrass	Strawberry	Unidentifiable	Other (only a trace unless otherwise indicated)
1a	0.08	0.03	—	—	—	—	—	—	Squash 0.01
1b	0.11	0.01	—	—	—	—	—	—	Squash 0.01
1c	0.11	0.01	—	—	—	—	—	—	Squash trace
1d	0.12	0.01	—	—	—	—	—	—	plant skin
1e	0.12	0.01	—	—	—	—	—	—	Squash 0.01
2a	0.02	0.01	0.11	—	—	—	—	—	Charcoal
2b	0.02	0.03	0.10	—	—	—	—	—	Charcoal
2c	0.02	0.02	0.11	—	—	—	—	—	Charcoal
2d	0.02	0.02	0.10	—	—	—	—	—	Charcoal
2e	0.02	0.01	0.12	—	—	—	—	—	Charcoal
3a	0.24	0.01	—	—	—	—	—	—	—
3b	0.26	0.01	—	—	—	—	—	—	—
3c	0.21	Trace	—	—	—	—	—	—	Charcoal, Grape 0.02
3d	0.24	0.01	—	—	—	—	—	—	Grape 0.01
3e	0.21	0.01	—	—	—	—	—	—	Charcoal
4a	—	—	—	0.24	—	—	—	—	Plant skin 0.03
4b	—	—	—	0.23	—	—	—	—	Plant skin 0.03
4c	—	—	—	0.18	—	—	—	—	Plant skin 0.04
4d	—	—	—	0.17	—	—	—	—	Plant skin 0.04
4e	—	—	—	0.14	—	—	—	—	Plant skin 0.05
5a	—	—	—	0.04	—	—	—	—	Plant skin 0.07
5b	Trace	—	—	0.02	—	—	—	—	Plant skin 0.10
5c	Trace	—	—	0.03	—	—	—	—	Plant skin 0.08
5d	Trace	—	—	0.01	—	—	—	—	Plant skin 0.12
5e	—	—	—	0.02	—	—	—	—	Plant skin 0.10
6a	—	—	—	—	—	0.15	Trace	—	—
6b	—	—	—	—	—	0.16	Trace	—	—
6c	—	—	—	—	—	0.17	Trace	—	—
6d	—	—	—	—	—	0.15	Trace	—	—
6e	—	—	—	—	—	0.14	Trace	—	—
7a	—	—	—	—	—	0.23	0.02	—	Plant skin
7b	—	—	—	—	—	0.22	0.02	—	Plant skin
7c	—	—	—	—	—	0.22	0.02	—	Plant skin
7d	—	—	—	—	—	0.20	0.02	—	Plant skin
7e	—	—	—	—	—	0.22	0.02	—	Plant skin

43

TABLE 5.2—(cont.)

Sample no.[b]	Chenopod	Sunflower	Iva	Hickory	Rubus	Maygrass	Strawberry	Unidentifiable	Other (only a trace unless otherwise indicated)
8a	0.20	—	—	0.10	—	—	—	—	Bone
8b	0.19	—	—	0.13	—	—	—	—	—
8c	0.19	—	—	0.10	—	—	—	—	Grape
8d	0.18	—	—	0.14	—	—	—	—	—
8e	0.19	—	—	0.11	—	—	—	—	—
9a	—	0.08	0.01	0.19	—	—	—	—	*Ilex* sp.
9b	—	0.07	0.01	0.20	—	—	—	—	Charcoal trace
9c	—	0.08	0.01	0.19	—	—	—	—	—
9d	—	0.10	0.01	0.16	—	—	—	—	—
9e	—	0.07	0.01	0.20	—	—	—	—	—
10a	0.17	—	Trace	Trace	—	Trace	—	—	—
10b	0.18	Trace	Trace	0.01	—	Trace	—	—	Charcoal trace
10c	0.14	Trace	Trace	0.01	—	Trace	—	—	—
10d	0.16	Trace	Trace	0.01	—	0.01	—	—	Charcoal trace, Plant skin trace
10e	0.17	—	Trace	0.01	—	Trace	—	—	—
11a	0.09	Trace	—	0.12	—	—	—	—	1 grass seed
11b	0.10	Trace	—	0.11	—	—	—	—	—
11c	0.09	Trace	—	0.11	—	—	—	—	Charcoal trace
11d	0.07	Trace	—	0.13	—	—	—	—	Charcoal trace
11e	0.11	0.01	—	0.08	—	—	—	—	—
12a	0.01	0.01	—	0.01	—	0.15	—	—	Plant skin trace
12b	0.01	0.01	—	0.02	—	0.14	—	—	Plant skin trace
12c	0.01	0.01	—	0.01	—	0.15	—	—	Plant skin trace
12d	0.01	0.01	—	0.01	—	0.15	—	—	Plant skin trace
12e	0.01	0.01	—	0.01	—	0.16	—	—	Plant skin trace
13a	—	—	—	0.02	—	0.20	—	—	—
13b	—	—	—	0.01	—	0.20	—	—	—
13c	—	—	—	Trace	—	0.23	—	—	—
13d	—	—	—	Trace	—	0.22	—	—	—
13e	—	—	—	0.03	—	0.18	—	—	—

Sample										Notes
14a	0.11	Trace	Trace	0.16	—	—	—	—	—	
14b	0.07	Trace	Trace	0.20	—	—	—	—	—	
14c	0.11	Trace	Trace	0.14	—	—	—	—	—	
14d	0.07	—	Trace	0.18	—	—	—	—	—	
14e	0.09	Trace	Trace	0.17	—	—	—	—	—	
15a	0.17	0.01	0.01	0.01	—	—	—	—	—	
15b	0.19	0.01	0.01	Trace	—	—	—	—	—	Charcoal trace
15c	0.21	0.02	Trace	—	—	—	—	—	—	
15d	0.19	0.02	0.01	0.01	—	—	—	—	—	
15e	0.19	0.01	Trace	0.04	—	—	—	—	—	Charcoal 0.01
16a	0.15	0.03	—	—	—	—	—	—	—	
16b	0.15	0.03	—	Trace	—	—	—	—	—	
16c	0.15	0.03	—	—	—	—	—	—	—	
16d	0.14	0.04	—	Trace	—	—	—	—	—	
16e	0.15	0.05	Trace	—	—	—	—	—	—	
17a	—	0.21	—	—	—	0.01	—	—	—	
17b	Trace	0.21	—	—	—	0.01	—	—	—	
17c	Trace	0.20	—	—	—	0.01	—	—	—	Charcoal trace
17d	Trace	0.21	—	—	—	Trace	—	—	—	
17e	Trace	0.21	—	—	—	0.01	—	—	—	Charcoal trace
18a	0.11	—	—	0.03	—	—	—	—	—	Charcoal trace
18b	0.10	—	—	0.08	—	—	—	—	—	Charcoal trace, Plant skin trace
18c	0.14	Trace	Trace	0.05	—	—	—	—	—	Squash trace
18d	0.14	—	—	0.02	—	—	—	—	—	Squash trace
18e	0.12	—	—	0.05	—	—	—	—	—	
19a	0.12	0.03	—	0.08	—	—	—	—	—	Plant skin trace, Amaranth trace
19b	0.13	0.03	—	0.04	—	Trace	—	—	—	Amaranth trace
19c	0.10	0.03	—	0.07	—	Trace	—	—	—	Plant skin trace, Amaranth trace
19d	0.11	0.04	—	0.03	—	Trace	—	—	—	Amaranth trace
19e	0.13	0.03	—	0.04	—	Trace	—	—	—	Amaranth trace
20a	0.09	0.01	Trace	0.05	—	—	—	—	—	Plant skin 0.01
20b	0.10	0.01	0.01	0.11	—	—	—	—	—	Plant skin 0.01, Amaranth trace
20c	0.12	0.01	0.01	0.02	—	—	—	—	—	Plant skin 0.01, Amaranth trace

TABLE 5.2—(cont.)

Sample no.[b]	Chenopod	Sunflower	Iva	Hickory	Rubus	Maygrass	Strawberry	Unidentifiable	Other (only a trace unless otherwise indicated)
20d	0.13	0.01	Trace	0.03	—	—	—	—	Plant skin trace, Amaranth trace
20e	0.12	0.01	0.01	0.04	—	—	—	—	Plant skin .01, Amaranth trace
21a	0.05	0.02	—	0.16	—	Trace	—	—	Charcoal trace
21b	0.05	0.01	—	0.21	—	Trace	—	—	Charcoal trace
21c	0.04	0.01	—	0.21	—	Trace	—	—	Plant skin trace
21d	0.08	0.01	—	0.12	—	Trace	—	—	Plant skin trace
21e	0.06	0.01	—	0.17	—	Trace	—	—	Insect fragment
22a	0.08	—	0.01	0.04	—	Trace	—	—	Grape 0.01
22b	0.09	Trace	0.01	0.01	—	Trace	—	—	—
22c	0.10	—	0.01	Trace	—	Trace	—	—	Charcoal trace
22d	0.10	Trace	0.01	Trace	—	Trace	—	—	—
22e	0.09	Trace	0.01	0.01	—	Trace	—	—	Charcoal trace
23a	0.01	0.16	—	0.05	—	Trace	—	—	—
23b	0.01	0.16	—	0.06	—	Trace	—	—	—
23c	0.01	0.13	—	0.11	—	Trace	—	—	—
23d	0.01	0.15	—	0.05	—	—	—	—	—
23e	0.01	0.17	—	0.05	—	Trace	—	—	—
24a	—	—	—	Trace	—	0.23	—	—	Plant skin 0.01
24b	—	—	—	Trace	—	0.23	—	—	Plant skin 0.01
24c	—	—	—	0.01	—	0.22	—	—	Plant skin 0.01
24d	—	—	—	—	—	0.22	—	—	Plant skin 0.02
24e	—	—	—	—	—	0.22	—	—	Plant skin 0.02, Frog bones, snake bones[c]

25a	—	—	—	—	—	0.23	—	—	Plant skin 0.01
25b	—	—	—	—	—	0.25	—	—	Plant skin 0.01
25c	—	—	—	—	—	0.24	—	—	Plant skin 0.01
25d	—	—	—	—	—	0.23	—	—	Plant skin
25e	—	—	—	—	—	0.23	—	—	Plant skin 0.01, Charcoal trace
26a	0.07	0.01	0.02	0.15	—	—	—	—	Plant skin trace
26b	0.07	0.01	0.02	0.09	—	—	—	—	Plant skin trace
26c	0.09	0.01	0.01	0.06	—	—	—	—	Plant skin trace, charcoal
26d	0.07	0.01	0.02	0.08	—	—	—	—	Plant skin trace, charcoal
26e	0.10	0.01	0.02	0.04	—	—	—	—	Plant skin trace, Charcoal trace
27a	0.04	Trace	—	0.13	—	—	—	—	—
27b	0.05	Trace	—	0.13	—	—	—	—	—
27c	0.05	Trace	—	0.11	—	—	Trace	—	—
27d	0.06	Trace	—	0.09	—	—	—	—	Charcoal trace
27e	0.06	0.01	—	0.09	—	—	—	—	—

[a] Five samples, each having a wet weight of 1 gm, were taken from each specimen. The figures for the constituents are dry weights; a "trace" means less than .01 gm.

[b] Portions of Specimens 3, 5, 9, 15, 16, 20, 23, and 24 were sent to Elizabeth M. Dusseau and Richard J. Porter, University of Michigan, for parasitological analysis (see Chapter 7).

[c] Dr. Barry Hinderstein, Sam Houston State University, has identified these snake bones as belonging to the subfamily Colubrinae.

Chapter 6

Pollen Analysis of Human Paleofeces from Upper Salts Cave

JAMES SCHOENWETTER

Arizona State University

Introduction

The identification and/or statistical analysis of pollen from coprolites and dung has been relatively ignored by palynologists. In North America, Laudermilk and Munz (1938) identified pollen from the ancient dung of Pleistocene sloths to supplement their identifications of macrofossil vegetal remains from such materials. Their objective was accumulation of data pertinent to the question of the diet of these extinct animals. Martin, Sabels, and Shutler (1961), dealing with the same issue but also with questions of paleoenvironmental reconstruction, related the analysis of pollen from coprolites of the Shasta ground sloth to a geochemical study. Whereas work has progressed with fecal remains from other animals along the same lines, these pioneering works served to outline two areas of concern for such studies: diet and paleoenvironment.

Archeologists rather quickly recognized the importance of this line of research. Martin and Sharrock (1964) investigated the pollen of prehistoric human feces from Glen Canyon. They concluded that dietary habits of archeological populations could be profitably studied in this fashion, and such pollen studies could be utilized to investigate other aspects of paleoethnobotany. However, they encountered such a wide range of variation in pollen spectra from their samples, and such obvious evidence of overrepresentation of pollen types because of dietary behavior, that they expressed great caution to those who would attempt to utilize such data for paleoenvironmental reconstruction.

The most extensive palynological study of human paleofeces has been accomplished by Kelso (1971). Kelso compared the results of pollen analyses of 37 fecal samples from Hogup Cave, Utah, with those from 13 specimens from Danger Cave, Utah. Thirty-four samples of cave fill from Hogup were also analyzed to reveal major distinctions in the pollen records from contemporaneous specimens of the two different sorts. Taken in combination with the study by Napton and Kelso (1969), a realistic picture emerges of the potential contribution to archeology of pollen analysis of human paleofeces.

Kelso's records for Hogup and Danger Caves illustrate a much closer relationship among the pollen spectra of contemporary paleofecal specimens than did Martin's and Sharrock's results. There is also a closer statistical relationship between contemporary paleofecal pollen spectra and cave fill pollen spectra at Hogup Cave than would be anticipated on the basis of the earlier, more limited studies. This suggests that human paleofecal pollen records may indeed yield data pertinent to paleoenvironmental reconstruction. At least, this may be so if a sufficient series of specimens is available and adequate demonstration of contemporaneity of samples can be provided. On this point, however, Kelso demurs. He suggests that consistent fluctuations in the paleofecal pollen records through time are predominantly functions of variations in cultural pattern and dietary practices rather than reflections of the paleoenvironmental situation.

This is a rather critical matter to the archeologist, for it is directly pertinent to the dating of human paleofeces and associated archeological materials through the technique of pollen analysis. Pollen dating relies on the assumption that pollen records indicating similar ecological patterns are more likely to be contemporary than not. This assumption is essentially justified in the same way archeologists justify the assumption that sherds of the same pottery type at different sites are more likely to be contemporary than not. Furthermore, pollen dating relies on the assumption that similar ecological patterns revealed by the pollen record are functions of regional climatic events of a sufficient magnitude that they can be isolated in relative time as horizon markers of temporal units. If the pollen records of human paleofeces are functions of dietary practices, or functions of cultural patterns, similar pollen records need not be contemporary. Even if they are contemporary, they need not be reflections of the climatic events used to isolate temporal units.

In my opinion, the picture is not quite so black as presently available evidence and interpretation would indicate. I agree with Kelso that the interpretation he has drawn from his data is well justified. However, I am heartened by the similarity between pollen spectra of contemporary paleo-fecal and cave fill samples. In time, as work progresses, I anticipate the discovery of statistical techniques that will isolate the climatically sensitive portion of such pollen spectra. I judge the principal reasons for similarities among the spectra to be functions of such effects rather than functions of cultural pattern and dietary practices. Until such techniques are established, however, the message of prior research is clear: Pollen analysis of human paleofeces best suits the archeologist's interest in reconstructing patterns of an ethnobotanical character. At present, it is particularly appropriate as an aid to the reconstruction of dietary practices.

An informal report by Benninghoff dealt with the first effort to extract and observe pollen from the human paleofeces of Salts Cave (Watson 1969: 51). No attempt was made to quantify these observations to present a pollen analytic study. Pollen of plants known to have been consumed (Chenopodiaceae—Amarantaceae; *Cucurbita*) was observed, and pollen of plants which are rare to nonexistent in the environs of Salts Cave (*Picea*; cf. Anthemidae or *Artemisia*) was also present. The former sort of pollen was tentatively interpreted as indicating dietary practices; the use of Chenopodiaceae and/or Amarantaceae species as pot herbs and ingestion of *Cucurbita* flowers. The latter pollen represented a possible extension of range of certain plants in prehistoric time, but the evidence was granted to be so weak as to be uninterpretable.

The pollen analysis of eight fecal samples reported here represents the results of a contracted research effort. The specimens were collected from Upper Salts Cave in July, 1969, quite apart from the series of 100 specimens analyzed for macrofossil content by Yarnell (1969). They were received at the Palynological Laboratory of the Department of Anthropology at Arizona State University early in September of that year.

Procedures and Methods

Nine paleofecal samples were submitted to the laboratory, with the understanding that eight would be used for pollen analysis; the ninth would serve as a "spare" in the case of laboratory error or sample loss. The proveniences of the samples within Upper Salts Cave were:

Sample 1:   10 m south of P72
Samples 2–5:   P71, Cairns passage
Sample 6:   P62
Samples 7 and 8: P60
Sample 9:   P50, south side of Mummy Valley

It was considered possible that provenience could be a controlling factor on the pollen record of the specimens, with the effect that samples collected in geographic proximity might be more similar to each other than those collected distant from each other. Sample 5 was selected as the "spare," as three other samples were collected from that provenience.

The specimens arrived at the laboratory in protective wrappings of metal foil. These had served to maintain sample integrity and to avoid contamination by modern airborne pollen beyond the confines of Salts Cave. To reduce the prospect of contamination by airborne pollen in the laboratory, the specimens were unwrapped within a fume hood. The specimens were then halved, and material amounting to approximately 15 cm³ volume was removed from the interior core to ensure that the matrix subjected to pollen study did not incorporate pollen that had fallen upon the exterior surface of the specimen after defecation. Because pollen is microscopic and windborne, even clean-room procedures do no more than reduce the probabilities of contamination of specimens. However, the procedures followed to minimize contamination were adequate to the point that such contamination as may have occurred in the field or the laboratory would be statistically insignificant. Pollen was extracted from the sample by the following process:

Step 1. Rinse with distilled water.
Step 2. Rinse with hot 10% KOH, followed by transfer through a sieve of 170 μm mesh to a clean centrifuge tube.
Step 3. Rinse again with hot 10% KOH.
Step 4. Rise twice with distilled water.
Step 5. Rinse with glacial acetic acid.

Step 6. Acetolysis, (Erdtman 1943) including 2-min boiling water bath.
Step 7. Rinse with distilled water.
Step 8. Rinse again with hot 10% KOH.
Step 9. Rinse twice with hot distilled water.
Step 10. Rinse with 95% alcohol.
Step 11. Transfer to storage vials with 95% alcohol.

Each step was followed by centrifugation and decantation of supernate. The remaining matrix was stored in glycerol. The samples are reasonably polliniferous, containing at least 300 grains of pollen per drop of processed matrix.

Observation and counting of pollen was undertaken at 600 magnifications. Pollen was often less frequent than fungal spores (especially Samples 6, 7, 8, and 9). Counts were halted after 200 pollen grains had been tabulated. The remainder of the microscope slide was then scanned to determine the presence of other pollen taxa. This produced results only with Specimen 8, in which a single grain of *Carya* (hickory) was observed.

Identification of the pollen was undertaken without benefit of a reference collection of local floristic types. This, along with the normal problems of taxonomic diagnosis in palynology, results in identifications on a less critical taxonomic level than is preferable.

In reference to Table 6.1:

A. Identification of the wind-pollinated genera is fully secure.

B. Palynological differentiation of the genus *Amaranthus* and many genera in the family Chenopodiaceae, particularly the genus *Chenopodium*, is not reliable without recourse to electron microscopy (Tsukada 1967). I have here combined such pollen under the category Chenopodiineae but believe that most of the pollen observed is of the genus *Chenopodium*.

C. The genera *Iva* (sumpweed), *Ambrosia* (ragweed), *Xanthium* (cocklebur) and *Franseria* (bursage) produce pollen which is very similar in morphology. Without reference materials of local representatives, I consider identification within the group unreliable, and so have combined all such pollen in the category Ambrosieae. Most of the pollen is probably of *Iva*, though *Ambrosia* may be strongly represented.

TABLE 6.1   Grain Counts of Pollen Observed in the Fecal Samples from Upper Salts Cave

Pollen type	Fecal specimen number							
	1	2	3	4	6	7	8	9
Wind-pollinated—anemogamous								
Pinus (Pine)	1						1	
Quercus (Oak)	6	8		1			12	2
Gramineae (Grass)	5	1		5	2	2	14	24
Chenopodiineae (Chenopod–Amaranth group)	4	4		95	130	28	8	2
Ambrosieae (sumpweed group)	5		2	86	66	165	6	11
Insect-pollinated—zoogamous								
Other Compositae (e.g., sunflower)	4		2	13	2	5	2	159
Opuntia (Cactus)	1							
Caryophyllaceae								1
Polygonum—tricolporate type	2							
Polygonum—periporate type	7							
Rosaceae			1					
cf. Liliaceae			8				157	
cf. Iridaceae—Amaryllidaceae			187					
cf. *Acorus* (sweet flag)	164	187						
Unknowns	1							1
Total number of grains	200	200	200	200	200	200	200	200

D. The pollen of cacti has been extensively, but not intensively, studied (Kurtz 1948; 1963; Tsukada 1964). For the genus *Opuntia* two pollen types are recognized, one referable to the Cylindropuntia (cholla) subdivision of this genus and the other referable to the Platyopuntia (prickly pear) subdivision. The pollen observed was of the Cylindropuntia type. Chollas do not presently occur in Kentucky or surrounding states, but they are quite common in Arizona. Since a range extension of chollas into Kentucky seems quite improbable, it would at first appear that this sample has become contaminated within the confines of the palynology laboratory. However this is not very probable either, because the pollen is of a zoogamous (non-wind-pollinated) genus. The prospect that a single airborne grain of a pollen type not adapted to such transport would happen to fall into the sample is somewhat more remote, I believe, than the prospect that a population of prickly pear plants in Kentucky may have once existed (or still exist) which produced Cylindropuntia-type pollen rather than Platyopuntia-type pollen. The pollen morphology of all species of prickly pears has not been

investigated, nor has there been much comparative study of geographic populations of the same species. I would thus be hesitant to interpret the occurrence of this pollen grain in the specimen as due to some other mechanism than ingestion of cactus fruit, but consider it probable that cholla cactus fruit was not involved despite the morphology of the pollen grain observed.

E. The two categories of *Polygonum* pollen refer to distinctions in pollen morphology. The periporate form is commonly attributed to the smartweed group within this genus (cf. *P. persicaria*).

F. The pollen type here attributed to Liliaceae is a monocolpate grain with microreticulate-psilate sculpturing. It was normally quite poorly preserved.

G. Pollen of genera in both the Iridaceae (iris) and Amaryllidaceae (amaryllis) families is similar and I am unwilling to offer a more exact identification. The pollen type is larger than pollen of most lilies.

H. *Acorus* is not a common pollen type of Midwestern floras. The *Acorus* (sweet flag) identification was made on the basis of a published description of this pollen (Kapp 1969: 86) and on concurrence in the diagnosis by Dr. A. Traverse, Associate Professor of Geology and Biology at Pennsylvania State University and principal editor of *Catalogue of Fossil Spores and Pollen.*

Results of Analysis

If the pollen of a fecal sample is considered as solid food waste, it should represent the food that an organism has ingested over a period of some 24–36 hours (Callen and Martin 1969: 329). Although paleofeces are normally fairly polliniferous, this limited time-span for accumulation of pollen in the sample creates a tendency for the pollen spectra of fecal remains to be species deficient. Anthropological conclusions to be drawn from the pollen records of human paleofeces must depend upon comprehension of the fashions by which pollen may be transferred from its sources to the human gut, since this species deficiency is an obvious function of dietary practices. Generally, there are four main means of transport:

1. Pollen ingested as, or eaten as a portion of, a food or beverage.
2. Pollen which, clinging to food in storage, is transferred to another food source in the storage container and ultimately eaten. The distinction between 1 and 2 is behaviorally important. Under condition 1 the pollen represents the food eaten; under condition 2 the pollen represents the food stored.
3. Pollen which rains out of the atmosphere onto food during preparation or consumption of a meal, and is ingested as part of the meal.
4. Pollen inhaled into the upper respiratory system from the atmosphere and swallowed along with saliva or drained into the stomach with mucous.

There is no way to determine the transportation mechanism of the pollen by direct observation. The surface of the pollen grain is highly resistant to chemical action and it is essentially unaffected by the mechanism of transport involved. Inhaled pollen could be very ancient, inhaled with dust from disturbed ground, and yet look no different from contemporary pollen of the same type. Ancient pollen could also be ingested together with dirt adhering to food or other objects placed in the mouth.

The analysis of 100 fecal samples from this locality (Yarnell 1969) provides two sources of information pertinent to this problem. First, it is clear that the majority of the pollen grains observed may be of types which provided the bulk of the macrofossil plant remains: Chenopodiineae pollen (potentially derived from *Chenopodium*), Ambrosieae pollen (potentially derived from *Iva*), and "other Compositae" pollen (potentially derived from *Helianthus*). Second, the macrofossil analysis of most specimens indicates a diet of stored food principally consumed during the winter months. This is the period of the year when flowering is minimal and little pollen is being released into the atmosphere. These data would tend to reduce the probability of conditions C and D being critically important in samples from the cave, and would support the idea that either condition A or condition B, or a combination of both, might be reflected in any given sample.

The pollen *spectra* (in distinction to the pollen *grains*) offer little evidence that conditions C or D account for a critical proportion of the pollen recovered. Five of the eight samples contain more than 79% pollen of zoogamous plants. Such plants release too little pollen to the atmosphere for inhalation in this quantity over the period of time represented by a single specimen of fecal waste. The three remaining samples contain sufficient pollen of anemogamous (wind-pollinated) types to allow the possibility that inhalation was important in producing the pollen spectrum. All have large quantities of Chenopodiineae and Ambrosieae pollen, which are produced by plants flowering in the late summer and early fall. However, all have very low frequencies of Gramineae pollen which is produced at the same time of year and released in abundance; they also contain quantities of zoogamous pollen equal to or greater than the quantity of grass pollen recovered, and they contain almost no pollen of the dominant anemogamous forest trees of the district. While such trees pollinate much before the Chenopodiineae and

Ambrosieae, it seems highly unlikely that their pollen would be less well represented in the atmosphere during the growing season than would the pollen of zoogamous plants.

An additional format of evidence pertinent to the problem is the known pattern of relationship between pollen dispersal and seed maturation for the plants represented in the pollen record. The pollination—fruiting relationships of *Chenopodium*, *Helianthus*, and *Iva* are such as to allow a great deal of pollen to be collected with the harvested seed. This is particularly true of *Helianthus* pollen, the majority of which probably never leaves the flower at all. The pollen of *Chenopodium* and *Iva* is released in great quantity within the recess of the flowers to ensure transferral to the female organs of these hermaphroditic plants. Thus it is reasonable to assume that the matured flower (containing the harvestable seed) would also contain much pollen of the species involved. Should a menu be principally composed of one or more of these seed types, the menu would also include pollen gathered with the seeds.

The pollination—fruiting relationships of *Quercus* (oak), *Carya* (hickory), and *Phalaris* (maygrass) are such as to allow a minimum of pollen to be collected with the harvested seed. *Phalaris*, like many other grasses, releases its pollen to the atmosphere from stamens exserted beyond the confines of the flower. Little pollen is thus entrapped within the confines of the area of the matured seed. *Quercus* produces male and female sexual organs in different flowers. The male flowers of *Quercus* do not contact the female flowers and the pollen is wholly disseminated through the atmosphere, so little *Quercus* pollen would be found clinging to mature acorns. Furthermore, hulling of the acorn would disperse any pollen clinging to the mature fruit, and the low frequency of acorn shell in the fecal samples indicates this was a common practice. The nuts of *Carya* ripen within a husk which opens for their release; pollen clinging to the husk would thus not occur with the harvested nuts.

In view of the pollination—fruiting relationships of the major food plants, it is very probable that the pollen spectra of half the samples represent pollen ingested with seeds of *Chenopodium* and *Iva* (Samples 4, 6 and 7) and seeds of *Helianthus* (Sample 9). There seems, in fact, little reason to presume that all the pollen observed was not ingested as a part of a food or beverage.

The macroanalysis of the fecal specimens from which the pollen spectra were obtained (Table 6.2) appears to belie this interpretation. No *Iva* seeds were observed in any of the specimens, for example, and certain samples that contained little by way of Chenopodiineae pollen (Samples 1, 2, 8, 9) contained more *Chenopodium* seed than could be expected. This lack of relationship between pollen spectrum and macrofossil plant remains in the same specimens could indicate that the pollen involved was not, in fact, consumed as part of the diet. A more plausible explanation, however, would be that the pollen, being lighter and smaller, is more quickly carried through the intestinal tract than seed fragments, pieces of nut shell and other more substantial foods. Thus the pollen of a fecal sample may represent a menu distinct from that of the solid waste with which it is associated. This explanation is open to controlled experimental verification, but has yet to be put to a direct test. It should be pointed out that the comparison of palynological and macrofossil remains from some of the human paleofeces at Glen Canyon (Callen and Martin 1969) gave similar results. In that study only two of eight samples showed a positive correlation between the two techniques of investigation.

The plants represented by the vast majority of the pollen in the remaining specimens (Samples 1, 2, 3, and 8) are zoogamous. In order to account for such a quantity of the pollen, one must postulate ingestion of the flowers, flower buds, and/or fresh pollen-contaminated foliage of the plants. The seeds of members of the sweet flag, lily, iris, and amaryllis families are perhaps palatable, but are probably not worth the effort of collection as food. I suspect that the pollen of these samples was mostly obtained through eating of the flower buds. Jonquil flower buds are relatively tasty. According to Yarnell (1964: 187), iris leaves were used as medicine by certain Indian groups. Were flower buds or flowers mixed with leaves for such a purpose, consumption of the greens and/or herbal tea made from them would deposit quantities of this pollen type in the gut. Members of the lily family were also used as medicine (Yarnell 1964: 164), but the portion of the plant involved is not known. *Acorus* is also known as an aboriginal medicinal plant (Yarnell 1964: 164), but it is the roots which are recorded as having been used for this purpose, not the flowers or foliage.

TABLE 6.2 Macrobotanical Constituents of Paleofecal Specimens Submitted for Pollen Analysis[a]

Sample number and Provenience	Components
1—10 m south of P72, Upper Salts	Chenopod
	Sunflower
	Hickory
	Maygrass
	Strawberry
	Fruit skin
2—P71, Cairns, Upper Salts	Chenopod
	Sunflower
	Hickory
3—P71, Cairns	Chenopod
	Sunflower
	Fruit skin
4—P71, Cairns	Chenopod
	Sunflower
	Hickory
	Squash
5—P71, Cairns	Chenopod
	Sunflower
	Maygrass
6—P62	Chenopod
	Sunflower
	Hickory
	Maygrass
	Strawberry
7—P60	Chenopod
	Sunflower
	Hickory
	Maygrass
8—P60	Chenopod
	Hickory
	Fruit skin
9—P50	Chenopod
	Sunflower
	Maygrass

[a] Data compiled by Robert B. Stewart. The specimens were prepared for analysis by soaking in ammonium chloride, which was found to be more effective than trisodium phosphate for breaking up packed masses of hickory nutshell.

Discussion

If it is granted that the vast proportion of the pollen of the fecal samples comes from food ingested, and represents the sorts of foods eaten, what conclusions may be drawn? These data may be used to help answer a series of questions: first, whether the food involved was eaten in any particular season; second, whether the food was fresh or stored; and third, what behavioral patterns may be inferred.

I have suggested that the majority of pollen recovered in specimens 1, 2, 3, and 8 was ingested together with the flowers, flower buds, or fresh pollen-contaminated foliage of the taxa involved. Flowering in these families occurs in the early spring. Iris, for example, is among the first plants to flower in the growing season. It is particularly interesting that neither oak nor hickory pollen occurs in quantity in the fecal specimens. Both are anemogamous taxa which yield much pollen to the atmosphere during their time of flowering. Both are extremely common plants in the modern vegetational pattern, and—judging by the frequency of hickory nutshell in the macrofossil record—both must have been locally frequent plants at the time these samples were deposited. It seems extremely unlikely that quantities of such pollen would not be inhaled and swallowed, or would not fall onto food during cooking and dining, during the period of flowering involved (April—May).

The interpretation of winter through very early spring seasonality offered by pollen analysis must be tempered, however, by the fact that so few samples have been analyzed and the knowledge that very short time periods (24—36 hours) are represented by each specimen. Yarnell (1969: 49) has argued that macrofossil evidence is consistent with an interpretation of year-round plant and small-animal consumption. Hence an all-season utilization of the cave seems reasonable. I feel that the pollen record does not serve to reinforce this conclusion, and am particularly impressed that at least half of the randomly selected specimens show evidence of March—April seasonality. It would seem that if year-round utilization of the cave did occur, it was less constant in the summer than in the late fall through the early spring period.

The macrofossil remains indicated that the diet represented by Salts Cave human paleofeces was predominantly of stored foods. Fresh foods (sumac, strawberry, viburnum, etc.) were present in only 20% of the specimens observed by Yarnell, and were only sparsely represented where they did occur. The abundant food types represented by macrofossils were of presumably stored foods. The pollen record reinforces this conclusion dramatically. In half the samples there is little pollen that is not likely to have been consumed along with stored seeds. In the remaining specimens, the predominant pollen is of types indicating a time of year when fresh plant food could not have provided the bulk of the diet. Thus, while the pollen record provides evidence of consumption of fresh plant foods to a higher degree than the macrofossil record, and while it adds to the list of known fresh plant foods in the diet, it again indicates the overwhelming importance of stored plant food in the menus of Salts Cave prehistoric miners.

Of all sources of information archeologists might utilize to reconstruct ancient culture, none would seem more obscure than the pollen contents of human paleofeces. But the palynological data, taken in the context of the macrofossil data and the archeological facts of spatial and temporal distribution, do seem to allow insight into the anthropology of the Salts Cave population that left these remains. With such a limited pollen record to go by, I am at this juncture not sufficiently confident to offer conclusions. But some conjunctions of data do appear to offer grounds for testable hypotheses regarding prehistoric behavior.

The most obvious conjunction is that of the occurrence of pollen representing very early spring consumption of fresh plant foods with fecal samples representing a diet of stored seeds and the presence of an activity pattern of the mining of emetic minerals. The mining of mirabilite for its medicinal properties seems wholly in keeping with the reconstruction of a high-roughage diet of stored seeds. The pollen record adds yet another dimension to this interpretation that the mineral had a medicinal role. The season of collection of the plants represented by these pollen records is the season when very little fresh vegetable food is available in the deciduous forest environment. By November, and certainly by December, the vitamin resources of fresh vegetable foods available to the prehistoric population must have reached a low ebb. This would perforce have continued until the time when such early germinating plants as are represented by *Acorus*, Lilliaceae and Iridaceae—Amaryllidaceae pollen was available. Vitamin deficiency diseases such as scurvy may not have laid an excessive stress upon the population by March, but it seems likely that they would have existed. The ethnobotany of more northerly districts, at least, involved medicinal remedies for scurvy (Yarnell 1964: 83, 145).

Thus I think it no accident that half the paleofecal specimens selected randomly from the cave contain pollen of early spring plants. I would suggest that this pollen had been consumed as a medicine, probably in the form of an herbal tea serving the same function as the patent medicine vitamin-charged tonics existing today on drug store shelves. The high frequency of specimens indicative of such "dosing" in the cave context could indicate two, not mutually exclusive, behavior patterns. (1) A pattern of multiple medication for the discomfort of illness (a "wide spectrum" approach not unknown to modern physicians) or (2) a pattern of systematic successive medications, amounting to a ritual, that may have been established for relief of illness or may have had social or religious values.

A second conjunction of data is the indication from both macrofossil and pollen studies that menus were rather limited. Of the hundred specimens investigated by Yarnell, 21 specimens had only one food type represented as very abundant or abundant and another 54 specimens had only two food types so represented. Only 5 specimens had four food types represented as very abundant or abundant, and no specimens exceeded this number of abundant food types. Two thirds of the pollen records also indicate only one to three food types being consumed. This simplicity of menus is in contrast with the macrofossil evidence of a wide availability of food resource types, and would appear to reflect some dietary strategy on the part of the population.

Two hypotheses come to mind. On the one hand, the strategy may be that of a sociological subunit, or special work group, of cavers. Thus what we see reflected in the data is the diet, perhaps the seasonal diet, of persons who knew the cave and could find their way around in it and exploit it efficiently. The high carbohydrate–high fat content of such a seed and nut diet, and its light weight and small bulk per calorie, seems admirably suited the demands of miners working the mineral deposits for a short period.

Alternatively, the dietary strategy may be that of a nonelitist group, perhaps simply those who were in the cave to obtain mineral for their own use or the use of a few others. We would expect if this were the case that the dietary strategy was that common to the group or groups of which these individuals were a part, but perhaps a seasonal strategy.

I favor the latter of these alternatives, since the evidence of consumption of medicines offered by the pollen record seems to me less likely an activity of a specialist group. Also, I am rather unconvinced of the functional necessity of a caver diet despite my feeling that the utilization made of the cave would tend to indicate its exploitation by people who were, for the most part, skilled and experienced.

If the dietary strategy is that common to a nonelitist group, some further inferences may be offered. If a given menu involved a small variety of stored foods, but a wide variety of stored foods was available for consumption, it would seem that the food storage containers were segregated by food type in large degree. Also, it would appear, only one or two storage containers were utilized for the preparation of any given meal. If different forms of food were mixed in the storage containers, or if many storage containers were tapped for food at a given time, menus would not so consistently evidence the abundance of only one or two food types.

A functional explanation, particularly if the diet represented in Salts Cave specimens is acknowledged as primarily a winter diet, is that the storage containers were carefully sealed to prevent food spoilage. Menu variety was thus sacrificed to reduce the loss of stored foods over the long period of the winter season. We seem here to witness, then, the sort of human group in which each food consumption unit (perhaps a nuclear family) has access to only one or two storage containers at a given time because its food resources must be conserved until the following season of harvest.

In view of the availability of a variety of stored foods, however, menu variety could have been obtained through sociocultural food distributive mechanisms. Such distributive systems are not ethnographically rare, particularly during seasons when food is not plentifully available. The effect of food distributive systems among the members of a group, predictably, would be menu variety and an increase in the number of types of food in relative abundance at any given meal. The kind of dietary strategy indicated by the Salts Cave paleofeces, then, may be indicative of a group either too small in size or too ineffectively organized to achieve the level of sociocultural cohesion in which food-sharing is a daily practice.

This leads to the suggestion that neither large group size nor village life was typical for the populations having access to Salts Cave in prehistoric times. Although this is an extreme anthropological conclusion to draw from the evidence of paleofecal analysis, it seems in keeping with the known archeological record of the region.

The data of the paleofeces also, of course, indicate a rather impressive reliance upon domesticated plant foods. There is no longer much antipathy to the idea that sumpweed, sunflower, chenopods, and perhaps squash were domesticated plants during the Early Woodland period and perhaps prior to this time in the American Midwest. The botanical evidence, combined with the archeological record, is fairly convincing (Fowler 1971). Even if biological domestication, involving genetic distinction from wild varieties, had not yet taken place, the probability of a cultural commitment having been made to these food resources through systematic growth encouragement (i.e., farming) and harvesting seems reasonably clear.

If the suggestion that Salts Cave populations were small-group, nonvillage populations is taken in the context of the conclusion that Salts Cave populations were also farming populations, some conflict may be thought to arise. Traditionally, food producing populations are archeologically recognized as village populations; the two behavior patterns are so functionally integrated ethnographically that their separation seems anthropologically inappropriate. But we are now aware that the earliest evidences of agricultural activity in the New World (cf. Byers 1969; Flannery 1970; Whitaker and Cutler 1971) occur in nonvillage contexts. Also, there seems to be a general pattern within specific areas of North America, such as the American Southwest (Dick 1965; Martin and Schoenwetter 1960) and the Central Mississippi Valley (Schoenwetter in prep.; Fowler 1971), that food production practices are first recognized in nonvillage settlement contexts. Whether the sort of behavior involved should be classed as "incipient" agricultural or horticultural is not relevant here. Just as we have discovered that the Childean model that directly correlates the introduction of ceramic technology with food production is not valid, so we now have evidence in growing abundance to indicate that a direct correlation of village settlement patterning with food production is not valid. The conflict of interpretation suggested in the first sentence of this paragraph, then, is more apparent than real. While the conflict may exist, it is not evidenced nor does it stand supported by anthropological example.

Summary

The principal concerns in the study of pollen records from human paleofeces are in the areas of dietary reconstruction, seasonality of food consumption, culturally controlled behavior and paleoenvironmental reconstruction. Of the four, the last area of interpretation is recognized as the most poorly interpretable. In this report, I have eschewed concern with the question of paleoenvironment because the sampling and analysis program was clearly inadequate to the demands of such a complex question.

As regards seasonality, it has been shown that the pollen record supports the conclusion of specific seasonality. All the data could be consistent with an interpretation of utilization of the cave between mid-October and mid-April. The only pollen record which could be considered consistent with an interpretation of cave utilization between mid-April and mid-September is that in which fresh cactus fruit consumption may be considered evidenced.

In the area of dietary behavior, the pollen record both reinforces and amplifies the conclusions drawn by Yarnell. A diet essentially composed of stored seeds and nuts is most consistent with both forms of record. The palynological data adds to the list of fresh vegetable foods consumed, but is most reasonably interpreted in terms of a contribution of such foods to the diet as rare occasionals (cactus fruit) or as components of medicines (sweet flag, lily, iris, and/or jonquil).

Through the conjunction of archeological, plant macrofossil and palynological data, this report has attempted something else in the analysis of pollen records from human paleofeces. It has offered three inferences of behavioral and cultural character that derive from the conclusions regarding diet:

(1) that the use of medicines was common in the population utilizing Salts Cave. These may have been functional medicines, for the relief of physiological stress, or they may have been ritual medicines;

(2) that the limited menus of the population are a reflection of either small group size or a noncohesive sociocultural pattern. I favor the interpretation that both alternatives refer to the same organizational phenomenon in the anthropology of the population: a nonvillage settlement pattern;

(3) that the economic base for the population or populations contributing to the paleofecal record was food production rather than food gathering. These inferences are submitted as hypotheses subject to independent testing which may illustrate the archeological potential of the pollen records of human paleofeces.

Chapter 7

The Search for Animal Parasites in Paleofeces from Upper Salts Cave

ELIZABETH M. DUSSEAU AND RICHARD J. PORTER
University of Michigan

Parasitological studies of 13 paleofecal specimens (3c, 5c, 9c, 15c, 16c, 20c, 23c, 24c, SCU 9, SCU 10, SCU 11, SCU 12, and SCU 13) from the area around survey station K31 which is 150 m north of the Cairns in Upper Salts Cave, have been completed.

Following reconstitution in 0.5% trisodium phosphate, extensive microscopic examinations were made of the suspensions, both directly and following concentration procedures.

All specimens are negative for evidence of parasitic infection with the possible exception of 23c. In this specimen, nematode larvae have been found which cannot be identified (Figure 7.1). They are not *Enterobius*. They could possibly be infective larvae of either *Strongyloides* or a hookworm. Available evidence indicates that all human hookworms now present in the Western Hemisphere were introduced from Europe and Africa in post-Columbian times. If population of the Western Hemisphere by human groups involved generations of migration through a temperate region, it is extremely unlikely that either hookworm or *Strongyloides* could have traveled with the migrant population. The lack of a specific date on 23c adds doubt to the situation. Accordingly,

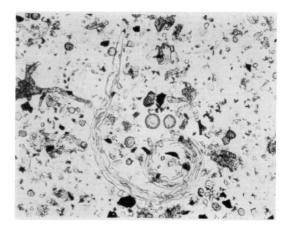

Figure 7.1 Nematode larva from Upper Salts Cave paleofecal specimen 23c.

it would be rash to postulate that this presumed nematode is either a hookworm or a *Strongyloides*.

At the time of deposition of specimen 23c, non-pathogenic nematodes might have been transported to the area in or on those Indians moving into and out of the cave. It is not inconceivable, therefore, that these larvae could be of a non-parasitic nature.

Chapter

8

Ovum and Parasite Examination of Salts Cave Human Paleofeces

GARY F. FRY

Youngstown State University

Eight paleofecal specimens from the vicinity of survey station K31 in Upper Salts Cave, Kentucky, were examined for parasites and ova. The samples were first rehydrated by soaking them in a 0.5% solution of trisodium phosphate (Na₃PO₄), after the method developed by Van Cleave and Ross (1947). Four examinations were made of each specimen: two after mechanical concentration utilizing a 125-μm sieve, and two after concentration using a modified formaline—ether technique (Fry 1970). An examination consists of standard transverse microscope scan of one or two drops of a sample plus one drop of Lugol's iodine solution.

One sample contained several eggs of what appear to be members of the roundworm genus *Ascaris* sp., probably species *A. lumbricoides*. The ova are typical of the fertilized eggs of this species being broadly ovoidal with a thick, transparent shell and coarsely mammilated outer layer (Faust *et al.* 1970: 337). Eggs vary from 45 to 75 μm in length by 35 to 50 μm in width.

Ascaris lumbricoides is the most cosmopolitan and common helminth (roundworm) and has been found in many parts of the world. It thrives in warm or temperate, moist climates where soil is polluted by infected feces. Infection is direct from feces-contaminated soil, food, or drink to mouth, with fertilized eggs remaining infective for many months. Infection in man is typically only with eggs from human sources, although infection is also reported from orangutan, dog, cat, sheep, muskrat, and squirrel. Infection by *A. lumbricoides* may cause toxic damage by absorption of the by-products of dead and living worms or traumatic damage causing nervousness and irritation, poor digestion, diarrhea, and acute inflammation of the bowel (Faust *et al.* 1970: 335—340).

In view of the sanitary habits of aboriginal visitors to the caves, it is not surprising that such infections were maintained among them.

Chapter

9

Observation and recording in
Middle Salts Cave: The Blue Arrow Passage

PATTY JO WATSON

Washington University

No collections beyond those noted in Watson *et al.* (1969) were made in this passage. However, detailed recording was carried out. Aboriginal traffic here was much heavier than in Indian Avenue or elsewhere in Lower Salts. We had collected 11 fecal specimens as well as fragments of squash and gourd from the Blue Arrow Passage previously (this passage is shown on Figure 3.1). Other remains of these types are still present, as are fragments of fiber ties, torch and fire material, pieces of charcoal, and mined areas. Several of the mined areas show extensive and intensive battering indicating that the Blue Arrow Passage—like nearly all of Upper and Middle Salts—was definitely exploited for its minerals. This is not true in Lower Salts, where traces of mining are sporadic, and, in many passageways, nonexistent.

The nature and density of remains in the Blue Arrow Passage is illustrated by the following description abstracted from the original notes on the B survey portion of that passage (see page 28 for a discussion of the recording technique).

The connection between Upper Salts and the Blue Arrow Passage is a rock-floored crawlway (survey stations B1 to B9) about 1 m wide and 0.75 m high that leads down through the breakdown to a canyon passage partially underlying Upper Salts (Figure 3.1). There is scattered torch material throughout the crawlway and two gourd fragments are lying on a ledge at the junction of the crawlway with the canyon at B9. Here it is possible to stand and to walk in an erect or nearly erect position along the passage. Torch debris and smudges are present here and throughout the entire passage. In terms of relative density they approach Upper Salts.

In addition the following items are present: 1 m north of B9 is a paleofecal fragment, and 4 m farther on is a small piece of cordage. At B11 there is a *Gerardia*[1] stalk with the seed pods intact lying on the floor near the west wall. Between B12 and B13 there is occasional battering on both walls. Three meters south of B13 there is a paleofecal fragment against the east wall under an over-

---

[1]*Gerardia* is here used in a broad sense and includes *Aureolaria* Raf. as well as related forms such as *Dasystoma* Raf. For a brief discussion of this plant in Salts Cave see Watson *et al.* (1969: 33).

hanging ledge, and there is another in a pile of cane near the west wall 5 m north of B13. One meter north of B14 are two fragments of charred wood, the larger of these is 8 by 10 cm. Two and one-half meters north of B15 is a fecal specimen *in situ* on a ledge on the west side of the passage (Watson *et al.* 1969: Pl. 10 upper). At B20 and B21 and between A62 and A59 there is battering on the walls indicating prehistoric gypsum mining.

Chapter 10 Lower Salts

PATTY JO WATSON
Washington University

Except for six fecal specimens and one mineral specimen removed from the F survey for analysis, and a worked mussel shell (probably a spoon or scoop; cf. Watson *et al.* 1969: Pl. 13E; Parmalee, Paloumpis and Wilson 1972: Figure 3) found in a crawlway near F25, no further collections have been made in Lower Salts. However, a considerable amount of time was spent tracing and recording aboriginal remains in a mazelike series of passages underlying the area of Upper Salts between Dismal Valley and Wilson's Accident. These passages are connected to Indian Avenue by a long canyon, the F survey, and were unknown to us at the time of publication of the 1969 report (Watson *et al.* 1969). At that time we knew only of Indian Avenue, and had to reach it by a 550-m-long crawl and crouch way beginning at the Corkscrew near Grand Forks in Upper Salts (Figures 3.1 and 10.1; Watson *et al.* 1969: 5 and Figure 3). As noted in the earlier report, the Indian route to Lower Salts was then a mystery to us. When the second phase of work in Salts Cave began during the early spring of 1969, Roger Brucker—Cave Research Foundation Member and Director—was asked to take charge of the project of locating the aboriginal route to Lower Salts. During March and April, 1969, he and several volunteers worked on this problem by means of altimeter readings, dye tracing, and—once the general area of the connection between Upper and Lower Salts was known—by rock pounding and shouting between parties on each of the two main cave levels. Finally, Brucker's parties, by moving some of the breakdown near survey station S10 in Dismal Valley and in the F survey of Lower Salts respectively, were able to open a direct route from above to F13 in Lower Salts. But this was not, of course, the exact route followed by the Indians. Brucker (n.d.) offers the following reconstruction:

The T-survey passage once continued beneath Dismal Valley in a sweeping S curve. It departed from under the north wall of the Valley near F13 and continued northward to Indian Avenue. Dismal Valley itself was filled to near its top with orange sand, to an elevation of 675 feet, probably at a time when the main part of Salts Cave was draining actively northward at an elevation of about 600 feet.

After the 600 foot level ceased to be the active drain, local drainage enlarged the T-survey passage,

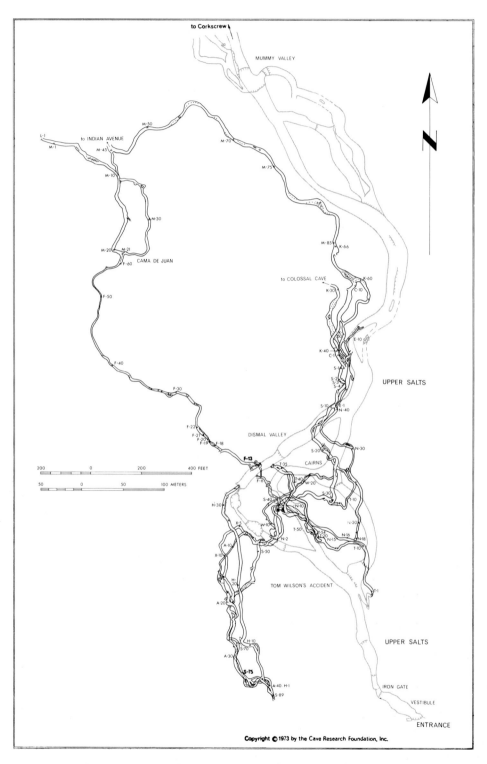

Figure 10.1 Map showing main area of aboriginal activity in Lower Salts.

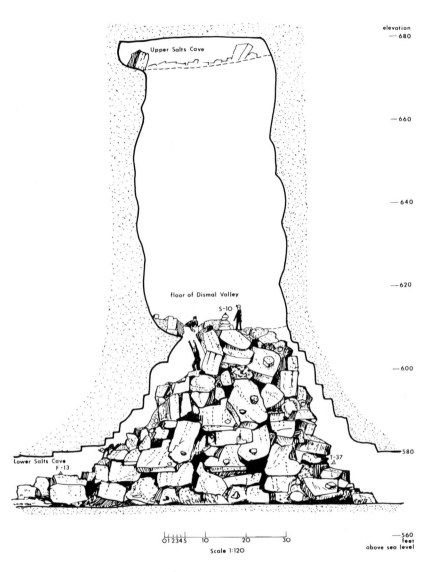

Figure 10.2 Section through Dismal Valley at station S10. (Original drawing by Roger W. Brucker.)

cutting it downward from its top at 580 feet to its bottom at 567 feet. The invading waters cut upward through the thin Dismal Valley floor, permitting the deep sand fill to wash downstream. Probably through alternate periods of flood and low water, the entire section of fill (100 feet long × 30 feet wide × 40 feet thick) went down the drain.

Where the sand fills are intact at both ends of Dismal Valley, the top surface is covered with a foot-deep layer of limestone breakdown. A similar layer on top of the now-missing fill was lowered to fill partially the T-survey passage canyon in the floor. . . . My guess is that small holes led to both T37 on the south side of Dismal Valley and F13 on the north side about 3000 years ago. Further, I believe it was possible to crawl at that time between the two in ledge-protected pockets ... Through the holes the aborigines could reach the water below, a scarce commodity in this part of the cave. The route also led to Indian Avenue.

The small holes were later blocked, perhaps by slumping of the breakdown, resulting in the current topographic situation in the area of the connection (Figure 10.2).

With the exception of human footprints—so far unique to Indian Avenue—the aboriginally traveled areas of much of Lower Salts are generally comparable to Indian Avenue insofar as archeological remains are concerned (cf. Watson *et al.* 1969: 25–31). These are all canyon passages, i.e., they are usually narrow (1–2 m wide) and often half or two-thirds choked with breakdown, although one can usually move along them in an erect or semi-erect position. The passages form a complex series of multilevel, superimposed, intermittently connecting canyon passages (Figure 10.1). The key to this confusing complex is the fifth-level canyon, which has been mapped by the Cave Research Foundation as the S survey (not to be confused with the Upper Salts S survey in Dismal Valley). The S survey connects to the north with Indian Avenue and runs on to the south for an as yet unknown distance. Indian material in the S survey is confined to the first 75 survey stations, however, possibly because the canyon becomes very wet south of this point so that debris would not have been preserved. Above the narrow, twisting S survey are four other, intermittently intersecting levels of canyon passages with a maximum vertical relief of some 25–30 m. Moving along the upper canyons requires considerable caution in the areas where lower passages and upper intersect, leaving one straddling a 2.5–3-m-wide slot that goes straight down 10 m or more. The Indians negotiated these areas freely for we find torch smudges and charcoal throughout, and occasional mined areas (the latter, however, only in places where the passage has a floor).

In a patch of sand in one of the upper canyons (at survey station X5) are approximately 40 enigmatic pawprints, identified by Cave Research Foundation biologist Tom Poulson as those of raccoon (Figure 10.3). The prints go both directions in the passage. The animal apparently wandered into the upper cave, became confused, and kept on into the interior to Dismal Valley and thence Lower Salts. Although his body has not been found, it is difficult to believe he ever got out. He may have

Figure 10.3 Pawprints at survey station X5 in Lower Salts Cave; the scale is a 15 cm rule.

reached the S survey and starved to death, then his body decomposed in this damper part of the cave. In any case, his trip may have antedated the passage of the Indians because four of his pawprints have bits of cane charcoal in them and one is overlain by a small fragment of fiber cord. If he did precede the Indians, however, it is hard to understand why there are no Indian prints in the same area.

Nature of the Aboriginal Remains in Lower Salts

The Indians explored all the passages of Lower Salts shown in Figure 10.1 except that part of the route to the Corkscrew that lies between M21 and the Corkscrew itself, and the K survey that leads from K45 to Colossal Cave. Judged by relative density of debris, the F, N, and A surveys received the most traffic, although none can compare with the Blue Arrow Passage or Upper Salts in quantity and variety of materials. Nineteenth and early twentieth century cavers did not visit or know about the part of the cave now called Lower Salts. Although Cave Research Foundation exploring and mapping teams had been in all these passages previous to our archeological recording trips (in fact it would be very difficult to accomplish the recording without survey points to tie to), recent traffic has been kept to a strict minimum, and the majority of debris is *in situ*.

The F survey is a passage running from N8 to Cama de Juan (M21; the M survey then continues to Indian Avenue at M45). Throughout most of its extent (F12 to F60) the F survey is a dry canyon with a rocky floor. In some places it is partially choked with breakdown. Between N8 and F6, however, the canyon is damp (a small stream is intermittently present) and sandy-floored. Near F5 is a small vertical shaft with water trickling down the sides and a pool in the bottom. At F6 the survey enters a low crawlway (60 to 75 cm high) opening about 1.3 m above the sandy-floored canyon. The canyon ends in a pile of breakdown, but the crawlway leads north under Dismal Valley to Indian Avenue.

What follows is an illustrative abstract of the original notes on a portion of the F survey (charcoal and torch/campfire fuel are scattered throughout the entire passage):

Six meters north of F18 is a fecal deposit on the floor just east of the trail; the passage at this point is half-choked with breakdown so one must crouch low to move along it. Bark fragments are present at both F19 and 20. [Some fragments of this bark were sent to Robert B. Stewart who identified it as oak; personal communication.] At F20 the gypsum crust on the ceiling is smoke blackened as are fragments of mirabilite coming off the ceiling between F20 and F21. Four meters south of F21 there are paleofecal fragments near the west wall together with weed stalks, cane, and a piece of wood. At F21 there is battering on both east and west walls as well as on the ceiling. One item of the torch/campfire fuel on the floor here is an unusually long (34 cm) *Gerardia* stalk (see footnote, page 63).

Seven meters north of F21 is a paleofecal specimen near the east wall. At F22 is a fragment of warty squash on a ledge on the east side of the passage; the wall opposite is battered. Three meters north of F22 is a fecal deposit on a ledge on the east side of the passage, and the ceiling is smoke-blackened at this point. One meter farther north there are squash fragments on the passage floor. At F23 is a 120 cm long weed stalk (probably *Solidago*) lying on a ledge on the west side of the

passage where there is a concentration of charcoal fragments.

On April 11, 1969, a crystal was collected at F25 and subsequently submitted to William B. White, Cave Research Foundation Chief Scientist, for mineralogical analysis. He reports in a personal communication: "An X-ray diffraction pattern showed the specimen to consist entirely of epsomite, $MgSO_4 \cdot 7H_2O$. There was no evidence for additional minerals." This is the only formal evidence so far for the presence of epsomite in Salts Cave, although it is common in Lee Cave (for White's earlier summary of Salts Cave mineralogy, see Watson *et al.* 1969: 79–82).

Discussion of two other passages will round out this summary description of the aboriginal activity areas in Lower Salts: the N and the S surveys.

The N survey is a more complicated canyon than F. It begins in an impressive room where the A, N, and S passages come together. The room is characterized by vertical relief up to 10 m in several places and by an array of large breakdown blocks, some the size of an automobile. The N survey is at an intermediate level between the A (high) and the S (low) passages. N1 is up at the level of A, but N2 drops some 6 to 7 m, and from there on the N is a narrow, twisting, dry canyon. This canyon often lacks a floor so that the cave-explorer, aboriginal or modern, is forced to straddle a 7 to 14 m drop as he makes his way along narrow rock ledges. This is conspicuously the case at several places between N2 and N8. Then the passage opens out into a sandy-floored tunnel with ledges on both sides, many of which contain charcoal and smudges from prehistoric torches. At N40, the N survey joins the S in another multilevel junction room.

An illustrative abstract of the notes taken in part of the N survey follows (torch/campfire fuel remains are present throughout the passage).

At N15 there is battering on both the south and north walls; sporadic battering continues on both walls between N15 and 16. At N18 there is a charred fragment of bark tie lying on a ledge on the east side of the passage. At N19 there is an unmapped cutaround passage on the east side that shows possible batter marks on the walls.

Five meters north of N20 there is battering high

on the east wall; it appears that the miner stood on a ledge projecting from the west wall and leaned across the passage to work on the opposite side.

Three meters south of N22 there are batter marks high on the east wall and again 5 m north of N22 the east wall has been mined. On the floor here are two fragments of uncharred wood and two pieces of a possible vine tie; nearby are a bark fragment and a fragment of a small branch.

The S survey is now the main or master passage in the Lower Salts complex. It is at a lower level than either the F or the N and is a damp canyon throughout most of its extent, becoming wet at about S80. From that point on, aboriginal debris is absent, either because the Indians did not go any farther, or because the water has destroyed the evidence of their passage. Remains in the S survey—unlike those in the drier parts of Lower Salts—consist almost exclusively of charcoal fragments and smudges: Aboriginal traffic was present but light. In the damp passages one cannot be certain of tracing the Indians' movements by means of charcoal scatters because the water, during periodic floods, easily shifts the charcoal from one place to another. However, soot smudges on the walls or ceiling are clear evidence that prehistoric cavers passed here.

The first and strongest impression one has when tracing the prehistoric people through these labyrinthine passages in Lower Salts is that they were extremely skilled and knowledgeable spelunkers. Even with the help of the marked survey stations it is impossible not to become confused and temporarily lost quite frequently until one becomes very familiar with the maze. Moreover, many places are difficult to negotiate even for a person with both hands free; it is hard to imagine working one's way along while carrying a flaming torch in one hand. Yet the Indians seemingly moved freely through the entire complex (although spending most of their time in the higher, drier canyons), pausing here and there to remove minerals from the walls but only rarely doing any intensive mining. It is possible that the remains here represent reconnaissance trips, and that the quantity of mineral available in Lower Salts was not adequate to justify regular work crews going there to remove it (for a discussion of the logistics of mining minerals in Salts Cave, see Watson et al. 1969: 57—64). Certainly there is no evidence that these passages received the amount of traffic that is evidenced in Upper and Middle Salts. Nevertheless, those who scouted out the twisting, intertwined canyons were consummate cavers whose exploits in the Flint Mammoth Cave System were unequaled for at least 3000 years.

Chapter 11

Excavations in the Vestibule of Salts Cave

PATTY JO WATSON
Washington University

In 1916, N. C. Nelson carried out a series of excavations in prehistoric midden debris still present at that time in the entry chamber, or Vestibule, of Mammoth Cave (Nelson 1917). During that same period, he visited nearby Salts Cave and noted sparse remnants of prehistoric debris in the Vestibule there (Nelson 1917: 30). The presence of middens or ash beds in Salts Cave Vestibule had been referred to earlier by Col. Bennett Young (1910: 305), and it is clear that these beds had been dug into and thoroughly disturbed by relic collectors during the late nineteenth and early twentieth centuries. No trace of them remained on the surface inside the Vestibule when we began our work in Salts Cave. However, during the second phase of investigations (1969–1972), we dug a test trench in the Vestibule to see whether prehistoric remains were present below the surface. This first trench was Test C, and it revealed enough aboriginal cultural debris to indicate that further excavation might provide stratigraphic and cultural information not available from the cave interior. Hence, several other test pits were dug in the Vestibule during 1969, 1970, and 1971. The results of the excavations are described in this section; see Figure 11.1 for a plan view of the Vestibule showing the locations of

the trenches. Light was provided by pressure lamps (one or two per person), and all excavation was done with trowel and grapefruit knife, except that of very rocky strata for which we also used short-handled, U.S. Army surplus pick-mattocks. Quarter-inch hand-screens were used during the excavation of trench D but not elsewhere. Because of the small scale and slow pace of the digging (plus the fact that a large sample of fill was being floated), it was decided that—for our purposes at that time—screening the moist, clayey sediment required more effort and manpower than the results justified.

Test Trench C

Excavation in the Vestibule began April 8, 1969, when a 1.5 × 3 m trench was laid out against the north wall (Figures 11.1 and 11.3). The trench was designated Test C (Tests A and B were two trenches dug in the cave interior in August, 1963; Watson *et al.* 1969: 20–25). Test C was excavated in 21 10–15 cm levels to a total depth of about 230 cm during the spring and summer of 1969. (Actual excavation dates were April 8–12, May 30–31, and June 28, 1969.) Although bone and

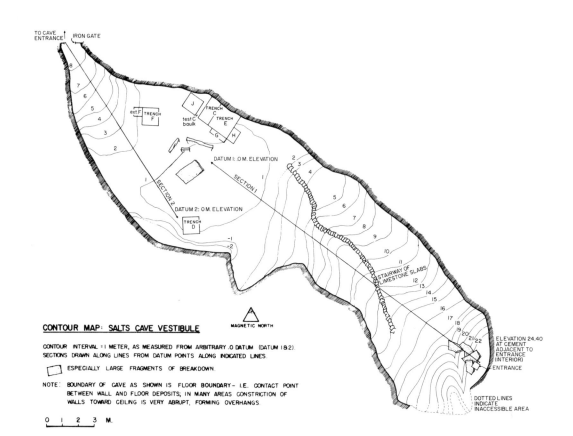

CONTOUR MAP: SALTS CAVE VESTIBULE

CONTOUR INTERVAL = 1 METER, AS MEASURED FROM ARBITRARY .0 DATUM (DATUM 1 & 2).
SECTIONS DRAWN ALONG LINES FROM DATUM POINTS ALONG INDICATED LINES.

☐ ESPECIALLY LARGE FRAGMENTS OF BREAKDOWN.

NOTE: BOUNDARY OF CAVE AS SHOWN IS FLOOR BOUNDARY – I.E. CONTACT POINT
BETWEEN WALL AND FLOOR DEPOSITS; IN MANY AREAS CONSTRICTION OF
WALLS TOWARD CEILING IS VERY ABRUPT, FORMING OVERHANGS.

0 1 2 3 M.

Figure 11.1 Salts Cave Vestibule. Plan view.

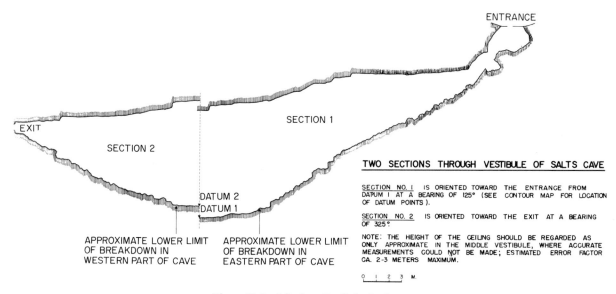

TWO SECTIONS THROUGH VESTIBULE OF SALTS CAVE

SECTION NO. 1 IS ORIENTED TOWARD THE ENTRANCE FROM
DATUM I AT A BEARING OF 125° (SEE CONTOUR MAP FOR LOCATION
OF DATUM POINTS).

SECTION NO. 2 IS ORIENTED TOWARD THE EXIT AT A BEARING
OF 325°.

NOTE: THE HEIGHT OF THE CEILING SHOULD BE REGARDED AS
ONLY APPROXIMATE IN THE MIDDLE VESTIBULE, WHERE ACCURATE
MEASUREMENTS COULD NOT BE MADE; ESTIMATED ERROR FACTOR
CA. 2-3 METERS MAXIMUM.

0 1 2 3 M.

Figure 11.2 Salts Cave Vestibule. Sections.

72

Figure 11.3 Salts Cave Vestibule. Beginning the excavation of Test Trench C; the photo is artificially lighted.

charcoal were present throughout the upper 150 cm of Test C, study of the profile resulted in the conclusion that two layers represent relatively intense periods of midden deposition: one at about 50–60 cm below the surface and the other about 100–120 cm below the surface. Below the second horizon was a series of sand, clay, and rubble layers which were sterile of cultural debris as far down as 230 cm where excavation was stopped.

Test Trench C/N

This designation refers to the northernmost meter of Test C, which was found to be covered with breakdown rock at a depth of 70 cm below the surface and left unexcavated until July 4, 1969, when the rock was removed. On July 4–5 and on August 24–25, 1969, excavation here resulted in the removal of 75 cm of sand and clay in seven levels to a total depth of about 150 cm below the surface.

Test Trench D

This 2 × 2 m square on the south side of the Vestibule was dug in 10 levels to a total maximum depth of 130 cm during the summer of 1969 (June 29 to July 4, and August 25). Deposition here is different from that in Test C. There is much more gravel and rock, indicating that water flow was

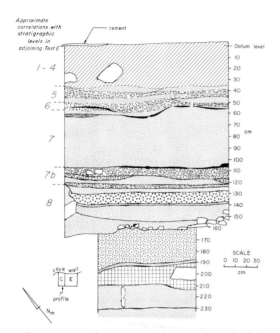

Figure 11.4 Salts Cave Vestibule excavations. South face of Test C profile. A key to Figures 11.4–11.10 appears on page 82.

greater in volume and velocity than at the north wall of the Vestibule. Cultural debris was scarce throughout, although a few pieces of chipped stone and some charcoal fragments were found in each level.

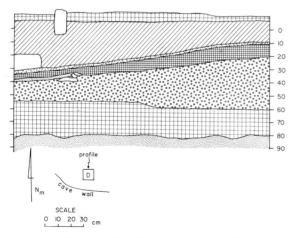

Figure 11.5 Salts Cave Vestibule excavations. North face of Test D profile.

Test Trench E

This began as a 3.0 × 2.5 m trench, later enlarged to 3 × 3 m, and lay immediately adjacent to the east wall of Test C. The trench was excavated during the late summer and fall of 1969 in nine stratigraphic levels to a maximum depth of about 150 cm (the excavation dates were August 23 to September 1, October 18–19, and November 28–30, 1969). The major midden levels found in Test C were encountered and excavated here also, yielding human and animal bone as well as several artifacts. The stratigraphy in general resembled that of Test C.

Test Trench F and F Extension

Test F was a 2 × 2 m square located a short distance upslope from Tests C and E. It was excavated on August 26, 1969, to a maximum depth of about 65 cm. Two superimposed ash beds were found in the northern part of the square, both within the upper 20 cm. The rest of the deposit consisted of dry, gray fill distributed around and among limestone breakdown rock. The latter occurred throughout the square beginning about 50 cm below the surface; it is because of this breakdown that excavation ceased here.

Test F Extension was a 1 × 1 m square laid out on April 4, 1970, adjacent to the northwest corner of Test F so that a controlled sample of the ash beds could be removed for flotation and sifting to recover carbonized plant remains.

Test Trenches G and H

These were small extensions of Test E to the south and east, respectively. Excavated levels in Test G were the same as in the main trench E. The stratigraphic situation in H was somewhat different and it was dug in four levels:

1. Breakdown debris and clay
2. Sandy clay with a lense of midden material (2A)
3. Thin layer of light brown clay, probably equivalent to level 6 in Trench E

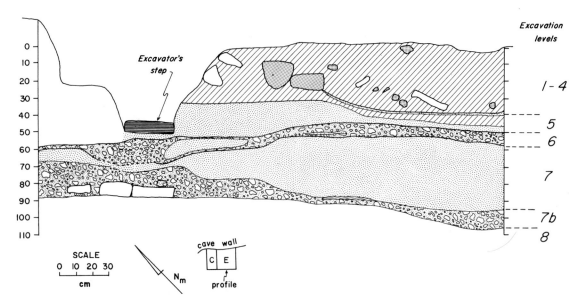

Figure 11.6 Salts Cave Vestibule excavations. South face of Test E profile.

4. A thin sandy layer, probably equivalent to level 7 in E, overlying a midden stratum corresponding to 7b in E.

Test Trench J

This is a 2 × 2 m square dug about 0.5 m west of Test C during the spring of 1970 and the spring and fall of 1971 (April 4–11, 1970; March 20, 1971; April 5, 1971; November 26–28, 1971). It was subdivided into four 1 × 1 m squares and excavated stratigraphically to a maximum depth of 230 cm. The nature of the deposition was a combination of that in the Test F pit and that in the Test C–Test E area. The first stratigraphic unit was the same as that of Tests C and E, but below that in the western half of the square the fill resembled that in Test F; excavation there ceased at a depth of 100 cm because breakdown rock filled that part of the square. In the damper, eastern half of the square the nature of the fill (sands and clays) was more like that in C and E.

Several artifacts and pieces of animal bone were found in this square as well as fragments of human bones and teeth. Excavated dirt below the uppermost stratigraphic unit from the 1 × 1 m square in the southeast corner (J IV) was saved, carried out of the cave, and floated to recover charred plant remains.

Stratigraphy of the Vestibule Trenches

In general, the Vestibule situation seems to represent an intermittent accumulation of garbage (largely the result of butchering and eating game animals), perhaps for the most part left by hunting parties. There does not seem to have been any intensive or lengthy occupation by large numbers of people, although the remains would be consonant with one or two longer-term occupations (a few months at most) by small groups.

The water-laid deposits in C, E, and the eastern part of J must be the result of an active, although small, stream flowing through this part of the Vestibule depositing clay, sand, and gravel in its bed and partially or completely covering the refuse left there by human occupants of the area. The fluctuating activity of this stream can be described with reference to deposits it left in the Test C and E areas. The following interpretation was worked out September 1, 1969, by Cave Research Foundation geologists Arthur and Margaret Palmer, Steve Wells, and John Bassett.

The lowest material exposed in the south face of Test C (Figure 11.4) has a high clay content but is mostly silt. There are some channel sands indicating velocities of 0.5−1 ft/sec for the stream that deposited them. This stratum also includes weathered limestone derived from the cave wall (most of the sandy material comes ultimately from the regional caprock: the Big Clifty Sandstone).

The next few units reflect a breakdown situation (between 190 and 210 cm below the surface in the profile, Figure 11.4) with resultant ponding of the water and stagnation (the clay stratum at 160−185 cm). The finely disintegrated charcoal that permeates the clay layer is a puzzling phenomenon possibly representing some local catastrophe like a brush fire in or around the Sink, water later washing the resultant charcoal into the Vestibule (this horizon was also encountered in Test J).

The sand deposits overlying the black clay indicate relatively high stream velocities, possibly a spring flood situation, with a fair amount of material coming in from the surface (again, largely sand derived from the caprock). These sandy and gravelly strata below the 120-cm mark are the remains of a meandering stream flowing in a channel-and-bar regime. The overlying midden-bearing clay strata reflect periods of stagnant water when the stream was drying up in this spot.

The thick brown and yellow sand deposit above the 105-cm midden layer represents renewed stream activity; the brown sand, darker because it is mixed with clay, was laid down under lower velocity stream conditions.

Similarly, the sand deposits interleaved with clay beds (containing midden debris) in the section between 35 and 55 cm are the result of alternating local wet and dry episodes. The thick capping material accumulated as clay, washed in from the entrance, was trapped in breakdown debris.

In general, it can be concluded that there was never a large amount of water running through this part of the Vestibule, and that the stream could not have moved stones larger than 3−4 cm maximum.

Stream activity is also evidenced in the northeast corner of Test E, where the attenuated midden material spills over the edge of what was once a small stream channel and is covered with gravels and sands (sometimes cross-bedded) laid down by a stream flowing against the cave wall. Above

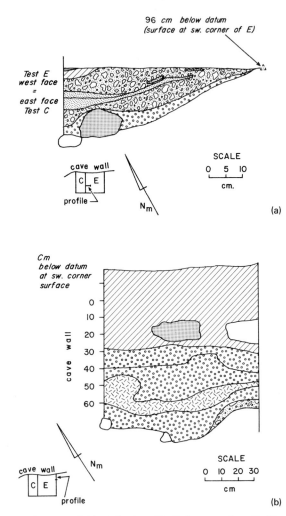

Figure 11.7 (a) Salts Cave Vestibule excavations. Profile of west edge of midden 7b at a point 1 m from the south wall of Test E. (b) Salts Cave Vestibule excavations. Profile of northeast corner of Test E.

these deposits, left by relatively rapidly flowing water, are large breakdown rocks and the capping zone of clay and rubble (Figure 11.7b).

Across the Vestibule, the profile in Test D (Figure 11.5) suggests that a rapidly running stream was often present near or against the south wall, and that its activity alternated with phases of breakdown (probably spalling off of weathered and decomposing limestone from the cave wall).

The archeological situation in Salts Vestibule is, then, a result of interaction between the depositional activities of two intermittently present factors: human groups and water. From time to time the water flowed into the cave entrance, down the slope, and across portions of the Vestibule floor, depositing sand and clay in flat places where they often partially or completely covered trash thrown, dropped, or scuffed there by the people camping in the drier areas of the Vestibule. The main midden deposit can be seen at its present highest point in Test F and in the south face of Test J (Figures 11.8 and 11.9). It overlies and is intermingled with fairly massive breakdown that gives way to the east (down slope) to water laid sands and clays. The transition zone between the higher, dry, breakdown-and-midden and the lower-lying, damp, stream-deposit-and-midden occurs half way across Test J. The midden spilling down from west to east over and through the breakdown overlies and is interleaved with stream sands beginning at just about the 1-m mark (Figure 11.9). In order to account for the sand beds sloping from west to east at

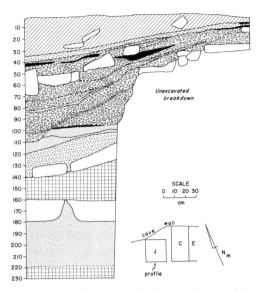

Figure 11.9 Salts Cave Vestibule excavations. South face of Test J profile.

this point, one must postulate that the stream was flowing from north to south, having veered south away from the cave wall to follow along the front of the breakdown pile underlying the western 1-m of J. The north face of Test J shows the same general pattern; midden debris over and among break-

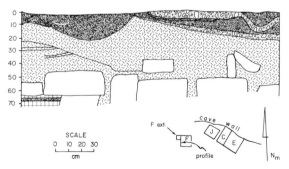

Figure 11.8 Salts Cave Vestibule excavations. West face of Test F profile.

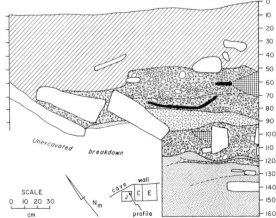

Figure 11.10 Salts Cave Vestibule excavations. North face of Test J profile.

down to the west, midden debris interleaved with stream deposits in the eastern one meter.

In the Test C area, stream deposits comprise a major portion of the profile. The midden debris that slopes markedly from west to east in Test J lies flat in the C profile, then slopes up gradually toward the east into Test E. At a point about one meter north of the south face of E, the profile of the western edge of 7b (Figure 11.7a) showed this midden layer sloping up and overlying a low sand and gravel mound (level 8 in Test E, the mottled sand at the 130-m level on the eastern side of the Test C profile). Sand lenses occur in the midden material here, and it seems clear that Test C covers an area that was a relatively major stream channel for the water running from north to south along the breakdown exposed in Test J.

The 7b midden material covers the earlier stream deposits of level 8, and—as noted on page 76— its northern edge laps into the major stream channel that ran east–west along the cave wall before turning south at Test C (Figure 11.7b).

We can summarize the sequence represented by all the available profiles as follows: The earliest events of which we have a record are breakdown (bottom Test J, 160 cm and below) and stream sands being laid down in front of the breakdown (bottom Test C, 190 cm and below). Next a catastrophic fire occurred in and around the Sink (perhaps), followed after an interval of uncertain duration by rainfall that resulted in much pulverized charcoal being transported into the Vestibule and eventually piled up by slowly moving water against and within the edge of the breakdown. This horizon is present in Test C (120—140 cm), J IV (160—185), and the southern part of J II (160 cm and below).

Later rain storms resulted in faster moving water laying down sand and gravel that was subsequently eroded (125–150-cm zone in C profile, yellow sand between 110 and 120 cm in J). More sand and gravel filled up the channel and was, for the first time, interleaved with midden debris (bones and charcoal). The stream dried and more midden accumulated in the C and E areas (at about the 100-cm level in J, C, and E) until a burst of stream activity occurred again and thick sands were deposited in C and E (60—100-cm horizon in

both), but only sand lenses in J IV (these do not show in the profile because they were present only in the northern part of the square).

The final event was once again breakdown and ponding in the C, E, and J areas, represented by the upper zone of breakdown debris and clay in all three trenches. It is probable that the ash beds mentioned by Young and Nelson were present only in the westernmost, premanently dry part of the Vestibule in the vicinity of Test F and the area south of it.

In conclusion, it may be noted that only once during the 3-year period we worked in the Vestibule did water invade any of our trenches (although it should also be noted that the cement platform covering the entrance diverts some water that would otherwise enter the cave directly). In March, 1970, after very heavy spring rains, enough rain ran through the grated entry (see Watson *et al.* 1969: Plate 2) and down the entrance slope to flood Tests C and E, collapsing portions of their south walls and of the west wall of C. More rain in the succeeding 2 weeks resulted in the collapse of the east wall of E (fortunately all these profiles had already been recorded). Under present conditions nearly all the water runs along the north wall of the Vestibule, but the entrance zone is a very active place and probably lcoked and behaved hydrologically somewhat differently 2000 years ago.

Concerning the Tables in This Chapter

All depth measurements were made by means of string and line level from a datum point on the surface for each trench except D. The datum for trenches C and E was the same: the cement layer at the southeast corner of C and southwest corner of E. The datum for J was the surface at the southwest corner of the trench which is the same level as the C–E datum.

All measurements in F were made from the surface at the southwest corner; the F area is 50—75 cm higher than the C–E–J area. Although the Vestibule floor in the Test D area is generally the same level as at Test C, it is quite rocky and uneven; here we measured depths from the surface aᵢ the center (because two of the corners were filled with breakdown) of each side of the square.

Absolute depths have very little meaning in the Vestibule because of the catastrophic nature of much of the deposition—created as it is by localized breakdown and its after effects—in combination with fluctuating stream activity. Depositional patterns are often very complex in the transition zone between dry breakdown and stream erosion and aggradation. J II and J IV are in this transition zone; C, D, and E are in the stream zone; F is above it in dry breakdown. Hence, it must be stressed that the depths given in the tables of this chapter are only approximations; the depth below

datum of any one stratum may easily vary 20 cm within a distance of 1 m or less. In the dry breakdown areas there may be a considerable depth of deposit that is simply a jumble of debris in, around, and under breakdown rock. In the areas reached by the stream, there are many discrete or discontinuous lenses and pockets of sediment contrasting in color and texture with the immediate surroundings. Therefore, the stratigraphic summaries are simplifications of the sequences in the various trenches, and the general correlation chart (Table 11.7)—although the basic relationships are correct according to present evidence—must be viewed as a diagrammatic rendering.

TABLE 11.1 Salts Cave Vestibule—Trench C Stratigraphic Summary

Nature of deposit Arbitrary levels	Approximate depth below surface[a] (cm)	Nature of deposit
1–3	0–35	Breakdown debris and clay
4	35–50	Stream sands
5	50–60	Brown clay, probable occupation horizon (people living or camping on top of earlier stream deposits)
6–10[b]	60–100	Stream sands
11	100–120	Brown clay, probable occupation horizon
12–15	120–160	Stream sands and gravels
16–17	160–185	Moist black clay containing much finely disintegrated charcoal; the result of a brush fire?
18	185–200	1–2 cm of red sand overlying hard, dry, gray clay (probably decomposed limestone indicating breakdown)
19–21	200–unknown (limit of excavation at 230)	Red orange sand with clayey patches

[a]See pages 78–79.

[b]The bottom 2–3 cm of level 10 are in the occupation horizon below the sand.

TABLE 11.2 Salts Cave Vestibule–Trench C/N Stratigraphic Summary

Arbitrary levels	Approximate depth below surface[a] (cm)	Nature of deposit
1–3	75–110	Clayey sand; stream deposit
4	110–120	Dark clay and sand; some occupation debris mixed with stream deposit
5	120–130	Clayey sand; stream deposit
6–7	130–unknown (limit of excavation at 150)	Stream sands

[a]See pages 78–79.

TABLE 11.3   Salts Cave Vestibule—Trench D Stratigraphic Summary

Arbitrary levels	Approximate depth below surface[a] (cm)	Nature of deposit
1—2	0—40	Upper 10 cm is decomposed limestone looking like hard, dry, gray clay; this is a breakdown deposit and it overlies 30 cm of general breakdown debris and clay like the upper stratum in C, E, J
3	40—50	5 cm of gray and brown clay overlying 5 cm of decomposed limestone like the top 10 cm in this trench; breakdown deposit
4—6	50—70	Yellow sand lense in NW corner at 50—55 cm, rest is gravel and sand; stream deposit
7	70—90	Gravel and sand with some decomposed limestone at north end of trench
8—10	90—unknown (limit of excavation at 130)	Gravel and sand

[a]See pages 78—79.

TABLE 11.4   Salts Cave Vestibule—Trench E Stratigraphic Summary

Stratigraphic levels	Approximate depth below surface[a] (cm)	Nature of deposit
1—4	0—40	Breakdown debris and clay
5	40—52	Breakdown debris and clay with sand
6	52—60	Brown clay; probable occupation horizon
7	60—95	Stream sands
7b	95—105	Brown clay; probable occupation horizon
8	105—unknown (limit of excavation in small test pit 160)	Stream sands and gravels

[a]See pages 78—79.

TABLE 11.5   Salts Cave Vestibule—Trench F Stratigraphic Summary

Arbitrary levels	Approximate depth below surface[a] (cm)	Nature of deposit
1—5	0—unknown (limit of excavation 65 cm)	Gray clay containing midden debris, ash, charcoal lenses; all overlying and intermingled with breakdown

[a]See pages 78—79.

TABLE 11.6 Salts Cave Vestibule—Trench J Stratigraphic Summary

Stratigraphic levels	Approximate depth below surface[a](cm)	Nature of deposit
J I, 1–3	0–50	Breakdown debris and clay
4	50–unknown (limit of excavation at 100)	Midden clay among breakdown
J III, 1	0–25	Breakdown debris and clay
2	25–40	Limestone rubble with midden clay and charcoal
3–4	40–100	Breakdown with interspersed midden
5	100–unknown (limit of excavation at 100)	Sand overlying breakdown
J II, 1–3	0–60	Breakdown debris and clay
4	60–70	Midden-bearing clay
5	70–75	Sand
6	75–105	Midden clay
7	105–110	Sand; in eastern part of square only
8	105–110	Midden clay same as level 6; in western part of square
9	110–115	Midden clay
10–11	115–125	Sand
12	125–130	Midden clay
13	130–135	Clay in northern 75 cm of square; midden?
14	130–135	Sand (in southern 25 cm)
15	135–unknown	Sand and gravel in northern 75 cm
16	135–unknown (limit of excavation at 160)	Moist black clay with much finely disintegrated charcoal like C 16–17 and J IV 20
J IV, 1–2	0–35	Breakdown debris and clay
3	35–40	Limestone rubble and sand with some interspersed midden
4–8	40–85	Midden bearing clay
9	85–90	Sand
10–11	90–105	Midden clay
12	105–110	Sand
13	110–115	Midden clay
14–17	115–130	Sand
18–19	130–140	Clay (midden?)
20	140–160	Moist black clay with finely disintegrated charcoal
21	160–185	Dry, decomposed limestone looking like hard, gray clay
22	185–220	Red brown silty sand
23	220–unknown (limit of excavation at 230)	Decomposed limestone

[a]See pages 78–79.

TABLE 11.7 Salts Cave Vestibule Trenches—Suggested Correlations of Levels[a]

East					Horizon	J II	J IV	J I	J III	West
C	C/N	E	G	H						F
1–3		1–4	1–4	1	Breakdown debris and clay	1–3	1–2	1–3	1	Not present
4		5	5	2	Stream sands Midden among breakdown	4	3–4	4–5	3–4	1–5
5–11	1–7	6,7,7b	6,7,7b	3–4	Midden-bearing brown clay alternating and interfingering with sand and gravel	5–13	5–13	Limit of excavation	Limit of excavation	Limit of excavation
12–21[b]		8	Limit of excavation		Breakdown debris alternating and interfingering with sand and gravel	14–16[b]	14–23[b]			
Limit of excavation	Limit of excavation	Limit of excavation				Limit of excavation	Limit of excavation			

[a]See pages 78–79.

[b]Levels C 16–17, J II 16, J IV 20 are equivalent and possibly represent a brush fire; see Tables 11.1 and 11.6.

KEY TO SECTIONS

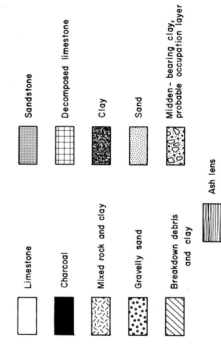

Limestone

Charcoal

Mixed rock and clay

Gravelly sand

Breakdown debris and clay

Sandstone

Decomposed limestone

Clay

Sand

Midden-bearing clay, probable occupation layer

Ash lens

Chapter 12

Prehistoric Cultural Debris from the Vestibule Trenches

PATTY JO WATSON

Washington University

The nature of the cultural debris mingled with the stream deposits in the Vestibule of Salts Cave conveys some information about the nature of the group responsible for it. Fragments of animal bone make up by far the largest proportion of material recovered, and indicate the hunting and eating of deer plus a series of smaller mammals (see pages 123–133). Together with the remains of game animals are many broken, splintered, and sometimes charred pieces of human bone (pages 146–159), giving one the strong impression that the Vestibule dwellers were at least part-time cannibals.

Also sparsely present in the debris are chert flakes and tools, plus a few bone and ground stone tools (see Tables 12.1–12.4).

The Vestibule chipped stone collection comprises only 131 pieces from all levels of all trenches; 69 of these came from Test D, which was more productive of chipped stone that any of the other excavations. It is possible that this variation is partially a result of the greater stream activity in this part of the Vestibule (that is, the chipped stone implements may have been washed in by the water together with the pebbles, sand, and gravel that was also excavated in Trench D). However, none of them shows any sign of having been rolled or battered, so they must not have been carried far, if at all. It is possible that the relatively greater density of worked chert in the Test D area at least partly reflects the behavior of the prehistoric people.

Although quantities are low, there are a variety of items ranging from cores, debitage, and fragments of unworked chert to projectile points and nicely prepared, chipped celts. The most abundant tools are utilized or slightly utilized flakes. The evidence for utilization usually consists of sporadic nicks and tiny flake scars along one or more edges. The flakes and chips classed as debitage do not show such nicking or chipping. Scrapers, on the other hand, are flakes with clear indications (a continuous series of flake scars) of persistent use and retouch along at least one edge. On two flakes, the scars are sufficiently regular and purposeful-looking to allow them to be classified as retouched flakes.

Projectile points vary in shape from lanceolate

TABLE 12.1 Salts Cave Vestibule Excavations Chipped Stone Summary

Pit and Level	Cores	Core fragments	Raw material	Slightly utilized flakes	Utilized flakes	Heavily utilized flakes	Retouched flakes	Scrapers	Chipped celts	Projectile points	Debitage	Limestone	Totals
C, 1													0
2													0
3			1										1
4					1								1
5								1					1
6											1		1
7													0
8													0
9											1		1
10													0
11								1		2[a]	1		4
12									1	1			2
13–21													0
	0	0	1	0	1	0	0	2	1	3	3	0	11
C/N, 1				1									1
2													0
3													0
4													0
5													0
6													0
7									2	2[a]	2		6
D, 1													0
2	1			1									2
3			1										1
4			2	2	2		1	1					8
5	1		3	1						2[a]	2		9
6	1		1					1		1[a]	3		7
7			2	3	2				2		4		13

	Total
8	5
9	15
10	7
11	1
12	1
D (subtotal)	**69**
E, 1	0
2	1
3	0
4	0
5	4
6	4
7	0
7b	8
Fea. 7D	1
8	0
E (subtotal)	**18**
F. ext. 1	0
2	0
3	2
F (subtotal)	**2**
G, 1	0
2	0
3	0
4	0
5	0
6	1
7	0
G (subtotal)	**1**
H, 1	0
2	1
3	1
4	0
H (subtotal)	**2**

TABLE 12.1—(cont.)

Pit and Level	Cores	Core fragments	Raw material	Slightly utilized flakes	Utilized flakes	Heavily utilized flakes	Retouched flakes	Scrapers	Chipped celts	Projectile points	Debitage	Limestone	Totals
J, 1													0
2					1						1		2
3							1						1
JI, 4	1												1
JII, 4				1	1						1		3
5													0
6				1	1						1		3
7													0
8													0
9	1												1
10					1				1				2
JIII, 4				1									1
JIV, 4				1								1[b]	2
5				1									1
6													0
7													0
8													0
9					1								1
10										2[a]	1		3
11–23													0
Subtotal	**2**	**0**	**0**	**5**	**5**	**0**	**1**	**0**	**1**	**2**	**4**	**1**	**21**
Grand total	**8**	**3**	**13**	**25**	**14**	**1**	**2**	**7**	**8**	**14**	**32**	**4**	**131**

[a] Projectile points from C, 11: 1 fragment, 1 nearly complete; C, 12: complete; C/N, 7: basal fragments; D, 5: complete; D, 6: fragment; D, 9: probably complete; E, 7b: 2 are tip ends, 1 has tip broken off; JIV, 1 nearly complete, 1 smaller fragment.

[b] Possible scrapers

TABLE 12.2 Salts Cave Vestibule Excavations Ground Stone[a]

Pit and level		Pestles	Celts	Atlatl weights	Tubular pipes	Totals
C,	10–11		1[b]			1
C/N,	5		1[b]	1		2
	6		1[b]			1
	7	1	2[b]	3[c]		6
E,	7b	1 fragment		1[c]	1	3
	8	1 fragment				1
J,	3			1		1
J II,	10		1[b]			1
J II,	12					
	baulk	1	1[b]			2
J IV,	4				1	1
Totals		**4**	**7**	**6**	**2**	**19** Grand total

[a] Identifications of the raw materials used to manufacture these artifacts were made by L. Greer Price, and verified by Stanley Sun and Harold Levin, all of the Earth Sciences Department, Washington University. The possible pipe fragments are clastic arenaceous limestone, the atlatl weights are oolitic limestone (C/N 5), and carbonaceous siltstone.

The celts are oolitic limestone (C 10–11; C/N 6; and the two from J II), finely crystalline limestone (C/N 5), gabbro, and calcareous sandstone (the two from C/N 7).

The pestles and pestle fragments are all limestone (the fragment from E 8 is clastic fossiliferous limestone).

[b] Celt dimensions: C, 10–11—20.0 × 7.0 × 5.5 cm
         C/N, 5—14.5 × 4.5 × 5.5 cm
             6—14.7 × 5.0 × 6.0 cm
             7—18.5 × 6.6 × 5.2 cm and 11.5 × 5.5 × 4 cm
       J II, 10—12.0 × 5.5 × 4.0 cm
       J II, 12 baulk—12.7 × 4.5 × 3.7 cm

[c] The atlatl weight fragment from E 7b fits with one from C/N 7 to form a single large fragment (Figure 12.6).

TABLE 12.3 Salts Cave Vestibule Excavations Worked Bone

Pit and level	Awls	Perforated teeth	Atlatl hook	Spatulates	Miscellaneous	Totals
C, 11	1					1
C/N, 3	1					1
4	1					1
5				1		1
6		2				2
7		2				2
E, 5					1 worked antler	1
7	1					1
7b	1				1 polished bird bone shaft	2
F, 1			1[a]			1
J II,3					1 needle	1
JIII,4	1					1
JIV,10					2; worked antler and bone bead	2
Totals	**6**	**4**	**1**	**1**	**5**	**17**

[a] This atlatl hook is made from a cylindrical bone rod (now broken at one end and with maximum length of 44 mm, diameter of 10 mm), deeply notched in an oblique cut that forms a small protruding tongue of bone: the hook that would have engaged the butt of an atlatl dart.

TABLE 12.4 Salts Cave Vestibule Excavations Worked Shell

Pit and level	Spoons or scrapers[a]	Pendants	Miscellaneous	Totals
C, 10	1			1
C/N, 7		1	2; scraper or pendant fragment & fragment of perforated shell	3
D, 4	1		1 bead?	2
E, 5	1			1
J I, 4			1 probable scraper	1
JIV, 8			1 probable scraper	1
JIV, 10			1 probable scraper	1
	3	**1**	**6**	**10**

[a]See Watson *et al.* (1969: Pl. 13 E), and Nelson (1917: Figs. 15a,b).

Figure 12.1 Projectile points from the Salts Cave Vestibule excavations. Proveniences: top left, trench D, level 9; top right, trench C, level 12; bottom left, trench E, level 7b; bottom right, trench C/N, level 7.

(see Figure 12.1) to tanged, the tang being more or less square-ended or triangular. All the points are fairly large, none of the complete ones being less than 6 cm long. Presumably these are all points for atlatl darts rather than arrowheads (a single atlatl hook was found, Table 12.4), and they compare very favorably with those found by us on the surface adjacent to Salts Sink, and with several in the Mammoth Cave National Park collections labeled as having been found near Salts Sink.

The chipped celts are very interesting implements that might have been used as butchering tools. Two of them, however, have clearly discernible sheen on one face near the bit; this sheen resembles the earth polish visible on some Mississippian chipped hoes. Several ground stone celts that were probably axeheads and hatchet heads were found in the Vestibule, so the chipped stone implements may indeed not have been used for woodworking.

Other artifacts recovered during the Vestibule excavations include bone tools, some fragments of worked shell, two complete pestles, seven celts, and five whole or fragmentary atlatl weights (Figures 12.2—12.6, Tables 12.2—12.4). Two of the celts are quite large (185 and 200 mm long). The other end of the size range is represented by a celt from Test C which is only 115 mm long. The latter shows edge wear comparable to that Semonov (1964)

Figure 12.2 Chipped celts from the Salts Cave Vestibule excavations. Proveniences: left, trench J II, level 10; center, trench E, level 7b; right, trench C/N, level 7.

Figure 12.4 Ground celts from the Salts Cave Vestibule excavations. Proveniences: left, trench J II, level 11 and right, trench J II, level 10.

Figure 12.3 Pestles from the Salts Cave Vestibule excavations. Proveniences: left, trench C/N, level 7 and right, trench J II, level 11 baulk.

describes as being indicative of use as an axe. All the celts were shaped by pecking and all have fine grinding only at the bit which was seemingly sharpened by abrasion parallel to the working edge.

The two pestles are bell-shaped (bell-shaped pestles were also found by N. C. Nelson at Mammoth Cave—Nelson 1917:65, Fig. 18a, b—and by Funkhouser and Webb in the rock shelters of eastern Kentucky—Funkhouser and Webb 1929:78, Fig. 34). Like the celts, they were shaped by pecking with some grinding around the edge of the bell. Both of the Salts Cave pestles show fracturing at the bottom edge of the bell, the fractures in a few places having been reworked by pecking. The basal ends of each show a circular working area (in the center of the bottom of the bell). The

Figure 12.5 An atlatl weight from the Salts Cave Vestibule excavations. Provenience: trench C/N, level 5.

Figure 12.6 Atlatl weight from the Salts Cave Vestibule excavations. Right portion is from trench E, level 7b; left portion is from trench C/N, level 7.

following observations were made by Gregory Swift during the course of an independent research project supervised by P. J. Watson:

> Examination of the working surfaces of the complete pestles from the Vestibule under a binocular microscope revealed some interesting facts.

The pestle from SCU-C/N, level 7, has an indentation worn in the center of the working surface; the working surface of the other is flat to slightly convex. On both implements the traces of wear are minute, although both seem to have been frequently used. On one of the objects (that from SCU-C/N 7) the striations are circular or curved in shape, on the other they are small, straight scratches, seemingly unconnected. There were only a very few marks on these surfaces which could be seen without magnification, and these seem to be, for the most part, accidental. There was no evidence of the working surface having been crushed by pounding and there were no foreign particles embedded in this surface.

It seems to have been the intent of the user of these tools to keep whatever he was working underneath the pestle. With one pestle (the one from J II 12) this was done by a back-and-forth motion or a series of glancing blows; with the other, the motion used was a limited circular or twisting motion [Swift n.d.: 3].

The Director of the St. Louis Museum of Science and Natural History, James Houser, kindly allowed us access to the Museum's collection of pestles, and—with the very generous and knowledgeable assistance of museum volunteer, Leonard Blake—Swift was able to make some detailed comparisons with the Salts Cave pestles. The following discussion is based upon his notes and drawings. Seven of the Museum specimens are bell-shaped pestles, although none is quite so pronouncedly bell-shaped as the two from Salts Vestibule. An eighth pestle, conical in shape, shows battering or pecking in a central circular area on the base rather than minute striations as on the bell-shaped pestles. The seven bell-shaped pestles all have central depressions; three exhibit curvilinear striations, two show straight striations, and one both curved and straight. The central depression is spalled off the seventh one. All these seven, like the two from Salts, show peripheral chipping around the edge of the bell. All but one of the Museum pestles also have chipped handles. These observations are summarized in Table 12.5; see also page 180.

In general, it appears that these bell-shaped pestles had rather special uses that involved some sort of grinding rather than straight up-and-down pounding. However, the bell ends of all of them were at least occasionally used as hammers to

TABLE 12.5 **Attributes of Wear on Some Pestles at the Museum of Science and Natural History, St. Louis, Missouri**

Designation of pestle	Nature of basal wear	Edge chipping (flake scars around basal periphery)	Chipping at top of handle
18X298; bell pestle from Clark County, Indiana	Central depression; some curved striations, some pounding marks	Present	Present
18–329; bell pestle from Tennessee	Central depression with curvilinear striations	Present	Present
18X1349; bell pestle, provenience unknown	Central depression with long striations parallel to edges of depression	Present	Present
18X289; conical pestle from Hardin County, Kentucky	Central part of base pecked or battered, no tiny striations visible	Present	Present
18X296; bell pestle, provenience unknown	Central depression with small straight radial striations around edge	Present, edge apparently reground	Not present
18X301; bell pestle from Floyd County, Kentucky, 1905	Central depression with circular and rounded striations	Present	Present
18X1350; bell pestle, provenience unknown	Central depression; straight and curved striations on base	Present	Not present
18X303; bell pestle, provenience unknown	Central depression, now spalled off	Present	Present

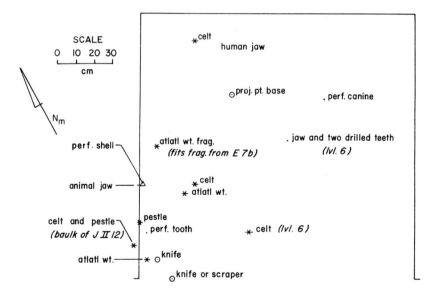

Figure 12.7 Salts Cave Vestibule excavations. Triangulated finds from trench C/N, levels 6 and 7, and from the adjoining baulk. *:ground stone artifact; △ : shell; ○ : chert; ● : bone.

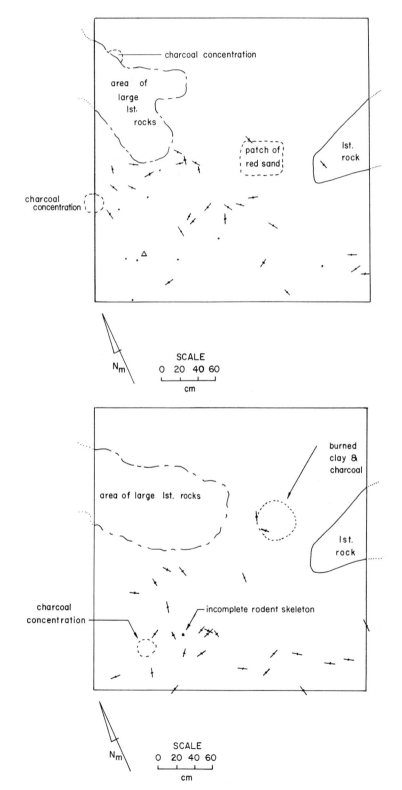

Figure 12.8 Salts Cave Vestibule excavations. Triangulated finds from level 5 of trench E. The angles of the lines drawn through the dots indicate orientations of the *in situ* items.

Figure 12.9 Salts Cave Vestibule excavations. Triangulated finds from level 6 of trench E. The angles of the lines drawn through the dots indicate orientations of the *in situ* items.

judge from the chipping and scarring along the bell periphery (but not on the base).

Distributions of the ground stone artifacts from the excavations are relatively meaningless because the number of items is so small. However, two points should be noted.

(1) A very high percentage of the celts and pestles came from an area with a maximum radius of 150 cm comprising the northwest corner of Test C plus J II and J II baulk (Figure 12.7). This is also true of the atlatl weights. Furthermore, these items were all found at depths between 120 and 150 cm below the surface. Thus the items might be part of a disturbed cache, although the individual pieces were scattered rather than clumped, except for one celt resting against a pestle in the J II 12 level of the baulk between C and J.

(2) The picture is somewhat complicated, how-ever, by the fact that one of the atlatl weight fragments from C/N 7 fits a fragment from E 7b: the former was found about 145 cm below the surface, the latter 86 cm below the surface, and the two were 345 cm apart.

Find spot and angle of orientation of the bones found in Test Trench E were mapped (Figures 12.8–12.11) in order to determine whether the pieces displayed any consistent orientations. This project was supervised by Charles L. Redman (1969). He found the bone orientations to be ran-dom; that is, the items measured seemed to be *in situ*, they did not seem to have been pushed or rolled by a flowing stream. Another point made clear by the distribution maps is the abundance of bone in the main midden layer, 7b, in comparison with the other levels (see Figure 12.12).

Bone in the smaller square, Test J, was less com-mon than in E (some levels yielded no finds of suf-

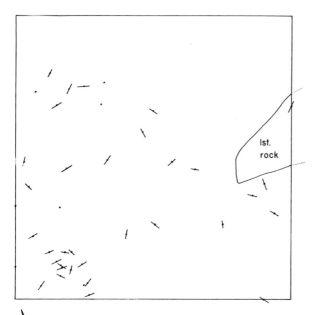

SCALE

0 20 40 60

cm

N m

Figure 12.10 Salts Cave Vestibule excavations. Triangul-ated bone fragments from level 7 of trench E. The angles of the lines drawn through the dots indicate orientations of the *in situ* fragments.

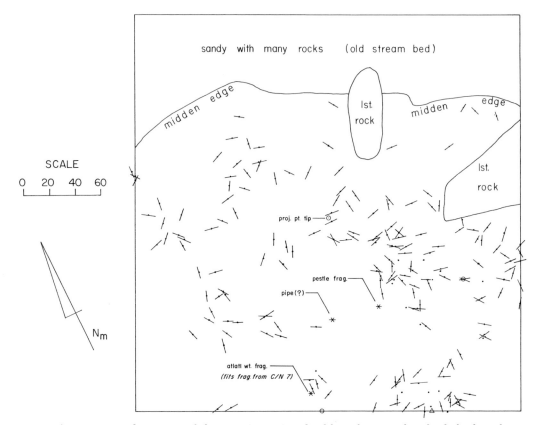

Figure 12.11 Salts Cave Vestibule excavations. Triangulated bone fragments from level 7b of trench E. The angles of the lines drawn through the dots indicate orientations of the *in situ* fragments. *: ground stone artifact; △: shell; ○: chert; ●: bone.

ficient size to be triangulated), and the distribution maps show no clear patterning. One reason for this, apart from the smaller area of the excavation, is that the midden beds here are sloping and often comprise material jumbled among the breakdown, whereas in E the midden horizons slope gently or are flat.

No architectural remains were found in any of the Vestibule trenches, although several pits and pitlike depressions were present in Test E, two possible post holes and several charcoal concentrations in Test C, and a few amorphous pits or pockets among the breakdown in J (Table 12.6). Most of the pits were recognizable by their contrast in color (the pit fill was darker) with the surrounding deposits but did not reveal any distinctive contents, a few bone fragments or pieces of stone in charcoal-bearing clay being the usual pattern. However, the flotation samples from these pits have not yet been analyzed. Two hollows or pockets among the breakdown in Test J did contain significant concentrations of turkey bone in one case and human bone in another (Table 12.6). The contents of these particular hollows may represent refuse discarded on single occasions.

The small series of artifacts found in the Vestibule excavations could fit with the general late Archaic to Early Woodland assignment of the cave activity given by Schwartz in his preliminary work at Mammoth Cave (Schwartz 1960, 1965) and by us for Salts Cave (Watson *et al.*

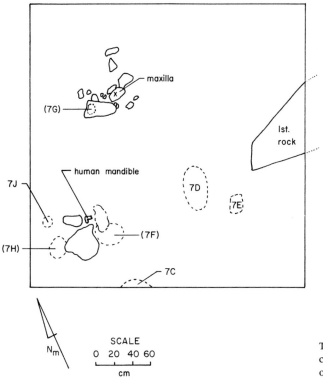

maxilla

(7G)

Ist.
rock

human mandible

7J

7D

7E

(7F)

(7H)

7C

SCALE

N_m

0 20 40 60

cm

Figure 12.12 Salts Cave Vestibule excavations. Trench E, level 7b features. Northwest stone/bone cluster at top, southwest stone/bone cluster at bottom of figure.

1969). The presently available radiocarbon dates for the Vestibule also fall within this vaguely defined time span (late second millenium to early first millenium B.C., see Table 31.2 and Figure 31.1). Unfortunately there are inversions in the determinations: The oldest figure of 1540 B.C. ±110 is from the highest dated stratum in Tests E and H, and the 7b dates (7b is the lowest dated stratum in Test E) are markedly younger than the levels above them (5 and 6). When considering these vagaries of the Vestibule charcoal dates from E and J, one should keep in mind that stream activity insufficient to move bones or stone artifacts could nevertheless transport bits of charcoal horizontally, and—if there were openings in the breakdown—possibly even vertically. For this reason we submitted some of the animal bone from

the Vestibule for radiocarbon dating, but the results are not yet available.

The oldest Vestibule dates (mid second millenium B.C.) are the oldest ones from Salts Cave, but are exceeded by a Mammoth Cave determination (twigs and weed stalks from Jessup Avenue, 2170 B.C. ± 70) and one from Lee Cave (2250 B.C. ± 65 on cane). See Table 31.1.

There are no dates on the prehistoric remains from Mammoth Cave Vestibule, but the materials recovered certainly seem generally similar to those from Salts Vestibule (Nelson 1917). The simplest explanation for both Salts and Mammoth is that the people who lived or camped occasionally in the entry chambers of these caves were also the people who explored and worked deep in the interior.

TABLE 12.6 Salts Vestibule Trenches—Feature Summary

Trench	Feature designation	Description
C	Possible postholes	130 cm below the surface in the south half of C were two possible postholes each 11 cm in diameter and consisting of dark sandy clay with numerous charcoal flecks; No. 1 was 70 cm from the west trench wall and 45 from the south, No. 2 was 60 from the west and 130 from the south. No. 1 was 15 cm deep, No. 2 was 10 cm deep (ending on a rock); the contents of both were floated.
E	7A—pit	Dug from level 6 in E into level 7, 20 cm deep, see Figure 12.12; eastern half of pit fill floated.
	7B—redesignated midden level 7b	Brown somewhat sandy clay with much charcoal and many bone fragments; 18.75 pounds floated.
	7C—pit	Dug from 7b; 15—20 cm deep; see Figure 12.12; fill sample floated.
	7D—pit	In 7b; see Figure 12.12; cuts into level 8 and is 15 cm deep. South half of fill floated.
	7E—pit	In 7b, about 7 cm deep; Figure 12.12
	7F—possible pit	In 7b, 20 cm deep; see Figure 12.12
	7G—pit	In 7b, 15 cm deep; see Figure 12.12
	7H—pit	Dug from 7b into 8, 25 cm deep, contents floated. See Figure 12.12
	7J—pit	In 7b, 12 cm deep; Figure 12.12
	NW stone/bone cluster	In 7b; see Figure 12.12
	SW stone/bone cluster	In 7b; see Figure 12.12
H and E	2A—midden lense	About 1—1.5 m in diameter, maximum thickness at center is 6 cm, at edges 1—2 cm. 70 cm below surface, covered the northwest corner of H and extended into E (on top of the large breakdown rock in the west wall and to the south of it). Sample floated.
J	Breakdown pocket containing turkey bone	In J II, levels 4—5; 40 cm maximum diameter, 15 cm maximum width, in north half of J II. In pocket was loose brown clay with charcoal and small limestone and sandstone rocks; turkey bone scattered through hollow.
	Breakdown pocket	In J II, 6—7; 45 cm from the north trench wall, 10 cm from the east; contained bone fragments scattered through clay fill.
	Breakdown pocket	In J II 10; pocket contained sand and charcoal plus bone fragments, a celt, and a chert flake. Location is 60 cm from the north, 32 from the east; 10 cm deep.
	Breakdown pocket	In J IV 8; pocket contained midden clay with a jumble of bone (some of it human). As originally found the pocket was about 25 cm in diameter and 25—30 cm deep, 80 cm from the south and 25 from the west trench wall.

KEY TO PLANS

⊙ Chipped stone   • Bone fragment

△ Mussel shell   ✎ Bone fragment (orientation indicated)

✳ Ground stone   (7A) Feature

Chapter

13

Pollen Analysis of Sediments from Salts Cave Vestibule

JAMES SCHOENWETTER

Arizona State University

Introduction

In August of 1972 the Palynology Laboratory accepted a contract to accomplish archeological pollen analysis of sediment samples submitted by the Cave Research Foundation through Patty Jo Watson. The Foundation submitted 17 specimens from the Carlston Annis shell midden locality (Bt-5) and 19 specimens collected from the south profile of Test Pit J in the Vestibule of Salts Cave. The Laboratory was requested to undertake as much analysis as could be accomplished during the equivalent of two weeks of laboratory research, and a priority system was provided for the samples. Of the 17 Carlston Annis specimens 13 were given first analytic priority, and of the 19 Salts Cave specimens 15 were given priority.

Methods

Extraction of pollen from the 28 samples was begun with the standard procedure utilized in this laboratory. This involves separation of the light (polliniferous) fraction of a large (75–150 cm³) volume of sediment through swirl flotation in an acid medium, decomposition of inorganic matter with hydrofluoric and nitric acid treatments, and decomposition of extraneous organic matter with dilute lye. Only one of the 28 samples provided sufficient pollen for analysis as a result of this extraction procedure. Microscope inspection of the samples revealed that reprocessing of the Carlston Annis extracts to reduce further the quantity of remaining inorganic and organic residues would not provide a sufficient concentration of pollen because so little pollen was contained in the specimens originally. In the case of the Salts Cave specimens, however, the pollen density was appreciably higher. Further processing offered prospect of obtaining statistically meaningful data from at least some samples.

The 14 Salts Cave samples were returned for further processing. Inorganic residues which had resisted a minimum of 48 hr rinse in hydrofluoric acid and a 30-min rinse in hydrofluoric acid heated in a boiling water bath were reduced by placing them in crucibles with hydrofluoric acid and heating the mixture to the boiling point for 45 min. After rinsing the result with hot water and cold nitric acid, organic residues were attacked with Erdtman's (1943: 28) acetolysis solution in a boiling water bath for 3 min. This was followed with hot water rinses and a 10-min rinse in a 10% lye solution. Further water rinses and the application of alcohol as an organic solvent completed the reprocessing treatment. This treatment reduced the specimens by about 60% volume in most cases, concentrating the pollen of the original 75–150 cm³ samples in an extract of about 0.5 cm³ volume.

At this juncture, the 2 weeks research period had been completed with only one pollen record achieved. Two students participating in a current course in archeological pollen analysis were pressed into the service of the project. As part of their classroom exercise, Rose Duffield and Jannifer Wyatt evaluated the reprocessed Salts Cave specimens through microscopic examination and obtained the pollen records of four samples. I found opportunity to observe the pollen of an additional three samples during this period. The eight pollen records provide all of the counts that can be obtained, given present technology, from the 15 Salts Cave specimens given highest priority.

Because of the low pollen density in the samples, specimens were evaluated as profitable for analysis if a pollen density of 40 or more grains per drop of extract was evident. Observation was halted after 100 grains had been tabulated from a specimen, or after all the pollen on one slide had been observed, which ever occurred first. The use of a 100-grain pollen count is not optimal, statistically speaking. However, obtaining higher counts would have expended more time and would not have allowed more confidence in interpretation. Although a given pollen frequency might then have been statistically evaluated within narrower confidence limits, the fact that only eight samples are available would still remain. Eight samples are hardly a firm basis for the sort of intensive statistical treatment that might be encouraged by larger pollen counts. This is especially true when it is recognized that each specimen represents a unique temporal horizon, because the samples were collected in vertical order.

Archeological pollen analysis is defined (Schoenwetter 1970: 35, 36) as the establishment of research designs to provide information of archeological character or to provide information pertinent to archeological interpretation. In the present case, the design selected is one that allows discrimination between the portion of the pollen record referring to the natural history of the Salts Cave area and the portion reflecting the activities of man. As will be seen, this design provides information useful to archeological interpretation of the Salts Cave Vestibule human population.

The first question at issue, of course, is the probability that both a "natural" and a "cultural" component of the pollen record in fact exist. The stratigraphy of the sampled profile in Test Pit J is essentially one of midden deposits (pp. 75, 81, Figure 11.9). All of the sediments observed *could* represent deposition during the period of Vestibule occupation. Thus, all of the pollen could have been contributed to the sediments by human agency. Furthermore, because the test pit is located far into the Vestibule, well beyond the point that sunlight directly penetrates, it is impossible for pollen-bearing plants ever to have grown at the sampled location. Thus, the pollen of the deposits cannot reflect an immediately local flora.

However, no evidence of human occupation is recovered from Test Pit J in levels 1 through 2, 14 through 19, or 21 through 23. These levels are of a lithological character distinct from those in which occupational evidence exists (the middens), and appear to be undisturbed decomposition products of the cave walls and floor, or sediment washed into the locus. Thus, there is at least equal probability that the pollen they contain is unaffected by human agency as that the pollen is so affected. Furthermore, Test Pit J is located in a topographic low area within the Vestibule, and the Vestibule entry is located in a topographic low area (Salts Sink) of the district. Both gravity fall and water transport would tend to transport pollen from the Vestibule entrance to the area of Test Pit J and concentrate it there. All the samples, then, potentially contain pollen provided by human agency and pollen provided by the "natural" agency of washing or blowing through the Vestibule entry.

There are two traditional procedures for discrimination of aspects of a single pollen record. The most direct is to obtain records of pollen rain from modern examples of ecological patterns of known character. These records reflect a known "present" that may be utilized to identify the character of an unknown "past" in compliance with the uniformitarian principle upon which all paleoecological research is based (Odum 1959: 96). The less direct procedure, which is more traditionally used, is to base interpretation of the fossil record upon the known ecology of the taxa observed, and the frequency variations of those taxa in the record. This approach presumes that the distribution of pollen taxa in a record reflects the distribution of the plant taxa in the preexisting vegetation in a substantially direct fashion.

In the present case, the direct procedure cannot be employed. No samples of pollen rain from the presently existing vegetation pattern of the region have been collected. Some surface sediment samples from southeastern Missouri have been subjected to pollen analysis (Fish n.d.) as have some from the Illinois River Valley (Schoenwetter 1966) and the American Bottoms of the Mississippi Valley (Schoenwetter 1964). But these do not serve as adequate controls. The Missouri series is too small and the Illinois series was collected from locales too ecologically and climatically distinct from the conditions of the Salts Cave area. Discrimination of the "natural" from the "cultural" components of the Salts Cave fossil pollen rain, then, has proceeded on the basis of internal evidence, the evidence provided by association with known cultural phenomena, and judgments regarding the ecology of the taxa represented in the pollen rain.

Analysis

The assumption has been made that pollen records occurring below and above the midden strata reflect no direct cultural impact on the pollen rain. This assumption is probably more justifiable for the record below the midden strata than the one above the middens, for we are aware that surficial deposits of midden and other materials reflecting human occupancy occur with-

in the Vestibule area. However, it seems a reasonable working hypothesis. The assumption has also been made that the stratigraphic series of pollen spectra accurately reflects a true passage of relative time. I recognize that the issue is debatable on two grounds: (1) cave stratigraphy is normally complex, such that instances of horizontal and reversed stratigraphy often occur which cannot be clearly discerned in test-pit excavations; and (2) reversed and horizontal stratigraphy would have a reasonably high probability of occurence in such artificial deposits as midden. A third assumption is that a test of significant difference at the 95% level of confidence is adequate for examination of hypotheses regarding these data. Following the argument of Mosimann (1965: 638), the simplest test of critical value to pollen studies has been applied here: that provided by the confidence interval for percentage frequency of binomially distributed variables (Mosimann 1965: 642–643). This test is also advocated by Faegri and Iversen (1964: 133). The test seems particularly appropriate because used with low pollen counts, as is the case here, it would tend to show *less* discrimination than other potentially applicable tests. Thus, a difference between two records which is accepted as significant is actually quite strongly indicated.

Comparison of the samples from levels 2 and 21 (Table 13.1) allows examination of statistically significant distinctions in pollen frequency that, granting the assumptions, must be distinctions of a natural order due to the passage of time. There may be some cultural influence on the frequency values of pollen types in the sample from level 2, but, if so, it is indirect and results from the effects of human activity in the area prior to the time of deposition of this sample. The comparison shows no significant difference in the *Quercus* pollen frequency, the Chenopodiineae pollen frequency, the Tubuliflorae pollen frequency, the Gramineae pollen frequency, or the unknowns pollen frequency. Significant difference *is* observed in the *Carya* pollen frequency and the Ambrosieae pollen frequency. Significant difference is *not* observed in the presence/absence distinction of *Castenea* pollen, or in the presence/absence distinction of *Ulmus* pollen. The changes due to temporal order of these

TABLE 13.1   Pollen Observed in the Sediment Samples from Test Pit J IV, Salts Cave Vestibule

Level	Depth below surface (m)	Pinus	Juniperus	Quercus	Carya	Castenea	Juglans	Acer	Ulmus	Morus	Populus	Cheno-podiineae
2	.20	4		33	1	3						11
3	.30	4	1	42	9			1			1	2
4	.35	1		27	6		3					14
Upper 5	.40			4	5							15
Lower 5	.50	2		6	2							26
6–7	.65	2		2	4							60
8–10	.75–.85					*Insufficient pollen*						
13	1.00	3		10	2		1		1	1		3
14–21	1.05–1.50					*Insufficient pollen*						
21	1.70	1		35	18				5			5
22–23	2.00–2.30					*Insufficient pollen*						

"natural" pollen rains, then, are twofold: (1) a change in the representation of hickory, and (2) a change in the representation of Ambrosieae.

The question of which, if any, of these changes may have been related to the occurrence, before the time horizon represented by level 2, of cultural activity in the area may be effectively answered by comparing the pollen rains of levels 2 and 21 with the pollen rains of the midden strata. The midden strata are the strata most likely to contain a reflection of cultural impact upon pollen records. Through comparison, we should be able to discern whether the changes involved occurred early in, during, or after the time periods represented by the midden strata. If a change occurred *early* in the period represented by the midden strata, there is some high probability that the introduction of human behavior affected the otherwise "natural" record and so was responsible for the change. If a change occurred *during* the period represented by the midden strata the probability that human activity caused the change is somewhat lower and would only be really likely in the event that patterns of cultural action relative to vegetation themselves underwent change. If the change occurred *after* the cessation of human activity, the probability is relatively low that the change is a function of the human actions.

The change in Ambrosieae frequency occurs *after* the occupation period. The confidence interval surrounding the 14.0% value for Ambro-

sieae of level 21 is the interval between 8.0 and 22.0%. The value of Ambrosieae in level 13 ($N = 43$) is surrounded by the confidence interval between 12 and 39%. Because the two ranges overlap, no significant distinction is evidenced. Significant distinction from the Ambrosieae value of level 21 is not, in fact, evidenced in *any* of the midden samples, according to the significance test used here. The significant change in Ambrosieae frequency occurs between levels 2 and 3. Thus, there is a low probability that this change is a reflection of the effect of human behavior on the pollen rain.

There are two significant changes that occur in the Carya pollen record. The value for Carya in level 13 is not significantly different from that of level 21, but the values of Carya in levels 6–7 and the lower sample from level 5 are distinct from that of level 21. This change occurs during the occupation period. However, the Carya values for the upper sample of level 5 and the samples of levels 4 and 3 are not significantly different from that of level 21. Thus, the significant change represented in the difference between Carya values in level 2 and those in level 21 occurs *after* the period of occupation. In fact, it occurs between levels 2 and 3. This change, like the change in Ambrosieae frequency, probably does not reflect cultural behavior. It would thus appear that the distinctions in pollen record between levels 2 and 21 are due to natural, not cultural, events.

Ambrosieae	Tubuli-florae	Anthemidae	Liguli-florae	Gramineae	Cercis	Ribes	Caryophyl-laceae	Umbel-liferae	Cyperaceae	Unknowns	N
35	7			4						2	100
31	4		3	2							100
30	9	1	1	5		1			1	1	100
17	3		1	2				1		2	50
19	18			26						1	100
12	12			6			1			1	100
12	5			3	1					1	43
14	6			13						3	100

The preceding discussion does not demonstrate that no cultural effect on the Salts Cave pollen record exists, however, and thus does not fulfill our objective of discriminating such cultural effects. It simply informs us that those distinctions that exist between the presumably pre- and post-occupational samples are not likely to be due to human activity. The essential purpose of the exercise has been to provide a base line of "known" to allow analysis of the "unknown." The pre- and post-occupational samples serve as controls. Where distinctions occur between either of these records and the records of the midden samples, an assessment must be made of the probability that the distinction is a function of human behavior. Where no distinction occurs between the pre- or post-occupation sample and one or more midden samples, no assessment need be made.

There is no statistically significant variation through the time range of the record in two of the pollen taxa that are regularly represented in the counts: *Pinus* and unknowns. A number of pollen taxa are represented by rare occurences: *Juniperus, Castenea, Juglans, Acer, Morus, Populus,* Anthemidae (cf. *Artemisia*), *Cercis, Ribes,* Umbelliferae, Caryophyllaceae, and Cyperaceae. As such, they have no statistical significance at all. To evaluate their effect on the pollen record these records were combined with those of *Pinus* and unknowns in each sample to determine if the cluster varied significantly through the time period

sampled. None of the resulting values is statistically greater or lesser at one or more time horizons. Such records, then, do not serve to discriminate cultural from natural events.

Two of the pollen taxa, *Ulmus* and Liguliflorae, are represented by statistically insignificant values, but occur in two or more adjoining records and thus appear to be reflections of some temporal phenomenon. In the case of Liguliflorae, this seems to be wholly a phenomenon of the period of later midden accumulation. It may be a natural event, but its association would lead one to suspect that it is a cultural event. Furthermore the pollen type involved is disseminated solely by zoogamous plants and thus is not adapted to long-distance transport. It is likely, then, to have been incorporated in the deposits as a result of cultural activity. The observed record of *Ulmus* pollen, on the other hand, seems more probably a function of natural events. There is no statistical difference between the value for *Ulmus* pollen in level 21 and in level 13, so the presence/absence change that occurs in the *Ulmus* frequency after the time represented by level 13 takes place during, rather than early in, the cultural period. However, the presence/absence change in *Ulmus* pollen is not significant at the 95% level of confidence.

Changes significant at the 95% level occur in the records of *Quercus, Carya,* Chenopodiineae, Ambrosieae, and Gramineae pollen. The cases of *Carya* and Ambrosieae have been discussed previously.

The first change that occurred in the hickory frequency (between levels 21 through 13 and levels 6−7 through 3) occurred during the occupation, while the second change (between levels 6−7 through 3 and level 2) occurred following the occupation. These changes thus most probably reflect natural events. The only significant change occurring in the Ambrosieae value occurs after the occupational period, and is thus interpretable as a function of natural events.

In the case of *Quercus*, there are also two changes. The earlier occurs early in the occupation in the significant distinction between the oak value of level 21 and the oak values of levels 13 through 5. This change has a high probability of being due to some cultural event. The later change, which occurs in the distinction between the oak values of levels 13 through 5 and the oak values of levels 4 through 2, occurs during the occupation and results in values not significantly distinct from those of the control records. This change has a low probability of being due to some cultural event.

Three significant changes in Chenopodiineae pollen values occur during the occupation period, showing up as wide fluctuations from sample to sample in the period encompassed by levels upper 5, lower 5, and 6−7. The disparity of these temporally sequential records, as well as their association with cultural materials, promotes assessment that the changes are due to cultural events. One significant change occurs in the Gramineae pollen value in the lower sample from level 5. The argument applying to the Chenopodiineae record also applies here, leading to the conclusion that this change is culturally induced.

The conclusion that the Chenopodiineae pollen record is culturally influenced has been drawn on pollen statistical and on associational grounds. This can be supported on the grounds of the archeological recovery of *Chenopodium* and *Amaranthus* macrofossils and microfossils in human paleofeces from Salts Cave, and on the grounds of pollination−fruit-harvesting relationships. These are both ecological arguments which propose that if in fact the occupants of Salts Cave were harvesting and eating *Chenopodium* and *Amaranthus* seed, there is every reason to expect that these activities would contribute substantial quantities of Chenopodiineae pollen to the domiciliary environment.

The conclusion that the grass pollen records are highly culturally influenced has also been drawn on both associational and pollen statistical evidence. This conclusion does not find independent ecological support of the same order as the Chenopodiineae record. Grass seed is known to have been consumed, but the pollen−fruit-harvesting relationships of grass seed and grass pollen are such that little pollen would be expected in the domiciliary area as a result of use of grass seed for food. I believe the power of the associational and pollen statistical evidence, in combination, to be great enough to justify the conclusion that the grass pollen variance is culturally induced. One might speculate that grass pollen may have reached the midden as an industrial waste, perhaps from the manufacture of a grass mat or bedding. But there is obvious need for independent testing of this conclusion.

The case for Liguliflorae pollen representing cultural events is based on associational evidence and on the ecological evidence of the known pollen dispersal mechanisms of the taxon. This conclusion must thus be regarded as weaker than that drawn for the grass pollen.

The pollen statistical evidence that one of the changes in the oak pollen record is culturally induced is countered by the evidence that another such change is naturally induced. Again, independent ecological support for the conclusion is lacking. In fact, there is reason to believe on ecological grounds that the conclusion of cultural inducement is erroneous. While oak did constitute a food resource, its pollination−fruit-harvesting relationships are more like those of *Carya* than of *Amaranthus*. Thus, we would anticipate its pollen record to be like that of *Carya*: a natural events record. Furthermore, we may note that in the case of Chenopodiineae and grass pollen, the pollen statistical variations occur as short-term fluctuations. This is not the case for oak pollen; once established, a change persists through continuous records. Thus it would appear that the conclusion that one of the changes in the oak pollen frequency is culturally induced is indeed quite weakly drawn. I have chosen to dsmiss it, substituting the conclusion that both of the significant changes in the *Quercus* pollen record are due to natural causes.

The arguments presented reasonably justify the

inference that variations occurring in the records of oak, hickory, and Ambrosieae pollen are due to natural events. There are too few samples of any temporal horizon, however, to provide a firm basis for argument regarding the *character* of those environmental events. Were the events more firmly fixed in absolute time, argument could be drawn by biostratigraphic reference to contemporary paleoecological and paleoclimatic fluctuations. Were the cultural–ecological relationships of the Salts Cave inhabitants understood in detail through the time span of occupation, the pollen records could be evaluated by reference to them. Had we a body of pollen records representing patterns of relationship between pollen frequencies and known climatological, ecological, or vegetational events, controlled comparison could be made which would provide such inference. But none of this information is presently available. Unable to work "from known to unknown" I am able only to speculate and offer hypotheses that may prove testable.

My speculations proceed from the presumption that the Salts Cave pollen record represents four temporal horizons of natural events (Figure 13.1). The youngest of these is represented by level 2, which is isolated by its distinctively low pollen value for hickory. The next youngest horizon (Horizon II), encompasses levels 3 through upper

5. The hickory pollen value is higher than in Horizon I, and the Ambrosieae values, while not higher than in Horizon I, are higher than occur in the contiguous samples of Horizon III. The oak values of the two upper samples of Horizon II are equivalent to those of Horizon I, while in the lowermost sample of Horizon II the oak value is equivalent to that of Horizon III. Although the statistical significance of the fact is nil, Horizon II may also be isolated by the occurrence of more pollen types than the other horizons.

Horizon III is isolated by the combination of hickory values higher than those of Horizon I, and low oak and Ambrosieae values. It is reflected in the samples of levels lower 5 through 6–7. Horizon IV is isolated by the combination of higher hickory values than occur in Horizon I, high oak values and low Ambrosieae values, plus the occurence of *Ulmus*. The frequency value for Ambrosieae in level 13 is not low, but because so few grains were observed this value is not statistically higher than the Ambrosieae values for levels 6–7 or 21.

I interpret Horizon IV as the expectable palynological reflection of a mature oak–hickory climax forest biotope. Within such an ecosystem the forest canopy would be generally closed and the range of plant associations would be small. Such habitat variations as exist in response to local-

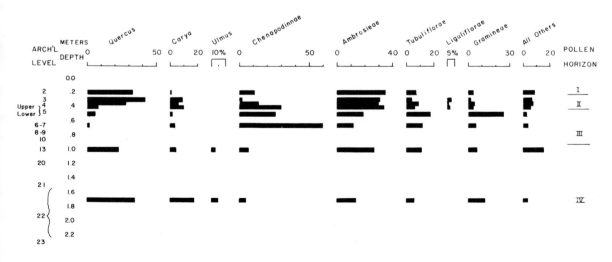

Figure 13.1 Pollen spectra of Test Pit J IV, Salts Cave vestibule.

ized conditions of substrate and microclimate would be generally masked by the monotony of the highly adapted oak—hickory plant association, to the effect that little species diversity would occur. In the present case, elm and perhaps walnut are possibly the only taxa consistently to be found as indices of habitat variations such as would be expected to occur near the Vestibule entry in the Salts Sink area.

With the advent of Horizon III the oak—hickory climax state of the local forest seems to have been disrupted. It appears that the hickory was immediately affected to a greater degree than the oak, but the latter diminished as well. The result was an opening of the canopy, allowing more frequent occurrence of light-tolerant taxa such as mulberry and red bud. During this period, elm seems to have lost its position as the prominent indication of habitat variability. On the whole, the pollen record of Horizon III seems to me most interpretable as a disclimax vegetation pattern, suggesting the advent of a climatic fluctuation.

The direction of the fluctuation is extremely difficult to attempt to reconstruct from these data. The earliest available radiocarbon dates indicative of Salts Cave occupation fall in the 1500—1400 B.C. range. If a disclimax-creating climatic fluctuation occurred shortly before we observe it represented in the midden stratum of level 13, and if this stratum does date to the 1500—1400 B.C. period, the fluctuation involved may be that which marks the end of the xerothermic (Hypsithermal) postglacial interval. However, Wright (1970) has presented a forceful argument that there was in fact no synchronous xerothermic interval throughout central and eastern North America, and that paleoclimatic reconstruction for various regions and districts within this large geographic area must be independently controlled and evaluated (see also Watts 1971 and Webb and Bryson 1972). In view of the present state of knowledge, it can only be pointed out that the temptation to make a biostratigraphic correlation linking the onset of environmental conditions of Horizon III at Salts Cave to paleoclimatic reconstructions elsewhere, and thus inferring the establishment of a more temperate paleoclimate, should be resisted.

I would reconstruct the conditions of Horizon II as an amplification of those of Horizon III: a further reduction in the general canopy and the establishment of greater species diversity. A weedy ground cover also seems indicated. The re-emergence of hickory as a forest dominant, and oak as such somewhat later, may be considered indicated at this time. To draw such an inference, however, would demand that we consider that neither taxon was a forest dominant during Horizon III. I think this is too extreme a reconstruction of the disclimax state during Horizon III. I believe both oak and hickory were the forest dominants in Horizon III. However, during that time I would say their dominance status was more a reflection of their earlier status as climax species than it was due to their innate capability to compete more effectively than other taxa for a dominance position. After the disclimax-creating environment became established, oak and hickory were less adapted to the new environment than they had been to the old. But no other taxa existed in the area in sufficient reproductive strength to achieve a dominance position in the local forest during Horizon III. Oak and hickory were not better adapted to Horizon II conditions than other taxa, but they were the taxa which, by virtue of a dominance position achieved under different conditions of environment, had the reproductive strength to maintain positions of dominance by default.

During Horizon III, however, other taxa could have generated sufficient reproductive strength to achieve dominance in Horizon II. They seem not to have done so. Perhaps this is because the environmental conditions of Horizon II were distinct from those of Horizon III, so oak and hickory were more favored as competitors. Alternatively, it may be that the stress of the disclimax environment served to generate a genetically distinctive, more adapted, population of oak and hickory by the time of Horizon II. I consider the latter somewhat more likely because of my feeling that the disclimax environment of Horizon II is an amplification of that of Horizon III.

I interpret Horizon I as reflecting the establishment of subclimax oak—hickory forest. Species diversity had become reduced relative to Horizons II and III. However, as the canopy was more open than it had been in Horizon IV (witness the higher

Ambrosieae pollen value), more ecotones and greater species diversity probably existed than had been the case during Horizon IV.

The reconstruction offered here is highly speculative. It cannot, in good conscience, be utilized as a basis for interpretation of cultural ecological patterns of the inhabitants of Salts Cave. But it does justify the hypothesis that the inhabitants of Salts Cave lived at the site through a time when ecological changes were occurring that could have dramatically affected the types, distributions, and qualities of the plant and animal resources upon which they were dependent for survival. If this is true, technological variations during the period of occupation may have been functionally related to these processes of environmental change. The reconstruction offered here, then, could be tested by analysis of technological variation if the artifactual materials from the Vestibule excavations were sufficiently abundant, but at the present time they are

not. Another test is afforded by the analyses of other forms of biological fossils (animal bone and charred vegetal remains) reported elsewhere in this volume. The present results of those analyses seem to support the reconstruction.

However, the reconstruction is tenuous enough so that little can be said regarding the relationship of conclusions drawn from this study and the study of pollen from samples of human paleofeces deposited in Salts Cave. The two types of pollen records have such distinctive points of origin and refer to such distinctive orders of elapsed time that comparison of almost any sort is inherently strained. None of the conclusions or inferences drawn independently from either study appears challenged by the data, inferences, or conclusions drawn from the other. However, there are also few instances in which the two studies operate mutually to confirm any of the conclusions or inferences reached.

Chapter 14

Flotation Procedures
Used on Salts Cave Sediments

PATTY JO WATSON

Washington University

In August, 1969, William Robertson[1] undertook trial flotation of some of the Vestibule sediments (from Tests C and E) as well as dry sediment from the cave interior to see whether they contained charred plant material not detectible to the excavator's eye. They did, and in sufficient quantity to indicate that a lenghy flotation series would be productive of considerable botanical material. Richard A. Yarnell agreed to examine such material as resulted from flotation. Robertson ultimately floated four series of samples beginning in August 1969, with the first lot from Tests C, E, and F in the Vestibule and several samples from the cave interior (Test A valley and Mumy Hall).

The second series was floated April 11 and 12, 1970 (F extension, several samples from features in Test E, and all the fill from J IV levels 4 to 11).

The third series was floated October 15, 1971, and comprised J IV levels 14 to 18; the fourth series was floated May 13, 1972, and included J IV levels 19 to 23.

Series I and II were floated at the Cave Research Foundation Flint Ridge camp in Mammoth Cave National Park. The procedure was as follows. The samples were carried out of the cave in double plastic bags, each one weighing at least 8–10 pounds, with several bags in the 15–20-pound the range. (A conservative estimate of the total weight of fill carried out of the Vestibule for flotation is 1500 pounds.) A foil-wrapped tag was placed in each bag and another tag was tied to the outside. The samples were then spread out in sheltered places in the shade to dry. The floating was done in large garbage cans somewhat smaller but roughly comparable to a 50-gallon oil drum. Two such cans were used when possible, because floating could continue in one while the other was being emptied of accumulated sediment. The other flotation equipment consisted of a metal bucket with its bottom replaced by window screen, and

---

[1]William Robertson IV has a Master's degree in botany, learned basic flotation techniques from Stuart Struever's staff at Kampsville, Illinois, and has had experience with flotation in the Near East (Turkey and Israel). He is presently on the staff of the National Academy of Sciences in Washington D.C.

a small scoop made by attaching brass carburator screen to the frame of a kitchen strainer. A piece of plank covered with a newspaper folded in half is laid across the garbage can or barrel, which is filled about ¾ full with water. The bucket is half submerged in the garbage can so the water mounts inside it through the screen bottom, and is twisted back and forth by the bail held in one of the floater's hands; the scoop is in his other hand. A second person slowly pours the sample dirt into the moving bucket. After a few seconds the floater skims off the charcoal, or light fraction, with the scoop and dumps it onto the newspaper (previously labeled with waterproof ink). After several passes at differing levels in the bucket, the floater pulls the bucket out of the garbage can and dumps the material (the heavy fraction) caught in the screen onto a second labeled newspaper. Both fractions are laid out to dry in a protected place out of the sun. The heavy fraction is sorted through and usually discarded (the Salts Cave heavy fractions were largely made up of gravel and small fragments of limestone and sandstone, but occasionally small rodent or fish bones or fish scales were present). The paper containing the light fraction is carefully folded over, sealed with masking tape, and labeled on the outside.

The Salts Cave samples were almost all sandy enough so that the separation of the charcoal from its matrix was quite good; very little charcoal was found in the heavy fraction.

Results of the analysis of Salts Cave Vestibule flotation samples are reported by Yarnell in the next Chapter.

Chapter 15

Intestinal Contents of the Salts Cave Mummy and Analysis of the Initial Salts Cave Flotation Series[1]

RICHARD A. YARNELL

University of North Carolina, Chapel Hill

As the title indicates, this chapter deals with two sets of analyses. Both are relevant to the previously reported results of analysis of 100 human paleofecal specimens from Salts Cave (Yarnell 1969). The materials analyzed are (1) intestinal contents of a desiccated cadaver from the cave interior and (2) 12 samples recovered by flotation of deposits excavated from test pits in the floor of the cave.

The intestinal contents are from the Salts Cave mummy ("Little Alice") which Louise Robbins has recently identified as the body of a young boy (Robbins 1971 and page 141 in this volume). Two samples were examined by Eric O. Callen (who had previously examined five of the Salts Cave fecal specimens). In the mummy samples he found *Iva* (sumpweed, marsh-elder) seeds, hickory nutshell, evidence of animal protein, pieces of pre-

adult insect cuticle, and fragments of carbonized material. I examined five samples of this material, utilizing low magnification, with results very similar to Callen's. Three samples were large enough for quantitative treatment. Their total weight was 11.14 gm, of which 4.75 gm (42.6%) was a residue which passed through a screen with 0.7-mm openings. Quantification by weight of the remainder yielded these results: 71.1% hickory nutshell, 25.4% sumpweed seeds, 2.3% carbonized material (mainly hickory nutshell), 0.6% chenopod seeds (about 100 seeds), and 0.6% unidentified material. In addition, one sample included three amaranth seeds. There was no trace of sunflower, squash, grass, or fruit seeds, the other major components of the fecal samples.

The intestinal samples are essentially the same in appearance and much the same in contents as many of the Salts Cave fecal samples analyzed and reported earlier. This should allay the suspicions of those who have had doubts about the human origin of the Salts Cave feces.

The flotation samples were weighed and then sifted through a graded series of nine standard screens with openings ranging from $\frac{1}{4}$ inch to 0.21

[1]This is the revised version of a paper read in a symposium, "Coprolite Analysis in North America," held at the XXXV Annual Meeting of the Society for American Archeology, Mexico City, April 30–May 2, 1970.

TABLE 15.1   Salts Cave Flotation Samples—Carbonized Plant Remains[a]

	Mumy Hall floor	A valley 10—20 cm	A valley 40—60 cm	F 1 0—20 cm	F 2 20—30 cm
Sample weight [b]	3.8	12.9	13.7	16.6	8.9
Quantified plant remains	*0.84*	*4.87*	*7.02*	*8.02*	*4.67*
Unidentified		0.02	0.09	0.15	0.07
Dicot charcoal	0.47	3.32	4.82	5.69	3.11
Arundinaria cane	0.37	1.53	0.38	0.35	0.49
Monocot stems			0.34		0.04
Plant food			*1.39*	*1.83*	*0.96*
Hickory nut			0.84	1.17	0.58
Acorn					0.08
Seeds			*0.55*	*0.66*	*0.30*
Sunflower			36	22	15
Sumpweed			76	100	10
Chenopod			705	760	445
Amaranth			23	7	13
Knotweed			2	1	3
Panic grass			4		
Maygrass			5	3	27
Unidentified grass			11	13	
Unidentified			40	55	25
Poke			17	6	19
Portulaca			1		
Sumac			1		
Blueberry				1	1
Ground cherry?					

[a]Locations F, E, and C are from the Vestibule, other samples are from deep within the cave.
[b]Weight excludes stone, bone, and noncarbonized plant remains.
Decimal numbers indicate weight in grams; whole numbers indicate number of seeds.

mm. Quantification of small seeds was carried out for size categories down to about 0.5 mm. Quantities of other materials were determined only to about 1.5 mm.

Eight flotation samples are from excavations in the Salts Cave Vestibule. Four samples were taken from floor deposits deep within the cave. Two of the deep-cave samples consist mainly of noncarbonized plant remains, primarily torch material. Plant remains in the other samples are all carbonized with the exception of a few berry seeds.

The carbonized material totals 52.5 gm. It includes 1.6% unidentified remains, 78.7% dicot charcoal (mainly stems and twigs). 6.4% *Arundinaria* cane, 0.8% other monocot stems, and 12.5% plant food remains. The 6.6 gm of carbonized plant food remains includes 71.3% hickory nutshell,

2.1% acorn, and 26.6% grain and berry seeds. The latter includes 2600 grain seeds, 240 unidentified seeds, and 47 berry seeds. In addition there are 160 grain seeds, 10 unidentified seeds, 20 berry seeds, and 5 bottle gourd seeds which were not carbonized. Except for 14 berry seeds, the noncarbonized seeds are from the two deep-cave samples which are mainly composed of noncarbonized torch remnants and contain no carbonized plant food remains.

With the exception of the gourd seeds this is entirely an assemblage of Eastern Woodland plant remains. There is no evidence here of *Cucurbita* and no evidence of *Lagenaria* from the Vestibule deposits. Otherwise the plant food remains in the flotation samples are very similar to the fecal contents, both in kind and in relative quantities.

In the feces and the flotation samples, hickory

E 1–2	E 4	E 5 40–50 cm	E 6	C 6 60–70 cm	C	A valley	Totals
1.0	9.0	12.9	8.6	2.2	5.4	7.2	102.2
0.42	*5.27*	*8.47*	*6.67*	*1.26*	*1.66*	*3.36*	*52.53*
0.06	0.06	0.07	0.18	0.02	0.09	0.04	0.85
0.34	4.93	8.10	5.00	1.12	1.35	3.09	41.34
	0.01	0.16	0.01	0.04		0.01	3.35
	0.03						0.41
0.02	*0.24*	*0.14*	*1.48*	*0.08*	*0.22*	*0.22*	*6.58*
	0.16	0.10	1.38	0.02	0.22	0.22	4.69
			0.05	0.01			0.14
0.02	*0.08*	*0.04*	*0.05*	*0.05*			*1.75*
	7			2			82
	2	3	8	3			202
	80	50	30	95	3	4	2180
			2	3			48
			1				7
			1	6			11
	9	3	9	12		2	70
							24
10	15	15	45	6	1	3	215
1							43
							1
							1
							2
		1					1

nut is relatively abundant, acorn is sparsely represented, but evidence of other nuts is absent. The total of 82 carbonized sunflower seeds in the flotation samples is less than expected relative to the totals of 202 sumpweed seeds, 2180 chenopod seeds (at least two species), 70 maygrass seeds, and 48 amaranth seeds. In addition, there are 11 panic grass seeds, 7 knotweed seeds, and 1 portulaca seed, all three of which are very minor fecal components and perhaps only incidental, though knotweed and portulaca, as well as chenopod, amaranth, and poke, may have been eaten as greens.

Carbonized berry seeds include 43 poke seeds, 2 blueberry seeds, 1 sumac seed, and 1 ground-cherry seed. Noncarbonized berry seeds include 8 ground-cherry seeds, 5 elderberry seeds, 4 blackberry seeds, and 1 grape seed. Noncarbonized grains include 1 sunflower seed, 8 sumpweed seeds, 140 chenopod seeds, 4 amaranth seeds, 5 maygrass seeds, 1 panic grass seed, 1 portulaca

seed, and 1 carpetweed seed (*Mollugo verticillata*). Neither ground-cherry nor elderberry seeds have been found in the fecal specimens. On the other hand, squash seeds and, in one case, viburnum seeds were fecal components but do not appear in the flotation samples. Otherwise the fecal contents and the flotation sample contents are remarkably similar.

Six Vestibule samples are from the main excavation at the base of the damp talus slope which extends down steeply from the cave entrance. These samples, plus one from the cave interior, are of the sort which might be expected to have come from an open site. They contain 45% of the total carbonized nut remains but only 14% of the total weight of carbonized seeds. The other three samples with carbonized plant food remains include one from the cave interior and two from an excavation on the dry inner side of the Vestibule. All three samples are from dry ash beds and contain a much greater abundance of carbonized grain seeds than any open flotation sample I have seen. In the dry ash bed samples, grain and berry seeds make up 36% of the plant food remains by weight. This figure is only 10% for the other seven samples with carbonized plant food remains, whereas it is an estimated 75% in the fecal samples. In the two cave interior samples with no carbonized plant food remains, seeds make up 75% of the total weight of plant food remains, if we disregard the five gourd seeds. Carbonized plant food remains in flotation samples from open sites generally contain more than 95% nutshell.

Attempts were made to identify 481 small pieces of wood charcoal with the following results: 11.3% unidentified diffuse porous woods, 17.3% unidentified miscellaneous woods, 27.9% white oak group, 7.7% red oak group, 18.3% walnut, 6.2% hickory, 5.8% chestnut, 3.5% beech, 1.2% cherry (probable), 0.4% "locust" (?), 0.2% ash, and 0.2% elm. The vast majority of these were small fragments of twigs and small branches which made identification difficult and frequently somewhat uncertain. Trees not represented here include tulip poplar, dogwood, sassafras, black gum, and maple, which may make up some part of the unidentified categories. It is difficult to understand why we find no evidence of walnuts, chestnuts, beechnuts, or cherries when these species are represented by 29% of the wood charcoal. Incomplete utilization of available food resources is strongly indicated.

Table 15.2   Salts Cave Flotation Samples—Noncarbonized Plant Remains[a]

	Mumy Hall floor	A valley 10–20 cm	A valley 40–60 cm	F 1 0–20 cm	F 2 20–30 cm	E 1–2	E 4	Totals
Noncarbonized plant remains	*10.25*	*9.04*						*19.29*
Unidentified	0.04	0.37						0.41
Dicot stems and twigs	4.80	7.20						12.00
Arundinaria cane	1.32	0.34						1.66
Monocot stems	0.04	0.10						0.14
Bark	2.45	0.63						3.08
Dicot leaf fragments	1.10							1.10
Gerardia pod	0.15	0.36						0.51
Human feces	0.11							0.11
Gourd seeds	0.20							0.20
Plant food remains	*0.04*	*0.04*						*0.08*
Hickory nut		0.01						0.01
Acorn		0.01						0.01
Seeds	*0.04*	*0.02*						*0.06*
Sunflower		1						1
Sumpweed	4	4						8
Chenopod	137	4						141
Amaranth	2	2						4
Maygrass		5						5
Panic grass		1						1
Portulaca		1						1
Unidentified	3	7						10
Ground-Cherry?		1	3	1	3			8
Elderberry			2	2	1			5
Rubus		2				1	1	4
Strawberry	1	1						2
Grape		1						1

[a]F and E samples are from the Vestibule; others are from deep inside.

Decimal numbers indicate weight in grams; whole numbers indicate number of seeds.

Chapter 16

Plant Food and Cultivation of the Salts Cavers

RICHARD A. YARNELL

University of North Carolina, Chapel Hill

Salts Cave is an unusual archeological complex in a number of respects, not the least of which is its extraordinary yield of data essential to the reconstruction of ancient patterns of subsistence and ecology. Earlier analyses and interpretation of materials and observations in this cave have been published (Watson and Yarnell 1966; Watson *et al.* 1969).

Recent excavations in the Salts Cave Vestibule have recovered a considerable quantity of carbonized plant remains. In particular, block J IV, measuring 1 m² and more than a meter deep, in part, was excavated for the primary purpose of controlled recovery of plant remains. The excavation penetrated 20 natural stratigraphic levels below a seal of breakdown rock and pounded clay 30 to 50 cm thick (see Table 11.6 and Figures 11.9 and 11.10). The levels are numbered 4 through 23 proceeding downward. All soil in the block was removed by stratigraphic level and subjected to water flotation with several samples (portions) to each level.

Few samples from levels 14 to 23 have been analyzed, but it appears that few plant remains and very few plant food remains were recovered from these levels. Only a few hickory nutshell fragments and chenopod seeds have been identified. Samples from levels 12 and 13 have not yet been examined.

Flotation of 283 kg of soil from levels 4 through 11 resulted in the recovery of 67 samples with a combined weight of 1277 gm. Analysis of these samples followed a standardized procedure. Each sample is weighed. It is then divided into 11 parts by careful sifting through a series of 10 standard laboratory screens graded as follows in millimeters: 6.35, 4.00, 2.83, 2.38, 2.00, 1.41, 1.00, 0.71, 0.42, and 0.21. This screening probably causes moderate additional damage to the delicate carbonized materials beyond that already caused by the cave inhabitants, natural forces, excavation, flotation, transportation, and handling. Each resulting sample fraction is composed of particles of approximately equal size. This greatly facilitates the separation of various components that is required for quantification. Each fraction is weighed and examined under low magnification (7× to 30×), but ordinarily only the fractions with particles retained above the 2 mm screen are entirely sorted and quantified by weight. There is little point to counting nutshell fragments, but otherwise seeds are counted by genus or species. All seeds are weighed together as one component, because their weight is ordinarily quite low. The vast majority of seeds pass through the 2-mm screen but not through the 0.7-mm screen. These seeds are counted and weighed, but the quantities of other plant remains in the 0.7–2-mm range are calculated on the basis of quantities determined for materials not passing through the 2-mm screen. Otherwise quantity determinations would be vastly more time consuming, even if nutshell and other fragments of this size could be identified with adequate confidence. Ordinarily the materials passing through the 0.7-mm screen are low in quantity (comprising about 8%) and largely unrecognizable, though a few very small recognizable seeds are sometimes recovered. The sample weight is revised to include only the total quantified material not passing through the screen with 0.7 mm openings. Quantities are expressed as percentage of total plant food remains by weight. Seeds of each genus or species are expressed as number per gram of plant food remains.

The J IV samples from levels 4 to 11 are composed of 1023 gm of identifiable carbonized plant remains. This includes 833 gm of wood and cane charcoal and 190 gm of plant food remains made up of 178 gm of nutshell, 11 gm of seeds and cucurbit shell, and less than 1 gm of rhizome and tuber. Other components include 4 gm of unidentified plant remains, 13 gm of bone, 2 gm of microflakes, 131 gm of stone, and 103 gm of residue of fine debris, sand, and dust (see Table 16.1).

The 21,384 seeds recovered are from squash (*Cucurbita pepo*), sunflower (*Helianthus annuus*), sumpweed (*Iva annua*), chenopod (*Chenopodium* sp., perhaps *C. hybridum*), maygrass (*Phalaris caroliniana*), panic grass (*Panicum* sp.), amaranth (*Amaranthus* sp.), knotweed (*Polygonum* sp.), ragweed (*Ambrosia artemisiifolia* probably), sumac (*Rhus* sp.), grape (*Vitis* sp.), strawberry (*Fragaria virginiana*), blackberry (*Rubus* sp.), blueberry (*Vaccinium* sp.), honey locust (*Gleditsia triachanthos*), pokeweed (*Phytolacca americana*), and purselane (*Portulaca oleracea*). In addition 391 doubtful, un-

known, or unidentifiable seeds were recovered. Nutshell is from hickory nut, hazel nut, and acorn. The rhizome and tuber are unidentified. Small rind fragments from gourd (*Lagenaria siceraria*) and squash were recovered.

There are at least two sets of questions to which these data can be usefully applied. One involves the implications of variations in composition of plant remains between levels. The other is relevant to the validity of making qualitative and quantitative estimates of actual subsistence and inferences about paleoecology on the basis of results from analysis of flotation samples. In both cases there appears to be some basis for encouragement and guarded optimism.

Stratigraphic Variation in Plant Remains

Plant food remains from level 4 to 11 are abundant and varied (see Tables 16.1 and 16.2). Interlevel comparison of their composition reveals variations, some of which appear to indicate developmental trends:

1. The relative quantity of wood and cane charcoal, expressed as percentage of total plant remains, increases from 72% to 93% from level 11 to level 7 and remains nearly constant to level 4 where it drops sharply to 69%. Inversely, hickory nutshell decreases from 27% to 7% from level 11 to level 7, remaining nearly constant to level 4 where it rises sharply back to 27% (see Table 16.2). The percentage variation of hickory nut may be simply a function of variation in quantity of wood and cane, or vice versa, thus accounting for the inverse variation. However, this assumes that one or the other remained relatively constant. Unfortunately, we are not yet in a position to say much about absolute quantities of plant materials utilized. One variable is cane which is obviously more abundant relative to wood in levels 4 and 5, but this would have the effect of depressing wood charcoal in level 4 even further, relative to hickory nutshell.

2. Hickory nutshell, as percentage of plant food remains, is constant at 98% to 99% in levels 11 through 8. Then it drops in the higher levels to 86%

TABLE 16.1 Salts Cave Vestibule J IV Flotation Samples: Contents by Weight in Grams

J IV level	Preflotation weight	Sample weight (excluding fine debris)	Sample components					Plant Food					
			Stone	Chert microflakes	Small bone	Unidentified plant remains	Wood and cane charcoal	Plant food	Hickory nutshell	Acorn	Hazel nut	Rhizome: 4 tuber: 10,11	Seeds and cucurbit
4	80,316	276.5	40.8	1.0	1.2	2.2	160.1	71.2	61.38	0.48	1.05	0.06	8.25
5	31,195	220.2	19.6	0.4	1.6	0.8	183.9	13.9	12.75	0.06	—	—	1.05
6	29,967	158.6	13.8	0.1	4.0	0.5	128.4	11.8	11.37	0.02	—	—	0.42
7	15,366	73.5	6.7	—[a]	1.5	0.1	60.6	4.6	4.43	0.04	—	—	0.09
8	52,390	128.5	8.7	0.1	1.3	0.2	98.8	19.4	19.15	0.02	—	—	0.28
9	9,073	16.4	0.8	—	0.1	0.1	12.3	3.1	3.04	0.01	—	—	0.02
10	41,590	147.2	12.1	—[a]	0.5	0.2	101.8	32.5	31.74	0.06	—	0.20	0.47
11	23,132	153.1	28.9	0.3	3.0	0.4	87.2	33.3	32.86	—	—	0.11	0.31
Total	283,029	1174.0	131.4	2.0	13.2	4.5	833.1	189.8	176.7	0.7	1.1	0.4	10.9

[a] Less than 0.05

115

TABLE 16.2 Salts Cave Vestibule J IV Flotation Samples: Contents as Percentage of Plant Remains

	Sample components					Plant food				
J IV level	Chert micro-flakes	Small bone	Unidenti-fied plant remains	Wood and char-coal	Plant food	Hickory nutshell	Acorn shell	Hazel nutshell	Rhizome: 4; tuber: 10,11	Seeds and cucurbit
4	0.4	0.5	1.0	68.5	30.5	26.29	0.20	0.45	0.03	3.53
5	0.2	0.8	0.4	92.6	7.0	6.42	0.03	—	—	0.53
6	0.1	2.9	0.3	91.3	8.4	8.08	0.01	—	—	0.30
7	—[a]	2.3	0.1	92.9	7.0	6.79	0.06	—	—	0.14
8	0.1	1.1	0.2	83.4	16.4	16.17	0.03	—	—	0.24
9	—	1.0	0.5	79.6	19.9	19.71	0.02	—	—	0.13
10	0.3	0.4	0.2	75.7	24.1	23.60	0.04	—	0.15	0.35
11	0.3	1.5	0.3	72.2	27.5	27.20	—	—	0.09	0.26
Total	0.2	1.3	0.4	81.8	17.8	16.71	0.06	0.10	0.04	0.93

[a]Less than 0.05.

in level 4 (see Table 16.3). The successive decreases of hickory nutshell relative to other plant food remains is presumably a result of increased utilization of other plant foods, especially from weedy and cultivated annuals. This interpretation is supported by the dramatic increase of seeds from sun-loving annuals, which is absolute as well as relative in the higher levels (see Tables 16.4, 16.5, and Figure 16.1).

3. Acorn shell relative to hickory nutshell, taken two levels at a time, increases successively from 0.1% in levels 10 and 11 to 0.7% in levels 4 and 5. It is not readily apparent why this successive relative change took place. (See Table 16.3.)

4. The changes in frequency of seeds (exclusive of nuts) can be expressed in various ways:

(a) Seeds remain at 0.5%, or less, by weight of total plant remains until level 4 where they increase to 3.5% (see Table 16.2).
(b) Seeds remain below 1.5% by weight of plant food remains in levels 11 through 8, then increase in the higher levels to 11.6% in level 4 (see Table 16.3).
(c) Seeds relative to hickory nutshell by weight, taken two levels at a time, increase from 1.2% in levels 10 and 11 to 12% in levels 4 and 5.

TABLE 16.3 Salts Cave Vestibule J IV Flotation Samples: Contents as Percentage of Plant Food Remains

	Sample components			Plant food				
J IV level	Small bone	Unidentified plant remains	Wood and cane charcoal	Hickory nutshell	Acorn shell	Hazel nutshell	Rhizome: 4 tuber: 10,11	Seeds and cucurbit
4	1.7	3.1	225	86.2	0.7	1.5	0.1	11.6
5	11.2	5.6	1327	92.0	0.4	—	—	7.6
6	34.0	4.1	1087	96.3	0.2	—	—	3.6
7	33.1	1.5	1328	97.1	0.9	—	—	2.0
8	6.7	1.0	508	98.5	0.1	—	—	1.4
9	4.9	2.6	400	99.0	0.3	—	—	0.7
10	1.5	0.8	313	97.8	0.2	—	0.6	1.4
11	9.0	1.1	262	98.7	—	—	0.3	0.9
Total	7.5	2.3	459	93.7	0.3	0.6	0.2	5.2

(d) Seeds, exclusive of chenopod, increase in number per gram of plant food remains from 1.1 in level 11 to 4 in levels 8 and 7 and to 34 in level 4.

(e) Seeds of annuals (cultigens and weeds), exclusive of chenopod, increase slowly in number per gram of plant food remains from 0.2 in level 11 to 2.2 in level 7 and then increase rapidly to 28.6 in level 4 (see Table 16.4 and Figure 16.1).

If relative frequency of seeds from cultigens and weedy annuals is an index of amount of cultivated land as expected, it appears that there were small increases in cultivation through level 7 and then successive large increases in levels 6, 5, and 4. Change in chenopod seed frequency, relative and absolute, is less even. It differs from the other annuals in the much larger number of seeds recovered and in the relatively large number of seeds recovered from level 10. Chenopod seeds per gram of plant food remains are more numerous in level 10 than in any other levels except 5 and 4. However, the increase of chenopod seeds from level 8 to level 4 is similar to, though not as spectacular as, the increase of the other annuals. The high incidence of chenopod seeds in level 10 is as yet unexplained, but it may turn out to be a primary indicator of intensity of occupation.

Otherwise the evidence indicates that remnants from those plants which would be found exclusively or most often in gardens show the greatest and steadiest increase through time relative to other plant food remains. It seems extremely unlikely that this increase was simply a result of fortuitous circumstances or of differential habitation site utilization, seasonality, climate, etc. These and other explanations are possibilities, but less likely and certainly less obvious than explanation in terms of changing habitat utilization and alteration of natural environment.

Further support for this conclusion is the recovery of blueberry seeds from levels 4 and 5 only. Blueberry is an indicator of forest clearance or thinning, especially by fire, as is hazel, the nutshells of which were recovered only from level 4. In addition, seeds of pokeweed, which grows only on highly disturbed sites, were recovered from level 4 only, as were the only nondubious knotweed seeds. Uncertainly identified knotweed seeds came from levels 6, 8, and 10.

It should be added that seeds of strawberry, blackberry (or raspberry), and sumac, also indicators of disturbance of mature natural environments (and all perennials), were recovered from level 11 as well as from higher levels. However, the incidence of sumac seeds increased strongly in level 5 and again in level 4. Ragweed seeds were restricted to levels 9 and 10, one seed in each.

Perhaps the most impressive indication of change in pattern of plant husbandry is the initial appearance of cucurbits in level 5 and their distinct increase in level 4. The remains consist of squash seeds and small rind fragments of squash and gourd. Gourd remains occurred only in level 4 and are considerably less frequent than squash remains in the Vestibule flotation samples. However, gourds are considerably more frequent than squash in the cave interior, presumably because of their greater suitability as containers.

The absence of cucurbits below level 5 has additional significance of far greater general interest. Corroboration by additional studies is needed, but we now have a strong indication that gourd and squash were absent from central Kentucky gardens during an initial period when the crops were chiefly sunflower and sumpweed, both of which apparently were initially brought under the care of man in central eastern North America (Heiser 1951, 1955; Black 1963; Yarnell 1972).

Our data indicate that the continuing intensification of sunflower and sumpweed cultivation increased considerably during the period represented by level 6 and continued to increase thereafter in levels 5 and 4 with the introduction of cucurbits. At the same time a vast increase of weedy herbaceous annuals, especially chenopod, amaranth, panic grass, and maygrass, which flourish on recently opened soils, is apparent. We can infer that there was considerable increase in activities that opened the soil surface to sunlight during the mid-first millenium B.C., presumably as a result of increased slash and burn preparation for garden plots and shifting cultivation of the soil which opened habitats suitable for useful weeds as well as for plants intentionally propagated (see Part VI).

TABLE 16.4 Salts Cave Vestibule J IV Flotation Samples: Seeds per Gram of Plant Food Remains

Grams of plant food	J IV level	Squash seeds	Sun-flower	Sump-weed	Grain seeds						Greens	
					Chenopod	Amaranth	Knotweed	Ragweed	Panic grass	Maygrass	Pokeweed	Purselane
71	4	0.1	2.6	5.7	179	2.7	0.1	—	3.6	13.6	0.2	0.1
14	5	0.1	1.2	4.2	110	1.1	—	—	3.8	8.7	—	0.1
12	6	—	0.5	2.0	66	0.9	—	—	1.9	2.9	—	—
5	7	—	—	0.9	45	—	—	—	0.4	0.9	—	—
19	8	—	0.2	0.7	24	0.1	—	—	0.1	0.6	—	—
3	9	—	—	—	25	—	—	0.3	—	1.0	—	—
33	10	—	0.1	0.2	71	—	—	—[a]	0.2	0.2	—	—[a]
33	11	—	0.1	0.1	19	—	—	—	—[a]	—	—	—
190	Total	0.1	1.1	2.7	98	1.2	—[a]	—[a]	1.8	6.1	0.1	0.1

[a]Less than 0.05.

The strong increase or initial appearance of sumac, blueberry, and hazel nut in the latest levels indicate increased forest clearing but not necessarily cultivation. In any case, the ecological changes which took place during the later occupations apparently did little to increase the utilization of fleshy fruits and nuts with the exception of blueberries and hazel nuts. The most significant change was the greatly increased availability of seeds and greens from herbaceous plants, available as a result of forest clearance and cultivation, relative to plant foods from more or less undisturbed plant communities.

Comparison of Flotation Samples to Paleofeces

Analysis of food remains in 100 human paleofeces collected at various locations in the Salts Cave interior yielded a grossly quantified spectrum of the Salts Caver diet (Yarnell 1969). Originally the relative quantities of the components of each specimen were estimated by assigning one of five values to each component. These are A—very abundant, B—abundant, C—moderate, D—scanty, and E—scarce. Numerical values were assigned as follows: A = 5, B = 4, C = 3, D = 2, E = 1. By adding the assigned values for each

component of the fecal samples, a point total was derived for each. These totals were then converted to percentages of the summation of point totals of all fecal components (Yarnell 1969: Tables 6 and 7).

At the time when the fecal component percentages were derived it was obvious that A was equal to much more than B plus 1, that B was equal to more than C plus 1, and so on. However, it was not until later that a more appropriate formulation was derived that provides a more realistic indication of relative quantities of the fecal components. This formulation is that A = 2B, B = 3C, C = 4D, D = 5E (A = 120, B = 60, C = 20, D = 5, E = 1 or reasonable approximations thereof). The formulation is based on the realization that this was essentially the basis for the original assessments of quantity and is justified in part by a number of actual seed counts from fecal samples (Yarnell 1969: Table 7). In any case, the new basis of quantitative evaluation is eminently more appropriate than the old one. However, the percentage changes resulting from changing the basis of quantification are somewhat smaller than was anticipated.

A comparison of the original and revised relative quantities of the fecal components, a modified revision, and food remains from the Vestibule block J IV is depicted in Table 16.5. The modified revision of fecal contents is taken as the best

TABLE 16.4—(cont.)

	Fleshy fruits						Totals				
Unidentified	Strawberry	Blackberry	Blueberry	Sumac	Grape	Honey locust	Total	Total minus chenopod	Grain minus chenopod	Cultigens	Fleshy fruits
3.7	0.1	—	0.1	1.0	0.1	—[a]	213	33.7	28.3	8.4	1.3
2.8	—	0.1	0.2	0.6	0.1	—	133	23.0	19.0	5.5	1.0
2.5	—	0.1	—	—	0.1	—	77	10.9	8.2	2.5	0.2
1.5	—	—	—	0.2	—	—	49	3.9	2.2	0.9	0.2
1.3	0.1	0.6	—	0.2	0.1	0.1	28	4.1	1.7	0.9	1.1
—	—	0.3	—	—	—	—	27	1.6	1.3	—	0.3
0.6	—	0.1	—	0.1	0.1	—	72	1.6	0.7	0.3	0.3
0.3	—[a]	0.1	—	0.2	0.1	0.1	20	1.0	0.2	0.2	0.5
2.1	—[a]	0.1	0.1	0.5	0.1	—[a]	114	16.1	12.9	3.9	0.8

estimate of food consumption by the Salts Cavers as evidenced by the contents of the 100 specimens published in 1969. (Results of wet analyses performed on both Mammoth and Salts Cave paleofecal specimens—pages 41–47, 193–202 of this volume—will eventually enable a further refinement of these estimates.) Various considerations entered into the process of arriving at the percentages presented in Table 16.5.

The estimate of 5% for animal food is least secure. It was arrived at partly as a matter of convenience, but not without some justification. Eric Callen found meat debris in only two of five Salts Cave feces which he examined (Watson *et al.* 1969: 44). Of the 50 largest fecal samples analyzed, 60% contain vertebrate remains, versus 20% for the 50 smaller samples. Thus, it is likely that at least half the meals contained animal flesh of some kind. The bulk of the evidence is for animal food from rodents and small fish which indicates that meat from larger animals was not abundant (see Duffield's account in Chapter 17 of this volume). In any case it seems unlikely that animal foods made up more than 10% of the total diet nor much less than 5%.

Other percentage increases in the modification of the revised calculation of fecal contents are for squash flesh, poke and purselane greens, acorn, hazel nut, rhizome, and honey locust fruit. The last three are represented only in the flotation samples. The 1% for rhizome (etc.?) was arbitrarily added. Acorn and hazel nut quantities were calculated on the basis of quantities of carbonized nutshell in flotation samples from levels 4 and 5 by using the following formula for approximate food equivalence: 1 gm acorn shell = 4 gm hazel nutshell = 20 gm hickory nutshell. Percentage reduction required in order to accommodate the increases are applied in proportionally equal amounts for sunflower, sumpweed, and hickory nut.

The same foods are represented in the flotation samples and in the feces, so far as could be expected. Rhizome, tuber, and perhaps other foods (animal and plant) are not likely to be represented by easily recognizable traces in feces or flotation samples. Honey locust seeds, hazel nutshell, and acorn shell are not likely to be ingested because they are easily separated from the accompanying food. They are much more likely to appear in flotation samples, although carbonized acorn shell is thinner and more fragile.

The food percentages are represented by only roughly equivalent quantities of seeds from the Vestibule flotation samples, although the correspondence is considerably closer than was anticipated. Food components from levels 4 and 5 are taken as the primary standard for quantitative

TABLE 16.5 Quantification of Salts Caver Foods

	100 Fecal samples			Seeds and weights from vestibule J IV levels			
	1969 percentage	Revised percentage	Modified percentage	4,5	6,7,8	9,10,11	Seed[a] size
Gourd seeds	0.8	0.4	3	Rind only	—	—	Very large
Squash seeds	3.3	2.3		11	—	—	Very large
Sunflower achenes	23.0	28.7	25	201	10	7	Large
Sumpweed achenes	17.9	16.4	14	461	41	10	Medium
Total cultivated	*45.0*	*47.8*	*42*				
Chenopod seeds	20.8	24.9	25	14,080	1,454	2,910	Small
Amaranth seeds	2.9	1.5		209	12	—	Very small
Knotweed seeds	0.7	<0.1		5	—	—	Small
Panic grass seeds	1.5	>0.1	2	305	25	7	Very small
Pokeweed seeds	0.1	<0.1		15	—	—	Medium
Purselane seeds				10	—	—	Very small
Unidentified seeds	(0.1)	(0.1)		300	62	29	Various
Maygrass seeds	4.0	5.1	5	1,091	50	9	Small
Strawberry achenes	0.7	0.2		5	1	1	Very small
Blackberry seeds	0.3	>0.1		1	13	5	Small
Blueberry seeds	0.1			12	—	—	Very small
Viburnum seeds		<0.1	1	—	—	—	Large
Sumac seeds	0.5			79	4	10	Medium
Grape seeds	1.0	0.2		7	3	8	Medium
Honey locust	—	—		3	2	3	Very large
Total seed weight				*9.30 gm*	*0.79 gm*	*0.80 gm*	
Hazel nutshell	—	—	1	1.05 gm	—	—	
Acorn shell	0.3	<0.1	2	0.54 gm	0.08 gm	0.07 gm	
Hickory nutshell	16.9	18.6	16	74.13 gm	34.95 gm	67.64 gm	
Rhizome: 4 tuber: 10,11	—	—	1?	0.06 gm	—	0.31 gm	
Animal remains	5.1	1.0	5?	2.74 gm	6.83 gm	3.66 gm	
Totals	*100.0*	*100.0*	*100*	*87.82 gm*	*42.65 gm*	*72.48 gm*	

[a]"Very large" means about 10 mm, "medium" about 3–6 mm, "very small" 1 mm or less.

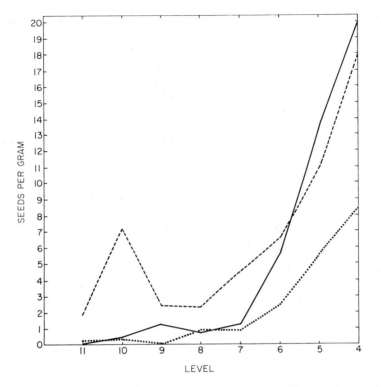

Figure 16.1 Salts Cave Vestibule J IV flotation samples: seeds per gram of food remains. (---) Chenopod × 0.1; (· · ·) Cultigens; (——) Grain minus chenopod and cultigens.

comparison with fecal components. Materials from levels 6 through 8 may be contemporaneous with some of the fecal samples, but it is less probable that any of the feces are as old as levels 9 through 11. This is indicated by the radiocarbon dates and by comparative composition.

The quantitative correspondence between the feces and the Vestibule J IV samples is with seed bulk rather than seed number. For instance, one sunflower seed was estimated to be the approximate mean equivalent of four sumpweed seeds. Thus, if 201 sunflower seeds equal 804 sumpweed seeds equals 25%, 461 sumpweed seeds equals 14.3% which is close to the fecal estimate of 14% (see Table 16.5). However, it is something else again to estimate food equivalence between sunflower seeds, seeds of plants eaten as greens (purslane and pokeweed), seeds from fleshy fruits, and

nutshell fragments (not to mention feathers and fish scales).

The food equivalence of grain seeds from Vestibule J IV samples and fecal percentage seem to match rather well with one major exception. On the basis of the 25% estimate for chenopod seeds in the fecal samples, only about half the observed number of seeds from J IV 4 and 5 would be expected. This means that chenopod is overrepresented in J IV and/or underestimated in the feces.

There are reasons for expecting overrepresentation (or a lessened underrepresentation) of various carbonized plant food remains. Some, being less delicate structurally, are less likely to be destroyed or distorted beyond recognition than others. Some, such as large fruit pits and nutshell, are likely to be discarded rather than ingested (yet, five fecal samples were literally packed with hickory nutshell). Small grain seeds are more likely to be lost in the fire than are the larger ones (but less likely to be recovered if flotation is not employed).

Chenopod seeds are especially vulnerable to loss during parching because they have a tendency to pop. In fact, most of the carbonized J IV chenopod seeds which are more or less intact have partially popped. The occurrence of these seeds in twice the expected quantity might be largely accounted for by seasonal parching of large numbers of them as a preparation for storage. Harvesting chenopod seeds on rainy days would be largely ineffectual. On days of inclement autumn weather the Vestibule would be an appropriate location for preparation of the harvest for storage. The small maygrass seeds, by way of contrast, apparently were consumed in season, for the most part, during late spring and early summer when activities would less likely be carried out within the cave (Yarnell 1969: 47, 49).

It should be noted that food production as a primary result of garden cultivation (cultigen husbandry) was a postulated 42% of total food, and that food production as a secondary result of gardening and other activities creating habitats for weedy seed-food and greens plants accounted for perhaps as much as an additional 32%. The vast abundance of chenopod seeds suggests that it was a protected garden plant, if not intentionally propagated, and a harvested crop. The bulk of the produce from maygrass, amaranth, pokeweed, and purselane may have been such, also. Knotweed appears to have been only incidental.

The indication is that garden production, fallow or otherwise, contributed two-thirds, more or less, of the total food supply. This estimate may turn out to be too high, but it should be obvious that the amount was somewhat greater than has generally been suspected for a subsistence pattern of this age in eastern North America.

Chapter 17

Nonhuman Vertebrate
Remains from Salts Cave Vestibule

LATHEL F. DUFFIELD

University of Kentucky

Nonhuman bone debris left by the prehistoric people who occupied Salts Cave can provide a considerable amount of information about the human group and its environment. It can tell, among other things, what animals the people killed, the relative importance of each species in the diet, and some details about butchering and food preparation. In addition to behavioral information, the debris can, especially in conjunction with information from other studies, aid in reconstructing the environment near the site at the time it was occupied.

This chapter presents basic information concerning the nature of the sample, procedures in analysis, and results. The latter includes a list of species identified and points out the relative importance of each. An attempt is made at environmental reconstruction using principally the animal bones.

Nature of the Sample

As already noted (pages 71–75), excavations in Salts Vestibule were carried out intermittently.

(Figures 17.1 and 17.2 show bone fragments *in situ* in Trench J.) The initial rough sorting of bones was made in the field and they were brought to the University of Kentucky after each fieldwork period. In the laboratory, the bones were dry brushed but no attempt at identification was made until all bones for each provenience unit were cleaned. At this stage, the human bones—many of which have much the same general appearance as the other animal bone and are equally fragmentary—were removed for separate analysis by Louise Robbins (Chapter 18 in this volume).

All bone, both human and nonhuman, was generally fragmentary but in good condition. For the most part, the periosteum was intact, and the bones were not heavily eroded or solution pitted. Conditions for preservation in the site were exceptionally good. Extremely thin and delicate bones, such as the metacarpals of bats and splint bones of the turkey "drumstick," were in amazingly good condition.

In all, over 2000 animal bones representing at least 13 species and 55 individuals were recovered. This latter figure represents the total number of individuals derived for the various horizons in the site.

123

Figure 17.1 Salts Cave Vestibule, trench J III, level 4. Bone fragments *in situ*.

Procedures in Analysis

The midden and its remains represents the end product of human and geological phenomena. By studying human aspects of the midden *some* of the behavior of the people can be reconstructed. Such reconstructions depend however, on one of the basic assumptions of this study: that the sample recovered from the site is representative. Thus, recovery of only a few bones is a reflection of cultural behavior. If people were not extensively utilizing animals and/or were not ceremonially or otherwise disposing of the bones at places other than the midden, then there should not be a large

number of bones. If this assumption is correct, a small bone sample becomes more significant and statements based on the sample should have greater relevance to a study of prehistoric human behavior. It is clear that if the sample is small because of sampling error, the assumption of cultural relevance is incorrect.

The bones were not catalogued, but were individually identified using the comparative osteological collection at the University of Kentucky. The identifications were recorded together with provenience for each lot of specimens. Those specimens which could not be identified with the comparative collection on hand were taken to the Osteology Laboratory in the Zoological Museum of the University of Wisconsin. Because the comparative collection at Wisconsin is extensive, it was possible to increase greatly the number of smaller animals identified. Thus, all identifications were made using comparative collections; keys or identification manuals were used only to acquire proper names of bones for an animal such as the turkey (Harvey *et al.* 1968). Bones were considered identified when they could be attributed to species and element. To make a species identification but not know the specific element seems incongruous and such an identification could undoubtedly be challenged.

In faunal identification, the investigator should indicate his degree of certainty in his identification. When a species name is applied with no qualification, it is assumed that the investigator is willing to withstand any challenge to his identification. Using the species—element approach undoubtedly results in a high number of unidentified specimens. For example, many unidentified birds bones probably are turkey, but the fragmentary nature of the bones did not permit specific identification.

Once the bones were identified, tables indicating species, minimum number of individuals, and pounds of meat per species were compiled (Tables 17.1 and 17.2). Minimum number of individuals was calculated largely on the basis of the maximum number of particular elements present, taking into account proximal or distal and right or

Figure 17.2   Salts Cave Vestibule, trench J II, level 6. Bone fragments *in situ*. (a) (left) General view. (b) (right) Close-up to show human skull fragment (the scale is divided into 2-cm units).

left. At times, information on maturity or immaturity was included in the calculation. For example, if two deer were indicated by the presence of the right distal humerus fragment of mature deer and there was also a left distal humerus of an immature deer, this was considered to represent three individuals.

Because the bones were not catalogued, all those fragments from one species were never laid out together during the analysis, and consequently it was not possible to use the paired comparison approach for determining minimum number of individuals (Krantz 1968; Chaplin 1971), nor was

it possible to see which specimens might be fragments of the same bone.

Once minimum number of individuals was calculated, pounds of meat supplied by each species could be determined. The base figures for the amount of meat that could be provided by each individual were taken from White (1953) and Parmalee (1965). Table 17.2 indicates the results of this determination. Normally tables such as this list the animals in zoological sequence; however, so few animals were found, the sequence was determined by the horizon in which they occurred. This has the disadvantage of placing box turtles

TABLE 17.1 Animal Bone from Salts Cave Vestibule: Specimens and Minimum Number of Individuals by Species and Horizon

Animal	Horizon I		Horizon II		Horizon III	
	Number of specimens	Minimum number of individuals	Number of specimens	Minimum number of individuals	Number of specimens	Minimum number of individuals
Odocoileus virginianus Deer	3	1	46	2	111	7
Meleagris gallopavo Turkey	4	1	63	4	151	11
Sciurus sp.? Squirrel	1	1	—	—	1	1
Cervus canadensis? Elk?	1	1	—	—	—	—
Bos taurus Cow	1	1	—	—	—	—
Terrapene sp.? Box turtle	1	1	1	1	2	1
Myotis sp.? Bat	4	—	15	—	5	—
Sylvilagus floridanus Eastern cottontail	—	—	5	1	7	1
Vulpes fulva Red fox	—	—	7	1	1	1
Procyon lotor Raccoon	—	—	10	2	13	4
Mephitis mephitis Striped skunk	—	—	1	1	1	1
Peromyscus sp? Field mouse	—	—	2	1	1	1
Sigmodon hispidus Hispid cotton rat	—	—	—	—	1	1
Oryzomys palustris Rice rat	—	—	—	—	1	1
Marmota monax Groundhog	—	—	—	—	1	1
Sciurus carolinensis Eastern gray squirrel	—	—	—	—	5	1
Urocyon cinereoargenteus Gray fox	—	—	—	—	2	1
Canis sp? Dog or wolf	—	—	—	—	2	1
Morone sp? Bass	—	—	—	—	3	1
Ictalurus sp? Catfish	—	—	—	—	2	1
Subtotal	*15*	*6*	*150*	*13*	*310*	*36*
Unidentified mammals[a]	20	—	225	—	902	—
Raccoon?	—	—	73	—	—	—
Rodent?	1	—	5	—	5	—
Bird	17	—	83	—	135	—
Fish	—	—	—	—	28	—
Totals	*53*	*6*	*536*	*13*	*1380*	*36*

[a] Horizon IV contained only 12 mammal bones, none of which could be identified.

TABLE 17.2   Relative Importance of Species in Terms of Pounds of Meat

Animal	Horizon I			Horizon II			Horizon III		
	individuals	lb	%	individuals	lb	%	individuals	lb	%
Deer	1	100.0	21.7	2	200.0	72.4	7	700.0	77.0
Turkey	1	8.5	1.8	4	34.0	12.2	11	93.5	10.2
Squirrel	1	1.0	Trace	—	—	—	1	1.0	Trace
Elk?	1	350.0	76.1	—	—	—	—	—	—
Box turtle	1	0.3	Trace	1	0.3	Trace	1	0.3	Trace
Cottontail				1	1.8	Trace	1	1.8	Trace
Red fox				1	4.0	1.3	1	4.0	Trace
Raccoon				2	35.0	12.6	4	70.0	7.7
Field mouse				1	?	—	1	?	Trace
Striped skunk				1	5.0	1.7	1	5.0	Trace
Hispid cotton rat							1	?	Trace
Rice rat							1	?	Trace
Groundhog							1	5.6	Trace
Gray fox							1		
Gray squirrel							1	0.7	Trace
Dog or wolf							1	25.0	2.7
Bass							1	1.0	Trace
Catfish							1	1.0	Trace
Totals	5	459.8	99.6	13	280.1	100.2	36	908.9	97.6

with mammals but it enables the reader to grasp quickly the differences among the various horizons.

Units of Analysis

Materials from excavation units C, C/N, E, G, H, J I–IV, and F were grouped together following the correlation chart provided (Table 11.7). Four horizons were defined on the basis of comparative stratigraphy in the various trenches (pages 75–78). For present purposes, these major stratigraphic groupings may be referred to as Horizons I, II, III, and IV, with I being at the top and IV at the bottom.

Bones from excavation unit D, on the south side of the Vestibule were analyzed, but the results do not play a role in the conclusions because the stratigraphy in D could not be correlated with that on the other side of the Vestibule. Thirty-two bones were found in levels 3–7 and level 9 of unit D. Species and minimum number of individuals in-

clude at least one deer, one raccoon, one chipmunk (*Tamias striatus*), and a box turtle.

Also excluded from the tabulations were the bones found on the surface and those whose provenience became lost through collapsing pit walls (page 78) or human error. On the slope south of the Iron Gate for example, bones of a turkey and a groundhog were found. On the north side of the Iron Gate, further into the cave interior, was a catfish ceratohyal, turkey bones, and deer bone fragments. Considering the fact that this was once a commercial cave not too much significance is attached to surface bones in the Vestibule area, although they may indeed be prehistoric.

The materials from wall collapse in unit E were quite interesting. A left mandible of a dog was found and the right proximal femur of an extremely small but mature raccoon was present.

Four features, 7A, 7C, 7D, and 7F, all found in unit E (page 94, Table 12.6) contained animal bone debris. Bones found in these features were not incorporated into the charts because their horizon of origin could not be precisely determined. In Fea-

ture 7A, the proximal end of a right ulna of a raccoon was present together with a thoracic vertebrae
of an immature deer, a head of a deer rib, unidentified bones from a large mammal (probably deer),
and bones from a small bird. A turkey rib bone was
also found.

Feature 7C had two bone fragments from a large
mammal. Feature 7D held the right distal humerus
of a turkey and a large number of unidentified
bone fragments. These include 57 mammalian
bones mostly from a large animal, and two bird
bone fragments. Feature 7F had six bone fragments from a large mammal.

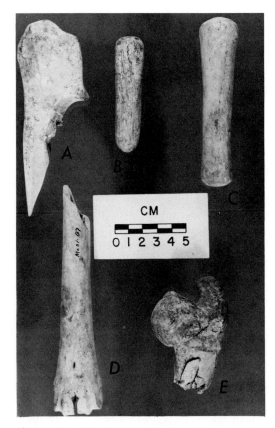

Figure 17.3 Salts Sink Vestibule: Animal bones. A, Ulna
awl; B, C, Unknown bone objects; D, E, bones showing fracturing.

Food Procurement

The principal animals hunted were deer, raccoon, and turkey. There is a low number of bones
from nonfleshy sections of deer probably indicating that these animals were killed at some distance
from the site. The mandible and front and rear legs
were the portions most often carried back to the
cave (Table 17.3). However, the occasional occurrence of vertebrae and rib bones indicates that a
deer was sometimes brought in fairly intact. It was
not often, however, that feet of any of these
animals appeared in the midden deposits.

The age curve of deer does not appear to be
normal. Teeth in four mandible fragments could
be aged using criteria illustrated by Harlow and
DeFoor (1962). One was about 7–9 months, another about 4.5 years, one 5.5 years, and one about
10 years old. Pathological alteration of some of the
bones suggests that the oldest individual may have
been arthritic. One would normally expect a large
number of young deer. Data from the Woodland
horizon at Tick Creek, Missouri, where 547 deer
mandibles were found, indicate that 68% of them
were from 0 to 4 years of age (Parmalee 1965:27).

The raccoon must have been a food animal to
judge from the fragmentary nature of the crania.
Had these animals died in the cave naturally, there
should be more post cranial bones in the deposits
and the crania should not be so crushed and fragmented. In general, there is a surprisingly small
quantity of post cranial elements of these animals
present. In addition to food, raccoons supplied
canines used to make canine tooth necklaces.
(Figure 17.4F).

Turkeys, on the other hand, must have been
carried to the site feathers and all, and many of
the turkey bones were eventually incorporated
into the midden. For example, different phalanges,
jugals, quadrates, premaxillae, mandibles, and
splints as well as humeri, femora, etc., attest to
the variety and degree of preservation of these
bones. Turkey bones in some cases were broken,
but generally were not so badly fragmented as
mammal bones. The sternum and pelvis, however,
did not fare so well and were never found whole.
The fragmentary nature of these bones may have

TABLE 17.3 Frequency Distribution of Deer Bones from Horizon III, Salts Cave Vestibule

Elements	Mature				Immature			Totals
	Right	Left	Axial	Fragment	Right	Left	Axial	
Antler				2				2
Cranium	1	1	1				1	4
Maxilla	2	1						3
Teeth						1		1
Mandible	3	7			1			11
Cervical vertebrae			4				1	5
Thoracic vertebrae			5				7	12
Lumbar vertebrae			1					1
Sternum			1					1
Ribs				21				21
Scapula	2	1				1		4
Humerus, proximal		1			1	1		3
Humerus, distal	2	3						5
Radius, proximal		1			1	1		3
Radius, shaft	2	1						3
Ulna		2			1			3
Unciform		1						1
Scaphoid	1							1
Metacarpal		2		2				4
Metatarsal	2			1	1			3
Splint				1				1
Pelvis	2	2	1					5
Femur, distal	2							2
Tibia, proximal	2							2
Tibia, distal	1							1
Tibia, shaft	3	1						4
Phalanges, 1st	2	1				1		4
Phalanges, 2nd	1							1
Phalanges, 3rd	1							1
Totals	*29*	*25*	*13*	*27*	*4*	*5*	*9*	*112*

inflated the minimum number of individuals because for Horizon III this number is derived from the eleven sterna fragments. The figure cannot be too far off, however, because there are eight right coracoids and eight right radii.

There were turkeys of various sizes and at least one of them was a hen. Most of the identified bones are from the anterior portion of the bird with less bones being identified from the posterior portion. The large number of "splints" however suggest that the femur, tarsometatarsus, and tibio-tarsus were broken up in food preparation and consumption, and therefore not readily identified.

Other animals are present, but not in any great quantities. The small numbers suggest that these animals were probably used as food, but were not intentionally hunted; that is, they were taken as the opportunity presented, although some animals, like striped skunk, red fox and gray fox might not actually have been food animals. They may have been in the site naturally. Foxes, raccoons, some snakes, and other surface dwelling animals oc-

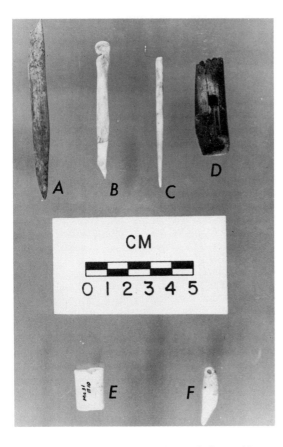

Figure 17.4 Salts Sink Vestibule: Worked animal bones. A, Splinter awl; B, Deer splint awl showing notching; C, Needle; D, Grooved bone; E, Bone bead; F, Perforated canine.

casionally wander deep into caves and in some cases become lost and die. When this happens the bones of the skeleton tend to be concentrated in a limited area unless they are washed away by flooding cave streams. If these animals were in the midden at Salts Cave due to natural reasons there should be a greater number of identifiable bones present.

Fairly complete skeletons of mice and bats suggest that they are in the midden due to natural causes, but judging from the human paleofecal analyses, some mice were eaten. Fairly complete skeletons of both *Peromyscus* sp. and the rice rat, as well as some unidentified skeletons of other small rodents, were present in the debris. In

addition to these more complete skeletons, there are some isolated elements. Bats, the size of *Myotis keeni* or *Myotis lucifugus*, were present and it is likely that the bat remains are there naturally.

Fish remains occur only in Horizon III and on the surface near the Iron Gate. Catfish and bass were noted in the excavated areas together with 28 bones that could not be specifically identified. Fish scales have been found in some fecal specimens (Yarnell 1969: Table 7; page 119 in this volume).

Food Preparation

As already suggested, there was some field butchering of deer, but once animals were brought into the cave they were further prepared for eating. Some deer bones exhibited cut and skinning marks, but there were so few intact bones that a detailed butchering and cutting analysis and description was not possible. Bones such as the astragalus, the scapula and parts of the skull had small cuts of the kind normally considered a result of the butchering process. Bones of most mammals, especially those of medium size such as foxes, dogs, etc. and the larger ones such as deer were battered and broken. Few very large specimens remained. Battering and crushing may have taken place before all flesh was removed, and thus bones could have been cooked with the meat and eaten. Some bone slivers occur in human fecal remains (Yarnell 1969: Table 6). The bones also could have been broken after defleshing and then boiled to produce bone butter (Leechman 1951), which could have been eaten or used in food preparation.

Another feature of bone utilization was the gouging out of the interior of long bones that contained cancelleous tissue. Bones such as the distal end of the tibia or the humerus have much of this soft, interior, bony tissue removed. In general, it appears that the inhabitants of Salts Cave were not blessed with an abundance of animal protein (Yarnell 1969; Table 7), and they were utilizing as much of the animal as was energetically feasible. This is in line with the fecal studies that indicate seeds and vegetable materials as being the most common dietary items.

Relative Food Values

Tables 17.1 and 17.2, showing the species found, suggest that turkey and deer were the most important animals in the diet in terms of actual numbers and pounds of meat. There is no doubt as to the deer's importance. One deer can provide 100 pounds of meat and from 126 to 197 calories per 100 gm (McCance and Widdowson 1940). In terms of pounds of meat the deer provides 78.8% of the meat that was once on the individuals found in Horizon III. If one translates this into calories per pound, he will quickly see that the importance of deer is quite substantial.

The role of the turkey as reflected in this table can be challenged. Despite the fact that in Horizon III turkey provides about 93.5 pounds of meat or 10.2% of the total, the caloric food values obtained from this bird are not so great as the raccoon which supplied 70 pounds or 7.7% of the meat. Caloric values for roasted turkey range from 116 to 176 calories per 100 gm (Altman and Dittmer 1968) while roasted raccoon has 255 calories per 100 gm (Watt and Merrill 1963). Converting to calories per pound demonstrates that raccoon is more important than turkey in the diet by as much as 8 to 5.

One of the nagging problems in examining the role of animals in the diet of the Salts Cave people is the role possibly played by human flesh. Human bones are fragmented and splintered in the same fashion as other mammal bones and exhibit butchering and skinning marks. Some are even worked into tools. They were found mixed with other animal bones in the midden (see pages 146–157 of this volume). Judging from the number of individuals found, the importance of human flesh in the diet—if those individuals were indeed eaten—might have been considerable.

Environmental Exploitation

The combination of animals found in various horizons in the site gives some indication of the kinds of environments being exploited by the people.

Horizon I contains a relatively small amount of identifiable bone (Table 17.1), and considering that this horizon contains some historic materials, the bones are not regarded as especially significant. One of the bones found has been extensively rolled and eroded. It resembles elk, but identification cannot be positive. There is also an intrusive molar of a cow present.

Those materials from Horizon I that could be prehistoric include turkey, deer, squirrel, and box turtle. These animals indicate deciduous woods, or a semiopen deciduous woods environment, perhaps a forest edge. Deer prefer edge environments, but can be found in the woods especially in the fall when there is an abundance of mast. Box turtles may be found in woodland situations as well, but they prefer the more grassy openings.

Horizon II reflects more or less the same situation—woodland or semiopen woodlands. The cottontail rabbit prefers brush areas and woodland margins. This is also the environment favored by the striped skunk, which is seldom found far from water. The red fox is also adaptable but prefers strongly rolling country with semiopen woodlands. The raccoon, most abundant in wooded river bottoms, is less abundant in the wooded uplands. They can be found in cliff areas. These animals feed at night and sleep in their dens during the day. Thus, if they were hunted or trapped, this may have been done at night.

Horizon III reflects a greater diversity of environments being exploited. At this time the people appear to have utilized not only dense, broadleaf deciduous woods and the semiopen woods or edge environment, but grasslands and riverine environments as well. The use of riverine resources is clearly reflected in the catfish and bass from the site (Table 17.1). The rice rat which may have been part of the diet, makes its home near water and readily takes flight across water if threatened.

Reaching the nearest point on the river from Salts Cave entrance involves a trip of about 1.5 miles, and then descent of a steep bluff directly to the water's edge. It is perhaps more likely that these people were utilizing the river in a place like that around Three Sisters Island where the shores are more accessible. The fish and the rice rat may have been acquired while the people were musseling.

The exploitation of dense woods is suggested by the presence of gray squirrel remains. The gray squirrel prefers heavy stands of timber with an abundance of undergrowth and brush. Such a situation could be present in either the bottom lands or in the more heavily wooded uplands.

The hispid cotton rat is predominantly a grass-land form. This little rat makes its nest in under-ground burrows or from grass and soft fibers on the surface, but under cover of some vegetation. Road-ways radiate from the nest and at times lead into marshes or onto damp ground, but generally not into areas that are flooded. These rats are fre-quently seen in cotton fields, hence their common name (Hall 1955: 136—138).

The hispid cotton rat seems to be anomalous at Salts Cave because these forms are found pre-dominantly further south. As of 1957 this rat was known as far north as Reelfoot Lake in Tennesse (Hoffmeister and Mohr 1972: 169). Salts Cave is just north of the present day distribution. If this was a more common form in the area at the time Horizon III was being deposited, the weather may have been slightly warmer.

Two charcoal radiocarbon dates, 990 B.C. $\pm$ 120 (GaK-2765) and 610 B.C. $\pm$ 100 (GaK-2622), if cor-rect, would suggest that this deposit dates during a time of climatic fluctuations that started around 940 B.C. and finally stabilized about 550 B.C. at the beginning of the Sub-Atlantic episode (Baerreis and Bryson 1965: 214—215).

Seasonal indicators are not especially abundant nor extremely diagnostic. The box turtle would tend to hibernate and thus not be readily avail-able in the winter. Sometimes, however, the shell of this animal is used as a container, and thus a broken carapace could be discarded at any time during the year. The squirrel and raccoon tend to be less active in the winter, but are known to come out during warm spells to forage for food. The groundhog—although a true hibernator—also follows this pattern. The presence of these animals together in a site suggests that the occupations took place at a time other than during the winter months. The presence of a mandible from a 7—9-month-old deer, however, suggests a November to January occupation.

The preceding discussion gives some indication of the materials recovered in the excavation units in the Salts Cave Vestibule. Analysis of the Salts Cave fecal specimens reveals that other animals were at least occasionally utilized as well. These include *Microtus* sp., a bird of the family Fringil-lidae (sparrow?), a small fish, and a salamander (*Ambystoma*?). While no bones of the bobcat were found, a hair from this animal has been reported (Yarnell 1969: Table 6).

Vertebrate Fauna from Nearby Sites

Material recovered in the excavation of Mam-moth Cave Vestibule are believed to date in the same time range as the Salts Cave material. Nelson (1917) reports some additional animals not found at Salts Cave. He notes black bear, opossum, por-cupine, brown bat, turtle (*Kinosternum*), and pos-sibly a crane. He provides positive identification of elk which is suggested from the Salts Cave materials. It is surprising that the pack rat was not reported from either cave since there is evidence of *Neotoma* activity in the area today.

The Jewell site in nearby Barren County, im-mediately southeast of Mammoth Cave, is a Mis-sissippian agricultural village. The faunal list from this site is somewhat the same as Salts Cave, but there are differences in frequencies. About 35 deer were found. This animal provided about 90.5% of all the meat for the village (Keller 1970: Table I). Turkey supplied about 2.2% and 5.7% came from black bear. The remainder came from many dif-ferent animals including box turtle.

This is an example of a focal economy (Cleland 1966: 43—44). Mississippian farmers in this area tended to concentrate their hunting efforts on deer while other animals had a relatively minor role in the meat supply. The Salts Cave people, on the other hand, had a diffuse economy (Cleland 1966: 43—44). It appears that hunting was an activity incidentally related to other food-getting pursuits. Some intentional hunting probably took place, but the evidence suggests that not a great deal of energy was expended in this type of activity. This would also suggest that animal resources were not especially abundant in the area. Scarcity of animals would have made it expensive, in terms of energy, to have spent much time in seeking out game.

Conclusions

The fact that Salts Cave people made extensive use of seeds and other vegetable materials is supported by several aspects of the site. Bones, while they constitute a large number of items recovered, seemingly are not too abundant considering the amount of earth moved. Furthermore, the animal inventory is sparse and many species are represented by only one specimen. These factors combine to sketch a picture of a society that spent little energy on stalking, capturing, butchering, cooking and eating of vertebrate animals.

Chapter 18

Identification of Subfossil Shell from Salts Cave

DAVID H. STANSBERY

Ohio State University Museum of Zoology

Twenty-three lots of shell were received for identification (Table 18.1). Of these all were ascertained to be freshwater bivalve (naiad) or terrestrial gastropod shell, 10 were or included terrestrial gastropod remains, 15 were or included naiad remains, no specimens of aquatic gastropods were included, two lots contained gastropods identifiable to species, seven lots contained naiads identifiable to species.

The most common naiad was the Common Mucket, *Actinonaias ligamentina* (Lamarck 1819). This species continues today as one of the three to five most abundant naiads of this section of the Green River. It is distinctly characteristic of the faster moving parts of the river (the riffles and runs). It is rarely found in the long natural pools or impoundments between the fast zones of the river.

Lampsilis ovata (Say 1817) is also characteristic of runs and riffles but, like *Ligumia recta* (Lamarck 1819) and *Elliptio dilatatus* (Raf. 1820), it is also found in the quieter, deeper parts of the river. It would seem that the Indians took the easiest and

quickest route to obtain naiad material—the shallows in the fast water.

It may be that all of the terrestrial gastropods are *Mesodon thyroides* (Say 1817), but this is not known with certainty. This species is widespread in shady, moist forests having herbaceous plants and litter over the forest floor. I have found it to be even more common on the flood plains of rivers or around alkaline swamps or bogs. It is frequently found within inches of the water itself and, under especially humid conditions, it may be found crawling about on herbs, dead limbs, and logs on the ground or some feet above the ground on tree trunks and rocks. It would not be surprising to find individuals around the mouth of a cave, especially if or when conditions were moist. I would not expect to find this species living any great distance underground.

All naiad species found are edible, although not especially tasty. In my experience they taste much like the water from which they come, and they can be very tough. All of the species recorded I have seen worked by prehistoric Indians. The *Lampsilis ovata*, "Pocket-book" to the commercial clammer, seems to have been a favorite scoop, bowl, or large spoon (Stansbery 1966: 42). A species having similar propor-

tions, *Lampsilis ventricosa* (Barnes 1823), apparently served the same function in areas—especially headwaters—where *L. ovata* was absent.

TABLE 18.1   Subfossil Shell from Salts Cave, Kentucky

Provenience	Number of pieces and description	Species
Upper Salts,	1 right valve	*Actinonaias ligamentina* (Lam., 1819)
P 54	1 left valve	*A. ligamentina*
	1 right umbo	*Lampsilis ovata* (Say, 1817)
	1 left posterior ventral disc	*L. ovata*
Upper Salts,	1 right valve	*Actinonaias ligamentina* (Lam., 1819)
P 54–55	1 left valve	*A. ligamentina*
Trench C,	1 right valve	*Ligumia recta* (Lam., 1819)
Level 6	2 fragments	Unidentifiable naiad
Level 7	many fragments	Unidentifiable naiad
	1 piece of disc	Unidentifiable naiad
Level 10	1 left valve	*Actinonaias ligamentina* (Lam., 1819)
Level 16/17	1 cardinal tooth	Unidentifiable naiad
Level 18	1 fragment (reflected lip)	Terrestrial gastropod
Trench C/N,		
Level 1	1 damaged shell	Terrestrial gastropod
Level 7	1 fragment	Unidentifiable naiad
	1 anterior right valve	Unidentifiable naiad
	1 right valve	*Ligumia recta* (Lam., 1819)
Trench D,	1 entire	*Mesodon thyroides* (Say, 1817)
Level 2		(a terrestrial gastropod)
Trench D,	4 fragments	Unidentifiable naiad
Level 5	1 fragment	Terrestrial gastropod
Trench D,	1 entire	*Mesodon thyroides* (Say, 1819)
Level 7	1 spire surface	Terrestrial gastropod
Trench D,	1 right umbo	*Elliptio dilatatus* (Raf., 1820)
Level 8	1 fragment	Terrestrial gastropod
Trench D,	1 spire	Terrestrial gastropod(s)
Level 9	1 fragment reflected lip	Terrestrial gastropod(s)
	several fragments (including reflected lip)	Terrestrial gastropod
Trench E,	1 right valve	*Actinonaias ligamentina* (Lam., 1819)
Level 5	several fragments of burned shell	Unidentifiable naiad
	1 fragment	Unidentifiable naiad
Trench E,	many fragments	Unidentifiable naiad
Level 7	1 disc center	Unidentifiable naiad
Trench E,	many fragments	Terrestrial gastropod(s)
Level 7b		
Trench F,	1 fragment	Unidentifiable naiad
Level 1		

Prehistoric People of The Mammoth Cave Area

LOUISE M. ROBBINS

Mississippi State University

Man has occupied caves in many parts of the world for literally hundreds of thousands of years. He has camped in caves for brief periods, lived in them for extended periods of time, and he has buried his dead in them. Many individuals, numerous for the time period during which they lived, have been removed by archeologists and geologists from caves in China, France, and the Near East in the Eastern Hemisphere. Fewer individuals have been found in caves in North and South America, but they are in sufficient quantity to attest to the fact that man utilized caves wherever they were to be found. The caves of western Kentucky prove to be no exception. However, the prehistoric occupation of the Kentucky caves introduces some provocative questions and presents some intriguing problems.

The prehistoric people of the Mammoth Cave National Park area are the focus of this part of the report because that area has received more scientific, and nonscientific, scrutiny than most other regions. Other sections of this volume concentrate on the nonbiological aspects of these people. This portion will examine the evidence that has been compiled on the people themselves in an attempt to identify the relationship of the "cave people" to populations inhabiting the regions adjacent to the caves.

Prehistoric humans have been found in both Mammoth and Salts Caves in the form of skeletal remains and exsiccated bodies, or "mummies" as they are more frequently known. From the time an early white settler found a mummy in one of the caves near Mammoth Cave, interest in searching for mummies in Mammoth and Salts has far exceeded the concern for other human bones in the Caves. (For the activities surrounding the location and subsequent disposition of the mummies, see Meloy 1971.)

The existence of aboriginal populations in the vicinity of Mammoth Cave is well known from the numerous site surveys, and in some cases excavations, made along the Green River (Webb and Funkhouser 1932). The Indian Knoll site, an Archaic shell mound on the Green River in nearby Ohio County, contained the most widely known prehistoric skeletal population in Western Kentucky, approximately 1250 individuals (Webb 1946; Snow 1948). Sites less well known, but of importance equal to Indian Knoll in terms of population, are the Chiggerville shell mound of Ohio County with a burial population of approximately 114 (Webb and Haag 1939); the Carlson (or Carlston) Annis site in neighboring Butler County, the most extensive of the Green River shell mounds, with a burial population of around 400 (Webb 1950a; Marquardt 1972); and the Read shell mound of Butler County that contained about 247 burials (Webb 1950b). Numerous surface sites have been identified within the boundaries of Mammoth Cave National Park, but few have produced burials (Sloan and Hanson, Field Notes, on file Museum of Anthropology, University of Kentucky).

There are two types of prehistoric human remains in Mammoth and Salts Caves: exsiccated remains of so-called mummies were discovered in both caves, and skeletal remains have also been found in both caves.

Mummies

The mummies have received widespread attention because of their exceptional state of preservation and the unusual circumstances surrounding the discovery of the Mammoth Cave mummy, "Lost John." The commercialization of Mammoth Cave has long included the presence of a mummy as a tourist attraction. Extensive research by Meloy (1971) on the mummies of Mammoth Cave reveals that of all the mummies displayed in that cave, only two have actually been found there. According to sources located by Meloy (1971: 18), a mummy was found in 1814 in Audubon Avenue but was reburied under stones until 1840 when it was found again. The weight of the stones had crushed the body so badly that it could not be used for public display. Nothing is known of the physical characteristics of this individual, nor whether it was a male or female, adult or child. It may be speculated that the Audubon Avenue mummy was a member of the same population from which mummies in other caves had come, but no clothing or other cultural items were found with the former to associate it with the latter.

The second mummy from Mammoth Cave was found in 1935, lying partially crushed under a boulder, in the interior of the cave. The location and subsequent extraction of Lost John from the boulder have received wide attention (Pond 1935: 27–35; 1937: 176–184; 1938: 7–9, 24; Meloy 1971: 14–20). Professionally trained archeologists were called upon to oversee the removal of the boulder and to record the cultural situation in which the mummy was found. It was observed that Lost John had not been buried in the cave, as were other mummies in the vicinity of Mammoth Cave, but that he was the victim of a prehistoric mining accident. The few cultural items found near him indicated his mining activities in the cave at the time of his death.

A physical anthropologist was called upon to examine Lost John for evidence of bodily damage at the time of death, physical characteristics, and populational affiliation (Neumann 1935, 1938: 345–353). Neumann estimated that the miner was kneeling when the boulder fell, its impact forcing the miner to fall on his right side. John attempted to brace himself against the fall by extending his right elbow outward, but the weight and force of the boulder caused the arm to break approximately one inch above the elbow joint, pushing the broken humerus into the sand. However, no blood from the injury was found in the vicinity of the right elbow. The major weight of the boulder rested against the left rear part of the neck and head, the left side of the chest, doubling it over the pelvis and breaking the tenth, eleventh, and twelfth rib shafts on the right side; the boulder also rested against the left side of the pelvis. Neumann noted an area of dried blood in the sand under the face and on the left side of the neck which he attributed to a fracture of the skull in the region behind the left mastoid process. Similar brownish material, assumed to be blood, was found on the skin of the pelvis anterior to the left ilium where it had been struck by the rock. Smaller limestone rock fragments beneath the body prevented it from being crushed entirely, although death probably resulted when the chest was crushed. A small space was found between the chin and neck which prevented pinching of the trachea or collapse of the larnyx, evidence demonstrating that John had not suffocated.

During the time the body was pinned under the rock it was damaged by rodent activity. The metacarpals and phalanges of the left arm had been severed from the lower arm and scattered, with some bones being found under the lower arm and others in the sand under the skull. Tooth marks were evident on the bones of the lower right arm, where rodents had severed the lower half of the arm and carried it away. Parts of the right scapula were destroyed by rodents, and an opening had been gnawed into the chest cavity.

The body of Lost John is well-preserved with flesh and internal organs present, although in a desiccated state, exceptions are those pieces removed by rodents, Figure 19.1. Desiccated external genitalia positively identify the body as male. He was around 45 years of age at the time of death, according to the external sutural closure pattern of the skull and degree of tooth wear. Plans to display the body for public viewing immediately after discovery heretofore prevented a comprehensive age analysis. Neuman (1938: 50–52) was able to take some measurements of the skull, and from these he calculated indices for much of the face. These figures and observations on John portray him as being round headed with a high cranial vault. The face is broad, but the forehead is narrow by comparison; statural estimates indicate that he was short, approximately 5 feet 3 inches tall. Neumann did not have techniques at his disposal to delimit precisely the time period during which Lost John had lived. However, the miner seemed to exhibit a close physical resemblance to a Woodland group from the Page site in Logan County, Kentucky, suggesting that John, too, had lived sometime during the Woodland period (Webb and Funkhouser 1930). The Page site material was reexamined by the writer and Neumann's claim seems justified.

The body of Lost John has not been subjected to any additional analysis since the metrical and morphological examination by Neumann. Arrangements are now being made by the writer for permission to X ray the body to determine the extent of internal injury resulting from the mining

Figure 19.1 "Lost John," the Mammoth Cave mummy, as he appeared when the boulder was lifted off his chest and neck.

accident. The X rays will also offer a means of double-checking the age assigned to John and of investigating the dentition and condition of the body prior to his death. Following the X rays, some tissue or bone will be removed from an unobtrusive part of the body and used to obtain a radiocarbon date for the time period during which he died. At the same time, a small dissection can be made in the region of the lower intestine and colon, from an area that will not show when the body is exhibited, to collect a sample of intestinal contents for a dietary analysis.

Although there are legends crediting Salts Cave with varying numbers of mummies, the only reasonably well-authenticated one was found in 1875 by two local men in the area. During a 1969 expedition into Salts Cave, the writer was a member of a party searching for evidence of the original burial place of the mummy. High upon a ledge of a passage leading off Mummy Valley, a limestone rock was found with an inscription attesting to the discovery of a mummy (Figure 3.2; see page 25).

Following the original disposal of the body, it was desiccated, or dehydrated, by the dry, cool atmosphere of the cave. After discovery in the nineteenth century, the small individual was dubbed "Little Alice," assigned an illustrative history, and became a familiar exhibit in some of the caves in the area (Meloy 1971: 7–13). Little Alice was on exhibit in Mammoth Cave, reported to be a mummy from that cave, when Lost John was found. Because there was no question of his claim to the title of "Mammoth Cave Mummy," he replaced Little Alice in that role and is to be found today in a display case a short distance inside the natural entrance to the cave. Little Alice was not to be seen by the public again. When the Salts Cave mummy was again placed on display in 1970 at the Museum of Anthropology, University of Kentucky, Lexington, it was in the role of "Little Al," a 9-year-old boy.

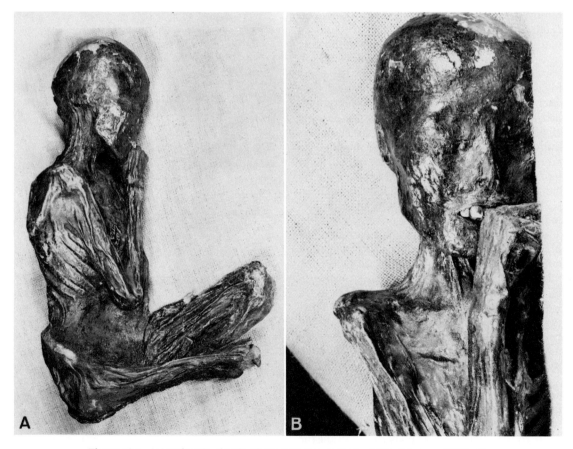

Figure 19.2   (A) Right side of Little Al, the Salts Cave mummy. (B) Facial view of Little Al.

When she was removed from the exhibit case at Mammoth Cave, "Little Alice" was placed in storage on the cave property until 1958. At that time she was transported to the University of Kentucky to another storage warehouse. In 1969, she was removed from storage and became the subject of a comprehensive examination as part of the research project then underway at Salts Cave (Watson *et al.*, 1969; Robbins, 1971).

A preliminary examination was made of "Little Alice" to record both the completeness and the condition of the desiccated body. The presence of external genitalia emphatically destroyed the mythical life history of "Little Alice"; the nickname was changed to "Little Al." The incomplete body exhibited what is assumed to be post mortem damage from being shuttled to and from public display sites and storage shelves. In addition, a light mold, or fungal growth, covered some areas of the body as a result of its being in an atmosphere where temperatures and humidities were higher than those of Salts Cave. Removal of the existing mold, and storage of the body with silica gel containers prevented a reappearance of the mold. The left humerus, left hand, and both feet were missing from the body. The ulna, radius, ilium and fibula from the left side and the tibia and fibula from the right side of the body were present, but disarticulated and devoid of flesh. All of the epidermis and much of the subcutaneous flesh was absent from the left side of the head and body (Figure 19.2A,B).

X rays were taken of Little Al primarily to obtain information for assessing his age because the flesh covering the face prevented direct examination of his dentition. The disarticulated bones contained no epiphyses, and nonfusion of the ilium to the pubis and ischium meant that the mummy was a young male; fusion of pelvic bones in males occurs around 14 years of age (Krogman 1962: 105—106). The X rays of the upper body, Figure 19.3, revealed the presence of deciduous teeth except for permanent teeth in the central and lateral incisor and the first permanent molar positions. The mandibular permanent canines appeared to be partially erupted which, taken in conjunction with the other permanent teeth present, suggested that Little Al was over 8 years of age (lateral incisor) but not yet 10 years old

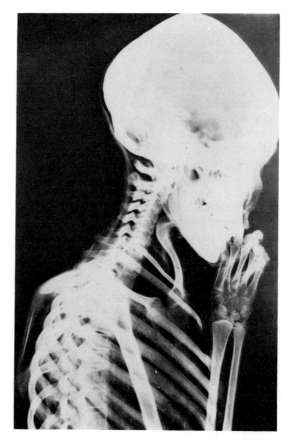

Figure 19.3   X ray of upper part of Little Al.

(Watson and Lowery 1962: 338—346). The bones of the right hand and wrist were also examined for their stages of ossification in an attempt to correlate dental age with wrist bone age and possibly narrow the age range of Al. According to the aging criteria developed by Greulick and Pyle (1959: 94—100), the hand and wrist bones yield an age range of 8 years 10 months to 10 years 9 months, giving a mean value of 9 years, the most frequently assessed age of the carpal bones. Johnston and Jahina (1965: 349—354) suggest that the carpal bones do not produce a reliable measure of a child's skeletal age, but it is believed that the combined dental and wrist age range justifies the 9-year-old age assignment to Little Al.

The X rays supplied additional information that had not been anticipated. They revealed that A1 had suffered no broken bones during his life, and only the distal end of the left tibia showed any growth arrest lines, possibly resulting from an injured ankle (see Figure 19.5). No evidence of bone pathology could be found in the X rays, nor did they reveal what may have caused his death.

An examination of the visible morphological characteristics of the body suggested that A1 was rather round headed with a high cranial vault and had a moderate to pronounced amount of lambdoidal flattening (Robbins 1971: 202). The artificial cranial deformation probably contributed to the mound-shaped torus of the occiput because the cranial bones of one so young are highly plastic and would yield to pressure applied to them. A slightly flattened area on the lower part of the bulging frontal bone also implies that contour modification occurred from binding pressure. Extreme midfacial and alveolar prognathism is present, but whether it was caused by the mixed dentition or was inherited is not known. The cranial morphology of A1, observed in the X ray of the upper body (Figure 19.3), resembles that of Adena peoples from the Robbins, Ricketts, and Wright sites in north central Kentucky (Webb and Snow 1945: 288–309) more closely than that of people from the nearby Page site in Logan County or the Stone-Grave people from the Duncan site in Trigg County, Kentucky (Funkhouser and Webb 1931). The Adena people supposedly did not occupy western Kentucky, and little is known of other recognized Woodland populations in that section of the state. From the present appearance of A1's body he lay or was placed in a flexed position, an atypical burial position for Adena or Stone-Grave populations, but one that is fairly common among many Woodland groups.

An estimate of A1's stature was determined from measurements of the exposed left femur and tibia, using the stature formula proposed by Trotter and Gleser (Krogman 1962: 163). The femoral length of 316 mm and tibia length of 264 mm yielded a stature of 4 feet 6 inches, an average height for a 9-year-old American boy who has attained about 78.6% of his adult height of 68.7 inches (Watson and Lowery 1962: 88–89). The degree of correlation between height and age suggests that Little A1's skeletal age may have been a year younger than his chronological age.

Tissue samples were removed from the lower thoracic and abdominal regions—20 gm from each region—for radiocarbon datings to determine the time period during which Little A1 lived. The samples, submitted to the University of Michigan Radiocarbon Laboratory, produced ages of 1960 ± 160 years (M-2258) and 1920 ± 160 years (M-2249), i.e., 10 B.C. and A.D. 30, respectively (J.B. Griffin, personal communication). These dates are more recent than those obtained from materials found in other parts of Salts Cave, which range from 290 B.C. ± 200 years (M-1573) for a paleofecal specimen from the cave interior to 1540 B.C. ± 110 years (Gak 2767) for charcoal from the cave Vestibule (Watson 1969: 69–70; page 235 of this volume). According to the radiocarbon dates obtained on Salts Cave materials thus far, it appears that the burial of Little A1 was the most recent prehistoric activity in the cave.

An attempt was made to determine the blood type of Little A1 by analyzing tissue removed from the lower thoracic area. Uncontaminated tissues from other areas of the body would have served equally well because, as noted by Glemser (1963: 437), blood cell antigens are found in most tissues of the body. After shredding the tough, fibrous tissue, it was washed first in distilled water and then in physiological saline solution numerous times to remove any phosphates or nitrates that might have been absorbed from the cave environment. The inhibition method of Boyd and Boyd (1939: 421–434) was used in testing for types A and B, the result being that neither appeared to be present. Additional testing of the tissue was conducted by means of the mixed cell agglutination technique used by Otten and Flory (1964: 283–285) on Chilean mummy tissue. The results of the test trials consistently indicated an O blood type for the tissue which, in view of a subsequent examination of comparable tissue by Zimmerman (1972), may be accepted as the actual blood type of the boy. Zimmerman found well-preserved red blood cells and lymphocytes in several veins of thoracic tissue from A1. The presence of these easily destroyed cells demonstrates the excellent

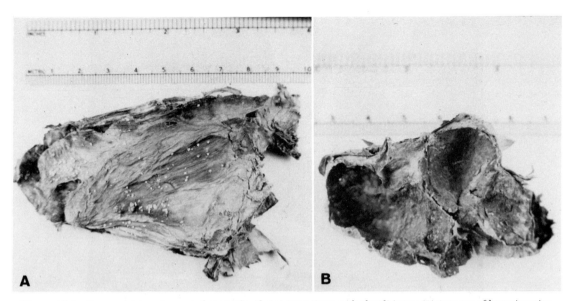

Figure 19.4 Preserved internal organs from Little Al. (A) Lung tissue with alveoli intact. (B) Segment of lower intestine.

preservation of the internal organ system of Little Al (see Figure 19.4).

Because X rays of the lower part of the body, Figure 19.5 revealed the presence of waste material in the lower intestine and colon, those organs were removed and examined for evidence of the diet of the boy, and indirectly, of his people. The stomach—desiccated but intact—was removed and examined for food debris. None was found; hence he must have died at least 4 hours after eating his last meal because that length of time is usually sufficient for food to pass through the stomach. In addition, the waste material in the lower intestine and colon probably represented his dietary intake of the previous 48 hours (Callen 1963: 189). Mirabilite crystals observed inside the kidneys and intestine of Little Al probably formed after his death. The quantity of fecal debris removed from Al suggested that he was in good health before he died and that his death was unexpected.

Yarnell analyzed fecal samples from the lower parts of the intestinal tract and upper region of the colon. He found mainly hickory nutshell, sumpweed, and chenopod (see page 109). Callen examined debris from the middle and lower regions of the descending colon and found mainly sumpweed with lesser amounts of hickory nuts, and some meat protein that may have come from grubs intermixed in the debris (Callen, personal communication). The plant remains in the fecal debris of Little Al are identical to plant remains in human fecal specimens found in other parts of Salts Cave (Yarnell 1969: 41–54). The early Woodland peoples of the region apparently cultivated local plants instead of relying on hunting as a primary food source, and this premaize agriculture continued with Al's population. It is hoped that analysis of Lost John's intestinal contents will contribute additional information on the primary food intake for the prehistoric people of the area.

After tissue was removed from Little Al for analysis, an exploratory dissection was made in an effort to discover the cause of death. No obstruction was found in the esophagus, which eliminated the probability of choking. No abnormalities were detected in the internal organs with the exception of an extensive amount of reddish brown material

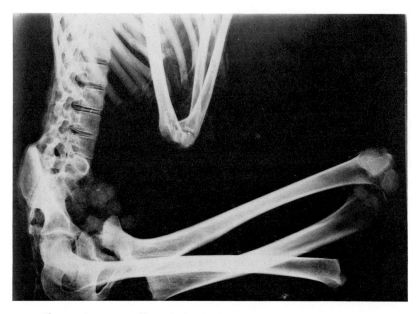

Figure 19.5   X ray of lower body of Little Al. Feces-laden intestine apparent.

in the vicinity of the aortic arch. The material was reconstituted and found to be blood. The aorta was examined for evidence of a rupture; while no rupture or tear of the aortic wall was found, it does not mean that one could not have been present. The writer was informed by two surgeons at the University of Kentucky Medical School that Little Al may have died from internal hemorrhage of the aorta which could have been ruptured by a strong blow to his chest or back. Such a blow would not necessarily damage the skeletal frame at the point of impact, and the X ray had revealed no evidence of bone damage in the thoracic region. In view of the results of the exploratory dissection, it is thought that Little Al probably died rather suddenly from an internal hemorrhage resulting from a fall or a blow to the thoracic area.

Other mummies have been removed from caves near Mammoth Cave National Park, but heretofore their relationship to the populations of Lost John and Little Al has not been investigated. The burial practices surrounding the interment of the mummies provide some indirect information of possible populational associations. Short

Cave in Warren County, Kentucky, a few miles south of Mammoth Cave, contained most of the other mummies, although all but one have been lost or destroyed (Meloy 1971). Little is known of the first Short Cave mummy other than it supposedly was a baby whose body, but not the skull, disintegrated when exposed to the noncave atmosphere (Meloy 1971: 22–23). There is no record of what happened to the skull. Significantly, the accounts of the baby's discovery reveal that it was wrapped in deerskin.

The second mummy from Short Cave, the famous Fawn Hoof, was found sitting in a stone-box grave, of the kind commonly found in Tennessee and neighboring counties in Kentucky to the south of Short Cave. She was arrayed in several finely fashioned skin burial garments and accompanied by a variety of grave goods, providing a rare glimpse of burial items that would not have been preserved in graves outside a cave (for a description of Fawn Hoof and her burial associations, see Nelson 1917: 23–25; Meloy 1971: 25–27). In physical appearance, the body of Fawn Hoof was well-preserved; the flesh was dry, hard, and dark in color. Two injuries were noted on the body, a wound between two ribs and an injury to one eye, but whether they were, in fact, injuries or represented rodent or other post-mortem damage is not known. A photograph of Fawn Hoof in Meloy's book (page 32) shows a loss of flesh from the left side of the head and body much like the area of missing flesh on Little A1. The marked similarity of the defleshed area of Little A1 and Fawn Hoof raises questions of how and when it happened. When Fawn Hoof was found, the body was perfectly preserved; there is no mention of flesh loss in any of the published reports of her. Consequently, she must have lost the flesh during her days of public exhibition. The loss of flesh from Little A1 was thought to have occurred when he was removed from Salts Cave. The assumption was that he had been buried in a flexed position on his left side, and the brain outline in the X ray seems to verify that burial position. When he was removed from the cave in 1875, the tissue on the left side may have adhered to the soil and been torn free of the body, exposing the skeletal frame. However, it now seems equally probable that Little A1 may have lost his flesh during the time he was being exhibited as Little Alice. If the body were exhibited lying on its left side with no attention given to the preservation of a dry atmosphere, the body may have absorbed moisture, especially the side that rested against the display case.

After being displayed as "The Mammoth Cave Mummy" for a time, Fawn Hoof was taken in 1817 to Worcester, Massachusetts, and became the acquisition of the American Antiquarian Society. Records show that while in Worcester, some cranial measurements were made on the skull of Fawn Hoof. Putnam (1874: 314–332) quoting Squier and Davis, *Ancient Monuments of the Mississippi Valley*, page 291, gives some measurements of a female "skull" from Short Cave (Kentucky). The stature for "the Mammoth Cave Mummy" was given as 5 feet 10 inches, but Putnam estimated it to be approximately 5 feet tall. In April 1876, Fawn Hoof was acquired by the U.S. National Museum and stored in the Archeology Division until transferred to the Division of Physical Anthropology in November, 1914 (see U.S.N.M. accession number 4789). At that time she

was defleshed, and her disarticulated bones stored for future anthropometric use (page 169 in this volume).

One other mummy from Short Cave is worthy of comment. There was some question whether this body—known as Scudder's Mummy—had been buried in a sitting position or on its left side in a flexed position (Jones 1876 4–5; Bushnell 1920: 66; Meloy 1971: 33–38). Deerskin wrappings on the body and deerskin items found with it suggest that it was from the same population as Fawn Hoof and the baby mummy. Scudder's Mummy, thought to be an adolescent boy, showed evidence of a fracture of the occipital bone that may have contributed to his death. Aside from the injury, the body was apparently well-preserved, being dark in color with dry, hard skin and hair that was thought to have been depigmented by the minerals in the cave.

The interment of the Short Cave mummies exhibits a pattern similar in some ways, yet different in others, to mummies found in Tennessee (Jones 1876: 1–3; Bushnell 1920: 66–70). Mummies in both areas were wrapped in deerskins and accompanied with grave goods. However, the Tennessee mummies differed in that some were disarticulated at the hips before being wrapped or dressed. Following the wrapping, they were placed upright in woven baskets. Wrapping the body before burial, and the kind of wrapping used, implies that the Short Cave and Tennessee mummies may have come from one population occupying a broad geographical area. The influence from Tennessee is most apparent in the stone-grave burial of Fawn Hoof, and some authorities (Nelson 1917: 27; Bushnell 1920: 69) attribute the cave burials to the Stone-Grave people of the region. If the Short Cave mummies were part of the Tennessee population, it is curious that the former were not disarticulated at the hips before burial. Why particular members of the population were selected for burial in the caves is another interesting question that leads to speculations concerning the social structure of the peoples, a question that the existing evidence is quite inadequate to answer. The same caves contain skeletal remains of individuals who apparently were defleshed before burial, but whether their population affiliation is the same as that of the mummies or is with a different group is yet to be determined.

Skeletal Remains

Skeletal remains were found in Mammoth and Salts Caves by several investigators. Putnam found a considerable amount of human skeletal material during his work in the caves for the Kentucky Geological Survey (Nelson 1917: 27–28), but no information can be found on the disposal of the skeletons.

Early reports comment on the discovery of numerous human skeletal remains by the saltpeter miners during the course of their work in the caves (Collins 1874: 158; Hovey 1912: 34; Meloy 1971: 16). Nelson (1917: 56) found some fragmentary skeletal material that he considered insignificant in his excavation of the Mammoth Cave Vestibule. Skeletal material discovered during recent excavations in Salts Cave, to be discussed later, drastically increases the significance of the bone fragments found by Nelson.

In 1930, workmen removed from the Vestibule of Mammoth Cave a single burial that was later studied by Neumann (1938: 340–346). The body had been flexed and placed in an oval grave lined with a fiber matting or burned grass. No grave goods were found with the body, nor was there any evidence of body wrappings. Neumann noted that the bones of the individual were in an excellent state of preservation, and once excavation damage was repaired, it was possible to make a comprehensive examination of the burial. The individual was a young female of about 18 years of age and exhibited small physical features. She was slightly long-headed with a high, small cranial vault and a narrow face. Neumann stated that her physical type was unlike any prehistoric population then known in Kentucky. Since Neumann's analysis of the skeleton, the nearby Archaic Knoll site has been excavated and its people studied (Snow 1948). A comparison of the cranial dimensions and indices of the Mammoth Cave vestibule female and the Indian Knoll female mean values (Snow 1948: Tables 8 and 10) reveals that the former falls within the range of metric variation for the Indian Knoll population. If, however, the metric values are not examined separately but as metric combinations of particular trait complexes, e.g., the face, or the cranial vault, then the Mammoth Cave skeleton exhibits less resemblance to the Indian Knoll people. A degree of morphological similarity exists between the Mammoth Cave cranium and the "long headed" Indian Knoll females, but only in the vault and upper facial region. This writer investigated the possible affiliation of the Mammoth Cave skeleton with Archaic and Woodland skeletal populations from Tennessee (Lewis and Kneberg 1961: 145–173; Fuller, n.d.). The Mammoth Cave skeleton most closely resembles Kentucky and Tennessee Archaic people who were small in stature, of light build, and who were long-headed with high cranial vaults, long narrow faces, moderately broad zygomatic bones, and a moderate degree of alveolar prognathism. The Woodland and Stone-Grave populations exhibit larger, broader, and more robust skulls and larger skeletal frames than is present in the Mammoth Cave skeleton.

Young (1910: 305) writes of finding human and animal remains mixed with the ashes of a large fire bed (presumably a midden deposit, see pages 71, 78) located in crevices at the foot of the steep entrance to Salts Cave. He noted the lack of order in the jumble of bone in the ashes and collected several skulls and a number of mandibles with teeth intact; a mixture of deciduous and permanent dentition indicated that some of the mandibles were of children around 6 years of age. Young comments on the damp soil from which the bones were removed and which contributed to their poor preservation. Upon exposure to the air, the bones apparently disintegrated, and no report was made of the physical characteristics of the crania or the mandibles.

No other complete skeletons are available for analysis from Mammoth or Salts Caves, but additional skeletal fragments have been removed from the caves. During the excavation of Mammoth Cave, Nelson found skeletal fragments consisting of a distal part of an adult femur and a patella; both fragments exhibited a deep longitudinal groove on the anterior surface. The left symphyseal surface of an adult female pubic bone, a partly charred cranial fragment, an adult metatarsal, an upper molar tooth, and two canine teeth, a child's mandible with deciduous teeth intact, and skeletal remains of a fetus were also found by Nelson.

During the excavation period of the Salts Cave archeological project, beginning in April 1969, a considerable amount of human skeletal material was recovered for analysis from Salts Cave. The unusual stratigraphic disposition of the bone, the fragmentation of skeletal parts, and the attention given "burials" before interment present some intriguing, challenging, and frustrating problems that have not heretofore been encountered in prehistoric populations from western Kentucky.

Nearly 2000 human bone fragments were recovered from the excavation of test trenches C, E, J, F, G, and H, and from collection surveys in the vicinity of the Vestibule (see Figure 19.6). The number of complete bones recovered was minimal, less than 50, and these were mainly mandibles, clavicles, or the small bones of infants. A stratigraphic analysis of the human bone was undertaken in an attempt to determine whether there was any pattern to the interment of the bone in the site (Tables 19.1 and 19.2). A curious picture unfolds, which makes the intentional interment of the human remains questionable. The recovery of human skeletal material from trench C is presented in detail to demonstrate the erratic distribution of the bones.

No human remains were found in Trench C until a depth of 50–60 cm (the upper occupation horizon of C, corresponding to level 6 in E), where the midshaft of an adult human radius was found intermingled with fragments of animal bone. At a depth of 80 to 90 cm, two rib fragments and a mandible were found. According to the dentition and robusticity of the mandible, it was from a male about 16 years old. A badly burned mandibular fragment was found in level 9 at a depth of 90 to 100 cm. In level 10, a mixture of burned and unburned human material was found including several fragments of an adult tibia, a third rib, a portion of an ulna, and a central incisor tooth.

Figure 19.6 Layout of human skeletal fragments from Salts Cave Vestibule excavations. Note the fragmented nature of the material.

There was a noticeable increase in the accumulation of burned human bone in level 11 (the lower occupation horizon of C and E), where an extensive amount of burned and unburned human material was found. Area A of that level (a bone cluster about 20 cm in diameter that lay 40 cm from the west wall and 170 cm from the south wall of Test C) contained the fragmentary remains of at least two individuals. One was an adult whose remains consisted of a right temporal bone, a portion of the occiput, and a section of the left parietal bone; the bones could be rearticulated. The other individual was a 6-year-old child,

TABLE 19.1 Human Bone Distribution in Salts Cave Vestibule Trenches[a]

C[b]	C/N	E	G	H	Horizon	J II	J IV	J I	J III	F
Levels 1–6 H = 43 B = 15 C = 2 W = 3	Levels 1–5 (Included in C)	Levels 1–4 H = 0 B = 0 C = 0 W = 0	Levels 1–4 H = 0 B = 0 C = 0 W = 0	Level 1 H = 0 B = 0 C = 0 W = 0	Breakdown debris and clay	Levels 1–3 H = 0 B = 0 C = 0 W = 0	Levels 1–2 H = 0 B = 0 C = 0 W = 0	Levels 1–3 H = 7 B = 2 C = 0 W = 0	Level 1 H = 0 B = 0 C = 0 W = 0	No level H = 0 B = 0 C = 0 W = 0
Levels 7–8 H = 72 B = 1 C = 8 W = 0		Level 5 H = 118 B = 44 C = 2 W = 1	Level 5 H = 0 B = 0 C = 0 W = 0	Level 2 H = 1 B = 0 C = 0 W = 0	Stream Sands / Midden among breakdown	Level 4 H = 15 B = 3 C = 0 W = 0	Levels 3–4 H = 22 B = 9 C = 2 W = 1	Levels 4–5 H = 3 B = 0 C = 0 W = 0	Levels 2–4 H = 23 B = 1 C = 1 W = 0	Levels 1–5 H = 6 B = 2 C = 1 W = 0
Levels 10–11 H = 120 B = 75 C = 0 W = 1		Level 6 H = 3 C = 1 B = 0 W = 1	Level 6 H = 28 C = 2 B = 12 W = 0	Levels 3–4 H = 0 B = 0 C = 0 W = 0	Midden-bearing brown clay alternating and interfingering with sand and gravel	Levels 5–13 H = 164 B = 30 C = 5 W = 0	Levels 5–13 H = 427 B = 72 C = 20 W = 1	Limit of excavation		
Level 12 H = 13 C = 0 B = 3 W = 0		Level 7 H = 15 B = 10 C = 2 W = 0	Level 7B,X,Y,Z & pit H = 305 B = 65 C = 18 W = 2	Limit of excavation	Breakdown debris alternating and interfingering with sand and gravel	Levels 14–16 H = 5 B = 5 C = 0 W = 0	Levels 14–23 H = 13 B = 3 C = 0 W = 0			
Limit of excavation		Limit of excavation	Level 8 H = 12 B = 4 C = 0 W = 0		Wall collapse	H = 17 C = 1 B = 4 W = 0				
			Limit of excavation			Limit of excavation				

[a] KEY: Bone totals in test areas. H: Human bone; B: Burned bone; C: Cut bone; W: Worked Bone;

[b] Tabulation of human bone from the debris of the collapsed west wall of Trench C: H = 17, B = 4, C = 1, W = 0.

according to the dentition of the left alveolar portion of the maxilla. Fragments of some long bones and a portion of a rib were found with the adult and child. Elsewhere in level 11, a substantial amount of burned bone, portions of temporal bones from two additional individuals and fragments of other cranial bones, i.e., sphenoid, zygomatic, and frontal sections were present. Numerous burned and unburned fragments of ribs, humerus, fibula, tibia, and jagged or slivered portions of lower arm bones were included. Many of the fragments had been exposed to varying degrees of heat. In still another part of level 11, most of the bone material was of human origin and was burned. Various fragments of the skull and limbs were burned entirely through, or completely charred. On the other hand, some long bone sections and rib fragments were not burned at all. A fragment of the rear part of a mandible had a different bone texture and density from most of the bone in the sample, suggesting that it belonged to a different individual. Hence, in that portion of level 11, two adult individuals seemed to be represented, and attrition of the available teeth suggested an age range of from 30 to 40 years for them at time of death. Included in the sample of human bone was a fragment of a bone awl fashioned from the shaft region of an adult human tibia (Figure 19.7). Level 12 produced a lesser amount of burned and unburned human material, mainly rib and occipital fragments.

In the excavation at the north end of Trench C, no human material was found until level N3 was reached at a depth of 100–110 cm. The human bone, the proximal end of an ulnar shaft, is unusual in that it has been fashioned into an awl. Markings on the polished surface indicate that it has seen considerable use (Figure 19.7). Level N5, contained unburned human bone in the form of a metacarpal bone, a rib fragment, and a section from the distal part of a tibia. The level also contained burned fragments of a rib and a radial or ulnar shaft from an infant. Level N6 contained two perforated animal teeth intermixed with burned human fragments of humerus, cranium, ulna, and a complete adult clavicle. Fragmentary unburned human bones at that level are from the humerus, cranium, vertebrae, and an adult mandibular

ramus with numerous cut marks on the condyle. Unburned long bone and rib fragments of an infant are also present.

Excavation of level N7 revealed an increasing amount of burned and unburned human bone. The burned fragments are from the skull, ribs, long bones of arms and legs, vertebrae, and feet. The petrosal part of a temporal bone and a talus bone are heavily calcined, but most of the burned fragments display lesser degrees of charring. These bones appear to be from adolescents and one, or more, adults. Some fragments—ulna, ribs, and a vertebra—obviously are from a young child or infant.

It was observed that some of the unburned cranial fragments in level N7 exhibit numerous cut marks. An unburned adult scapular fragment was found in level N7 of Trench C, and a burned axillary portion of an adult scapula was recovered from level 7Z of Trench E (the Z refers to the southernmost 1 × 3 m strip of the excavation). Whether the scapular fragments are from the same individual cannot accurately be determined, but the bone texture is similar. Three unburned perforated animal canine teeth are present with the human remains in level N7 of Trench C, which implies the people may have included ornaments if the remains reflect intentional burial practices. The burned shaft of a long bone from an immature individual was recovered from level 11 together with some unidentifiable bone chips. The only other human material from that level is a fragment of a bone awl that appears to have been fashioned from a tibial shaft.

Rather than give a minute description of the human bone found in each stratigraphic level of Test Trench E, I will discuss in detail only the bone from level 7b, the main midden horizon. Trench E was subdivided into 1 × 3-m sections labeled X, Y, and Z from the cave wall southward. Human material from the main midden or occupation horizon, 7b, sections X and Y, consists of the fragmentary remains of three age groups—infant, adolescent, and adult. The bones from sections X and Y are not sufficiently dissimilar to warrant separation into different groupings. Infant remains consist of a deciduous incisor, a canine with the enamel burned off, two deciduous molars, one of

TABLE 19.2 Stratigraphic Distribution of Recognizable Age Groups in Salts Cave Vestibule Trenches

C^b	C/N	E	G	H	Horizon	J II	J IV	J I	J III	F
Levels 1–6	Levels 1–5	Levels 1–4	Levels 1–4	Level 1	Breakdown debris and clay	Levels 1–3	Levels 1–2	Levels 1–3	Level 1	No level
A	A	A						F_1 F_1		
	A	i						a		
	i							a		
	A	A						A		
	i	i								
		Level 5	Level 5	Level 2	Midden among break-down	Level 4	Levels 3–4	Levels 4–5	Levels 2–4	Levels 1–5
A		f A				A M_5	A F_1	F_1	A	A
A	a	C F		A	Stream Sands	a i	M		a F_5	a
C a		a				iorf $A M_2$	F_5 $A M_2$	F A	a_1	a_1 A
a	Level 6	Level 6				f M_3	C_3 M_3		M_2 M_2	M_2 A
	A $F_6 A_1$	i_1 $F_6 A_1$					M_4		a_1	a_4
	A i_1								a	

Levels 3–4

Midden—bearing
brown clay
alternating with
sand and gravel

Levels 5–13	Levels 5–13	Limit of excavation
F_2 M_1	F A a	
F A_3	F i	
F_3 C_1 F_2 a_1 A_3 a_1 F		
A M_3 A	C_3 A_3	
	M_3	
i_2 C_2 F_3	A_3 i	
A_3F a_1	M_4 A C	
a_1 F_2 F_2	M_3	
M_1 i_2	F M F_4 C F	
	A_4 a_4	

Levels 14–16	Levels 14–23
A A A	A A F_4
A	A_4
	Wall collapse
F_2	A $\begin{matrix}M\\A_4\end{matrix}$ F_4
	A_4 C

Breakdown debris
alternating and
interfingering with
sand and gravel

Limit of excavation

a A A

Level 7 b,X,Y,Z & Pit

i iA C
a A_1 A
i A A_2 A
A i i
a i C
A_1 A_2

Levels 7–8	Level 7
A A_2	A A_1
i a	a C
—	i_1
a_5	i A_2
	A i
	A a_5

Levels 3–4

Level 8	
	A_2
A	
Limit of excavation	

Levels 10–11
A i A
  i_3
a_5 a
  i_3 Ai

Level 12
i_3 A
i
A a_5

Limit of
excavation

Limit of
excavation

a Key to Age Groups. Adults: Female, F; Male, M; Sex Unknown, A. Adolescents, a. Children, C. Infants, i. Fetuses, f. (Subnumerals indicate remains of single individuals.)

b Tabulation of human bone from the debris of the collapsed west wall of Trench C (page 78): $\begin{matrix} M \\ A A_4 C \end{matrix}$ F_4

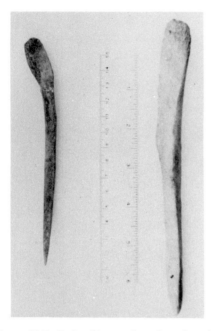

Figure 19.7 Tools of human bone from the Salts Cave Vestibule excavations. Proveniences: Trench C/N, level 3 (left), trench C, level 11 (right).

A proximal section of a fibular shaft has been reworked and polished to form an awl-like implement. Additional unburned fragments are from femora, humeri, fibulae, and ulnae or radii. No attempt was made to identify precisely how many individuals are represented in the bone sample because most of the fragments are too small, but individuals of different age groups are represented.

The human remains recovered from level 7bZ, in Trench E resemble the material from other parts of level 7b. Burned and unburned bone fragments and teeth of adults and infants were recovered. Charred and calcined fragments of an adult humerus and fibula exhibit numerous cutting marks. Markings on one humerus may represent an incised motif, but other parts of the possible motif could not be found. Fragments of radii, ulnae, femori, ribs, and tarsal bones show evidence of having been burned. Other fragments of the same bones exhibit no evidence of heating, although some of them have cutting marks. Burned and unburned portions of the frontal, sphenoid, parietal, occipital, zygomatic, maxilla, and temporal bones of adults were noted; parts of an infant maxilla and temporal bones were mixed in with the adult bones. Some of the unburned cranial bones show cut marks, the marks being most apparent on the left portion of a frontal bone and on a zygomatic bone. Many postcranial fragments were found, and several of them have the familiar cut marks. Only two teeth, a permanent incisor and a premolar, were among the bone fragments.

An incised fragment of a radial or ulnar shaft was recovered from the middle depth of level 7b. Other human bone from that provenience include a heavily calcined fragment of sphenoid bone and nonburned parts of humeri and ribs. Tibial shafts from two individuals exhibit marks that appear to have been caused by tearing flesh from the bone and damaging the periosteum in areas of muscular attachment. One tibial shaft shows marks of being cut and fractured or crushed as a result of a blow on the bone.

In the lower part of level 7b, most bone fragments of adult, adolescent, and children, are unburned. Bone fragments from an arm and a mandible of a child approximately 3 years old

which is burned, a nearly complete ilium, some ribs, and a complete clavicle exhibiting numerous cutting marks on the shaft, Figure 19.8a. The adolescent remains include the proximal end of a left femur with detached femoral head, a humerus epiphyseal cap, humeral shaft fragments, and fragments of a left scapula. Most of the infant and adolescent bones have not been burned, but burned and unburned fragments of adult bone are present. The charred, browned, and calcined fragments are from the femur, humerus, ribs, radius or ulna, and the temporal region of the skull. Two incisor teeth are badly burned with the enamel fractured and flaking off. Unburned adult bone fragments are from numerous bones of the skull: mandibular fossa, petrosal section, mastoid process (with cut marks), sphenoid parts, and frontal fragments. Fragments of the sternum are present as are numerous pieces of vertebrae and ribs, some of the latter showing cut marks. The distal portion of a well-preserved fibula also shows cut marks.

were recovered; bone fragments from adults include long bones, ribs, skull, scapula, and ilium. Burned fragments came from the radius, humerus, tibia, ribs, and skull of adults. Pits D and F (Features 7D and 7F) dug in the lower part of level 7b, contained adult and infant bone fragments like those in other parts of this level.

Excavation of Test area F and the ash bed in F extension, located upslope from Trench C, exposed a partially burned fragment of a sphenoid bone, two other small cranial pieces, and unburned shaft of a radius or ulna that shows multiple cutting marks. A polished and incised, badly charred deer antler fragment was intermixed with the human bone. The ash from F extension contained a small cranial fragment and the burned distal portion of an adolescent left tibia with the epiphysis missing; it was later found that the tibial section is part of an individual from level 13 of Trench J IV.

Excavation of test area G, a south extension of Trench E, uncovered two humerus fragments from the same individual. A small bone fragment from the shaft of a fibula was found in Test H, an eastward extension of E.

Human skeletal fragments were found throughout all levels of Trench J. Fewer fragments were present in the upper levels, but by level 6, a considerable amount of human bone began to appear (Figure 19.8b). The bone was like that previously encountered in the other trenches and test areas; some fragments were charred, others were exposed to lesser degrees of heat, and still other fragments were not exposed to heat at all. There appears to be a broader age range of individuals represented in the human material from Trench J; bone from both adult males and females is present, and sexual distinctions can be made in some of the bone fragments from adolescents. There was a noticeable increase in the amount of bone from infants and children, and for the first time, fetal bone is present.

Burned fragments of human origin were recovered from all levels of Trench J. A crushed phalange was found in level 6, J II; in level 8, J II, a frontal bone, with the nasal bone attached, of a female was found with cut markings on it. A distal fragment of a right clavicle from the same level

shows evidence of disease on the periosteum.

In level 4 of J II, cut marks were found on a distal anterior shaft fragment of a left humerus from a young adult, and the body of an adult cervical vertebra (C-6 or 7) shows evidence of osteoporosis on the anterior surface. These bones were intermingled with bone fragments of other adults and at least one adolescent individual. Level 4 of J IV also contained bone showing evidence of cutting and crushing. A mandibular gonial angle from an adolescent female has some cut marks on the exterior surface. The proximal end of a young adult left femur exhibits cut marks on the neck of the bone and depressions on the femoral head which seemingly contributed to the breakage around the head. An adult midshaft femoral fragment has been polished to a high gloss.

Level 5 of J IV contained burned and unburned bone fragments of an adult female and an unburned tibial section of a fetus. More unusual, however, was the recovery of a calculus, or kidney stone. There is a close resemblance between the Salts Cave stone and the calculi found by Snow, and described by Smith, in the Indian Knoll Site (Snow 1948: 510—512). The Salts calculus is thought to be from the kidney, also.

In level 6 of J IV, the medial half of a child's clavicle, bearing cut marks, was found, but the condition of the bone was more unusual than the marks on it. The clavicle fragment was the only human bone found that was extremely dry; when handled it tended to flake off periosteum which disintegrated into a white powdery dust. The bone had not been burned but rather was like bone long exposed to the sun and weathering elements.

Cut marks on bone fragments from the humerus and cranium appear in level 8 of J IV, but none is present in the level 9 material. One bone from level 9, however, is worthy of note. A right femoral midshaft fragment from an adult male had the distal end blackened, rounded, and smoothed as though it had been refashioned for a particular purpose, other than stirring coals of a fire. Cut marks on bone and crushing of some bones continue to appear in the baulk section of J IV 10, and in levels 11, 12, and 13. No particular part of the body and no particular age group seemed to be preferred. In general, the quantity of human

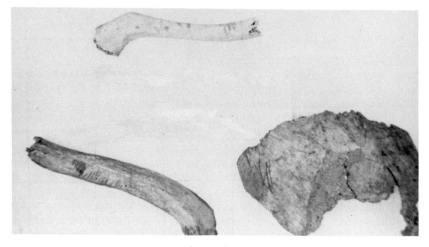

Figure 19.8a

Figure 19.8b

Figure 19.8c

Figure 19.8d

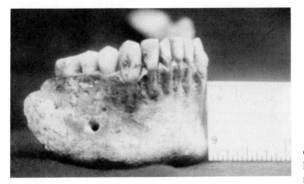

Figure 19.8e

Figure 19.8 Cut marks on human bone from the Salts Cave Vestibule excavations. (a) Upper—infant clavicle; lower left—adult clavicle; lower right—adult frontal. (b) Left—mandible; right—pelvis fragment. (c) Skull fragment. (d) Pelvis fragment. (e) Anterior portion of adult mandible.

bone fragments in trench J is greatest in the lower midden levels of J II (levels 8 to 10) and J IV (levels 8 to 13), reaching a peak in J IV 13 where 148 fragments were found representing at least four different individuals.

Additional human bone was recovered from flotation of soils from the different levels in Trench J. A lithoid object, much like the one found in level 5, J IV, was recovered from level II materials, but whether the calculus is a kidney or bladder stone has not yet been precisely determined.

One item recovered from level 13 of J IV greatly mystified the writer when it was received for examination. It was a blackened, charred, amorphous mass. The mass was fragile and when exposed to the atmosphere outside the cave it crumbled easily when attempts were made to remove soil from its many porous cavities. The internal cavities had a shiny, glazed appearance when the adhering soil was removed from them. The porosity of the mass contributed to its light weight of 26 grams. The writer attempted to simulate the mass by burning a wide variety of natural and synthetic materials in wood and in charcoal fires. None of the experiments duplicated the mass, but a slight approximation was achieved with a fatted section of pig skin burned in a hot wood fire. Well's (1960: 36) "curious clinker" is the only object found in published accounts that resembles the Salts J IV mass. After finding the unusual brownish mass in a number of the Early Saxon Illington urn burials, Wells noticed the presence of a similar substance during his observation of modern crematory remains. The substance was usually found under the head after cremation. Wells suggested that the mass is formed by transformed keratin from the hair after the hair had been infiltrated with fat or tissue fluids during the process of cremation. The mass from Salts Cave may contain transformed melanin, in addition to keratin, which contributes to its ebony black coloration. If we acknowledge Well's proposal for the origin of the "curious clinker," then the presence of such a "clinker" in the Salts Cave site may represent cremation residue. The writer has no knowledge of a similar mass being recovered in an eastern U.S. prehistoric site whose inhabitants practiced cremation of their dead. Some of the cranial fragments—two parietal fragments—found in association with the blackened mass were only slightly charred, while a petrosal fragment of the right temporal bone was not burned at all. An interpretation of this curious situation will be presented in a later section.

Once the human remains from the different test trenches were cleaned, and their stratigraphic placements recorded, an attempt was made to reconstruct as many bones as possible. It was soon apparent that the distribution of human bone followed no obvious stratigraphic pattern, and that—although approximately 25% of the human bone fragments were burned—the differential burning of the bones followed no recognized pattern of intentional cremation. Some bone fragments were burned while other fragments, of the same individual, were unburned. Skeletal fragments from a single individual came from several levels and sections of Trench J. Bone from J II and J IV were found to belong to one person, and bone from J II, level 6, and J III, level 4, belonged to one

individual. Bone fragments from level 3 of F extension and fragments from level 13 of J IV were reconstructed to form the shaft of a radius from a single individual. In addition, bone fragments from Trenches C and E could be reconstructed for several individuals; similar reconstructions were made of fragments from different stratigraphic levels of trenches E and J. The skeletal remains of a single individual were seldom restricted to one stratigraphic level unless only a few fragments of the person were recovered, as in the case of the fetuses (see Table 19.1).

During the time the trenches were being excavated, survey parties combed the breakdown areas around the trenches searching for additional human skeletal remains. Bone fragments of an adult individual were found against the east wall north of the Iron Gate beyond the excavation trenches. Fragments of a rib, radius or ulna, sternum, and head of a humerus were found in the rock breakdown against the east wall below an Edmund Turner signature. The bones were dry and well preserved, but their break patterns were comparable to the skeletal fragments being recovered in the trench excavations. Because evidence of pack rat activity had previously been noted in the cave, the fragments were examined closely for teeth marks of rodents; none was observed, so it is unlikely that the bones were carried by pack rats to the location where they were found. It is also unlikely that the fragments were left behind by someone who removed a complete skeleton from the cave in more recent times. Hence, it is probable that the bones were deposited in prehistoric times more or less where we found them.

Portions of an adult male individual were found about halfway up the west wall to the south of the Iron Gate. Fragments of a scapula, ulna, and humerus were found in association with a complete second cervical vertebra, a metacarpal, and a large first metatarsal bone. A hickory nutshell, displaying marks of rodent teeth, was also found with the bones, but no rodent teeth marks appeared on the bones. Size, robusticity, and texture of the bones indicated that they belonged to one individual.

Isolated fragments of human bone were found

farther along in the interior of Salts Cave. The manner in which they were transported is left to conjecture, but in this case it was probably the result of rodent activity. In at least two instances, human fragments were not only found along pathways leading to pack rat nests, but also exhibited gnawing marks.

Discussion of Human Remains

The analysis of skeletal remains recovered from the Salts Cave excavations and adjacent area surveys offers a challenge. The bones were too badly fragmented to permit extensive reconstruction for comparisons with other populations in Western Kentucky. Hence, it became necessary to place greater emphasis upon the burial practice surrounding the interment of the bones. Utilizing techniques proposed by Gejvall (1964: 383−388) and Brothwell (1963: 16−19) for identifying broken, cremated remains, an attempt was made to identify the number of individuals in the population and to approximate their age and sex ranges. The bones of 41 individuals were sorted out with some degree of certainty; the age distribution of the group was three fetuses, five infants, six children from 6 to approximately 10 years of age, at least four immature or adolescent individuals, six adult males, eight adult females, and nine adults whose sex could not be determined. Numerous bone fragments could not be assigned to particular individuals or age groups, but the population probably consisted of around 41 to 44 individuals.

Explicit cultural practices surrounding the interment of the dead were difficult to delineate. Numerous bones bear cutting marks made by a sharp implement and not by gnawing of rodents. The marks occur on some bone fragments in areas of muscle origin or insertion and seem to represent a method of defleshing the bones before burial. However, on other fragments, the markings are found in areas lacking muscle masses and the marks appear to have been randomly made. Cutting marks on some frontal, parietal, temporal, and occipital fragments tentatively suggest a scalping practice, but whether the practice was part of

a defleshing ritual or has other significance cannot be demonstrated because the bones could not be reconstructed to form even partial cranial vaults. The antiquity of scalping has not been resolved, although Neumann (1940: 287−289) identified the practice in a Central Illinois Middle Mississippi group from the Crable site (F 896), and Willoughby (1922: 61) observed the practice in the Ohio Hopewell group from the Turner Earthworks site.

The way in which the human and animal bones in the salts site were broken and burned presents the most difficult problem for discussion and interpretation. A substantial amount of human bone was heated, and some fragments were calcined, but they do not seem to represent the intentional cremation of primary burials. Broken bones of animal and of human origin were found intermingled with charcoal in most stratigraphic levels of the site, and some fragments, animal and human, were burned while other fragments of the same bone, or same individual, were only slightly heated or entirely unburned. The breakage patterns of human and animal bone exhibit no distinguishable differences, whether the bone is burned or unburned. Deep longitudinal and transverse fracture and splinter patterns occur with some bones being crushed near the broken edges (this seemed to increase the degree of serration along the break line). The broken edges of some burned bones exhibit minor warpage but no checking, while completely calcined fragments exhibit checking but may or may not exhibit warpage. Many of the charred fragments, once cleaned, have a glazed, or high gloss, appearance, but some of the charred pieces are glossed on the periosteal surface while the endosteal surface is only slightly heated.

An extensive search was made through the literature on crematory practices and on secondary burial practices in an attempt to gain information that might aid in the interpretation of the Salts Cave skeletal remains. Published accounts of crematory practices are not numerous, especially for eastern North America. Merbs (1967: 498−499) notes the major figures in the United States and Europe who have studied cremated remains so their contributions will not be reiterated here. Krogman (in Webb and Snow 1945: 188−189),

Baby (1954), and Binford (1963: 98—110) have analyzed prehistoric cremated remains in Kentucky, Ohio, and Michigan, respectively, but in each case, the cremations came from identifiable graves or recognized crematory pits. Each investigator attempted to determine whether the population under analysis had cremated their dead in a fleshed or defleshed condition, but the results of their studies provide little data applicable to the interpretation of the Salts Cave material. In a report on the Sims Creek site in the Fish Trap Reservoir of eastern Kentucky, Dunnell (1966: 188—189) observed that burned human fragments were intermingled with animal remains of deer, turtle, and turkey in the refuse deposits of food wastes. Refuse removed from an earth oven, feature 56, contained human cranial and long bone fragments together with remains of turtle and deer which Dunnell thought may have represented cannibalism. Occupation of the Sims site is attributed to pre-Fort Ancient peoples, but whether the site dates as early as the habitation levels of Salts Cave is questionable.

Snow (1948: 523, Figure 52) observed cut marks on some of the Indian Knoll human and animal remains and attributed them to the butchering practices of the people. However, he found the marks only in areas of tendon or ligament attachment. Some Indian Knoll graves, especially in the area disturbed by Moore's earlier excavation, contained disarticulated remains which obviously had been defleshed before burial. Consequently, Snow viewed the cut marks as a part of the burial preparation. None of the Indian Knoll remains had been exposed to fire, but some of the cut marks are similar to those found on the Salts bones.

The Adena people of Kentucky (Webb and Snow (1945: 70—82) cremated their dead, but there is little similarity in their treatment of the dead before cremation, or in the total range of their burial practices, to the situation found in Salts Cave.

During his excavation of Mammoth Cave Vestibule, Nelson (1917: 56) recovered fragmentary human bone in the same burned and broken condition as that found in Salts Cave. He proposed that the condition of the bone was not the result of cannibalism because the bones exhibited no evidence of having been cut, scraped, or torn. Jones (1876: 1) reports the presence of skeletal remains in Tennessee caves, but none of the remains are in the broken or burned condition characteristic of the Salts bone. Fowke (1922: 1—100) examined many caves in the Ozark region of Missouri that contained human skeletal remains. Some burials were obviously primary interments while the condition of others, because of the arrangement of the bones or incompleteness of the skeleton, indicated secondary interments. Miller's Cave, Pulaski County, Missouri (Fowke 1922: 57—81), contained a considerable amount of human bone with much of it being found in a scattered, disarticulated array. Some disarticulated remains of children were burned and found in kitchen refuse intermixed with shell, charcoal, burned animal bones, and ashes. Fowke suggests that the flesh of the burned human bones was used as food "like the flesh of any other animal" (Fowke 1922: 71, 73, 77). In view of the broken, burned condition of the bone, and the *in situ* presence of human bone intermixed with animal bone in the kitchen midden, the writer recognizes the ease with which Fowke might interpret the situation as one offering evidence of cannibalism; alternative explanations for the presence of the bone, its condition, its location, and the associated animal remains, are no less questionable.

Significant differences exist, however, between the skeletal remains of Miller's Cave and those of Salts Cave. The Missouri cave contained primary and secondary burials of complete skeletons in addition to the broken and burned human remains, and as yet, the only apparently unbroken and unburned skeletal material discovered in Salts Cave was that removed by Young. The burned remains in Miller's Cave were mainly of young, subadult, individuals, while the bones of individuals of all ages, including fetuses, exhibit evidence of burning or heating in Salts Cave. In addition, evidence of cutting, crushing, and fracturing, so frequently visible on the Salts Cave bone, apparently was not observed on any of the Miller's Cave material. The time period during which Miller's cave was occupied cannot be ascertained from Fowke's report. The cave appears to have been utilized by peoples who occasionally used stone slabs in the construction of graves but who usually buried their dead in the soil and ash of the cave. The recovery of pottery from the cave would tend to place occupation at a time more recent than the non-pottery occupation of Salts.

Some of the so-called "Ash Caves" (Funkhouser and Webb 1929) and rock shelters (Funkhouser and Webb 1930: 296–298; Webb and Funkhouser 1936) of eastern Kentucky contain numerous layers of prehistoric ash deposit, vegetal remains, and many well-preserved fabric items that duplicate items found in Salts Cave. However, skeletal remains in the shelters and ash caves are usually few in number, of females and children, poorly preserved, and represent primary interments. The partially cremated fragmentary remains of a young child were found in a crevice of the Newt Kash shelter, but after examining the remains, the writer suspects that the cremation was unintentional and not part of the usual burial practice of the people dwelling in the shelter at the time the child died. More probably, later occupants of the shelter built a fire over the shallow grave of the child, thereby heating portions of the burial in a manner that simulates partial cremation.

Skinner (1919: 52) found human bones in the kitchen midden of the pre-Iroquoian Mud Lock site in New York. He attributed the fragmentary condition of the bone to the cannibalistic tendencies of the inhabitants because the human bone "was split, cracked, and charred in the same way as those of the beasts," i.e., deer, elk, bear, birds, turtle, and fish. The refuse heap was located in a cemetery from which were recovered 10 burials, most of them in a flexed position. Hence, disposition of human remains at the Mud Lock site more closely resembles the Salts Cave situation than do other sites in the cave vicinity.

The writer has examined skeletal material, and reviewed field notes, from sites in Kentucky (materials housed in the Museum of Anthropology, University of Kentucky) for evidence of burial practices that resemble the circumstances in which the Salts and Mammoth Cave skeletal remains were found. The cave sites are found to be unique, relative to other sites in the state, and the skeletal remains of the caves were found to be no less distinctive.

Nature of the Human Population in the Caves

Prehistoric peoples left evidence of their presence in many passages of Salts and Mammoth Cave in the form of cane torch fragments, cane caches, burned-out campfires, moccasins, gourd fragments, footprints, and fecal deposits. The radiocarbon dates from fecal specimens and other remains establish man's presence in the caves at particular times, but the dates provide no information of the consistency with which the caves were used. That is, we do not know whether the caves were visited regularly by prehistoric peoples from the Archaic through the Woodland cultural periods, or whether occupation occurred sporadically at just a few intervals by different groups of people. That information becomes significant when trying to identify the specific time periods when the mummies were placed in the caves or when the skeletal remains were buried there. Any attempt to reconstruct the cultural environment that influenced the disposition of the dead members of the populations, whether fleshed bodies or fragmentary bones, must rest in part on speculation.

Looking first at the so-called cave mummies who were intentionally placed in the caves, we find no record of Little Al nor the Audubon Avenue mummy having been buried with cultural materials, clothing, or artifacts. That is in direct contrast to the extensive amount of cultural material found in association with the Short Cave mummies. Lost John, although not intentionally buried, had few cultural items—a mussel shell pendant and a short robelike breech cloth—with him at the time he was killed. Assuming John was wearing clothing and ornaments typically worn by adult males in his society, it would appear that little attention was given to clothing beyond its utilitarian function of covering or warming the body. On the basis of this assumption, it might be inferred that his people would not have an elaborate burial practice surrounding the interment of the dead. The Audubon Avenue mummy and Little Al may have belonged to such a population, but why these particular individuals were selected to be placed in caves is an open question. Their interment is probably not the typical method of burial commonly practiced by their respective populations, if indeed they were from different groups.

The prehistoric people also used the caves occasionally as a burial ground for skeletal remains. Individuals buried near the entrance of Salts and Mammoth caves may have been primary burials, although the incompleteness of some skeletons suggests that they had been defleshed before interment. The drying atmosphere of the cave interiors would have preserved tissue adhering to bone, although the damper atmosphere of the Vestibule entrances would hinder tissue preservation. However, human skeletal fragments from both parts of the caves were clean of flesh which implies that the defleshing process probably occurred outside the caves. If so, then the bodies were not buried outside the caves is another open question. One possible explanation for placing fleshed individuals and defleshed skeletal remains in the caves is that climatic conditions outside the caves may have precluded soil interment at the time of death, e.g., frozen ground or rainy season. From the high proportion of plant-seed content in the fecal debris of Little Al, it was assumed that he died during the fall season, but if his people practiced food storage, he may actually have died during the early winter months.

The interpretation of the burned and fragmented skeletal remains of Salts, and indirectly of Mammoth Cave, presents the greatest challenge. Other caves in the area have not yet revealed a site comparable to Salts with regard to the stratigraphic deposition of fragmented, burned, and cut human bone; nor have implements fashioned from human bone been recovered from the other caves. It is improbable that the skeletal remains recovered by Young at the bottom of the Salts entrance breakdown and the skeletal fragments recovered from the 1969–1970 excavations are from the same populations because of the differential treatment given to the two groups of skeletons. The evidence is admittedly tenuous, especially when an alternate claim that Young's group represented the "diners" and the stratigraphic group the "diet" might seem equally tenable.

After examining the Salts human remains intensively, the context in which they were found, and the treatment given them, the writer offers two hypotheses with regard to the interpretation of the circumstances surrounding the remains.

Evidence against the proposal of cannibalism having occurred in Salts comes from the analyses of human fecal specimens found in the cave. None of the specimens had a high meat protein content; on the contrary, the people who left excrement in the cave apparently consumed a variety of plants as their primary food source. The cut marks noted on many of the bone fragments might be acceptable as evidence for a defleshing burial practice of the people, similar to the practice suggested by Snow for some of the Indian Knoll people. As noted earlier, Snow found cut marks on some Indian Knoll bones which he thought were made as the bodies were being defleshed preceding their burial. The cut Indian Knoll bones were not widely distributed through the site, and therefore perhaps they represent a change in burial practice, or even a brief occupation of the site by a group other than the Archaic shell mound people, i.e., a Woodland population. After examining the Indian Knoll skeletons numerous times, the writer is of the opinion that more than one population is represented in the series, but that the different groups were not of equal size nor did they occupy the site for the same length of time.

The Salts population may have defleshed deceased members outside the cave, broken the bones, and brought the remains to the cave for burial in the softened soil of the kitchen midden. Indiscriminant burning of the bones may have occurred accidentally after burial when the soil was stirred to remove ash accumulation in and around fires.

The other interpretational hypothesis offered by the writer is that cannibalism did occur in Salts Cave. The 1969–1970 excavations produced a variety of animal bones, ranging from small rodents to rabbit, turkey, and deer, proving conclusively that the people who inhabited the site included some meat in their diet. The diverse kinds of animal bones, however, suggest the food animal population of the region did not provide a consistent food source; the people apparently ate any animals that could be caught. Such an unpredictable source of animal protein might be viewed as paving the way for cannibalism.

Garn and Block (1970: 106) maintain the nutritional value of cannibalism is subject to question because an individual weighing 110 lb yields only about 66 lb of edible muscle mass. Consequently, one individual would barely supply the protein requirement for 60 people for a single day. The authors agree that less frequent cannibalism might serve as a protein supplement in a population suffering protein malnutrition. Vayda (1970: 1462) also suggests that irregular cannibalism might occur, and have nutritional significance, among people who suffer food shortages upon occasion. He offers the theory, but does not pursue it, that infrequent cannibalism may be more prevalent in populations that do not have ready access to high-quality protein food animals.

Walens and Wagner (1971: 269—270) observe that most populations in the world have a protein-deficient diet yet do not practice cannibalism, even upon the dying members of the population. The investigators emphasize the social question of cannibalism over the nutritional importance of the consumed flesh.

Randall (1971: 269) recommends that, instead of emphasizing the biological criteria of cannibalism, the comparability of nutritional value of human flesh and the flesh of other "game" animals should be examined. However, evidence could be collected from most populations, including our own, to demonstrate that man's cultural values influence his dietary selections regardless of the nutritional value of the selections.

Wells (1964: 138—140) takes a more objective approach to skeletal evidence that seems to be the result of cannibalistic practices. He maintains that cannibalism is an acquired taste, noting that most known cases are associated with particular ritualistic practices or with famine. He adds that there is little substantial evidence to support the claims of cannibalism as explanation for the dismemberment of skeletons in graves. He does accept two characteristic pieces of evidence in the diagnosis of cannibalism: the unnatural scattering of bones in a site and the splintering and crushing of bones.

The indiscriminant scattering of broken and burned human bone throughout most levels of the Salts site suggests that all parts of an individual were not buried, or discarded, at one time; or if so, a great amount of soil disturbance occurred after burial. The soil and bone disturbance could have resulted from water action in the site or from individuals stirring the soil when scattering debris from the fires. However, the stratification and other characteristics of the deposits do not lend support to either of these suggestions (see pages 75—79).

The identical pattern of breaking animal and human bones further suggests that the people who broke them gave no special attention to either kind of bone. Since both human and animal bones were fashioned into implements, and both had motifs incised on them, it would appear that the people utilized whatever bone was accessible, be it animal or human. The cut marks on human bone have already received comment, but an additional note might be taken of the similarity in the markings on both animal and human bones.

Whether human flesh may have provided an irregular meat source or whether it was ritualistically consumed after some event, e.g., a battle, cannot be readily determined. The parts of the human body most frequently represented in the skeletal fragments from Salts are the skull, long bones, and ribs, with long-bone fragments being most numerous. Snow (1948: 530) suggests that some of the incomplete Indian Knoll skeletons may have been victims of enemy trophy collectors, who, after injuring or killing the Indian Knoller, partially dismembered the body taking various portions with him. Whereas such an explanation may seem plausible for the incomplete adult males in the Salts stratigraphy, it seemingly would not account for the number of young people in the site. Knowles (1940: 151—225), however, cites numerous reports in which individuals of all ages and both sexes were tortured, burned, or killed during warfare between Indian groups. Skeletal remains of females, and occasionally children, killed by violently inflicted wounds and injuries have been recovered from archeological sites.

It might well be that the 41 individuals sorted out from the skeletal fragments do not represent the population living at the site but, rather, represent portions of 41 individuals brought into the camp for human consumption. Such a theory does not fully account for the presence of fetal or infant skeletal fragments, however, unless one presumes a fondness for tender meat.

Prehistoric occupation zones have been excavated in numerous rock shelters in Kentucky and Tennessee, but there are no published accounts of any situation comparable to that found in Salts Cave. The strongest evidence for the cannibalism hypothesis seems to be the absence of sites with fragmentary skeletal remains that would compare with those recovered from the excavations in Salts and Mammoth Cave. Whether the Salts site is actually unique or whether its seeming uniqueness is a result of the comprehensive analysis of materials recovered from it remains to be investigated.

As frequently happens, the analysis of the Salts skeletal fragments raises many questions and emphasizes the need for further investigation of other caves in the area. Prehistoric remains from rock shelters in the general vicinity of the caves need to be examined for evidence that might contribute to a definitive interpretation of the habitation circumstances of Salts and Mammoth Caves.

Chapter 20

Dental Remains from Salts Cave Vestibule

Stephen Molnar and Steven C. Ward
Washington University

Salts Cave Vestibule excavations yielded 77 teeth from 14 proveniences (Table 20.1). Some of these proveniences were closely associated and probably contain remains from the same individual. For example, a right mandibular fragment from Trench E, level 7b (number 17, Figure 20.1) and a left mandibular fragment (number 6) from Trench C/N, level 6 are both broken at the symphysis and can be reconstructed as a single mandible. Of the 77 teeth, 49 were found in maxillary or mandibular fragments representing approximately 10 individuals (Table 20.2).

The total dental remains represent an estimated 14 individuals of varying ages. The ages were estimated on the basis of tooth wear and of apical development of the tooth root. The condition of the permanent and deciduous teeth indicate that at least 6 of the 14 persons were young children (nine deciduous teeth) or adolescents (identified by partially developed tooth roots or unerupted third molars). Few of the teeth were markedly worn, and only four individuals could be classified as older adults. One of the maxillae from Trench E, level 7b (number 15) has a worn M_3 with large areas of dentine exposed, as does a mandible from the same level (number 16). The M_1 in a mandible

from Trench C (number 6) has perhaps the heaviest wear and shows evidence of secondary dentine development. Trench C also yielded a mandible with a worn second molar that could be evaluated as that of an older adult (number 3). On the basis of the wear evaluation system of Molnar (1971), 15 teeth show wear equivalent to class three or greater. The present, somewhat sparse and fragmentary evidence, indicates that the dental remains from Salts Cave Vestibule are mostly those of children and young adults.

Dental Measurements

The crown diameters were measured by standard techniques using a bolie gauge. The mesial–distal and the buccal–lingual diameters fall well within the range of the diameters reported for a large sample of North American aboriginal remains from Dickson Mounds, Illinois (Table 20.3). The Salts Cave teeth are neither strikingly larger nor smaller in size than those from Dickson Mounds, and morphologically they have no outstanding features. A possible exception is represented by enamel pearls present on a

TABLE 20.1   Dental Remains from Salts Cave Vestibule

Laboratory number	Provenience (trench and level)	Dental remains
1	C 8	Maxilla with 2 deciduous teeth and 1 permanent tooth
2	C 10	Isolated tooth, C^R
3	C 11	Mandibular fragment with M_2
4	C/N 3	Isolated tooth, I^{2R}
5	C/N 5	Isolated deciduous teeth, dm_{1R} and dm_{2R}
6	C/N 6	Mandible fragment with 8 teeth
7	C/N 7	Mandible with 13 teeth
8	C/N 7	Right maxillary fragment with PM^1, PM^2, M^1; crowns separated from roots and lost
9	C/N 7	Isolated tooth, I^{2L}
10	C/N 7	Isolated tooth, M^{1L}
11	C/N 7	Isolated tooth, M_{1L}
12	E 6	Mandibular fragment with M_{1R}
13	E 6	Two isolated teeth, unidentified
14	E 7b	Mandibular fragment of child with M_1
15	E 7b	Maxilla with five teeth
16	E 7b	Mandibular fragment with M_3
17	E 7b	Mandibular fragment with 6 teeth and PM_{2R} in crypt (Figure 20.1)
18	E 7b	Maxilla with five teeth
19	E 7b	Isolated deciduous tooth, c^L
20	E 7b	Isolated deciduous tooth, dm^{1L}
21	E 7b	Isolated tooth, I^{1R}
22	E 7b	Isolated teeth; PM^{2R}, M^{2L}, C^L
23	E 7b	Isolated tooth, PM^{1R}
24	E 7b	Isolated teeth; M_{3R}, PM^{1R}, I^1
25	E 7b	Isolated teeth; PM_2 and unidentified
26	J II 4	Isolated tooth, I^{2R}
27	J III 4	Isolated teeth; I_{2R}, PM_2
28	J III 4	Isolated tooth, PM^{2R}
29	J IV 11	Isolated tooth, unidentified
30	J IV 13	Isolated teeth; PM^{1L}, PM^{2L}, PM^{1R}, M^{2L}
31	J IV 13 baulk	Isolated I_2

lower first molar from Trench C/N, level 7 (number 7). Several maxillary incisors were shovel-shaped as is often the case among North American Indians.

The Salts Cave teeth are largely free of disease; there are no caries, and only two examples of enamel hypoplasia were found. Several teeth were sectioned and examined under a transmitted-light microscope. They are histologically sound, showing a minimum of enamel or dentine imperfec-

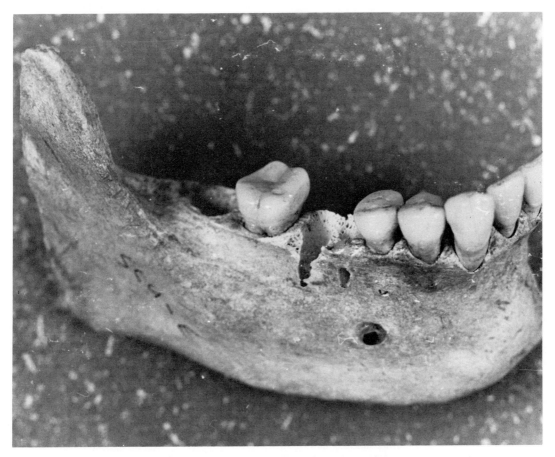

Figure 20.1 Mandible fragment from Trench E, level 7b (see also Figure 12.12, p. 95).

tions, and are much healthier than those in a series from prehistoric archeological sites in Michigan and the Southwest recently examined by us. The Michigan and Southwestern teeth show a high frequency of dental caries and many hypoplastic lesions of enamel and dentine, whereas the Salts Cave teeth—to judge from the condition of enamel and dentine—came from a rather healthy population. Although the young age of the Salts Cave population is surely an important factor, the data are not yet sufficient to support detailed speculation concerning the reasons for these contrasts.

TABLE 20.2 Teeth Associated with Bone

Laboratory number	Bone	Identification of teeth	Number of teeth	Comments
6	Mandible[a]	I_{1L} to $M_{3\ L}$	8	Left half of robust mandible, probably male; no pathologies.
17	Mandible[a]	I_{1R} to PM_{2R}, M_{2R}	6	Right half of robust mandible; probably male; no pathologies. M_1 and M_3 lost post mortem. (Figure 20.1).
14	Mandible	M_{1L}	1	Horizontal rami with PM_2 developing in crypt.
7	Mandible	I_{1R} to M_{1R}	13	Mandible, lacking right ascending ramus; M_3 unerupted.
16	Mandible	M_{3R}	1	Right ascending ramus with M_3 attached.
12	Mandible	M_1	1	
3	Mandible	M_{2R}	1	
5	Mandible[b]	m_1, m_2	2	Mandible fragment of child
15	Maxilla	PM^{1L} to M^{3L}	5	Robust left maxilla, teeth in poor condition.
1	Maxilla[b]	m^{1L}, m^{2L}, M^{1L}	3	Left maxilla of child; M^{1L} recently erupted.
18	Maxilla	$PM^{1R}, PM^{2R}, C^L, PM^{2L}, M^{2L}$	5	Complete juvenile maxilla; M_3 unerupted
8	Maxilla	PM^1, PM^2, M^1	3	Right maxilla fragment; crowns separated from roots and lost.

Total number of teeth associated with bone: 49
Maximum number of individuals: 10

[a] These mandible halves, both broken at the symphysis, fit well together and are probably from the same individual.
[b] Possibly from the same individual.

TABLE 20.3 Comparative Measurements of Teeth from Salts Cave and Dickson Mounds

	Dickson Mounds			Salts Cave		
		Crown diameters (mm)			Crown diameters (mm)	
Tooth	No.	M–D	B–L	No.	M–D	B–L
I_1	103	4.5–7.2	3.75–6.8	3	5.2–6.2	6.0–6.1
I_2	101	5.6–7.7	5.2–7.15	5	5.0–6.5	5.2–6.6
C	123	6.15–8.5	6.6–9.55	4	7.0–7.6	7.9–8.4
PM_1	126	5.92–8.7	6.7–8.95	4	6.9–8.0	8.2–9.0
PM_2	120	6.40–10.75	7.0–10.30	6	7.1–8.8	7.4–10.7
M_1	134	9.9–13.10	9.8–12.85	6	9.9–11.9	10.7–12.3
M_2	118	9.6–13.50	9.65–12.6	3	10.2–12.0	10.5–11.7
M_3	101	8.65–13.90	8.10–12.90	2	11.8–12.8	10.9–11.7
I^1	116	7.85–9.95	6.10–8.75	1	9.5	7.0
I^2	108	6.0–9.0	5.6–7.92	2	7.1–7.6	6.4
C	113	7.10–9.4	7.45–10.15	4	7.0–7.6	7.9–8.4
PM^1	103	5.9–8.6	8.7–11.5	7	7.0–8.0	9.8–10.2
PM^2	108	5.5–8.11	7.98–11.35	5	6.5–7.6	9.1–10.2
M^1	140	9.2–13.0	10.0–13.83	3	9.9–12.4	12.0–12.3
M^2	119	7.9–12.0	10.0–14.75	3	8.4–11.3	11.7–12.3
M^3	88	7.2–11.8	8.9–13.8	3	9.7	—

Salts Cave (and Related) Material in East Coast Museum Collections

PATTY JO WATSON

Washington University

As indicated earlier (page 22 and Watson *et al.* 1969: 12–13), a large quantity of prehistoric cultural material was removed from Salts Cave (and a few other nearby caves including Mammoth Cave) during the nineteenth and early twentieth centuries by collectors or by local Kentuckians who sold it to collectors. A Kentucky resident, Col. Bennett Young, amassed a large collection from Salts Cave and described many of the articles in his impressive *Prehistoric Men of Kentucky*. Much, if not all, of his collection went eventually to the Museum of the American Indian, Heye Foundation, in New York where it is still stored.

Other Eastern museums that acquired significant kinds or quantities of items from the Mammoth Cave area are the United States National Museum in Washington, D.C., the American Museum of Natural History in New York, and the Peabody Museum of Archaeology and Ethnology in Cambridge, Massachusetts.

Douglas W. Schwartz, during his study of Mammoth Cave National Park prehistory in 1957 and 1958, visited some of these museums (the Heye Foundation, the Peabody, and apparently also the American Museum of Natural History). However, his manuscript (Schwartz 1958e) is not published nor did he include in it much detail beyond the catalog descriptions of the objects. Because the remnants of items now left in the caves are so fragmentary, it seemed desirable to study the more complete museum objects, and to quantify them insofar as possible. Consequently in the spring of 1969, the following visits were made:

June 13	Department of Anthropology, U.S. National Museum of Natural History, Smithsonian Institution, Washington, D.C.
June 16	American Museum of Natural History, New York
June 17–18	Museum of the American Indian, Heye Foundation, New York
June 19–20	Peabody Museum of Archaeology and Ethnology, Harvard University, Cambridge, Massachusetts

Department of Anthropology
U.S. National Museum of Natural History
Smithsonian Institution

Here there are the following relevant items and collections:

1. Catalog # 87279, stored in a drawer labeled "Edmonson County, Kentucky." A large paleofecal specimen exactly like those from Salts and Mammoth Caves, but the label reads, "Lumps of pounded seeds. Indian Cave, near Mammoth Cave, Kentucky. Frs. Klett." Indian Cave is now owned by Mrs. Lucy Ferguson, proprietor of a souvenir shop at the south edge of Mammoth Cave National Park. Indian Cave lies just south of Highway 70 southeast of the Park boundary. Frances Klett was manager of Mammoth Cave for a time during the late nineteenth century (Bridge 1969). This paleofecal specimen (which actually may be from Mammoth Cave) is 14.5 cm long with a maximum diameter of 5 cm.

2. Also in the Edmonson County, Kentucky, drawer are fragments of a slipper from Indian Cave (# 87277) and a nearly complete one (22 cm long) from Mammoth Cave (#416634); both are chevron twined (see Figure 21.1).

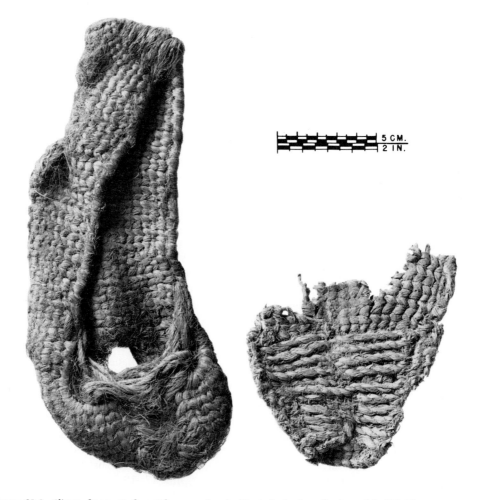

Figure 21.1 Slipper fragments from Edmonson County, Kentucky in the collections of the U.S. Museum of Natural History, Smithsonian Institution. *Left*: Slipper from Mammoth Cave, catalog number 416634. *Right*: Toe fragment of slipper from Indian Cave, catalog number 87277.

3. #87276. This number designates several fragments of gourd and squash shells also in the Edmonson County drawer. Some of the gourd fragments are charred in spots.

4. #4789 (also filled under #21610). The cleaned bones of a female mummy "Fawn Hoof" from Short Cave, acquired March 2, 1876. Short Cave lies on private property not far from Mammoth Cave but just outside the southern boundary of the Park. It was intensively mined for saltpeter in 1812–1814 at which time a number of aboriginal burials were found by the miners (Watson *et al.* 1969: 67; Meloy 1971). The History Card for Fawn Hoof reads as follows:

> This mummy of a female Indian was found in a cave about 4 miles from Mammoth Cave, Warren County, Kentucky, in 1814 by Mr. Charles Wilkins and given by him to the American Antiquarian Society of Worcester, Massachusetts. In exchange for anthropological material, the U.S. National Museum received the specimen during the year 1876. [The Museum records relating to this accession are very meager. There is nothing to indicate the number of accessories that accompanied the mummy but these which have been identified have been numbered and recorded under the above accession number.]
> Transferred to Division of Physical Anthropology for dissection, Nov. 11, 1914.

Fawn Hoof is the only one of the cave mummies known to have been accompanied by grave goods. These were rather carefully described by a tourist who visited Mammoth Cave in 1813, Ebenezer Meriam (Meriam 1844; see also Meloy 1971: 25–27).

The Archeology catalog card says: "Known accessories: 21610*a*—wooden bown, dia. 8" h. 4½"; *b*. small lot threaded seeds and deer hoofs and charred bone fragments; *c*. 2 strings of threaded seeds; *d*. threaded feathers of Cooper's hawk (*accipiter Cooperi*). Accessories retained by Archeology when body transferred to PA."

At least some of Fawn Hoof's grave goods went to the Peabody where the catalog lists them as follows:

8238 Pieces of 3 kinds of cloth made of _____ [here the cataloger obviously meant to fill in the blank when the material had been identified, but never did so].
8239 Rope made of _____
8240 Rope made of _____
8241 Fine string made of _____
8242 Seeds of _____ strung as beads
8243 Horn of a young deer's foot from necklace
8244 Piece of skin painted white
8245 Feathers from headdress

> Numbers 8238 to 8245 are portions of the several articles found on and with the so-called Mammoth Cave Mummy. Now in the American Antiquarian Society (Worcester). The body was not found in Mammoth Cave but in Short Cave.
> These fragments were given me by the American Antiquarian Society on my making the examination

at their room in Worcester. The mummy was collected about 1813 by the nitrate workers in Short Cave.

The preceding extract is from the Peabody catalog, Volume 2, and was apparently written by F. W. Putnam. In a marginal note he refers the reader to his article in the *Proceedings of the Boston Society of Natural History* for an account of the cataloged articles (Putnam 1875). Several of these items were seen at the Peabody Museum on June 19, 1969, as follows:

75-2 Fragments of open twined cloth. The warp strands are
/8238 touching and are made up of braided elements each about 5 mm wide. The weft strands are about 2–2.5 cm apart.
  Another fragment is somewhat finer; the warp strands are two-strand, S-plied seemingly, the wefts are about 1 cm apart, and both warp and weft strands are approximately 2 mm wide.
  A third fragment also has twisted warps (probably S-plied), the wefts are about 1 cm apart, and the warp and weft elements are about 3 mm wide.
/8239 Long piece of braided rope 6–7 mm in thickness:
/8240 Long piece of two-strand, Z-plied rope 7 mm thick, looks curiously fresh.
/8241 Several bits of twisted cordage 3 mm of less in thickness; those well enough preserved to be diagnosed are Z-twist.
/8242 Small brown seeds, each about 3 mm long, strung on a two-strand, Z-plied thread. If the latter were all in one piece instead of being broken into several, it would be about 25–30 cm long.

Fawn Hoof has never been dated (the flesh is now gone so radiocarbon determination on that is impossible, but a radiocarbon determination on bone collagen from the skeleton could still be obtained), hence it is impossible to say whether the burial was approximately contemporaneous with Lost John of Mammoth Cave and Little Al(ice) of Salts Cave, or belonged to a later—possibly even protohistoric—period.

American Museum of Natural History

Here, in a number of drawers in an old exhibit hall on the third floor, is a body of miscellanous items from Salts and Mammoth Caves and a collection of chipped stone from some surface sites in Eaton Hollow (Eaton Valley) between Mammoth Cave Ridge and Flint Ridge. The Mammoth Cave and Eaton Valley material was obtained by N. C. Nelson during the period of his work at Mammoth Cave beginning in 1916; the objects from Salts Cave were acquired in 1913, but no collector's name is given. (Only the Eaton Valley material is listed in the main file of acquisitions.) The Salts Cave material is described in what follows, surface collections from Salts Cave Fields and those from Eaton Valley have already been referred to (page 18), and the items from Nelson's Mammoth Cave Vestibule excavations are discussed in Chapter 26.

Contents of Drawer #586, "1913–12 Salt Cave Kentucky #1 Edmonson Co. (?) Possibly Hart" [This last is a pencilled notation]

1. 20.1/5771 A log fragment without bark, charred at one end and hacked at the other; 24 × 7 cm.
2. 20.0/5771G A debarked log, broken at one end, charred at the other; exhibits some rather fine hack impressions (dents) that may be recent; 51 × 5 cm.
3. 20.0/5772 Fragment of a small log with bark, broken at one end (and moldy) and charred at the other; 17 × 7 cm.
4. 20.0/5772 Another log fragment, charred at one end, broken at the other, bark partly removed (seems to have been hacked at in the center of the fragment); 26 × 7.5 cm.
5. 20.0/5773 Bundle of dried grass tied with modern string, stems and heads present; bundle is about 3 cm in diameter and is 55 cm long.
6. 20.0/5774 Smooth, barked stick with small twig lashed to it by fiber cord and modern string; cord is two-ply, S-plied. Neither stick looks worked, nor are they burned except for one charred spot on the twig; the larger stick is 71 cm long and 2 cm in diameter, the other 21.5 cm long and 2 cm in diameter, the other is 21.5 cm long and 0.5 cm in diameter.
7. 20.0/5775 Bundle of faggots consisting of about 20 sticks and one thin cane fragment. The cane is charred on one end, the sticks are not, although one or two have charred spots on them. All are tied together with modern string and a piece of rag; the bundle is approximately 72 cm long, and has a diameter of 7 cm.
8. 20.0/5775 Box of ashy cave fill including bits of charcoal, charred cane and twig fragments, bits of tie fiber.
9. 20.0/5776 Small bundle of 11 canes tied together with modern string, all charred at one end; biggest is about 1.7 cm in diameter, smallest is 0.6 cm in diameter. There is no trace of grease or oil on any of them. The bundle is about 20 cm long (although one cane is 26 cm long) and 5 cm in diameter.
10. 20.0/5777 Box of leaves (about 20 of them plus some broken fragments) which look like those found in Indian Avenue of Lower Salts Cave (Watson *et al.* 1969: 27); they are leaves of some species of white oak, possibly *Quercus muhlenbergii* or *Q. prinus*, with *Castanea pumila* as a less likely possibility. In the same box is a fragment of grass tie with a looped square knot.
11. Unnumbered odds and ends:
    Six cane fragments all charred at one end
    Five stick fragments all charred at one end
    One stick worn and charred at the small end, worn and broken at the other end (45 × 3 cm)
    One stick charred at one end (20 × 2.5 cm)
    Small bundle of twigs tied with modern string; bundle

is 25 cm long by 3.5 cm in diameter, some of the twigs are charred
Three fragments of a bark tie (6 cm inside diameter)
Three fragments of grass ties; one loop is 5 cm in diameter and has a square knot, the other is 4.5 cm in diameter and is tied with a bow knot.

Contents of Drawer #587, "1913–12 Salt Cave Kentucky #2 Edmonson Co. (?) Possibly Hart"

1. 20.1/8059 Cigarette box with about four small fragments of vegetable fiber slippers in it, all chevron weave.
2. 20.0/5763 Box with pile of short burned sticks and weed stalks in it; 22 sticks ranging from twigs to four which are 2–2.5 cm in diameter, two *Gerardia* stems 0.75 to 1 cm in diameter.
3. 20.0/5764A is written on a card in a cigar box containing fragments of several fiber slippers; other cards also in the box say "#5766 Twined cloth," "#5766 cloth," and #5765 child's moccasin." The 5764A card has the legend "Moccasin, both elements apparently of grass, 8½ inches long." There are seven fragments of slippers in the box representing a minimum of two different slippers, one done in chevron weave with elements 0.4–0.5 cm wide, the other simple weave (over-one, under-one) with elements 0.5–0.6 cm wide. The latter slipper is represented by five fragments, one of which is a piece of the toe with remains of two "laces" (two-strand, S-plied). Another card in this box contains an abbreviated description of the child's moccasin including the maximum length (6 inches, outside measurement).
4. 20.0/5770 Small cigar box with several grass ties and a torchlike collection of small twigs and *Gerardia* stalks, many of them charred. The twigs and weeds are loose, but if bunched up would make a bundle 18 cm long by 3–4 cm in diameter. Distinguishable among the bundle of ties are: one grass tie with looped square knot, inner diameter 6 cm; one grass tie with two square knots and inner diameter of 15 cm; several fragments of bark ties including one loose square knot.
5. 20.0/5778 Five fragments of squash (three of the fragments fit together to make one with a peduncle and inner diameter of about 15 cm maximum). One other fragment looks as though it was the top of the rind and had been made into a vessel by cutting out a circle around the stem; the wall of the vessel is 0.4 cm thick.
6. 20.0/5778 Three large fragments of gourd; two of these fit together and form what was probably a large container made of half a gourd sliced open longitudinally. The inside diameter of this gourd was 24 cm and the walls are 0.8 cm thick; 3 cm below the rim on one side a 2-cm hole has been burned through the wall.
   The other fragment is from the upper part of the original fruit near the neck, the wall is 0.5 cm thick.

7. Unnumbered items:

One small bunch (about 8 cm by 4 cm) of fine grass, the individual blades are about 2 mm wide

One bundle of coarser grass; bundle is 20 cm by 4.5 cm, individual blades are 0.5 to 1 cm wide

Another bundle of coarser grass, 12 cm by 8 cm, with individual blades 0.5 to 1 cm in width.

The coarser grass might be raw material for making slippers, the finer grass could have been used for twisting into cordage.

A box of bone and one slightly utilized chert flake labeled "Salts Cave, Kentucky, N.C.N. 1916". At least three fragments of human skull and one very worn human molar are included with the bone. The rest of the fragments (total about 50) consist of broken and splintered animal bone.

Research Annex of the Museum of the American Indian, Heye Foundation

All of the items listed and described here[1] are stored at the Research Annex (3401 Bruckner Boulevard in the Bronx), not at the Museum itself. There is an exhibit in the Museum that includes some of the Salts Cave material, but it was not possible to see the latter because the exhibit was being reorganized and the objects were packed away.

Slippers and Textiles

5/2201   Small, complete slipper; 20 cm long measured on the bottom, 6.7 cm wide at ball of foot, worn through at the heel. Chevron twining, elements 2–3 mm wide; tie arrangement apparently like that of 5/2203.

5/2202   Complete slipper; 22 cm long on bottom, 9 cm wide at ball of foot, worn through at toe and heel. Chevron twining, elements 3–4 mm wide, ties present.

5/2203   Complete slipper; 21.5 cm long on bottom, 8.5 cm wide at ball of foot. Chevron twining, elements 3 mm wide or less. Ties consist of braided strand 6–7 mm in diameter pushed through rim of slipper on both sides and tied over instep where it is wound around or tied to tassel formed by ends of woven material from toe seam (see 5/2214).

5/2204   Nearly complete slipper; 23 cm total maximum length on bottom, 7.5 cm wide at ball of foot, worn through at toe and heel. Chevron twining, elements 3 mm wide, ties present.

[1]Items number 4/6104 to 5/8650 were acquired in 1916; 5/8651 to 7/3219 were acquired in 1917. All the material listed here is from Col. Bennett Young's collection and all is from Salts Cave.

5/2205   Slipper about two-thirds complete, much of heel missing; originally was about 23 cm long by 8–8.5 cm wide, worn through at toe and heel. Chevron twining, elements 4–5 mm wide.

5/2206   Complete slipper; 23.5 cm long on bottom, 10 cm wide at ball of foot, worn through at heel and broken at toe (maybe partly from wear). Chevron twining, elements 4 mm or slightly more in width; stuffing in the toes, thick braided tie.

5/2207   Complete slipper; 22 cm maximum length on bottom, 10 cm wide at ball of foot, worn through at heel and very much so at the toe. Coarse chevron twining, elements 4–5 mm wide, ties present.

5/2208   Nearly complete slipper; 20.5 cm long on bottom, 7 cm wide at ball of foot, worn through at toe and heel. Chevron twining, elements 3–4 mm wide, ties present.

5/2209   Fragment of side of a slipper; coarse plain weave, elements about 5 mm wide.

5/2210   Nearly complete slipper; 21.5 cm long on bottom, 10 cm wide at ball of foot, worn through at the toe. Chevron twining, elements 4–5 mm wide, ties present. The area near the heel is burned away.

5/2211   Slipper about half complete. Toe completely worn through, heel is broken off. Plain weave, elements 4 mm wide, width across ball of foot 9.5 cm; tassel present at toe but ties gone.

5/2212   Nearly complete slipper; 23 cm long on bottom and about 8 cm wide across ball of foot, sole is gone and slipper was probably worn out. Chevron twining, elements about 3 mm wide, ties broken off one side. There was apparently mud on the bottom of the slipper, some of it is preserved on the lower parts of the sides.

5/2213   Slipper fragment, part of the side and bottom near the toe; coarse plain weave, elements 5–6 mm wide. One tie is intact and consists of a neat two-strand, Z-plied cord 3 mm in diameter.

5/2214   Complete slipper; 24 cm maximum length on bottom, width at the ball of the foot about 10 cm, worn through at toe and heel. Chevron twining, elements 3–4 mm wide. This slipper exhibits the tying mechanism very well; the tie is the end of the fiber mass that forms the inside of the slipper rim. On this example, this fiber is formed into a two-stand, S-plied cord which is passed to the opposite side of the slipper, pushed through that side then brought back to tie over the instep. Also at the center of the instep is a tassel formed by the ends of the fiber that was woven into the body of the slipper. This wad of material was twisted together and tied around with a fiber strand (and might then be tied to the laces).

5/2215   Nearly complete slipper; 19.5 cm long on the bottom, approximately 7.5 cm across the ball of the foot, toe and heel worn through. Coarse chevron twining, elements 4—5 mm wide.

5/2217 Three-fourths complete slipper; toe worn through and heel missing. Chevron twining, elements about 3 mm wide.

5/2218 Slipper fragment, the rim is preserved all the way around but there is no sole; maximum length 26 cm, 10.5 cm maximum width. Plain weave, elements 5—6 mm in width. This slipper was rather clumsily made in comparison with the others; dried mud is stuck in the weave on the outside of it.

5/2219 Fragment of the side of a slipper; chevron twining, elements 3—4 mm wide.

5/2220 Nearly complete slipper; 20.5 cm long on the bottom, 9 cm wide at the ball of the foot, worn through heel and toe. Chevron twining, elements 3—4 mm wide, ties broken but toe tassel intact. Dried mud on the bottom.

5/2221 Nearly complete slipper, but is squashed flat and part of the sole is gone; 23 cm maximum length on the bottom, perhaps about 8 cm wide at the ball (difficult to tell because of the flattening). Chevron twining, elements 3—4 mm wide, ties broken off one side but toe tassel is well preserved.

5/2222 Nearly complete slipper; worn through toe and heel (length and width not accurately obtainable because heel is partly broken away and slipper is flattened). Chevron twining, elements 3 mm wide or less, ties and toe tassel present.

5/2223 Fragments of the side and sole of a slipper; plain weave, elements 4 mm wide (warp seems to be two-strand, S-plied). Dried mud on the bottom.

5/2224 Nearly complete slipper; 23 cm long on bottom, 10 cm wide at the ball. Chevron twining, elements 3—4 mm wide, ties gone but part of toe tassel intact.

5/2225 Possibly the sole of a true sandal (a sole with bound edges, 16.5 cm long by 4.5 cm wide); plain twining.

5/2226 Fabric fragment identified by the catalog as the braided end of the weave from inside the toe of a slipper; 25 cm long and tapering from 3.5 to 1.5 cm in width.

5/2227 Identified by the catalog as a tangled mass of weaving material from inside the toe of a slipper.

5/2229 Two fragments of a slipper, sides and part of the sole. Chevron twining, elements 3 mm wide.

5/2230 Four fragments of slippers mounted on a card, plain weave with elements 4—5 mm in width; tie attached to one fragment is two-strand, S-plied.

5/2230 A second card with four more slipper fragments mounted on it; all are plain weave (but one fragment has one row done in chevron twining) with 5—6 mm wide elements.

5/2232 Two fragments of tightly rolled slippers, one is charred on one end, both are chevron twined. These were probably torch or fire fuel (there is a similar rolled slipper in the collection at the Visitor Center, Mammoth Cave National Park).

5/2236 Two cards, each with a large fragment of open-twined textile mounted on it; one piece is 20 × 18 cm, the other is 23 × 24 cm. The elements are about 2 mm wide. The catalog lists these as having been found near "Big Pit" by W. A. Elliott. I do not know what the Big Pit is, but the finder of the textile fragments is 'Major" Elliott of the Neville Salts Cave expedition (Watson *et al.* 1969: 11).

5/2237 About nine fragments of open-twined textile once glued onto two cards, the largest piece is 14 × 18 cm. The fabric is very similar to that of item 5/2238.

5/2238 Fragments of a bag made of open-twined fabric. (This item was described by Orchard 1920: 17ff.)

5/2239 Fragments of a smaller bag also open-twined fabric, referred to by both Orchard (1920) and Young (1910).

5/2240 Small fragment of a twilled (over-three, under-three) basket, glued to a card. The elements are probably cane splints and are 3—4 mm wide.

5/2241 Two cards on which are mounted several fragments of rather badly preserved open-twined textile.

5/2242 Four fragments of slippers (all seem to be from the sides); one plain weave plus two rows of chevron twining, one chevron, two plain.

5/2256 Four fragments of fabric mounted on a card; one is close twining, two are probably chevron, the fourth may be close twining, also. The catalog says "twine warp" as an identification for the items on this card, and the warp of one fragment does seem to be twisted.

5/2257 Several (25—30) small fragments of slippers; all seem to be plain weave except for one that is partly twined, elements are 4—5 mm wide or more.

5/2258 Sixty-five fragments of slipper fabric (seven of the larger fragments are mounted on cards); 63 are chevron twined, two are plain weave.

5/2269 Basket fragment 10—13 cm in diameter inside, twilled plaiting (over-three, under-three usually but sometimes over-four, under-four and sometimes over-two, under-two), elements 3—4 mm wide. The fragment consists of the top of the basket, the maximum amount of side left is 5.5 cm. The rim is a bundle with the basket elements wrapped around it. (Schwartz also saw a larger basket with this catalog number, 20—21 cm in diameter; Schwartz 1958e: 10, 21.)

Cordage and Bundles of Fibrous Raw Material

5/2231 Well-made braided cord with a square knot tied in it; the cord is 8 mm in diameter and probably about 1 m long (the specimen is looped up and mounted on a card) plus a separate fragment, also with a knot.

5/2233   Cordage very similar to 5/2231 but with a larger and less neat knot, was probably 50—60 cm long; mounted on a card.

5/2234   Several large knots; the catalog says "Knotted strands of raw material."

5/2235   Three fragments of knotted, braided cord; the cord is 6—8 mm in diameter.

5/2243   Hank of fine grass about 14 cm long and 4.5—5 cm wide maximum, individual strands approximately 0.5 mm wide.

5/2246   Fragments of four bark ties; one has a square knot and an inner diameter of 10 cm (the strip itself is 1.5 cm wide), inner diameters of the others are 15, 13, and 7 cm.

5/2247   Seven grass ties; one has a square knot and is 5 cm in inner diameter, inner diameters of the others are 5, 4 (tied with a square knot), 4.5 (tied with a square knot), 5.5 (tied with a square knot), and 6 (tied with a square knot) cm.

5/2248   Eight grass knots from ties, most are plain or looped square knots.

5/2249   Fragments of three bark ties (two with square knots, the third indeterminable) and two grass ties (one with a square knot, the other with a looped square knot).

5/2250   Ten hanks of grass strands; most are 8—9 cm long by 4—5 cm wide and 2—3 cm thick, but one is smaller (5 × 2.5 × 1 cm) and three are larger (9.5 × 4.5 cm, 11 × 5 cm, 13 × 6 cm); individual strands are 2—3 mm wide.

5/2251   Hank of bark 14 × 3.5 cm; charred at one end.

5/2252   Two hanks of bark 15—16 cm long by 2—3 cm wide.

5/2253   Five hanks of bark, four of them are 13—15 cm long by 2.5 to 5 cm wide, the other is 7 × 1.5 cm and the strips are 6 mm wide.

5/2254   Five clumps of fine grass (slipper stuffing? tinder?).

5/2225   Hank of grass 12 by 2 cm, 6—7 mm wide blades.

5/2260   Five fragments of cordage, all two-strand, S-plied, diameters range from 3 mm to 1 mm.

5/2261   Forty-eight fragments of cordage, all two-strand, 33 are S-plied, 15 are Z-plied; diameters of the cords range from 1 to 5 mm.

5/2262   Twenty-seven fragments of braided cord varying in diameter from 4 to 10 mm.

5/2263   Seventeen fragments of cordage, all braided, diameters from 5 to 10 mm.

5/2264   Two fragments of braided bark or grass (because of the preservative that covers it, it is difficult to identify), both are about 15 mm in diameter.

5/2265   Fragment of a braided strap about 9.5 × 1.5 cm.

Canes

4/7711   A series of charred canes 1 cm or more in diameter (one is 2.5 cm and another is 2.75 cm).

4/7712   Ten lots of cane, nine of them tied in bundles with wire, each bundle apparently representing a torch:

  1. 6 canes in a bundle about 25 cm long, cane diameters 1—2 cm

  2. 6 canes in a bundle about 24—25 cm long, cane diameters 1—2 cm

  3. 9 canes in a bundle about 38 cm long, cane diameters 1—2 cm

  4. 15 canes in a bundle about 36 cm long, cane diameters about 1 cm

  5. 9 canes in a bundle about 48 cm long, cane diameters 1 cm or more

  6. 10 canes in a bundle about 38 cm long, cane diameter 1 cm or more

  7. 8 canes in a bundle about 29 cm long, cane diameters 1 cm or more

  8. 10 canes in a bundle about 28 cm long, cane diameter 1 cm or more

  9. 5 canes in a bundle about 55 cm long, cane diameters 1 cm or more

  10. 14 loose canes which if bound into a bundle would make a torch about 45 cm long; the canes are 1—2 cm in diameter. Many of these canes are charred at one end.

Wood

4/7715   Four fragments of wood; one is a piece of a small log about 16 cm × 5 cm, burned at one end and broken at the other. The other three fragments seem to have been worked or used as tools. One is a stick 20 cm long by 2.5 cm in diameter, charred on one end, the other end tapers to a blunt point which appears to have been used as a pounder. The other two are both charred; one is smoothed all over and is 36 × 2.5—3 cm (cf Young 1910; 299, 317); the other is another possible pounder 17 × 2.5 cm.

Wooden Bowl

4/7716   Fragment of a wooden bowl which was originally square or rectangular. The preserved fragment is of the end or side with two rounded corners; the maximum dimension (between the corners) is 13 cm; the maximum length of the original vessel was probably 23—24 cm (Figure 21.2).

Squash, Gourd, and Corn

5/2267   Two fragments of warty squash and five fragments of gourd. The squash fragments may have been parts of vessels. One is the entire half of a squash fruit with stem; original diameter of the fruit was about 14 cm, the wall is 3 mm thick, and charred on one side. The other is the bottom two-thirds of the squash fruit, about 15 cm in diameter, and wall 3 mm thick.

  The gourd fragments include one nearly complete small one 8 cm in maximum diameter and 8 cm high;

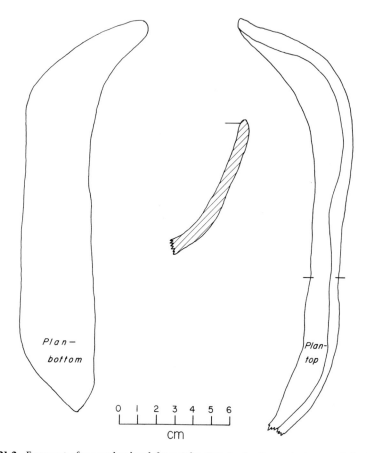

Figure 21.2 Fragment of a wooden bowl from Salts Cave in the Research Annex of the Museum of the American Indian, Heye Foundation. The catalog number of the bowl is 4/7716.

the side is broken out and the top has been cut or broken off to leave an opening some 3 cm in diameter. The other gourds are large pieces of rind; one looks as though it might have been part of a longitudinally split gourd like one seen at the American Museum of Natural History (20.0/5778, page 170). The maximum diameter of this specimen is about 17 cm and it would have stood about 21 cm high, walls are 4–5 mm thick. The other three are all large fragments of the bodies of gourds with diameters of about 16 cm (walls 3 mm thick), 19 cm (walls 5 mm thick), and 16 cm (walls 4 mm thick). All the gourds are brown or reddish brown, while the squashes are yellowish white.

4/7719 Five modern looking cobs, 16–18 rows, 18–20 cm long by 7–8 cm in diameter.

Mussel Shell

4/8214 Two mussel shell halves, nearly complete. All cal-
and careous crust has been removed and only mother-of-
4/8215 pearl is left. 4/8214 has two small (3 mm diameter) perforations near the hinge edge, one is drilled from both sides, the other from one side.

Bone and Antler

4/7718 Large fragment of antler, basal end intact, point broken off. Maximum dimensions 18 cm long by 3 mm in diameter; does not appear to be worked.

4/8210 Two fragments of long bone; one perhaps deer, but the other looks like the shaft of a human tibia. Neither has articular ends, both have been rodent gnawed.

4/8211 Fragment of animal bone identified by the catalog

as a bone smoothing tool; but it does not look worked.

5/2270   Three fragments of worked bone, two fragments of worked antler. The bone fragments appear to be animal toe bones with one end cut off, the whole piece being whittled and hollowed out (dimensions are 3.5 × 1 cm). One antler fragment has been trimmed somewhat (the outer surface cut off), dimensions 5.5 × 1.3 cm. The other piece of antler is referred to in the catalog as a knife handle. It is 5 × 2 cm, the larger end has had a 2.3-cm-deep hole hollowed out of it, and a narrow groove has been cut in one side very near this end. The opposite end is broken off but looks as though it had been perforated transversely, a groove is visible in section at the top of this end. The outer surface of the piece is smoothed all over.

Ground Stone

4/8189   Complete chipped hoe (five are listed in the catalog, and Schwartz saw two, but there is now only one), probably limestone. Maximum dimensions 13 × 7.5 × 2 cm. The implement is flaked all over both sides and is notched in the middle, presumably to make it easier to haft; possible sheen, like earth polish, on one end but very faint.

4/8191   Two bell-shaped pestles; both have slight central indentations on the bases which are not battered (see page 180).

4/8192   Fully-grooved, greenstone axe 13.8 × 8 × 4.8 cm; bit is battered.

4/8193   Two full ground celts with polished bits; one is 15.5 × 6 × 4.5 cm, the other is 10 × 4.8 × 4 cm, both have axelike rather than adzlike bits. The butt of the larger one is battered.

4/8205   Black slate gorget? Badly broken and has been restored with plaster; the central portion is completely missing so it is impossible to say whether it was perforated. Maximum dimensions are 12.3 × 4.5 × 0.5 cm; the object is oval in shape.

4/8221   Red slate gorget, rectangular in shape and with two central perforations each about 0.5 cm in diameter (cf. the gorget found on the surface near Salts Sink, page 17). Maximum dimensions are 9 × 3.7 × 0.5 cm.

4/8223   Pendant looking in plan view like an animal canine tooth. Maximum dimensions 5.5 × 1.5 × 0.3 cm; perforation at one end is singly-bored and is 3 mm in diameter. The catalog says this object is made of shell, but it looks like limestone.

Chipped Stone

4/8219   Large chert knife blade with serrated edges, 10.5 × 4.5 × 0.9 cm.

Peabody Museum of Archaeology and Ethnology[2]

Slippers and Textiles

75-2 /8229   Three complete or nearly complete slippers. One is 23 cm long on the bottom, 10 cm wide at the ball of the foot, worn through at toe and heel. Chevron twining, elements 3—4 mm wide, braided tie present and toe tassel intact. The second slipper is 23.5 cm long on the bottom, 10—11 cm wide at ball of foot, worn out at toe and heel. Chevron twining, elements 3 mm wide. Ties go from rim of slipper at toe to hole in the side, then cross over to the other side, through an opening at the slipper rim there, then back to the center where they are tied in a square knot.

The third slipper is 23 cm long on the bottom, 10 cm wide at ball of foot, worn out at toe and heel, Chevron twining, elements 3 mm wide, ties missing but tassel present.

According to the Peabody Catalog (Vol. 2), these slippers together with several other items were collected November 2, 1874, and received January 8, 1875. The collection and recording were done by F. W. Putnam.

75-2 /8230   Nearly complete, but broken, slipper. Chevron, twining, elements 3 mm wide or less, tassel intact and most of the ties are present. Ties are braided and fastened in a square knot. The slipper seems to have mud on it both inside and outside. Collected by F. W. Putnam on November 2, 1874; received January 8, 1875.

75-2 /8231   Nearly complete slipper, part of heel gone, worn through at toe. Chevron twining, elements 4—5 mm wide, tassel and ties intact; ties are attached in two places on each side and tied in a lump in the center.

A second nearly complete slipper; 22 cm long, but width indeterminate, worn through at toe and heel. Chevron twining, elements 3—4 mm, tassel intact as are some of the ties which went through two places on each side of the slipper.

The third slipper is broken; part of toe present with sides and parts of the sole. Chevron twining, elements 4 mm wide, long tassel present, ties broken; mud on the bottom of the sole.

Collected by F. W. Putnam on November 2, 1874; received January 8, 1875.

---

[2]Nearly all of the items listed here are to be found in six drawers of Case 62 in the storage area of the Museum. The exceptions are five items kept with the type specimen collections in the Putnam Archaeological Laboratory.

/8232   Fragments of nine slippers:

One consists of pieces of the sides and part of the toe. Chevron twining with elements 3—4 mm wide except for one small fragment which is plain weave.

Second slipper consists of pieces of side and sole. Chevron twining, elements about 3 mm wide, mud on the bottom.

Third slipper comprises fragments of sides, part of sole and part of toe; coarse plain weave (elements 6—7 mm wide).

Fourth slipper is nearly complete; 21 cm long, worn through at toe, ball, heel. Chevron twining, weft about 3 mm wide, tassel intact as are ties (latter braided and drawn through a hole in each side).

Fifth slipper is fragment of side and toe with one tie and part of tassel. Chevron twining, elements 3 mm wide.

Sixth slipper is nearly complete; 21.5 cm long, about 8 cm wide at ball of foot. Chevron twining, elements 3 mm wide, tassel and ties present (ties are S-plied and pass through one hole in each side).

Seventh slipper has parts of toe and heel missing. Chevron twining, elements 4 mm wide, part of tassel and ties present.

Eighth is a complete slipper; 20 cm long, 7.5 cm wide, worn through heel and toe. Chevron twining, elements 3 mm wide, tassel and ties intact (latter pass through one hole in side of slipper).

Ninth slipper is nearly complete but crushed from side to side; 24.5 cm long, Chevron twining, elements 2—3 mm, tassel and ties present.

The catalog notes that these items were found uncataloged and belong either with the 75—2 group or with another series of items collected in 1882 by W. D. Cutliff that have Accession Number 82—58.

8232A   Several small fragments of slipper fabric, perhaps all from one slipper; chevron twining, elements 3 mm wide. Catalog note same as above.

/8233   Two slippers; one nearly complete, 22 cm long, width indeterminate. Plain weave, elements 5 mm wide, tassel and ties mostly present, ties go through one hole on the side.

Second slipper is also plain weave, elements 6 mm wide, parts of tassel and some fragments of three-ply cords present, latter presumably ties. Catalog note same as for 8232.

A third slipper with this catalog number is separated from the first two and is stored in the Putnam Archaeological Laboratory. It is not complete, and is woven in a very unusual (for Salts Cave) technique: coarse open twining, elements 5—6 mm wide.

75-2-10   Bag of open twining, 14 × 17.5 cm, complete with
/8328[3]   handle of thin (about 3 mm diameter) two-strand, Z-plied cord. Weft cords about 0.5 cm apart; warp two-strand, S-plied cord.

82-58   Nearly complete slipper; 22 cm long, 9 cm wide,
/28378   worn through at toe and heel. Chevron twining, elements 3 mm wide, tassel intact and parts of ties present.

/28379   Nearly complete slipper; 19.5 cm long, 8.5 cm wide. Chevron twining, elements 3 mm wide, tassel and tie parts present.

/28380   Several fragments of a badly broken slipper; pieces of the toe, sides, sole, tassel, and ties. Chevron twining, elements 3 mm wide.

/28381   Parts of the side and sole of a slipper; chevron twining, elements 3 mm wide.

/28382   Parts of the toe and sides of a slipper, also some of the tassel and part of the tie; chevron twining, elements 4 mm wide.

/28383   Fragments of the sides and bottom of a slipper; chevron twining, elements 3—4 mm wide.

/28384   Fragments of the side, toe, and sole of a slipper; chevron twining, elements 4 mm wide.

/28385   Small fragments of a rather poorly made slipper; plain weave, elements 5 mm wide.

/28386   Fragments of the sides of a slipper; chevron twining, elements 3 mm wide.

/28390   About 10 fragments of open twined cloth.

/28392   Tassel from slipper toe.

(Numbers 82-58/28378 to 82-58/28398 represent items that, according to the Peabody Catalog, Volume 7, were "Bought from Wm. D. Cutliff of Mammoth Cave, 1882". They are all from "Salt Cave Near Mammoth Cave, Kentucky." The slippers are "braided from the leaves of the cattail rush *Typha*. No label (in Putnam Archaeological Laboratory): Two complete slippers; one is 22 cm long, 9.5 cm wide at ball, heel and toe worn through. Chevron twining, elements 3 mm wide, tassel and ties intact (latter go through one hole on each side of the slipper). The other is 21 cm long, 8.5 cm wide, heel and toe worn through. Chevron twining, 3 mm wide elements, tassel and

---

[3]The catalog refers to item 75-15-10/8328 as a bag collected from "Salt Cave," Edmonson County, Kentucky, by "Lucien Carr (Mr. Lee)," in August, 1875, and received in November, 1875.

ties intact. (These slippers may belong with 75/2-8230; the catalog lists three specimens under this number but there is only one slipper in the storage drawer.)

Cordage and Raw Material

75-2 /8236 — Approximately 17 fragments of braided (11) and twisted (two S-twist, four Z-twist) cord.

/8236A — Eleven fragments of twisted cord (five S-twist, six Z-twist), most are 3—4 mm in diameter. Catalog note same as for /8232.

/8236B — Three fragments of braided cords on a card; diameters of cords 6—8 mm. Catalog note same as for /8232.

75-2 /8237 — Wad of bark fibers; also—in Putnam Archaeological Laboratory—small hank of grass, fragments of bark and bark tie with a square knot, and fragments of braided cord.

75-22 /56795 — Length of braided cord, 6—7 mm in diameter.

81-34 /24874 — Braided rope about 8 mm in diameter; catalog says (Vol. 6) "Collected by William Cutliff Aug, 28, 1881; Received October 1881." The rope is from "Salt Cave, Kentucky."

82-58 /28387 — Fragment of braided cord, 4—5 mm in diameter. Catalog (Vol. 7) says "Braided strings from shoes"; the item was bought from William D. Cutliff in 1882.

/28388 — Fragments of S-twist Cord, about 2 mm in diameter. Bought from William D. Cutliff in 1882.

/28389 — Bunch of S-twist cord. Bought from William D. Cutliff in 1882.

Squash and Gourd

75-2 /8226 — Several gourd fragments and half a squash. The squash was almost certainly a vessel. The original fruit has been split exactly in half longitudinally, so that part of both stem and base are present; it would have been 13—14 cm in diameter and 12—13 cm high when whole. The walls are 3—4 mm thick, and are charred nearly all around what is now the rim.

Four of the gourds were clearly parts of big bowls as indicated by the rims. Two of these were large bottle gourds from which the stem and upper portion had been cut to form a vessel; the walls are 4—5 mm thick on these fragments, one of which is charred extensively. The other two gourd vessels were formed by cutting the fruit longitudinally, but leaving the immediate stem area intact; both of these have charred spots on the walls.

One other fragment is the base of a small gourd, what is left of it does not look worked, diameter 14—15 cm. There are seven other fragments, two of which fit together. Four others appear to be from the same thin gourd, so probably only three fruits are represented. All are red-brown in color; wall thicknesses are 6, 3, and 2.5—3 mm (stem and base of this one both present).

These squash and gourd fragments were collected in November, 1874, by F. W. Putnam and received at the Museum on January 8, 1875.

82-58 /28393 — Large gourd fragment, upper part and stem missing but specimen is probably two-thirds intact; 18 cm diameter, 20 cm high. According to the catalog, Volume 7, this was bought from William D. Cutliff in 1882 and is a gourd vessel from "Salt Cave, Kentucky."

/28394 — Gourd complete except for stem which is broken off; stands 17 cm high and has a maximum diameter of 17 cm. Catalog note same as for 28393.

/28395 — Stem of a gourd. Bought from William D. Cutliff in 1882.

Canes

75-2 /8219 — Eight canes and one *Gerardia* stalk bound together with wire so presumably representing a torch bundle. The bundle is about 38 cm long, the canes are 1 cm or more in diameter, the *Gerardia* stalk is 0.75 cm. All are charred at one end except two that are broken. The torch bundle was collected in November, 1874, by F. W. Putnam and received by the Museum January 8, 1875.

Wood

75-2 /8217 — Faggot bundle about 75 cm long and 12 cm in diameter. The bundle is tied with copper wire but a fragment of bark tie is till present; about 25 sticks are included. The catalog says these are "sticks for light," collected in November, 1874, by F. W. Putnam, received by the Museum January 8, 1875 (see Watson *et al.* 1969: Plate 9, lower, page 37).

/8218 — Charred stick 21.5 cm long by 2.5 cm in diameter; charred at one end, hacked at the other. The catalog says "burnt stick cut by flint axe," collected in November, 1874, by F. W. Putnam, received by the Museum January 8, 1875.

Feathers

75-2 /8220 — Five or six feathers in a cellophane wrapper, the longest being 37 cm in length. With them is a small fragment of two-strand, S-plied cord about 1 mm in diameter. These were collected in November, 1874, by F. W. Putnam and received by the Museum January 8, 1875; in the catalog note Putnam suggests the feathers may be turkey.

Paleofeces

75-2   Paleofecal specimen; dimensions 11 × 4.5 cm maxi-
/8221   mum. Collected in November, 1874, by F. W. Putnam,
           received at the Museum January 8, 1875.

82-58   Two fragments of human paleofeces, each 6.5–7 ×
/28397   3.5 cm. Bought from William D. Cutliff in 1882.

Bark

82-58   Fragment of bark (14.5 × 2.5 cm); bought from
/28389   William D. Cutliff in 1882.

Wooden Bowl

75-2   Fragment of a small rectanguloid wooden vessel; the
/8225   piece preserved consists of a corner, and part of an
           end and a side, 15 cm long maximum. There is a
           small perforation near the rim and part of the bottom
           is charred. The general shape is similar to the
           wooden vessel fragment seen at the Heye Foundation
           Research Annex (4/7716). The Peabody fragment
           was collected by F. W. Putnam in November, 1874,
           received at the Museum January 8, 1875.

"Cornstalk Beads"

81-34   Sections of some big pithy weed like giant ragweed
/24875   or horseweed rather than cornstalk; each piece is
           13–17 mm in diameter and about 20 mm long.
           Three of them are strung on a Z-twist string 2 mm in
           diameter. There are 15 of these "beads" which, ac-
           cording to the catalog (Vol. 6) were collected in
           "Salt Cave, Ky." by Wm. D. Cutliff on August 28,
           1881, and received by the Museum in October, 1881.

**Kentucky Building Museum, Western Kentucky
University, Bowling Green**

I am indebted to Jack M. Schock, Department of Sociology
and Anthropology, Western Kentucky University, for the
following information on some items from Salts Cave that
are displayed in the Kentucky Museum on campus:

The school museum (The Kentucky Building) has five items
from Salts Cave. These are one whole gourd container, four
sandals or slippers, and a small amount of vegetative
material. They were donated in the summer of 1925 by the
following individuals:

> Mr. Roy Owsley
> 1005 Ata Vista Road
> Louisville, Kentucky 40205

> Mr. Cecil Wright
> 3308 Crestwood Drive
> New Albany, Indiana 47150

Both individuals are supposedly alive and living at the
above addresses. They were accompanied by a Miss Gabie
Robertson who lives at 1341 State Street in Bowling Green.
[From a letter dated December 5, 1969.]

Discussion

A final comment is in order concerning the differences and similarities between my notes and
Schwartz's for those materials that we both saw.
In his 1958 manscript Schwartz provides a very
comprehensive listing of the relevant items at the
Heye Foundation from the Salts Cave Young collection, from Edmonson County, and from a few
specific proveniences within Edmonson County.
He does not include any details on the slippers or
the ground stone, however, but simply lists the
items with their proveniences. For example:

"4/8205 Slate gorget. Salt's Cave, Young Collection"

"5/2202 Fine twined weave sandal. Salt's Cave,
Young Collection"

"5/2211 Sandal. Salt's Cave, Young Collection"
Of the 100 items he lists from Col. Bennett
Young's Salts Cave collection, 19, plus one of the
two basketry fragments he listed (5/2269), could
not be located at the time of my visit, but I was able
to see and make notes on the others.

The situation is basically similar for the Peabody
Museum items except that a number of stone implements that came from Indian Hill according to
the catalog have been attributed in Schwartz's list
to Salts Cave (items 81-34/24858 to 81-34/24872,
pages 17–18), and a series of perishable items
(slippers, cordage, gourd fragments, etc.) from
Salts Cave according to the catalog are listed as
"Mammoth Cave Dist., collected by W. B. [sic]
Cutliff in 1882."

Schwartz does not include in the 1958 manuscript any information on material he may have
seen at the American Museum of Natural History,
and he did not visit the U. S. National Museum,
hence there is no overlap on study of the collections at those two places.

In conclusion, I would like to present some
generalizations concerning the various categories
of museum materials:

Slippers (see Watson *et al.* 1969:36–41; Schwartz
1958a; Orchard 1920). The equivalent of approximately 68 slippers from Salts Cave were recorded,
most of them at the Research Annex of the Museum
of the American Indian and the Peabody Museum

of Harvard University. Of these, 30 are sufficiently complete to enable determination of the length, and for 26 of them width at the ball of the foot could be measured. The range in length is from 19.5 to 26 cm (there is one reported length of 15 cm, but this slipper was not seen: American Museum of Natural History 20.0/5765, page 170); the mode is 22–23 cm. The width distribution is bimodal with the main peak at 10 cm and a lesser but definite peak at 8 cm. The distribution of length with respect to width is shown in Table 21.1. It is apparent that, perhaps as one would expect, the broader feet also tend to be the longer feet.

In the context of these measurements the lengths of most of the footprints in Lower Salts, Indian Avenue, and in the Upper Crouchway of Crystal Cave (Watson *et al.* 1969: 29, 62, 64) indicate feet at the upper end of the size range for the Crystal Cave prints (26 and 24.5 cm), and nearly the full range for the Indian Avenue prints (19, 21.5, 23, 24, and 24.5 cm). (It should be remembered, of course, that the slipper lengths are longer by an unknown amount than the feet that once wore the slippers; whereas in Lower Salts and the Upper Crouchway of Crystal, measurements are of prints left by the bare aboriginal feet themselves.)

Nearly all the slippers are twined; the few exceptions are plain weave, over-one, under-one. All six of the Salts Cave slippers in the collection studied by Schwartz at the Mammoth Cave National Park Visitor Center are twined, whereas of the 64 fragments from Mammoth Cave, 21 were plain weave and 43 chevron twined. Of the ten slipper fragments found by us in Salts Cave (Watson *et al.* 1969: 36–39), two show plain weave, the rest are chevron or plain twined (see King's study, Chapter 4 in this volume).

The presence of the slippers in the cave is probably to be largely attributed to loss and discard by the prehistoric cavers (a very high percentage of the more complete ones have holes worn through the sole at heel and toe). But they apparently were also used, at least sometimes, as fuel (5/2232 at the Research Annex of the Museum of the American Indian, page 172 in this volume). The manner in which they were tied onto the foot is fully demonstrated by several of the complete museum specimens (5/2203 and 5/2214 at the Research Annex and 75-2/8229 at the Peabody; pages 171, 175).

Cordage and Ties. Cordage includes well-made braided and twisted fibers of varying dimensions; among the twisted cords, S-twist predominates.

The ties presumably once held torch or faggot bundles. These are made of both bark and grass. The distribution of diameters for whole or nearly whole tie loops agrees with that obtained by us in Salts Cave (Watson *et al.* 1969: 33), and is summarized in Table 21.2.

The hanks and bundles of grass and bark raw material at the Museum of the American Indian and the Peabody are interesting, and their relative abundance in these collections (although there seem to be none left in the caves now) suggests to

TABLE 21.1 Length–Width Measurements of Some Salts Cave Slippers in Museum Collections

Lengths (cm)	
7.5–8.5 cm wide	9.5–10.5 cm wide
19.5	21.5
19.5	22.0
20.0	22.0
21.0	23.0
21.5	23.0
21.5	23.0
23.0	23.5
23.0	23.5
23.0	24.0
23.0	26.0

TABLE 21.2 Diameters of Salts Cave Ties in Museum Collections

Diameter inside the loop	Number of examples
4.0 cm	1 (grass)
4.5 cm	1 (grass)
5.0 cm	2 (grass)
5.5 cm	1 (grass)
6.0 cm	3 (1 bark, 2 grass)
7.0 cm	1 (bark)
10.0 cm	1 (bark)
13.0 cm	1 (bark)
15.0 cm	2 (1 grass, 1 bark)

Schwartz that they may have been stored in the cave interior. Perhaps some of them were also included in equipment carried by the prehistoric miners for the fabrication of torches (or for repairing their slippers).

Other Categories. As clearly evidenced in the museum collections, both squash and gourd shells were used as containers. The fact that so many of the larger museum specimens are charred suggests they may also have served as fuel when worn out or discarded.

The corn at the Museum of the American Indian (4/7719, page 174) is almost certainly modern. No evidence for corn has yet been found in the long series of paleofecal specimens examined by ethnobotanists Yarnell and Stewart (a total of 174 specimens from both Salts and Mammoth Caves).

The ground stone objects at the Museum of the American Indian compare favorably with those recovered from Salts Sink and Salts Vestibule. While recording the bell-shaped pestles (catalog no. 4/8191) of the Young collection, I was unaware of the complex of wear and use marks shown by our Salts Cave pestles (page 90), and so did not look for it. However, the Curator of the Research Annex, U. Vincent Wilcox, very kindly provided me with the following information (in a letter dated November 15, 1972):

> *Specimen 1:* Base generally shows regular roughened wear typical of grinding. In center of base, however, is a marked circular depression with a high degree of polish rendering it quite distinct from the rest of the basal surface. Edges and sides show no signs of battering, or flaking due to use as a hammer.

> *Specimen 2:* Of finer grained stone than the first. Most of base is ground quite smooth. A slight depression is apparent in the center, but is not nearly as distinct or as regular as in specimen 1. The depression does, as in specimen 1, show a markedly high degree of polish distinct from the rest of the basal surface. Base also shows a series of parallel linear striations transversing the surface, possibly the result of one-time use in grinding associated with a linear push-and-drag movement. At one place along the edge appear a few medium-sized flake scars suggestive of occasional or one-time use as a hammer.

> I briefly examined other bell-pestles from our Kentucky collections and noted that the polished depression feature was a frequent attribute.

Thus it appears that these two Salts Cave pestles from the Young collection (and various other bell-shaped pestles at the Museum of the American Indian) show the same general pattern of use as those we found in our Vestibule excavations, the central depression being the most distinctive characteristic.

Part

MAMMOTH CAVE

III

Mammoth Cave Archeology

PATTY JO WATSON
Washington University

Archeological investigations in Mammoth Cave previous to ours have been formally undertaken by N. C. Nelson (1917), Alonzo Pond (1937), and Douglas Schwartz (1958a–g, 1960). Their results are summarized in *The Prehistory of Salts Cave, Kentucky* (Watson *et al.* 1969). N. C. Nelson also notes in a manuscript at the American Museum of Natural History (Nelson 1923) that John M. Nelson did some digging in the Mammoth Cave Vestibule in 1899. N. C. Nelson's own finds from his 1916 excavation in the Mammoth Cave Vestibule are still available for study at the American Museum of Natural History (see pages 169–171).

It appeared from the work of these men that— like Salts Cave—Mammoth Cave had not only served as a source of minerals for the prehistoric inhabitants of the local area, but that the Vestibule was also a dwelling or camping place for some of them. As described by these authors, the remains in Mammoth Cave interior are, in general, identical with those in Salts Cave although the Mammoth Cave material was apparently more abundant and the cave more intensively used than Salts.

In order to obtain some detailed comparative information on use patterns and chronology in the cave, and on the diet of the ancient cavers, we began systematic investigations in Mammoth Cave during May, 1969. At that time a Cave Research Foundation mapping party in the Ganter Avenue area of Mammoth Cave discovered a complete split-cane basket that seemed to be aboriginal (Figures 22.1 and 22.2a,b). On May 31, 1969,

Harold Meloy—Mammoth Cave historian and National Park Service Collaborator as well as a Member of the Cave Research Foundation— guided an archeological party to the find spot of the basket, which lies upside down in a cutaround passage near survey station A54 (see Figure 23.1).

Our next visit to Mammoth Cave was February 13, 1970, when five paleofecal specimens were collected from the Ganter Avenue area (survey stations A54 and A51). On May 10, 1970, we collected some 23 more fragments from the A51 passage to be sent to ethnobotanist Robert B. Stewart for quantitative analysis.

More intensive recording and study of the still remarkably plentiful aboriginal debris in the Ganter Avenue area of Mammoth Cave was undertaken by a Washington University crew during April, 1971. We worked in Mammoth Cave April 6, 7, and 8 taking notes and making collections in the A, B, F, E ("Boiled Egg Passage"), and L surveys and in Jessup Avenue and Flint Alley (see Figure 22.4). On May 27, 1971, similar work was carried out in the K and E (western section of Ganter Avenue) surveys, and on May 28 a trip was made from the Violet City Entrance to the Historic Entrance in the main cave.

Detailed summaries of our findings are given in the chapters that follow. Although Mammoth Cave has been intensely commercialized for nearly 150 years, a surprising amount of prehistoric material is left there; future work is planned to obtain as full documentation of it as possible.

Figure 22.1 Probable aboriginal basket in Ganter Avenue cutaround passage near survey station A54, Mammoth Cave.

Figure 22.2 Close-up views of Mammoth Cave basket. Note repair cords at corner in photo on left.

Chapter 23

Observations in Upper and Lower Mammoth

PATTY JO WATSON
Washington University

Upper Mammoth: The Main Passages between Violet City and the Historic Entrance

Much of the route between the present-day Violet City Entrance and the Historic Entrance of Mammoth Cave has long been commercialized. Violet City—discovered in 1908 by cartographer Max Kämper and his guide, Edward Bishop—(see Figure 23.1) is a complex of vertical shafts opening by means of an artificially enlarged entrance on the surface only a few hundred feet from another artificial entry, the Carmichael Entrance. From the Violet City Entrance one descends a long flight of steps (Albert's Stairway) past a set of spectacular domes and enters Kämper's Hall, then Ultima Thule, and Anzer's Hall. The area around the domes and shafts is wet and if there were aboriginal activity here, the evidence has been destroyed by water. However, beginning in Anzer's Hall and continuing the length of

Mayme's Stoopway are remains left by aboriginal cavers: cane fragments, scattered bits of charcoal, charcoal smudges on the walls, and occasional evidence of mining on both sides of the commercial trailway. Some of the surface breakdown in these passages apparently postdates the Indians' use of them for several of the rocks overlie cane and charcoal. A small room in the breakdown at one side of Mayme's Stoopway has been partly mined and contains a scatter of cane and charcoal.

At Hain's Dome gourd fragments are lying on a flat rock beside the trail, obviously left there by some cave guide or explorer. The walls of the gourd are about 5 mm thick. Near it is some wood, perhaps aboriginal, and possibly a mining tool (see Watson *et al.* 1969: 59—60). Some of the walls of the dome are mined, and a pole that leans against the west wall, although probably not *in situ*, may be prehistoric.

At least three of the small passages leading out of the dome show remains of Indian traffic: cane, charcoal, smudged walls and ceilings.

There is another pole leaning against the wall and more traces of mining as well as cane and charcoal fragments at St. Catherine City. A low crawlway (60–75 cm high and about 6–7 m wide) leading off the main passage just north of St. Catherine City contains cane fragments.

Chief City is a huge room floored—like much of the rest of the cave—with piles of breakdown rock on and among which the aboriginal debris is strewn. Near the trail was found a 15 cm long, two-strand, Z-plied grass cord, probably dropped there by earlier tourists. According to local Kentuckians, the quantity of Indian materials (probably mostly cane, dry weed stalks, and wood) in Chief City was once very great, so great that early guides used to heap it up and ignite it to light the big room for the benefit of tourist parties. In 1935, the Mammoth Cave mummy—Lost John—was found on a ledge near Chief City.

There are mining tools near the west wall of Bryan's Pass between Chief City and Potter Hall. Some smudges are present on the west wall of Potter Hall but other remains are scarce here. In Wright's Rotunda there is further evidence of mining as well as a scatter of cane and charcoal. Another mining tool is lying on the breakdown at the east wall of the S Bend, and there is a paleofecal specimen nearby. There is evidence of mining of the east wall and of an alcove in that wall in the S Bend area.

In Kinney's Arena there is a large pile of cane against the east wall where someone has also collected together several paleofecal fragments and pieces of torch or firewood ties. These items are in and near another alcove in the east wall. Also here are two *Gerardia* seed pods and half of a hickory nut shell (35 mm maximum length).

Farther along, in the vicinity of the Snow Room, is a large fragment of warty squash (17 × 12 cm, walls 6–8 mm thick), and there are paleofecal specimens along both east and west walls.

There is another pole near the west of the Snow Room. Beside the trail on a ledge someone has placed a paleofecal fragment and the peduncle end of a large gourd (24 × 19.5 cm with walls 4 mm thick). There are traces of mining as well as cane and charcoal fragments from Kinney's Arena through the Snow Room. Beyond this point aboriginal remains are sparse and then cease altogether, having been obliterated by the intense nineteenth century and early twentieth century activity (including trail building and saltpeter mining) near the Historic entrance.

It is probably the case that most of the prehistoric material remaining in these highly traveled parts of Mammoth Cave has been disturbed; certainly nothing can be assumed to be *in situ*. However, the quantity and quality of the remains are impressive considering the amount of recent disturbance, and testify to the intensity of the aboriginal activity here which possibly surpassed that in most parts of Upper Salts.

Lower Mammoth: Jessup Avenue and Flint Alley

Shortly after leaving the present commercial route at the Wooden Bowl Room in the main cave (see Figure 23.2) and before reaching Ganter Avenue in Lower Mammoth, one passes the openings of two large passages in the right (south) wall. The first of these is Jessup Avenue, the second is Flint Alley, and both were traveled by the Indians. It is quite possible to go in one passage, past and through the pits at the south end, and come out the other passage, but because of the wetness in the area of the pits we cannot determine whether the Indians made this loop or not. In any case, they entered the drier ends of both passages and mined them for gypsum as well as chert (which is the "flint" of "Flint Alley"). Abstracts from our notes on these passages will serve to illustrate the nature of aboriginal material remaining in them:

Most of Jessup Avenue is a sand-floored walking passage. Torch smudges and a scatter of charcoal, charred cane, and weed stalks are present from the mouth of the passage at C1 to C22. Near C4 are two fecal fragments on the floor partly concealed by a breakdown rock. At C7 charcoal and wood fragments are lying on a ledge on the west wall. A bundle of small sticks was lying on the floor near the east wall, and these were collected for radiocarbon dating. The sticks were not tied together, but were resting near each other, some overlying others, and looked undisturbed. The

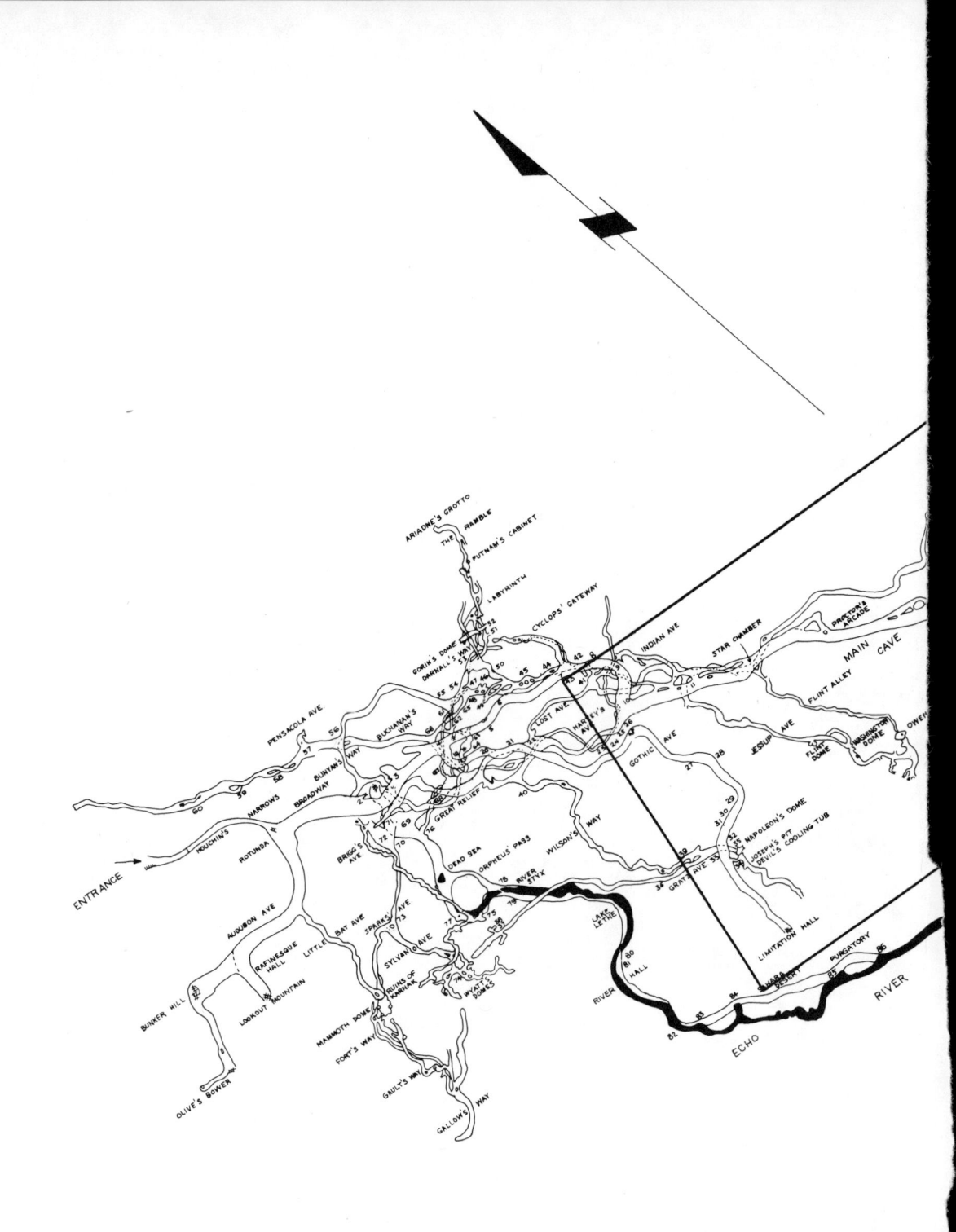

Figure 23.1. Map of the Mammoth Cave section of the Flint Mammoth System, including ar
ferred to in the text. Portions enclosed in rectangles are shown in greater detail in the Ganter A
maps. (Based on a map by Max Kämper, 1908, from the files of the National Park Service, and
fied by cartographers of the Cave Research Foundation.)

FEET

0   330   660   990   1320

0.00   0.125   0.25

MILE

APPROXIMATE SCALE

eas re-
venue
modi-

INDEX

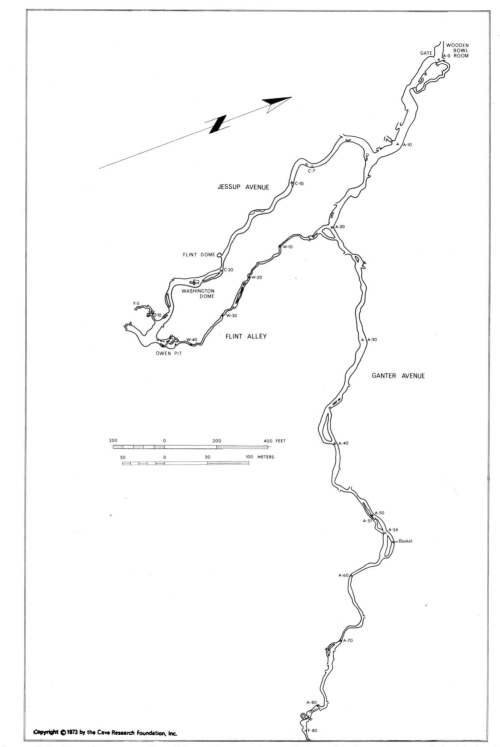

Figure 23.2 Map of western section of Ganter Avenue, Mammoth Cave, showing main areas of aboriginal activity.

resulting determination is 2170 B.C. ± 70 (Table 31.2).

At C10 there is a vertical shaft with both nodular and tabular chert outcropping in it and near it. Tabular chert occurs outside the main pit and nodular chert inside. Both kinds are of good quality and chunks of both have been smashed and battered out of the wall.

Indian remains are no longer visible past Washington Dome at C22 where the passage becomes appreciably wet. After crawling around the edge of Owen Pit, one finds the W survey of Flint Alley and, beginning at about W29, the aboriginal materials are visible once more. Flint Alley is a much narrower and rockier canyon than Jessup Avenue; torch/campfire debris and smudges are present from the junction with Ganter Avenue at A20 to W29, but are denser between A20 and W17 than they are south of W17. Thus, it seems likely that the Indians entered Flint Alley via Ganter and not from Jessup Avenue and Owen Pit.

At W29 there is evidence of mining on the east wall; between W22 and W21 there is battering on the west wall. From W20 to W4 seams or veins of chert as well as chert nodules are present on one or both walls. At W14 there is a small cutaround passage on the west wall that has been mined for gypsum. Between W10 and W7 the gypsum crust (1—1.5 cm thick) has been stripped from the west wall over an area 30—45 cm wide, and there is more mining at W4.

Lower Mammoth: Observations in the Eastern Portion of Ganter Avenue

Systematic observation and recording in the areas of Mammoth Cave not now commercialized was begun April 6, 1971, when an archeological crew went in the Historic Entrance, out to the Wooden Bowl Room and through the gate there, past Jessup Avenue and Flint Alley, and into Ganter Avenue (Figure 23.3). Ganter has not been shown to the public since the National Park Service took over management of the cave, but was much visited for many years before that. Late nineteenth and early twentieth century cave lighting consisted of candles, and lard oil or kerosene

lanterns, all of which emitted considerable smoke and soot so that several of the smaller passages in Mammoth Cave look like well-used chimneys. Unfortunately for us Ganter Avenue is one of these. This recent soot readily transfers itself from the cave to the caver and his accessories (notebooks, maps, etc.), so that within a few minutes of entry into such a passage everyone and everything is smudged and blackened. What is even worse is the fact that this uniform black coating makes things much harder to see. As one moves east, however, away from the main cave, the soot lessens gradually, and finally by the time the B survey is reached it is scarcely present.

From the Wooden Bowl Room along the easily traveled canyon past Jessup Avenue and Flint Alley to A54 there are smudges and places where the walls have been mined. The cutaround passage near A51 seems to have been a prehistoric latrine to judge from the quantity of paleofecal fragments here, 23 of which we collected for analysis (see pages 193—202). In a 60—75-cm-high crawlway cutaround at A54 is the probably aboriginal basket noted earlier (page 183, Figures 22.1 and 22.2). It was covered with recent soot and sitting upside down on a breakdown rock when found; after recording it was replaced in its original position. It appears to be made of split cane and is 14 cm high; the squared bottom is 18 cm on a side and the rim is 31 cm in outside diameter (28 cm inside). The individual splints are 5 mm wide and are woven in over-two, under-two twill (cf. item 5/2269 at the Museum of the American Indian, page 172). The rim, like that of the Museum basket, was formed by wrapping around a bundle. There are several old breaks in the basket bottom and in one place a partial repair has been made with fine (3 mm thick) two-strand, Z-plied fiber cord. In another place, two-strand, S-plied heavier cord (4—6 mm thick) was used in combination with untwisted fiber ties.

The rest of the remains in the Ganter Avenue A survey are similar to those of Salts Cave and Upper Mammoth Cave: cane, weed stalks, occasional fragments of wood or twigs, and charcoal scattered along the passage floor and on ledges, a few paleofecal deposits, some gourd fragments, occasional places where gypsum has been mined

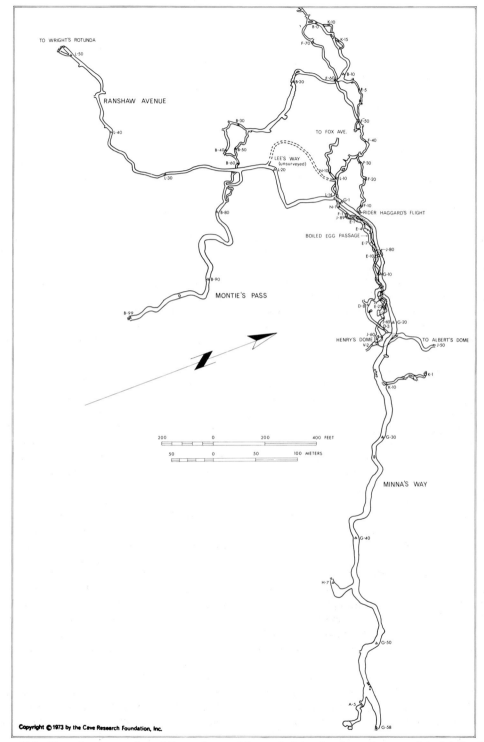

Figure 23.3 Map of eastern section of Ganter Avenue, Mammoth Cave, showing main areas of aboriginal activity.

from the walls. In some places the mining was very intense. An illustrative abstract from the notes on a portion of the A survey follows:

There is mining on both walls at A69 where the gypsum crust is 1–2 cm thick; the battering on the west wall is 2.5 m above the floor. At A70 there is sporadic battering on the south wall. Between A70 and A71 there is mining on both walls and a large stick (45 cm long by 2 cm in diameter) is lying on a ledge on the south wall. On a second, higher ledge on this wall is a paleofecal specimen lying near some fragments of cane and sticks. A small passage opening just east of the fecal specimen shows evidence of mining. At A71 there is mining on both walls and a paleofecal specimen on a ledge opposite the survey station. Between A71 and A72 is a cutaround passage on the south of the main passage, and this cutaround has been mined. Five meters west of A72 is a crawlway cutaround opening in the south wall that contains a gourd fragment; the crawlway has been mined. Between A74 and A75 is another cutaround passage on the south; there is a paleofecal specimen in it and evidence of mining on both walls. Between A75 and A76 a 1–1.5-cm-thick gypsum crust has been removed from the wall in a strip 50–60 cm wide over a length of 2.5–3.0 m. At A76 is a paleofecal specimen. At A77 evidence of intensive mining (wall stripping) begins and continues to A79–80.

The A survey meets the F survey at A84 (F81). A short distance further east, the B survey branches to the north while the F continues east to Rider Haggard's Flight (Figure 23.2). The B survey passages were much frequented by the Indians (and are much less obscured with recent soot than the A survey). Remains are like those of the A survey, and the cave is a relatively open canyon, also like the A survey. A clam shell lying on a ledge at B0 might be *in situ*; mirabilite is present around B8. At B10 a piece of wood—a fragment of a large branch about 5 cm in diameter and 15–20 cm long—was collected for radiocarbon dating. The resulting determination is 1050 B.C. ± 70 (Table 31.2).

At B18, on a low ledge in the passageway, propped against the wall is a limestone mining tool with the words "Indian hammer" scratched on it. On another ledge to the left are two paleofecal specimens and a clam shell, probably left there by early cave guides. At B19 the walking passage ends in a small room, approximately 1.2 m high by 3 m wide, that has been mined; torch and campfire debris is strewn about on the sandy floor. A 60–75-cm-high crawlway leads from this room and continues to B46. Remains left throughout this crawlway by the prehistoric cavers include seven fragments of charred hickory nuts (representing a maximum of five nuts) at B26. In the walking passage beyond, there is Indian debris all the way to B95 in Montie's Pass. Here the remains consist only of cane charcoal and the passage begins to be somewhat damp. It ends at B99 in terminal breakdown; there is cane charcoal between B95 and B99 but it has probably been moved by water coming in through the breakdown (we did not find any smudges here).

Two other passages surveyed by the Cave Research Foundation lead off the first part of the B survey: K (branching off at B3) and E (at B11). We examined these on May 27, 1972. Recent soot is present in the part of K near its junction with B, but there is much less of it than in Ganter between the Wooden Bowl Room and A54. Near K19 was a clam shell, and at K19 itself there are many torch smudges. The remains in the rest of the K survey are much like those in the A and B passages, torch debris and smudges are present throughout. Following is an illustrative abstract of the notes on a portion of the K survey:

In the K13 area, the Indians were moving along ledges on an upper level 3 or 4 m above the canyon floor. At K13 there is battering on the south wall. Sporadic battering is present from K13 to K12; between K12 and K11 the Indians climbed down to the canyon floor and 3 m north of K11 there is some battering on the walls. At K10 there is evidence of mining at the upper level again on both walls with some stripping of the gypsum crust on the south wall. Among the torch debris lying on the floor at K10 is an unusually large cane fragment (30 cm long by 1 cm in diameter). Between K10 and K9, still at the top level, a 2 × 1 m area on the south wall has been stripped of gypsum. At K9 there are a few batter marks on the south wall and intensive mining of the north wall including some stripping at a level 2.5–3 m above the floor.

On the floor is a log fragment 23 cm long and 2.5 – 4 cm in diameter.

At the end of the passage (K1–2), one can climb up into the F survey emerging at about F77. At F60, 100 m to the south, there is evidence of intensive mining near a junction with the B survey (B12). The K and E surveys both underlie the B and F passages somewhat in the manner of the stacked, intersecting canyons in Lower Salts.

The E survey begins at B11 as a crawlway with charcoal on the floor and sporadic battering on the walls. Between E3 and 7 the trail has been artificially built up and improved (probably in the nineteenth or early twentieth century). The aboriginal remains in the rest of the E survey consist of a little torch debris and some smudges. There is a good deal of modern wall battering at E12, probably as the result of passage improvement contemporaneous with the trail building at E3–7. At E20 one can climb up to join the F survey at F47.

The F survey is a through passage to more remote parts of the cave by way of Rider Haggard's Flight. This is a winding stone stairway, constructed in the 1880s for the benefit of tourists, that leads from the upper level (F) past a middle level (E) complex, to lower lying canyons N (Fox Avenue) and J. The N survey or Fox Avenue runs back to the main cave at Serpent Hall, not far from Cascade Hall and Echo River. The J survey is actually the lowest of a complex of superimposed canyons like those of Lower Salts. The E or "Boiled Egg Passage" (so called because of an ancient boiled egg—uneaten remnant of some tourist's or guide's lunch—cached in a small cleft at the junction of this passage with Rider Haggard's Flight) is the middle level of the complex, and the G is the upper level. It is possible to climb from E to J via an unsurveyed canyon that intermittently runs along between these two levels, but there is no negotiable connection between E and G.

Aboriginal remains in the F survey between B0 and F66 are much like those already described for the B, K, and E surveys in western Ganter. There is plentiful evidence of mining, and the usual scatter of torch debris is present in the main canyon as well as in a cutaround passage between F75 and F74. Beginning at F66 the trail has been recently dug out and improved all along the

canyon to about F46. There are places here where the walls are battered but it is likely that the battering is to be associated with the recent trail improvement rather than with the Indians. At F33 is the junction with the L survey, beginning as a crawlway leading to Lee's Way and Ranshaw Avenue. The prehistoric cavers traveled these passageways (see page 192) and also continued along the main F survey canyon to negotiate the large cleft now easily climbable by means of Rider Haggard's Flight of stone steps. Leading off to the left about halfway down the twisting Flight is the Boiled Egg Passage. The Indians seem to have gone along this narrow canyon and the intermittently present, unsurveyed one just below it, dropping some torch debris into the J survey at the bottom of this set of stacked canyons, but probably not actually moving along it. At any rate, places where the gypsum crust has been mined off the walls (there are also gypsum flowers and needles present in some places), smudges on breakdown rocks and on the walls, and a litter of torch debris on the floor occurs in E and the intermittent canyon below it, but in J there is only such material as seems to have dropped from above.

The following is abstracted from the notes on a part of the Boiled Egg passage:

Between E1 and E2 the passage is a narrow canyon with many climbable ledges. There is no evidence of mining but there is charcoal on the ledges, and on the south wall ledge opposite E2 are three pieces of bark tie. Between E3 and E4 charcoal is scattered along the sand floor of the canyon and also is present on a ledge running along the south wall. A fragment of bark tie is also lying on the canyon floor. Two meters west of E4 there is another bark tie fragment as well as cane charcoal (up to 3–4 cm long and 0.5 cm in diameter), and two pieces of what is probably *Gerardia*.

Between E4 and E5 there is charcoal on a ledge on the south wall as well as on the floor, and smudges on ledges on both walls as well as the ceiling. At E5 there are fragments of a possible vine tie as well as charcoal on the ledge on the north wall. At E6 there is charcoal on the ledges on both walls and on the floor. At E7 there is evidence of mining on the north wall and charcoal on the ledge there. At this point in the passage the canyon floor drops 6—7 m down and three pieces of charred cane are lying there (one piece is 15 cm long, the others are 6—7 cm in length). At E8 and 9 there is charcoal on the north wall ledge. Below the E survey here is a second (unsurveyed) canyon, and then the J survey below that. In the unsurveyed canyon is a scatter of charcoal and a fragment of charred wood about 10 cm square together with five pieces of charred cane each about 12 cm long.

Between E9 and E10, there is cane charcoal on a ledge of the south wall and uncharred *Gerardia* stalks on the north wall ledge. At E10 there is possible mining of the south wall. Between E10 and E11 there is charcoal on the ledge that serves as floor of the E survey here (the real floor is some 12 m down in the J survey). At E12 there are three piles of charcoal on the north wall ledge, including pieces of completely charred cane 5 cm long by 1 cm in diameter.

After E25 the Boiled Egg Passage intersects the J survey and Indian remains were not noted. The passage becomes wetter until it ends at a large pit (Henry's Dome) that had water up to 15 cm deep in it at the time of our visit (April 22, 1972). It is possible that the Indians went to Rider Haggard's Flight and out the Boiled Egg Passage to reach water in the Henry's Dome area. They do not seem to have gone beyond the Flight into Fox Avenue.

The Indians did explore the leads off the F survey before reaching Rider Haggard's Flight, however, the longest of these being the L survey crawlway—beginning at F33—and Ranshaw Avenue. From L1 to L14 is a rather unpleasant, rocky-floored crawlway connecting the F survey with Ranshaw, which is a wide crouchway mined and fairly intensively visited by the Indians. Remains in the L1 to L14 crawlway comprise charred cane and cane charcoal (items abundantly present in Ranshaw as well, where we also noted a fragment of a bark tie), a few paleofecal specimens, two pieces of hickory nut and one of acorn. The aboriginal debris decreases as one moves up to the L20s (at L23 there is a junction leading to the B survey in Montie's Pass). There is a thin scatter of cane charcoal extending to the vicinity of L38; the passage ends at L50 in breakdown below Wright's Rotunda.

If one goes north in Ranshaw beyond L14, he comes to the G survey, which was also explored by the Indians at least as far as G16. There is cane charcoal between G1 and G10 and some indication of mining. At G16 there is a climb up through breakdown to G17 where there is a torch smudge on a breakdown rock, but no further traces as the passage becomes wetter (there is a pit and small waterfall at G23).

In conclusion it may be stated that aboriginal patterns in Lower Mammoth are very similar to those in Lower Salts, but indicate a greater intensity of use in nearly every place we have investigated so far. Although all these passages were also explored by many persons in the nineteenth and early twentieth centuries, the prehistoric remains are clear and unmistakeable. Only in a few places (F66 for instance) have they been obliterated by recent activity. The Indians were certainly mining gypsum throughout the Ganter area much more intensively than in any passage yet discovered in Lower Salts.

Chapter 24

A Statistical Analysis of Constituents in Human Paleofecal Specimens from Mammoth Cave

WILLIAM H. MARQUARDT

Washington University

Twenty-seven human paleofecal specimens were examined for food remains by Robert B. Stewart. The specimens had been deposited in cave passages by aboriginal explorers who were probably engaged in mining activities.

According to Stewart, the separation procedure used was as follows:

Each specimen was divided in half (if possible along the longitudinal axis).

One half of the specimen was placed in about 100 ml of a solution of sodium phosphate (1 gm sodium phosphate diluted with 200 ml water), and left there until it broke down.

The solution was screened and the liquid that came through the screen was placed in a bottle for pollen analysis (see page 204).

From the damp seeds of the specimen remaining in the screen, five samples of 1 gm each (weighed when damp) were placed in separate bottles and about 40 ml of the solution of sodium phosphate was added.

Each sample was allowed to soak for a few days to enable further breakdown.

While still in solution, the different kinds of seeds were separated from one another in each sample.

The separated seeds were allowed to dry, and each seed type was then weighed separately.

The materials were separated according to genus and species where possible, and the dry weights for each category were recorded for each of the 135 subspecimens. Quantities weighing less than 0.01 gm were recorded as "trace," and in the case of seeds weighing less than 0.01 gm, the actual number of seeds was recorded when possible.

The variation in quantities of plant remains among subspecimens was generally very small. Only in specimens No. 5 (chenopod, $p < 0.001$), No. 20 (hickory nut, $p < 0.05$), and No. 21 (*Rubus* seeds, $p < 0.001$) were there statistically significant variations among the randomly selected subspecimens.

Excluding the categories "unidentified" (Stewart states in correspondence with P. J. Watson that the "unidentified" category consists of plant parts, apparently often consisting of crushed chenopod seeds) and "animal remains," the Mammoth Cave material is dominated by hickory nutshell (6.09 + gm), chenopod seeds (5.89 + gm), maygrass seeds (4.17 + gm), sunflower achenes (1.66 + gm), and plant and fruit skin (1.12 + gm). Together these five substances make up 96.7% of the (dry) gross weight, with charcoal, sumpweed (*Iva annua*), squash, blackberry/raspberry, strawberry, and grape seeds making up the remaining 3.3%. In terms of the number of specimens in which each substance was found, charcoal ranks first with 20 occurrences of 27 specimens. Chenopod occurred 18 times, followed by hickory nutshell (17), sunflower (17), plant/fruit skin (15), sump- weed (12), animal remains (11), maygrass (9), *Rubus* (6), strawberry (3), squash (1), and grape (1).

One hundred human paleofecal specimens from Salts Cave were analyzed for plant and other remains by R. A. Yarnell (1969). In contrast to Stewart's quantification by weight, Yarnell ranked the occurrences of each food material for each specimen according to one of six categories: very abundant, abundant, moderate, scanty, scarce, and absent. In Yarnell's table of modified percent- ages (Chapter 15, Table 15.1), sunflower achenes, chenopod seeds, sumpweed achenes, hickory nut- shell, maygrass seeds, and squash and gourd seeds together make up 88% of the bulk of the samples analyzed. Nearly half of the total bulk was com- posed of the remains of cultivated plants (gourd, squash, sunflower, sumpweed), and this total becomes 67% if one adds chenopod to the list of probable cultigens. From certain associations Yarnell was able to infer that hickory nut, sun- flower, sumpweed, squash, chenopod, and acorn were stored in the autumn for later consumption. Maygrass, although storable, was apparently con- sumed in the summer, when harvested, together with such spring and summer favorites as straw- berries, blackberries, raspberries, blueberries, and, as well, viburnum, grape, sumac, and poke berries. Although Yarnell's data were ordinally scaled in terms of relative abundance, his analysis was

apparently carried out by first examining the significant associations of certain plant foods, based on a presence/absence scale, rather than an ordinal one. Then, the information on relative abundance was used to augment these inferences and to elucidate significant associations (see Yarnell 1969: 47–49).

The data obtained from Stewart's examination of the Mammoth Cave specimens (summarized in Table 24.1) differ from those of Yarnell for the Salts specimens in two respects: (1) Stewart's data are expressed in weights of food substances for each specimen; (2) the number of specimens from Mammoth Cave (27) is much smaller than the number from Salts Cave (100). Alternatives were sought to the contingency analysis of Yarnell be- cause first, Stewart's data, expressed in actual weights, could be analyzed with statistical tech- niques other than those operating on a dichotom- ous scale, and second, contingency methods, such as χ^2, may be adversely affected by small sample sizes. Because of the availability of Yarnell's orig- inal data (Yarnell 1969: 42–43), and the above- mentioned contrasts in the quantification techniques and sample sizes of the Salts and Mammoth speci- mens, there seemed a good opportunity to compare the results of different analytic techniques applied to the same data. Therefore, the Mammoth Cave data were analyzed not only in 2 × 2 contingency tables, using the χ^2 technique, but also a correla- tion coefficient was calculated for each variable pair. Finally, as an additional experiment, a principal components factor analysis was carried out on the correlation matrix and the results were compared to those obtained with contingency and correlation techniques. The results of the contin- gency, correlation, and factor analytic techniques will be discussed in succession.

In the first analysis, the data for the 13 categories of materials found in the 27 samples were reduced to a presence/absence scale, and the 78 nontrivial contingency tables were generated. Table 24.2 illustrates the general form.

In Table 24.3, the observed associations (pre- sence of both variables) for each combination are given in the lower half of the matrix, and the expected associations are given in the upper half of the same matrix. For comparative purposes this

TABLE 24.1 Contents of Mammoth Cave Human Paleofecal Specimens[a]

Specimen number[b]	Hickory nut	Charcoal	Chenopod	Sump-weed	Maygrass	Sun-flower	Rubus	Squash	Grape	Unidenti-fied	Plant or fruit skin	Animal remains	Straw-berry
1	0.46		0.32	0.01+[c]		0.18	0.02+			0.23			
2	0.18	0.00+	0.38			0.04+				0.05	0.01+	0.00+	
3	0.10	0.00+	0.46	0.05						0.06	0.01+		
4		0.00+	0.00+								0.50	0.05+	
5	0.00+		0.56	0.06+		0.01+	0.00+		0.00+	0.22+	0.00+	0.00+	
6		0.00+	0.38	0.00+		0.12				0.22	0.00+	0.00+	
7	0.55	0.00+	0.07			0.06				0.10	0.02+		
8			0.00+		0.77						0.00+		
9		0.00+				0.04+				0.23	0.21		0.00+
10	0.24	0.00+	0.48		0.00+	0.00+	0.00+					0.04	
11		0.00+			0.53						0.00+	0.00+	
12	0.00+	0.00+	0.00+		0.78			0.07					
13		0.02+			0.52	0.01+					0.04+		
14		0.01+			0.53		0.00+				0.31		
15	0.31	0.01+	0.83			0.21						0.00+	
16	0.72	0.00+	0.40	0.00+		0.12						0.00+	
17		0.00+									0.00+	1.07	
18		0.00+			0.55							0.00+	
19	0.35	0.00+	0.34	0.03+		0.13					0.02+		
20	1.24	0.00+	0.00+	0.00+		0.40					0.00+		
21	0.04+	0.00+	0.41	0.03+	0.00+	0.05	0.01+						0.00+
22	0.41	0.00+	0.28	0.05		0.00+							
23	0.57	0.03+				0.00+							
24	0.00+	0.02+	0.66	0.01+		0.22					0.00+	0.00+	
25		0.00+										1.61+	
26	0.90	0.00+	0.32	0.06		0.07							
27	0.02+	0.00+		0.00+	0.49		0.00+						0.15

[a] All weights in grams. With respect to the "Plant or fruit skin" category: Samples 2, 3, 4, 5, 6, 7, 8, 9, 11, 13, and 14 contained fruit skin, whereas samples 17, 19, 20 and 24 contained plant skin.

[b] Specimens 1 through 23 were collected from the immediate vicinity of survey station A51 in Ganter Avenue; specimens 24 through 27 were collected from the area around survey station A53, Ganter Avenue.

[c] Values followed by "+" symbol indicate the recording of "trace" for one or more subspecimens.

TABLE 24.2 Two-by-Two Contingency Table for Variables Hickory Nut and Charcoal

Charcoal	Hickory nut		
	Present	Absent	*Totals*
Present	13 (12.59)[a]	7 (7.41)	*20*
Absent	4 (4.41)	3 (2.59)	*7*
Totals	*17*	*10*	*27*

$\chi^2 = 0.007$; $p = 0.93$ (not significant)

[a]Expected frequency given in parentheses.

table is similar to Yarnell's (1969:47) presentation of the Salts Cave data.

At the 0.05 level of confidence, there are only five significant relationships. These are the association of hickory nut with chenopod ($\chi^2 = 7.17$, $p = 0.008$), the association of hickory nut with sumpweed ($\chi^2 = 4.36, p = 0.035$), the association of hickory nut with sunflower ($\chi^2 = 3.87, p = 0.046$), the dissociation of charcoal with *Rubus* ($\chi^2 = 4.22, p = 0.038$), and the dissociation of maygrass with sunflower ($\chi^2 = 3.87, p = 0.046$).

Objections can be raised to such an analysis in terms of both efficiency and reliability. Of 78 tests, only five relationships can be demonstrated statistically significant, a rather meager basis for any sort of edifying generalization. Such a technique also makes no use of the information on relative abundance. Maygrass, for example, tends to be either absent, or present in abundance; only in Specimens 10 and 21 are the maygrass remains reported as "trace." Yarnell (1969:47) also found this to be the case with the maygrass found in the Salts Cave material. Charcoal, by virtue of its occurrence in 20 of 27 specimens, is the most frequently occurring material, yet it ranks tenth in terms of total weight of materials found in all specimens. The contingency analysis on the nominal, dichotomous data is not capable of taking into account these potentially interesting observations.

Also, comparisons of results from different analyses are often awkward when restricted to isolated, pairwise associations. For example, Steven LeBlanc undertook a brief statistical analysis of associations among the food constituents of

the 100 Salts Cave paleofecal specimens examined by Yarnell (reported in Watson 1970). He made a series of 2×2 comparisons as I have done for the Mammoth Cave data, and found three statistically significant associations—sumpweed with chenopod, hickory nut with chenopod, and fish scales with chenopod, and two dissociations—maygrass with chenopod, and maygrass with hickory nut. Thus, LeBlanc elicited only one combination (hickory nut with chenopod) that also occurs in the Mammoth Cave contingency series. At first glance, then, the contingency results might seem to indicate only scant affinity between the Salts and Mammoth materials. It will be shown later that this inference, based on a cursory examination of the statistically significant associations between certain variable pairs, will not withstand the scrutiny of more expedient analytic techniques.

The next step in the analysis entailed the calculation of correlation coefficients among all nontrivial pairs of the 13 constituents. Although the data are generally continuous, they are in the strict sense neither ratio scale nor interval scale in nature. This is due to the presence in some samples of an amount of identifiable material so minute that weighing is not feasible; such occurrences are recorded as "trace." The data are, however, ordinal in scale; "trace" is clearly greater than zero and less than 0.01 gm, but cannot be assigned an exact value in order to make the data continuous. For the calculation of correlation coefficients, then, "trace" was given the very small value of 0.001 gm. The Pearson product—moment coefficient is generally inappropriate for noncontinuous data. In lieu of Pearson's r, Kendall rank—order correlation coefficients were calculated (see Table 24.4).

Moderate positive correlations are observed for the pairs hickory nut—chenopod, sumpweed—sunflower, sumpweed—grape, *Rubus*—squash, *Rubus*—grape, and grape—unidentified. High positive correlations are noted for the pairs hickory nut—sumpweed, hickory nut—sunflower, chenopod—sumpweed, and chenopod—sunflower. Moderate negative correlations are observed for the pairs hickory nut—plant/fruit skin, charcoal—*Rubus*, chenopod—maygrass, sumpweed—may-

TABLE 24.3 Observed and Expected Associations of Materials in 27 Paleofecal Specimens from Mammoth Cave

Observed associations	Hickory nut	Char-coal	Cheno-pod	Sump-weed	May-grass	Sun-flower	Rubus	Squash	Grape	Unidenti-fied	Plant or fruit skin	Animal remains	Straw-berry
Hickory nut	13.0	12.6	11.3	6.9	6.3	10.1	3.8	0.6	0.6	5.0	9.4	6.3	1.9
Charcoal	13.0		13.3	8.2	7.4	11.9	4.4	0.7	0.7	5.9	11.1	7.4	2.2
Cheno-pod	15.0	13.0		7.3	2.9	10.7	4.0	0.7	0.7	5.3	10.0	6.7	2.0
Sump-weed	10.0	7.0	10.0		4.1	6.5	2.4	0.4	0.4	3.3	6.1	4.1	1.3
May-grass	5.0	7.0	5.0	2.0		5.9	2.2	0.4	0.4	3.0	5.6	3.7	1.0
Sun-flower	13.0	13.0	13.0	9.0	3.0		3.6	0.6	0.6	4.7	8.9	5.9	1.9
Rubus	4.0	2.0	3.0	4.0	4.0	3.0		0.2	0.2	1.8	3.3	2.2	0.7
Squash	0.0	0.0	0.0	0.0	1.0	0.0	1.0		0.0	0.3	0.6	0.4	0.1
Grape	1.0	0.0	1.0	1.0	0.0	1.0	1.0	0.0		0.3	0.6	0.4	0.1
Unidenti-fied	6.0	6.0	7.0	4.0	1.0	6.0	2.0	0.0	1.0		4.4	3.0	0.8
Plant or fruit skin	7.0	10.0	10.0	5.0	5.0	8.0	3.0	1.0	1.0	7.0		5.6	1.6
Animal remains	5.0	7.0	6.0	2.0	3.0	5.0	2.0	1.0	1.0	2.0	5.0		1.2
Straw-berry	2.0	2.0	1.0	2.0	1.0	2.0	1.0	0.0	0.0	1.0	2.0	0.0	

TABLE 24.4 **Kendall Rank-Order Correlation Coefficients between Pairs of Materials Found in 27 Mammoth Cave Paleofecal Specimens, with Levels of Significance**

Correlation coefficients	Hickory nut	Charcoal	Chenopod	Sumpweed	Maygrass	Sunflower	Rubus	Squash	Grape	Unidentified	Plant or fruit skin	Animal remains	Strawberry
										Levels of significance			
Hickory nut		0.822	0.046	0.009	0.005	0.001	0.691	0.161	0.742	0.999	0.033	0.072	0.807
Charcoal	0.03		0.615	0.225	0.624	0.295	0.013	0.055	0.055	0.162	0.952	0.735	0.305
Chenopod	0.27	0.07		0.001	0.043	0.002	0.774	0.140	0.072	0.154	0.340	0.507	0.159
Sumpweed	0.36	-0.17	0.43		0.014	0.024	0.093	0.262	0.020	0.227	0.228	0.038	0.506
Maygrass	-0.39	-0.07	-0.28	-0.33		0.001	0.079	0.051	0.356	0.009	0.540	0.348	0.903
Sunflower	0.45	0.14	0.42	0.31	-0.47		0.636	0.159	0.934	0.115	0.774	0.210	0.844
Rubus	-0.05	-0.34	-0.04	0.23	0.24	-0.06		0.019	0.019	0.272	0.460	0.297	0.510
Squash	-0.19	-0.26	-0.20	-0.15	0.27	-0.19	0.32		0.778	0.426	0.723	0.235	0.617
Grape	-0.05	-0.26	0.25	0.32	-0.13	0.01	0.32	-0.04		0.017	0.723	0.235	0.617
Unidentified	0.00	-0.19	0.19	0.17	-0.36	0.22	0.15	-0.11	0.33		0.053	0.149	0.500
Plant or fruit skin	-0.29	0.01	-0.13	-0.16	-0.08	-0.04	-0.10	0.05	0.05	0.26		0.533	0.248
Animal remains	-0.25	-0.05	0.09	-0.28	-0.13	-0.17	-0.14	0.16	0.16	-0.20	-0.09		0.053
Strawberry	-0.03	-0.14	-0.19	0.09	-0.02	0.03	0.09	-0.07	-0.07	0.09	0.16	-0.26	

TABLE 24.5 Eigenvalues and Percentages of Variance Accounted for by Each of Nine Factors in the Complete Principal Components Solution[a]

Factor	Eigenvalue	Percentage of variance	Cumulative percentage of variance
1	2.52973	28.1	28.1
2	1.69196	18.8	46.9
3	1.23162	13.7	60.6
4	0.96484	10.7	71.3
5	0.72467	8.1	79.4
6	0.60474	6.7	86.1
7	0.53643	6.0	92.0
8	0.44909	5.0	97.0
9	0.26692	3.0	100.0

[a]Only Factors 1 and 2 were extracted for consideration (see Table 24.6).

grass, and sumpweed—animal remains. High negative correlations can be seen for the pairs hickory nut—maygrass, maygrass—sunflower, and maygrass—unidentified. All other pairs can be considered essentially uncorrelated.

It can be seen that the correlation method provides more useful information than the contingency procedure. Even when only the seven pairs having correlation coefficients of magnitude greater than 0.35 are considered, a quite clear and reasonable pattern emerges. The coefficients indicate strong positive associations among the four variables hickory nut, sumpweed, chenopod, and sunflower, and show this group of four to be, in turn, dissociated from the variable maygrass. Also, maygrass is dissociated from the "unidentified" category, a variable probably consisting primarily of crushed chenopod seeds. Rank—order correlation methods can measure a relationship between two variables (in this case a "variable" is a single identifiable food substance), expressing the relationship in an easily understandable number ranging from −1.0 ("perfect" negative correlation) to +1.0 ("perfect" positive correlation); significance levels for given correlation coefficients are also easily obtained. The data are used to better advantage, and more subtle data interrelationships can be evaluated with little computational effort.

In order to define the patterns of data variation, a principal components factor analysis was performed on the rank-order correlation matrix. The variables "unidentified" and "plant/fruit skin" were excluded from the factor analysis because of uncertainty of the exact contents, and "squash" and "grape" were excluded because each occurs only once. In the principal components solution to the nine-variable correlation matrix, the first two factors together account for 46.9% of the variance (see Table 24.5). Factors 3—9 were discarded for the analysis, and the resulting factor matrix is presented as Table 24.6.

Both factors are bipolar group factors, and are nonoverlapping. The first factor is loaded negatively on the familiar group hickory nut/sumpweed/ chenopod/sunflower, and positively on maygrass. All five of these foods were potentially storable in the summer and fall, but the undeniable dissociation of maygrass from the other four foods appears to confirm Yarnell's (1969: 47) observation that there was apparently little surplus maygrass available for storage. As mentioned before, maygrass tends to be either present in quantity in the specimen, or completely absent, and was perhaps consumed immediately when discovered. Because maygrass can be expected where the soil has been disturbed, it is equally reasonable to suggest that it grew in or near the gardens, and was eaten in the early summer before the late summer— early fall harvesting of cultigens and the gathering of hickory nuts began. In his analysis of stratified Salts Cave material reclaimed by flotation, Yarnell —speaking of the upper levels of the excavation—

TABLE 24.6 Unrotated Factor Matrix for Nine Variables, Principal Components Solution[a]

Variables	Factor 1	Factor 2	Communality
Hickory nut	−0.71797[b]	0.05897	0.51896
Charcoal	−0.09875	−0.57269	0.33772
Chenopod	−0.65173	−0.16415	0.45170
Sumpweed	−0.67682	0.43487	0.64720
Maygrass	0.68138	0.26211	0.53298
Sunflower	−0.77457	−0.07164	0.60510
Rubus	0.08179	0.70866	0.50890
Animal remains	0.22503	−0.55433	0.35792
Strawberry	0.01139	0.51105	0.26130

[a]Only the first two factors were extracted for consideration.
[b]Loadings greater in magnitude than 0.50 are italicized.

reports "a vast increase of weedy herbaceous annuals, especially chenopod, amaranth, panic grass, and maygrass, which flourish on recently opened soils [page 117 of this volume]."

Factor 2 presents an opposition of animal remains and charcoal to *Rubus* and strawberry. Factor 2 is not readily interpretable, although one might tentatively suggest as an explanation for the bipolarity that blackberries, raspberries, and strawberries were not roasted before eating, hence would not be expected to load with charcoal, or with animal remains, which may represent material cooked before being eaten.

Rotating the two-factor matrix to the simple structure solution (Table 24.7) makes possible a graphical representation of the orthogonal factors (Figure 24.1). Again, considering loadings greater in magnitude than 0.50, the variables hickory nut, chenopod, sumpweed, and sunflower cluster together to the extreme right of the graph, dissociated from maygrass, the only variable with a high negative loading on factor 1. *Rubus* and strawberry appear near the top of the graph, in opposition to animal remains and charcoal, which appear at the extreme bottom. I do not consider it appropriate at this point to affix names to the two factors delineated in this analysis, nor is the factor analysis intended to test any particular proposition. I wish, however, to emphasize the consistency between the factor-analytic results and the correlation coefficients from which they are derived, as well as the convenience of the graphical representation of the orthogonal factors. At its

present stage of anthropological utilization, factor analysis can be more helpful in describing data interrelationships than in testing the validity of specific propositions.

Summary and Discussion

Quantitative data on materials from 27 Mammoth Cave human paleofecal specimens were analyzed with contingency, correlation, and factor analytic techniques. The correlation method is preferred over the contingency approach because the correlation coefficients are easier to interpret, and the correlation method takes better advantage of the ordinal scale in which the data are expressed. The factor analysis provides additional insight into the patterning of the variation and clustering of the variables.

A comparison with Yarnell's (1969) results indicates more similarities than differences. Rank–order correlation coefficients (Table 24.8) were calculated for the Salts Cave data given by Yarnell (1969: 42–43) for the ten variables common to the Salts and Mammoth Cave specimens. Correlations common to both Salts and Mammoth Cave data are the positive associations of the pairs chenopod–sumpweed and sumpweed–grape and the dissociations of the pairs hickory nut–maygrass, charcoal–*Rubus*, chenopod–maygrass, and maygrass–sunflower. Correlations noted in the Salts, but not the Mammoth material were the positive associations of the pairs charcoal–chenopod, charcoal–sumpweed, chenopod–grape, maygrass–*Rubus*, and maygrass–strawberry, and the dissociations of the pairs chenopod–strawberry, sumpweed–*Rubus*, sumpweed–strawberry, sunflower–*Rubus*, and sunflower–strawberry. In the Mammoth, but not the Salts data, were the positive correlations of the pairs hickory nut–chenopod, hickory nut–sumpweed, hickory nut–sunflower, chenopod–sunflower, sumpweed–sunflower, *Rubus*–squash, and *Rubus*–grape, and the negative correlation of the pair sumpweed–maygrass. In no case are there contradictory significant associations. Constituents found in the Salts paleofecal specimens, but not in those from Mammoth Cave are amaranth, panic grass, knotweed, sumac, gourd, blueberry, viburnum, and poke seeds, in-

TABLE 24.7 Varimax Rotated Factor Matrix for Nine Variables

Variables	Factor 1	Factor 2
Hickory nut	0.71408[a]	0.09513
Charcoal	0.12752	−0.56697
Chenopod	0.65918	−0.13105
Sumpweed	0.65401	0.46847
Maygrass	−0.69374	0.22739
Sunflower	0.77720	−0.03247
Rubus	−0.11745	0.70363
Animal remains	−0.19677	−0.56498
Strawberry	−0.03717	0.50982

[a]Loadings greater in magnitude than 0.50 are italicized.

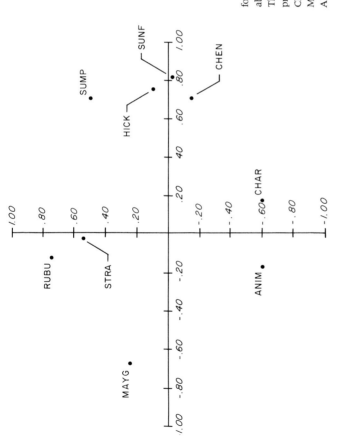

Figure 24.1 Graphical representation of factor loadings for rotated factors. Loadings on factor 1 are plotted along the abscissa, and those for factor 2 are plotted along the ordinate. This graph was drawn directly from the printed output of program FACTOR. Abbreviations: HICK = Hickory nut, CHAR = Charcoal, CHEN = Chenopod, SUMP = Sumpweed, MAYG = Maygrass, SUNF = Sunflower, RUBU = Rubus, ANIM = Animal remains, STRA = Strawberry.

TABLE 24.8 Kendall Rank-Order Correlation Coefficients between Pairs of Some Materials Found in 100 Salts Cave Paleofecal Specimens, with Levels of Significance[a]

Correlation coefficients					Levels of significance					
	Hickory nut	Charcoal	Chenopod	Sumpweed	Maygrass	Sunflower	Rubus	Squash	Grape	Strawberry
Hickory nut		0.115	0.845	0.983	0.001	0.350	0.168	0.247	0.968	0.450
Charcoal	0.11		0.019	0.016	0.359	0.925	0.003	0.536	0.622	0.487
Chenopod	−0.01	0.16		0.001	0.001	0.917	0.057	0.850	0.003	0.001
Sumpweed	−0.00	0.16	0.24		0.104	0.408	0.012	0.085	0.046	0.002
Maygrass	−0.34	−0.06	−0.24	−0.11		0.003	0.001	0.400	0.933	0.001
Sunflower	−0.06	−0.01	−0.01	−0.06	−0.20		0.010	0.058	0.119	0.031
Rubus	−0.09	−0.20	−0.13	−0.17	0.31	−0.17		0.083	0.515	0.632
Squash	−0.08	0.04	0.01	−0.12	0.06	0.13	0.12		0.770	0.906
Grape	0.00	0.03	0.20	0.14	−0.01	−0.11	−0.04	0.02		0.298
Strawberry	−0.05	−0.05	−0.30	−0.21	0.25	−0.15	−0.03	−0.01	−0.07	

[a]Data from Yarnell (1969: 42–43).

sect fragments, snail shell, and acorn shell. Because he was using a wet-method analysis, Stewart was able to identify plant skin, fruit skin, animal skin, and meat. Small amounts of fish scales, fish bones, and small animal bones were found in both the Mammoth and Salts Cave specimens. Unusual discoveries in the Mammoth Cave materials were the foot of a small turkey in Specimen 5 (identified by Joel Cracraft, University of Illinois at the Medical Center, Chicago), a small stone in Specimen 10 and small stones in Specimen 25, and a piece of mica in Specimen 17.

The correlation and factor analytic results compare favorably to LeBlanc's findings (already discussed). The positive associations of sumpweed with chenopod and hickory nut with chenopod, and the dissociations of maygrass with chenopod and maygrass with hickory nut are paralleled in the Mammoth Cave results (see Table 24.4 and Figure 24.1)

When compared with the 100 samples analyzed by Yarnell, the Mammoth Cave data corpus is smaller in both number of specimens and number of identified food materials. Despite the smaller amount of available information, the analyses carried out seem to suggest close similarity in subsistence strategies between the aboriginal Mammoth Cave explorers and those who mined gypsum and mirabilite in Salts Cave. On the basis of present evidence, we have no reason to suspect fundamental differences between the human groups that explored these two caves and exploited the environmental resources of the Mammoth Cave area.

Technical Notes

The χ^2 analysis of the presence/absence data was done by program CHICHI, version 3, a WATFIV FORTRAN program in the personal library of the writer. Yates's correction for continuity was applied in the calculation of the χ^2 values. Program CHICHI, version 3 is a modified and augmented version of a program originally published by Veldman (1967: 334–337). A source listing of the program will be sent upon request.

The Kendall rank-order correlation coefficients were calculated by program NONPAR CORR, from the Statistical Package for the Social Sciences (SPSS), Level H (Nie *et al.* 1970: 143–156). Two-tailed tests of significance for the Kendall coefficients were made by comparing each to the normal distribution with a standard deviation equal to

$$\left[\frac{(4n + 10)}{9n(n-1)}\right]^{1/2}$$

where n is the sample size. The test of significance is also carried out by program NONPAR CORR.

The factor analysis used was subprogram PA1 of program FACTOR, SPSS. Level H (Nie *et al.* 1970: 208–244, Nie and Hull 1971, 1972).

All programs were run on the IBM System/360-50 computer at Washington University.

Chapter 25

Pollen Analysis of Prehistoric Human Feces from Mammoth Cave

VAUGHN M. BRYANT, JR.
Texas A & M University

Introduction

In 1917 the principle of pollen analysis became accepted as a research technique following Lennart von Post's demonstration of its potentialities in the analysis of Scandinavian peat bogs (Faegri 1956). Since that time the techniques of pollen analysis have been utilized effectively in solving research problems in a number of diverse fields. However, it was not until 1938 that anyone demonstrated the usefulness of palynological data in the analysis of mammalian coprolitic remains (Laudermilk and Munz 1938). Even though this initial study was of nonhuman fecal material it showed that vertebrate digestive processes do not harm or destroy the durable exine, or outer wall, of pollen and spores.

The recognition that pollen analyses of human feces could serve as valuable clues to the understanding of prehistoric diet preferences, seasonal usage of camp sites, and as insights into the cultural use of plants was first noted by Martin and Sharrock (1964). Since their study, there have been a number of other palynological investigations of prehistoric human feces. In 1969 I conducted an analysis of 44 prehistoric human fecal specimens collected from archeological sites in the Amistad Reservoir area of southwest Texas (Bryant 1969); Napton and Kelso (1969) published the results of their pollen analysis of human fecal specimens from Lovelock Cave, Nevada; finally, this volume contains the results of Schoenwetter's analysis of eight paleofecal specimens from Salts Cave and my own examination of 17 specimens from Mammoth Cave.

The material examined in this study was collected from Mammoth Cave in 1970. The fecal specimens were originally sent to Robert B. Stewart, who conducted an analysis of their macrofossil contents. As part of our joint project I examined the same specimens for their microfossil (pollen) contents. Stewart's results are presented in the preceding chapter, but I have drawn upon some of his data in order to demonstrate certain apparent correlations in these paleofecal specimens between pollen contents and related macrofossil evidence.

Extraction and Identification

The 17 paleofecal specimens examined for their pollen content were recovered in a dried condition and were reconstituted into a moist state using the method developed by Callen and Cameron (1960). After the specimens had been reconstituted they were screened through a 20-mesh (841 μm) and a 65-mesh (210 μm) brass screen to recover plant and animal fragments such as seeds, bone, and hair. The liquid fraction recovered beneath the screens was processed for pollen contents using standard pollen extraction techniques consisting of a three step procedure: (1) removal of carbonates using hydrochloric acid; (2) removal of silicates by hydrous hydrofluoric acid; and (3) removal of nonpolliniferous organic materials by acetylation (a mixture of nine parts acetic anhydride with one part concentrated sulfuric acid). During the reconstitution and extraction process great care was exercised to prevent pollen contamination of the samples.

Identifications of pollen types in this report are based upon morphological comparisons with pollen samples in the Texas A & M Modern Pollen Reference Collection which is permanently stored in the Palynology Laboratory located on the Texas A & M University campus.

Analysis

A standard 200-grain pollen count was attempted for each sample as first suggested by Barkley (1934). Each identifiable pollen grain was counted and then recorded on tabular sheets. Grains so badly crushed or deteriorated as to be unidentifiable, fungal spores, and cryptogamic spores were excluded from the pollen counts. Well-preserved pollen that could not be identified was included in the counts as "unknowns."

The data from these pollen counts are presented in tabular form in Table 25.1. Pollen types are listed along the top of the table and the individual samples are indicated along the left side of the table. The total number of pollen grains counted in each sample is indicated along the right-hand side of the table. All numbers in the table indicate individual pollen percentages and *do not* represent the number of individual pollen grains counted in each category.

Pollen recovered from these samples were relatively scarce except in four samples (numbers 2, 3, 5, and 14) that produced 200-grain counts. Sample 13 did not contain any pollen and the amount of pollen recovered from the remaining twelve samples varied from 100–175 individual grains.

There are a number of possible explanations as to why some of these specimens contained abundant pollen while others contained either none or scarce amounts. The direct ingestion of pollen either by purpose or by accident can lead to a high abundance of pollen in fecal material. Absence of pollen suggests either seasonal absence of pollen (winter) or ingestion of foods not containing pollen. In human paleofecal samples from southwest Texas I found that the presence of high percentages of zoophilous (insect pollinated) pollen from plants such as agave and yucca were associated in the same samples with the recovery of crushed and broken anther fragments suggesting that flowers were a part of the diet. Similar high abundance of certain pollen types in other specimens from that study also suggested a spring and/or summer season when pollen production would be at its peak. Martin (1965) has suggested that total or near total absence of pollen in fecal samples suggests a winter season when few or no plants are in flower. In such cases the only major sources of pollen during the winter months would be restricted primarily to the previous spring and summer's pollen fallout now found mixed into the soil surface. On the other hand, absence or near absence of pollen may not always be an indicator of seasonality. In my analysis of prehistoric human fecal material from southwest Texas I discovered that the majority of specimens containing little or no pollen represented instances where meals had consisted primarily of one item such as bark, cactus pads, quids, and/or meat. Because each of these items is available during all seasons of the year their ingestion, coupled with a lack of pollen, clearly does not always indicate a winter season.

Pollen Types

Some of the pollen types such as pine, oak, hickory, and hackberry represented in these fecal

TABLE 25.1 Percentages of Pollen Observed in Prehistoric Human Feces from Mammoth Cave

Pollen types

Sample no.	Pinus	Carya	Quercus	Celtis	Betula	Populus	Ulmus	Juglans	Salix	Liquid-ambar	Cheno-Ams	Gramineae	Malvaceae	Ericaceae	Rosaceae
1	3	2									11.5	1	1		3.5
2											5	1		0.5	
3		1									38	1.5			
4	1	3									80	4			
5		0.5									2				
6			1				2				22.5	8	2	4	
7						1					54	9			
8		6									26	65			
9	8						8			0.5	9				
10	43		23	7.5	1.5					3	7.5				
11	8		11.5		0.5							44.5			2
12	28	43	13				1	4				4			
13	NO POLLEN														
14	53	20.5	5	1				2		1					
15	6	6				0.5			0.5		54	6		1	
16	1	10									52	4	5		2
17	3	3	6									4.5			

Pollen types

Sample no.	Onagraceae	Cyperaceae	Caryophyllaceae	Ranunculaceae	cf. Rhamnus	Ambrosiaceae	Liguliflorae	Artemisia	Other Composites	Acorus	Liliaceae	Unknowns	Total percentage	Pollen counts
1	1	0.5				26	48		2.5				100	137
2						1				92.5			100	200
3						59.5							100	200
4						7			4	96		1	100	141
5						1			0.5				100	200
6						59.5			3				100	102
7						11			22				100	100
8						2			1			.	100	101
9						28.5			44.5				100	129
10		5.5				6		0.5	2.5			1	100	162
11		2				23			11				100	112
12						3			1			1	100	151
13						NO POLLEN							100	
14			2.5	1	2	1			2				100	200
15						15			9				100	100
16			1			6			30		83		100	116
17									0.5				100	175

samples probably do not have cultural significance. Instead those pollen types are present as a result of accidental ingestion. In some cases those pollen types can lead to speculations about seasonality, but such speculations must be made cautiously. Other pollen types, such as Chenopod—Amaranths, found in these fecal specimens are more significant as indicators of diet or of other possible ethnobotanical usage of the specific plants involved. In the following annotated list of pollen types I offer comments as to which types might fit into each of these two categories, and suggest what possible significance each pollen type might have.

Arboreal Pollen

Pinus. Pine pollen is present in ten of the samples yet it appears as a dominant type in only three samples (numbers 10, 12, and 14). Pines, in general, produce an abundant amount of pollen all of which is light and well-suited to airborne travel. Pine pollen can easily travel great distances and can sometimes dominate the pollen rain even in areas where pines are not a floral component of the immediate local vegetation (Bent and Wright 1963). It is probable that most, if not all, of the pine pollen found in these fecal samples was ingested accidently. The significant percentages of pine pollen found in Samples 10, 12, and 14 could be interpreted as a clue to seasonality.

Carya. The *Carya* pollen could have come from either hickory or pecan trees in the vicinity of Mammoth Cave. Like pine, *Carya* pollen is adapted to airborne travel and is abundantly produced. The macrofossil analyses of these specimens (pages 193—202 and Table 24.1) indicate the use of hickory nuts as a food item. However, the presence of hickory pollen in the specimens should not be used to infer the eating of hickory nuts. Hickory trees bloom in the early spring and the fruits mature in the fall at a time when little, if any, hickory pollen would be in the atmosphere or still adhering to leaf or branch surfaces. In these fecal samples the high percentages of *Carya* pollen in samples 12 and 14 correlate with similar high percentages of pine pollen in the same samples and thus suggest deposition in the spring.

Quercus. Oak pollen is another of the anemophilous, or airborne, pollen types which one would expect to find in paleofeces from a region such as central Kentucky where oaks are a component of the local vegetation. As is characteristic among anemophilous plants, oak is a heavy pollen producer and its pollen is suited for airborne transport. The presence of oak pollen in six of the samples should not be considered as an indicator of acorn usage. Acorns, like hickory nuts, mature in the late summer and early fall and would be collected at a time of minimum oak pollen availability. The relatively high values of oak pollen in at least two of these specimens (10 and 12) seem to indicate seasonality.

Other Arboreal Pollen Types. Seven other arboreal, or tree pollen, types are represented in these Mammoth Cave paleofeces. In most cases their presence suggests accidental ingestion. *Celtis* (hackberry) pollen occurs in two specimens yet in one of them (Sample 14) it is represented by only a single grain. In Sample 10, however, I found 7.5% hackberry pollen which correlates with high percentages of pine and oak pollen in the same sample suggesting spring or early summer seasonality. No inference of hackberry seed usage should be derived from the presence of its pollen in these fecal specimens. Like oak and hickory, hackberry seeds are produced long after the pollen is dispersed. In tests made with the fruits of cactus and the leaves of agave (Bryant 1969) I found that the period between flowering and maturation of the fruits was sufficient for the total loss of pollen from the leaves, stems, and fruits of the plants studied. By the time of full maturation, rain, wind, and other disturbances had dislodged any pollen grains that might have accidentally fallen on the plant during its pollen dispersal period.

The occurrence of *Betula* (birch), *Populus* (poplar), *Ulmus* (elm), *Juglans* (walnut), *Salix* (willow), and *Liquidambar* (sweetgum) pollen in these specimens seems to be the result of accidental ingestion because all of them occur in low percentages. These pollen types are, for the most part, airborne and are capable of being carried long distances from their source. In addition, it is quite possible that in the late fall or winter a few of these grains could be recycled from the soil surface into the atmosphere by winds or other forms of disturbance. Therefore, specific inferences as to seasonality should not be attempted for these six arboreal pollen types when represented by low percentages.

Nonarboreal Pollen Types

Chenopod—Amaranth. Pollen analysts tend to lump many genera of the Chenopodiaceae with the genus *Amaranthus* since their pollen grains are morphologically similar and almost impossible to distinguish from one another with the use of a light microscope. Plants from this group such as goosefoot and amaranth are known to have been used throughout many areas of North America as an important food source. The Mammoth—Salts Cave region is no exception. Yarnell (1969) reported the remains of *Chenopodium* (chenopod) seeds in 87 of the 100 Salts Cave paleofecal specimens he examined and Stewart found chenopod seeds in 18 of the 27 Mammoth Cave specimens he examined. My analysis disclosed Cheno—Am pollen in 12 of the 17 samples; in four of those (Samples 4, 7, 15, and 16) Cheno—Am pollen reached frequencies greater than 50%. Bohrer (1968) reported that examination of modern surface samples show Cheno—Am pollen percentages exceed 50% only in areas where dense thickets of *Chenopodium* are the only major anemophilous pollen producer. Whereas accidental ingestion seems to be the probable source of pine, hickory, oak, and hackberry pollen in the Mammoth Cave samples, the high Cheno—Am pollen counts seems to be directly correlated with the eating of *Chenopodium* seeds. In the examination of human fecal material from southwest Texas I found that samples with high percentages of Cheno—Am pollen also contained abundant *Chenopodium* seeds. This suggests that *Chenopodium* seeds, collected and winnowed by primitive methods, contain abundant concentrations of *Chenopodium* pollen. This fact undoubtedly accounts for the 92% correlation I found between the presence of Cheno—Am pollen and that of *Chenopodium* seed remains in these Mammoth Cave paleofecal specimens. Of the 12 specimens that contained Cheno—Am pollen, all but one also contained *Chenopodium* seeds (compare microfossil and macrofossil contents of Samples 1—17, Tables 24.1 and 25.1).

Gramineae. Grass pollen was found in 12 of the 17 samples and none of it was from domesticated species such as *Zeas mays* (maize). Grass is an anemophilous plant, thus its pollen is dispersed by the wind. As such it could be expected to occur in limited quantities in any of the specimens. In the only sample (8) containing a high percentage of grass pollen (65%), chewed stems and leaves of *Phalaris caroliniaria* (maygrass) were abundantly present. A similar correlation between high percentages of grass pollen and presence of chewed grass stems and leaves in prehistoric human fecal remains has been noted by Martin and Sharrock (1964).

Ambrosieae. Plant species of this group of composites are anemophilous and are abundant pollen producers (ragweed and sumpweed are two of the better known members of this group). The presence of this pollen type in paleofecal matter does not necessarily indicate ethnobotanical usage of the plant, although in some isolated cases it might suggest such usage. In the present series, 15 of the 17 samples contained some Ambrosieae pollen. The two specimens with over 50% Ambrosieae pollen (3 and 6) also contained sumpweed seeds. This correlation may or may not be accidental; only a larger sampling could determine statistical validity.

Liguilflorae. Dandelions represent one of the major types in this group of composites. Dandelion pollen was present in only one specimen (1) where it comprised almost 50% of the total pollen. No recognizable dandelion plant parts, other than the pollen, were found but crushed flower petals could have passed unnoticed or may have been located in the portion of the specimen not selected for examination. Dandelion pollen is not normally airborne and is rarely ingested accidentally by humans. I believe that the high occurrence of dandelion pollen in Sample 1 represents the purposeful eating of flowers and/or leaves containing pollen that had fallen from the flowers.

Other Composites. Helianthus (sunflower) pollen is included in this category together with other composite pollen of similar morphology. These plants produce low quantities of pollen and depend upon insects to disperse it. Therefore only minor amounts of their pollen is usually found in the atmosphere. I found this type of composite pollen in 14 of the 17 samples I examined. In three of these (Samples 7, 9, and 16), where it reaches significant levels, there is a 100% correlation between the presence of high percentages of *Helianthus*-type pollen and the presence of sunflower seeds in the same specimens. Like the other composites already discussed, this apparent correlation between pollen and seed remains seems to be fairly reliable but must be tested further to obtain true statistical significance.

Liliaceae. In one specimen (number 17) 83% of the pollen came from an unidentifiable plant member of the lily family. Plants in this family are low pollen producers and are insect pollinated. In studies of prehistoric human fecal material from sites in southwest Texas I found that high percentages of liliaceous pollen were directly correlated with the presence of crushed anther fragments in the same specimens. Thus in some cases high percentages of liliaceous pollen result from the eating of floral parts and/or inflorescenses. I believe this may be the explanation for the very high percentages of liliaceous pollen in Mammoth Cave Sample 17.

Acorus. Sweetflag is a herbaceous plant that grows best in wet meadows, swamps, and on the banks of streams. Sweetflag, like the liliaceous plants, is insect pollinated and its pollen does not normally become airborne. Thus, the high percentages of sweetflag pollen in paleofeces Samples 2 and 5 undoubtedly represent the eating of flower parts and/or inflorescences. Schoenwetter, in his analysis of paleofeces from Salts Cave (Chapter 6 in this volume), also notes the presence of high percentages of sweetflag pollen in two samples. This confirms that these flowers were sometimes used as food in the Salts—Mammoth Cave area. Because sweetflag blooms in the late spring and early summer, its flowers could be eaten at anytime during these periods. Storage of sweetflag flowers for use in later months seems unlikely.

Other Nonarboreal Pollen Types. In addition to the types already discussed there were nine other pollen types found during the course of this study. For the most part each occurrence of these other pollen types can be attributed to probable accidental ingestion since none of them occurs in frequencies greater than a few percent.

Seasonality. Spring seasonality can be inferred from the pollen contents of at least three specimens. Specimens 10, 12, and 14 contain a dominance of pollen from arboreal plants that bloom in the spring. Because these pollen types would not be eaten with the seeds of these plants, it must be assumed that the pollen represents accidental ingestion from other sources, such as drinking water. Such high percentages of arboreal pollen most likely would be present in available water sources only during peak pollen dispersal periods in the spring.

Late spring and/or summer seasonality can be assumed for four of these paleofecal deposits (Samples 1, 2, 5, and 17). Sample 1 is dominated by dandelion pollen that probably resulted from the eating of flowers. Dandelions bloom over a long period beginning in the early spring and lasting until late fall, hence Sample 1 must have been deposited within this period of time. I believe that the high percentages of monocot pollen in Samples 2, 5, and 17 also resulted from the eating of flowers. Because most monocots tend to bloom in the late spring and/or the early summer, I presume these three samples were deposited at that season.

Winter seasonality is more difficult to determine. In human paleofeces the absence of pollen altogether, or the presence of pollen from such storable economic plants as composites, chenopods, and grasses generally suggest winter seasonality. Using these criteria, with caution, I suggest that six of the samples (3, 4, 6, 7, 15, and 16) may represent late fall and/or winter seasonality.

Seasonality for the remaining four paleofecal samples (8, 9, 11, and 13) should not be inferred from their pollen contents alone. Instead, it is necessary to examine the pollen evidence in light of what macrofossils also were present in each sample. Sample 8, for example, contains abundant maygrass pollen in conjunction with maygrass and chenopod seeds. There is no clear pollen or macrofossil evidence in Sample 8 to suggest any season other than late fall and/or winter. In general, the present evidence suggests that maygrass was not stored but was primarily harvested and eaten immediately as it ripened during the months of June and July (Yarnell 1969, Marquardt this volume). Thus it is possible that Sample 8 may represent a summer deposit. Nevertheless, I contend that because maygrass and chenopod seeds are both storable, Sample 8 could just as easily represent a fall or winter deposit. Sample 9 is dominated by composite pollen combined with the seeds of sunflower and wild strawberry. Wild strawberries are not well suited for storage and were probably eaten fresh. With that assumption in mind, I suggest paleofecal Sample 9 is a spring season deposit. Sample 11 contains abundant maygrass pollen coupled with blackberry and/or raspberry, maygrass, and squash seeds. The presence of blackberry and/or raspberry seeds indicates summer seasonality since they, like strawberries, were probably eaten fresh. Paleofecal Sample 13 had no pollen but did contain both maygrass and sunflower seeds. The only other macrofossil evidence in Specimen 13 is the outer skin of some as yet unidentified fruit. Taken as a whole, the evidence is too inconclusive to indicate seasonality. As already stated, absence of pollen may, or may not, represent winter seasonality; presence of storable seeds suggests, but does not confirm, winter seasonality because they

can be eaten during any season of the year; and, the presence of an unidentified fruit skin may or may not suggest summer seasonality depending upon the species of fruit and whether or not it was storable.

Summary

The examination and analysis of these 17 prehistoric human fecal specimens from Mammoth Cave are significant because the results can be used to infer certain probable diet practices and seasonality. The pollen evidence suggests that dandelion flowers and/or their leaves may have been eaten as part of the diet. Pollen from the flowers of a liliaceous plant and the flowers of sweetflag indicate that these flowers also were used as food. Composite pollen in some specimens corresponds well with the presence of composite seeds in the same specimens. This apparent correlation adds strength to the assumption that both sumpweed and sunflower seeds were occasionally eaten. However, the strongest correlation in the paleofecal remains between any specific pollen type and seeds from the same plant is that of chenopod. As noted earlier, there is ample evidence to support the conclusion that the presence of large amounts of Cheno—Am pollen in paleofecal material is generally an excellent clue to chenopod seed usage.

Chapter 26

Mammoth Cave Materials in Museum Collections

PATTY JO WATSON

Washington University

Much of the material collected by N. C. Nelson during the period of his excavations in the Mammoth Cave Vestibule is stored in three drawers in an old exhibit hall on the third floor of the American Museum of Natural History. The drawers are labeled:

#583 1916–55 Mammoth Cave, Kentucky Nelson #1 Edmonson Co.

#584 1916–55 Mammoth Cave, Kentucky Nelson #2 Edmonson Co.

#585 1916–55 Mammoth Cave, Kentucky Nelson #3 Edmonson Co.

Each drawer contains a rather heterogeneous array of objects:

Drawer 583, Nelson #1

20.1/136 A, B, and D—Three big sticks 2.5–3 cm in diameter and 38, 24, and 21 cm long, respectively; all are battered on one end as though they had been used as pestles (the longest one is battered on both ends).

20.1/137 A—Small bunch of modern cane tied with a string, probably from the torch-burning experiments Nelson mentions (1917: 36, footnote). One piece is charred at one end.

20.1/137 A to O—Seemingly aboriginal canes tied in a bundle with string and all fairly large (1.2–2 cm diameter), all but one charred at one end.

20.1/138 A to D—A, B, and C are sticks, D is the bark tie around them (but it is loose as though the original bundle was larger). The tie is made of several loops (with a square knot) and is about 5 cm in diameter. The sticks are about 33 cm long, 0.5—1.4 cm in diameter, and all are charred at one end.

20.1/139 Bark tie with a square knot.

20.1/140 Three fragments of cordage, all two-ply Z-plied, one is very neat and only 2 mm thick, the others are frazzled and worn.

20.1/141 About nine gourd fragments.

20.1/143 to 145—Fragments of chert nodules in two boxes labeled: "143–5 *M. C. Interior* Some Illustrated"; perhaps these came from Flint Alley.

20.1/146 Bone punch or flaker.

20.1/151 Hollow bone shaft with both ends sliced off.

20.1/154 Bone awl made from a small ulna (maximum dimensions 9 × 1 cm).

20.1/155 Bone punch or flaker.

20.1/166 Box of chipped stone; about 75 pieces of chert,

211

mostly nondescript flakes. One is a poor core, one large flake might have been a scraper.

20.1/167   Two bell-shaped pestles, probably limestone; the
20.1/178   bottoms are not battered.

20.1/182   A small bone awl.
20.1/189   Fragment of worked shell; a piece of clam shell from near the hinge worked into an object 5 × 0.7 cm, pointed at both ends.

Miscellaneous Unnumbered Items

In the same box with the worked shell (20.1/189) are two clam shells, unworked, and a note that says "Mammoth Cave digging. Some illustrated." (The ulnar awl, 20.1/154 is also in this box.)

In another box with a few numbered bone tools (20.1/146, 151, 155, and 182) are eleven awls on large splinters of long bone, three antler tips, and a pin or awl made of a long thin piece of bone.

Finally, there is a box containing fine-grained, red, sandy cave fill; the box is labeled, "*Mammoth Cave* Laminated Red Earth below Indian Refuse."

Drawer 584, Nelson #2

20.1/150   Long, polished bone shaft.
20.1/175   Awl made of what is probably a deer ulna.
20.1/192   A polished antler.
20.1/202   A box containing many dozens of charred sunflower seeds. Twenty-one separate achenes are mounted on a card labeled: "*Helianthus annuus* Mammoth Cave, Ky. Verified C. B. Heiser 6/49 N. C. Nelson." There is a litter of fragments, all charred, in the bottom of the box and three clumps of seeds accompanied by a note reading . . . "Large mass soaked in Duco solution (will soften with acetone) 1947. Sample sent to Dr. Charles B. Heiser, Jr. Asst. Prof. Botany, Indiana U. June 1949. See correspondence." Another note in the box reads: "Charred seeds from Mammoth Cave. Collected by N. C. Nelson, Trench W-III. These have been dipped in acetone–duco cement solution and can be softened with either acetone or amylacetate. *Helianthus annuus*, cult. 'sunflower' C. B. Heiser 1949."

Miscellaneous, Unnumbered Items

Two boxes of "cave refuse" from Mammoth Cave Trench III, each side "Top cover to Indian Refuse (to be carefully examined)."

Drawer 585, Nelson #3

20.1/216   Modern looking corn cob.
20.1/142   a and b—One large fragment and one small fragment (the latter probably broken off the former) of human paleofeces; the larger fragment is approximately 8 × 3 cm.

Miscellaneous, Unnumbered Items

Twelve boxes of various kinds of mussel shells; the identifications (which Nelson published in his 1917 report) are in the boxes on paper slips.

Lying loose in the drawer and filling nearly half of it is animal bone and antler labeled "By Products of Food Mammoth Cave, Kentucky 1917 N. C. Nelson"; included with this bone is a very large vertebra with a process 19 cm long (it was even longer originally, there is a break at the end of it).

A small box containing some tiny bones, some stone chips, and cave fill labeled "Mammoth III. Among rocks below Indian refuse 3½–4 ft."

With Col. Bennett Young's collection in the Research Annex of the Museum of the American Indian is a single slipper from Mammoth Cave:

5/2216   Nearly complete slipper; 19.5 cm long on the bottom, 7 cm wide at the ball of the foot, worn through at heel and toe. Chevron twining, elements 4–5 mm wide, ties present.

The slipper from Mammoth Cave at the U. S. National Museum was mentioned earlier (page 168). It is about 22 cm long, chevron twined, and is accompanied by the following note: " 416634 Gift of Rev. Dr. T. Peterson 2189 From Mammoth Cave Kentucky Collector Dr. Peterson, C. S. P. One Indian Sandal. Entered May 14, 1920." (See Figure 21.1).

Part IV ABORIGINAL USE OF OTHER CAVES IN MAMMOTH CAVE NATIONAL PARK

Chapter 27   Lee Cave[1]

PATTY JO WATSON
Washington University

It was not until very recently that any large caves were known to exist in Joppa Ridge, southwest of Mammoth Cave Ridge, in Mammoth Cave National Park. However, in 1968 Gordon L. and Judith E. Smith of the Cave Research Foundation found the entrance to a major Joppa Ridge cave that includes a large portion of main trunk passage similar to parts of Upper Salts (Figure 27.1). Within this passage is a complex and abundant series of cave minerals (see Table 27.1) as well as archeological materials reminiscent of those in Salts and Mammoth Caves

The cave was named for T. E. Lee, a famous local cave explorer of the 1870s [and one of the discoverers of Little Al(ice)], whose name is inscribed on the wall of a canyon passage at the bottom of the pit entrance.

The prehistoric remains in Lee Cave occur only in the eastern portion of Marshall Avenue, the long, dry, main trunk passage. The Indians probably entered Marshall Avenue from Deer Park

Hollow at the eastern end of this avenue where it now terminates in breakdown. At any rate, they did not enter as we do now by repelling, or climbing a cable ladder down a pit opening in Sand Cave Hollow, then squeezing through a 20—30-cm-wide, 5-m-deep canyon to wet breakdown chambers and a crawlway leading to the west end of the big walking passage. Near this junction, at Cave Research Foundation survey station J25, is a partially burned, 4-m-long log, 20 cm in diameter. A radiocarbon determination on charred fragments of this log was made by the UCLA Institute of Geophysics and Planetary Physics. The resulting reading is 4100 B.C. ± 60 (Table 31.2), nearly 2000 years older than the date on cane from K83 in Marshall Avenue (2250 B.C. ± 65; see Table 31.2). It is probable that the log predates Indian exploration of Lee Cave, and was probably carried into the cave by a big flood of nearby Green River (Freeman, Smith, Poulson, Watson, and White 1973). The river is now some 85 feet lower in elevation than the log, but floods of 60 feet have been recorded for Green River more than once in the past 20 years.

Undeniable remains of aboriginal human activity begin at survey point J56, but there is also

[1]For a detailed summary description of Lee Cave geology and biology see Freeman, Smith, Poulson, Watson, and White 1973.

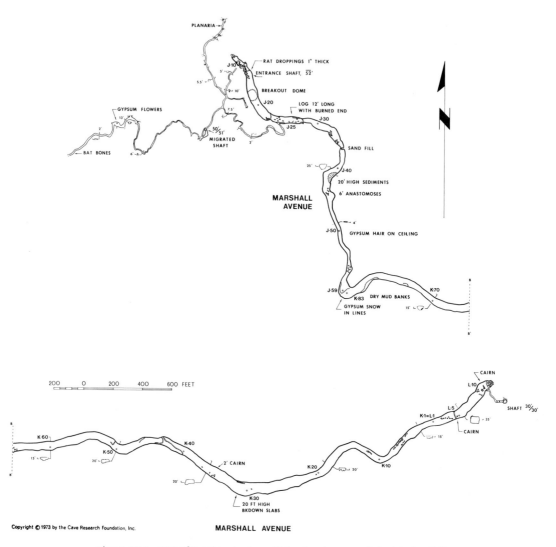

Figure 27.1 Map of Lee Cave in Joppa Ridge showing area of aboriginal activity.

evidence here of pack rat and stream activity. Clearly *in situ* material begins at K84 where cane fragments and cane charcoal are strewn along the floor in the center of the passage (cf. Figure 27.2). There is also cane along the south wall and charcoal scattered on the breakdown near the north wall. Canes for radiocarbon dating were collected from the center of the passage at K83; as already noted, the resulting determination is 2250 B.C. ± 65 (Table 31.2).

At K82 charcoal and cane are scattered along a ledge on the south wall (including cane fragments more than 30 cm long), charcoal is present on the breakdown near the north wall, and canes and charcoal are strewn down the center of the passage.

At K81 cane and charcoal continue in the center of the passage and along the south wall; there is charcoal along the north wall and three fragments of cane (all about 1 cm in diameter and less than

TABLE 27.1 Sulfate Minerals Identified from Lee Cave[a]

Mineral	Formula	Occurrence
Gypsum	$CaSO_4 \cdot 2H_2O$	Floor crusts Loose and curved crystals Wall effervescences
Epsomite	$MgSO_4 \cdot 7H_2O$	Mainly wall effervescences
Hexahydrite	$MgSO_4 \cdot 6H_2O$	Wall effervescences
Blödite	$Na_2Mg(SO_4)_2 \cdot 4H_2O$	Main constituent of floor crusts
Mirabilite	$Na_2SO_4 \cdot 10H_2O$	Accessory mineral in floor crusts

[a]From Freeman, Smith, Poulson, Watson, and White 1973: Table 1.

cane and charcoal are also present along the north wall and in the center of the passage. Sulfate minerals are conspicuously present on both walls here. Between K79 and K77 mineral is piled in drifts on the floor near the north wall; cane and charcoal are present throughout the passage. At K76 there are three long pieces of cane (1 m long by 1 cm in diameter) near the south wall and cane and charcoal in the center of the passage; mineral fragments are still present on and below the north wall. From K75 to K73 the breakdown slope to the north wall is steep and there is very little charcoal or cane on it. These items are most abundant in the center of the passage. Between K73 and K68 cane and charcoal are concentrated in the passage center on the surface and beneath breakdown rocks. At K68 there is a scatter of cane and cane charcoal, and a grass tie fragment (with

30 cm long). This pattern persists from K81 to K80. Six meters west of K79 cane and charcoal become more abundant along the north wall where there are canes up to 60 cm long. At K79 there is a pile of eight canes 15—30 cm long near the south wall;

Figure 27.2 Lee Cave. Cane and charcoal fragments on the floor of Marshall Avenue.

Figure 27.3 Lee Cave. Pile of extraordinarily long canes *in situ* near north wall of Marshall Avenue; survey point K57.

square knot) on top of the breakdown on the north side of the passage.

Between K64 and K59 it appears the Indians were walking along the center of the passage and also on top of the breakdown to the left, as was perhaps the case between K79 and K76. Between K84 and K79 most of the traffic was along the south wall and center, whereas between K75 and K64 almost everyone kept to the center of the passage, although at K63 there is a pile of cane and a tie fragment near the right wall. At K58, behind a rock and up the breakdown slope on the left, is a bundle of about 18 brushy small canes approximately 55 cm long and 1 cm in diameter; they are all charred at the larger ends but there is no tie. At K57, also near the north wall, is a pile of about 30 canes 2.5 m long; the individual canes are 1–2 cm in diameter (Figure 27.3).

A sample of organic substance found in the center of the passage at K29 was given to Yarnell for identification because at first it was thought to be paleofecal matter; it is not paleofecal matter, but a positive identification has not yet been made.

Between K35 and K36 is a crude cairn of limestone rocks; it is covered with fallen sulfate crystals and has several fragments of cane charcoal on it, so is seemingly aboriginal. There is a second cairn of loosely piled rock at L10, the foot of the terminal breakdown (Figure 27.4). Under the edge of one of the rocks in this cairn is a small fragment of cane charcoal and there are a few other charcoal bits on the cave floor around the pile. Both cairns are probably aboriginal; there is no trace of visitors to Marshall Avenue between the time the Indians left it and its discovery by Cave Research Foundation explorers. However, the purpose of the cairns is quite unclear. (A third possible, but much less obvious, cairn is present near survey point L5.)

As one continues from the K30s toward the

Figure 27.4   Lee Cave. Seemingly aboriginal cairn at survey station L10 in Marshall Avenue.

breakdown that terminates the eastern end of Marshall Avenue, debris becomes more and more sparse. From about K20 to the breakdown there are only scattered bits of charcoal along the passage floor. Despite this fact, aboriginal entry to Marshall Avenue at this point before the breakdown sealed the passage seems the most likely suggestion. There is a chert outcrop in the left wall at K11 but no clear-cut evidence that it was mined in prehistoric times.

Thus, it seems the Indians went into Marshall Avenue of Lee Cave perhaps to remove some of the exotic minerals, but did not use the cave intensively nor visit it often. The material they left there is cane torch debris for the most part, plus some wood and bark, a few grass ties, and the enigmatic cairns. The abundance and size of the cane suggests a ready source near the cave, probably a canebrake in Deer Park Hollow. The single radiocarbon determination from undeniably cultural remains is older than any from Salts or Mammoth Caves.

Chapter 28

Bluff Cave

PATTY JO WATSON

Washington University

Bluff, on the eastern end of Joppa Ridge, is a small cave (Figure 28.1) whose present entrance—wet and rather dangerous—is in the breakdown at the foot of a sink in Doyle Valley. Although this sink and breakdown arrangement is an unstable one in that new pieces of the sandstone caprock break off from time to time and old ones shift position as weathering—chiefly by water—progresses, it seems likely that the aboriginal entrance was approximately similar to the present one. The cave has long been inhabited by pack rats, but none of their leavings seems particularly fresh.

Evidence of pre-Columbian Indian use of this cave consists of some mining and smoke blackening on the walls plus a fairly thick scattering of torch debris among and under the small-sized limestone breakdown that covers the floor. Most of this torch debris comprises dry stalks of *Gerardia*, although some wood and cane fragments are also present.

As usual in these caves, there are no noticeable remains in the wet area around the breakdown, but beyond that is a short, dry passage running southwest from the sink. A short distance beyond the sink entrance, this passage becomes a crawl-way ending at survey station A8. There is charcoal in the crawlway, and beginning at A8 there are clear traces of mining on the walls (the gypsum crust is about 1 cm thick) as well as smoke blackening in some areas. On the floor are occasional fragments of *Gerardia* and a few possible *Solidago* stalks and wood fragments. By picking up the small breakdown rocks forming the passage floor, one can find many more pieces of charred material, especially

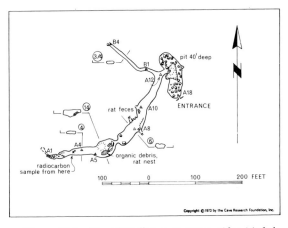

Figure 28.1 Map of Bluff Cave in Joppa Ridge (circled figures indicate ceiling heights in feet)

221

Gerardia in 8—10-cm lengths (some specimens found were as long as 21 cm). At one spot 33 *Gerardia* fragments (5—15 cm long and 0.2—1 cm in diameter) were recovered in about 30 min by removing one 8 × 30 cm rock, then picking through the smaller rocks and fine dust below it.

In the vicinity of A5 is another narrow squeeze-through where there are abundant pack rat remains (nut fragments, sticks and twigs, droppings, and a grass nest). Evidence of mining continues to A1 where there is a very tight squeeze into the cul-de-sac that ends the cave; the Indians almost certainly did not go beyond A1.

A sample for radiocarbon dating was taken on April 23, 1972, by collecting *Gerardia* stalks from under breakdown rocks over an area about 5 × 6.5 m near the A3 survey point. The determination from this sample is not yet available.

In sum, prehistoric Indians entered this rather uncomfortable little cave and mined gypsum from it using weed stalk torches for light (presumably there was no nearby cane stand). So far, no textile fragments, squash or gourd remains, human paleo-fecal specimens, or other artifacts have been found in Bluff Cave, but it is possible that intensive and extensive removal of breakdown would reveal some of these items.

Part **WYANDOTTE CAVE, INDIANA**

V

Chapter 29 Wyandotte Cave

PATTY JO WATSON
Washington University

Wyandotte Cave on a tributary of the Ohio—the Blue River—in southern Indiana (nine miles west of Corydon in Crawford County) contains evidence of aboriginal use reminiscent of that observed in the Mammoth Cave National Park caves some 75 miles to the south. Accordingly, trips were made into Wyandotte Cave to record the prehistoric remains and, if possible, to obtain material for radiocarbon dating.

One of the earliest historical documents referring to Wyandotte Cave is a letter written in 1818 (Adams 1820), in which reference is made to the presence in this cave of large quantities of epsom salts. Like many other caves in the general region, part of it had been mined for saltpeter during the War of 1812, and it was formerly called "the Indian Saltpetre Cave" and "Epsom Salts Cave." There is still an abundance of what seems to be epsomite in Wyandotte, and this may have been an attraction for the prehistoric people of the area just as it was for some of the early white settlers.

Fairly detailed early descriptions of Wyandotte Cave may be found in Stelle (1864) and Blatchley (1899). George Jackson, a member of the staff when the cave was privately owned and com-

mercialized, has published a more recent description of Wyandotte with photos of some of the prehistoric remains (Jackson 1953); Richard L. Powell (1968) provides an excellent geological summary.

Four thousand acres of land including the cave were bought for $1.25 an acre in 1820 by H. P. Rothrock, whose descendants retained the property until 1966 when the Indiana State Department of Natural Resources purchased Wyandotte Cave (and nearby Little Wyandotte Cave as well) with some 1100 acres of forest.

The entrance of Wyandotte is said by Blatchley to be 20 feet wide and 6 feet high; inside the opening is a large vestibule known as Faneuil Hall. Hence, the general situation is similar to both Salts and Mammoth Caves where there is a commodious room just inside the entrance, well sheltered but admitting some daylight. From here there is a tunnel-like passage—Columbian Arch—leading to Washington Avenue, the first big chamber of the cave interior and the first place where possible aboriginal remains are noticeable. These comprise woody material (twigs, sticks, branches) and many fragments of bark (probably from the shagbark hickory) as well as occasional tie fragments. These

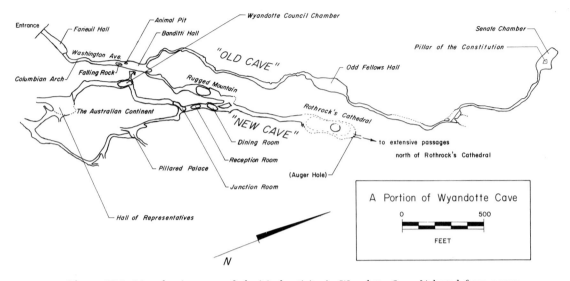

Figure 29.1 Map showing areas of aboriginal activity in Wyandotte Cave. [Adapted from a map prepared in 1966 by the Bloomington Indiana Grotto of the National Speleological Society.]

torch and campfire materials—bark fragments in particular are nearly ubiquitous—are strewn around and in the breakdown nearly everywhere in what is known as "the Old Cave" and in that part of the "New Cave" (discovered by the local white settlers in 1850) up to the Auger Hole at the north end of Rothrock's Cathedral. There are old reports of presumed moccasin tracks in some passages of the New Cave as first seen by whites, but there are no traces of these now nor of other aboriginal remains beyond the Auger Hole. Hence, the reports are hard to evaluate.

We were not able to check the southern extent of prehistoric debris, but the cave guides assured us it does not continue far beyond the south end of the Continent (Figure 29.1).

Besides the prehistoric and early historic remains in Washington Avenue and Banditti Hall, there are numerous fecal deposits left by some small animal, possibly raccoon. Much of the dung is packed with fish bones.

Two trips were made into Wyandotte. On the first we went to the left (west) out of Banditti Hall through the Old Cave to the Senate Chamber and the Pillar of the Constitution. The latter is an enormous stalagmite of white-banded aragonite 10 to 12 m in diameter.

Blatchley's account of his investigations in the Senate Chamber are reproduced at length here not only because he describes the excavations he made there, but also because that room and the Pillar are now much altered by the 75 years of human traffic since he visited them:

> The entire column is composed of "satinspar"—a rather soft, white, striated mineral, the purest form of carbonate of lime. From one side, near the base of the column has been removed by the Indians, or some prehistoric race in ages past, hundreds of cubic feet of this material.
>
> Up to 1877 it was generally supposed that the whites had made this excavation. . . .
>
> Prof. Collett, in 1877, found 3 glacial bowlders in the Senate Chamber, which, "from indications, such as wear and bruises, had been used as hammers or grinding pestles, and proved conclusively that that part of the Old Cave had been visited, if not occupied, by men of the Stone Age.
>
> Rev. H. C. Hovey, in 1882, first claimed that the excavation had been made by Indians "more than 1,000 years ago," and that the "round or oblong bowlders" of granite rock were the implements with which the ancient quarrymen wrought, being used "in breaking from this alabaster quarry blocks of a portable size and convenient shape."
>
> H. C. Mercer, in 1894, visited the quarry and mentions the finding, by Mr. Rothrock, of a pick

made of stag's antlers and states that 'the proof of Indian work at the spot was satisfactory and of a character never noticed and studied before the discovery of the site."

These constituted the recorded observations of the quarry up to the time of my first visit in July, 1896. It was then noted that the quantity of spalls and flakes of the material thrown over the side of the hill was very great, and that no digging had been done to discover the nature or thickness of the debris on top of the hill, nor to more fully verify the statement that the work had been done by Indians. My time being limited, no excavations were made at this visit, on a subsequent one, in November, 1896, I secured the services of a workman and shovels and again visited the place. Careful measurements showed that above the debris a space 8 feet long, 6 feet high and 5 feet wide of the hill on which the column rests was found to be covered with an area 14 feet square of the debris and through this, close alongside the base of the column, a trench was dug, 8 feet long, 3 feet wide, and to the solid stalagmite beneath. It averaged four feet 3 inches in depth—i.e., at that point the debris or pieces of quarried material and other matter was that thick. A perpendicular section through this trench disclosed the following layers:

1. Ashes in a compressed, damp bed, with occasional flakes of stalagmite intermingled — 14.0 inches
2. Charcoal — 1.0 inch
3. Ashes, with flakes of rock — 3.5 in.
4. Rectangular flakes of stalagmite or satin-spar, varying in size from an inch or 2 square to pieces 8 × 3 × 1 inches, or even larger, with occasional traces of charcoal intermingled — 28.0 in.
5. Charcoal — 0.5 in.
6. Flakes of stalagmite — 4.0 in.

Six quartzose bowlders, weighing from 3 to 6 pounds, were found scattered through the mass which we threw aside, 2 of them within a few inches of the bottom. They were worn with use, and on the surface of 2 or 3 of them were depressions which appeared to be finger marks due to excessive use. At any rate, they must have enabled the workman to retain the rock hammer more firmly in his grasp.

The remains of horns of five different deer, which mostly crumbled when disinterred, and numerous small bones, also too much decayed to identify to what animals they formerly belonged, were found at intervals in the trench.

By digging in a few other spots it was found that an area 14 × 14 feet, on top of this hill and at the base of the column, was covered to an average depth of three and one-half feet with the particles of stone quarried. In addition to this, no less than twenty tons of the material had been pitched over the hill. Much if not all, of this additional space was formerly occupied by stalagmitic material, the base of the column flaring outward on this side, and when the space already mentioned as having been quarried *above* the debris is taken into consideration, there is little doubt but that more than 1,000 cubic feet of the stalagmite has been broken loose.

In October, 1898, I visited the quarry for the third time, and dug in the debris for several hours. Eight additional bowlders of quartzose and many pieces of horn, crumbling bone and baked clay, were brought to light. Five wedge-shaped pieces of rock, one of flint, the others of limestone, were also found among the flakes of stalagmite. These had irregular notches in their edges showing that they, together with the horns found in the debris, were most probably used as wedges to pry loose the pieces of satin-spar after the latter **had been** cracked by the stone hammers. Such horns and wedges of stone have been found in a number of caves in Europe, where, ages ago, they were put to similar use [Blatchley 1899:147–151].

If Blatchley's description of his finds is accurate, then it seems quite possible that the quarrying of the Pillar of the Constitution was done aboriginally. The ash beds, charcoal layers, and especially the animal bone and antler are reminiscent of discoveries made in the excavations of Salts and Mammoth Cave Vestibules. Perhaps, however, there was also pottery in the Senate Chamber (the "baked clay" Blatchley mentions).

Although the area has undergone heavy disturbance over the past several decades, one can still see from looking at the Pillar that an appreciable amount of it has been hacked away, but it is certainly not possible to ascertain from inspection when this occurred nor who did it.

On our second trip into Wyandotte, we visited the outcrops of Lost River chert in the passage walls near the Pillared Palace. These chert beds played an important role in the geology of Wyandotte Cave (Powell 1968: 243), and were probably exploited by the prehistoric inhabitants of the area. The chert is dark gray, of reasonably good working quality, and occurs both in nodules and as a continuous seam or band in the lime-stone wall. Although chert is present in various parts of the cave, especially in the Dining-Room—Reception-Room passage north of the Continent, a room adjoining the Pillared Palace seems the least disturbed. Here there are masses of shatter and debitage on the floor, 15 cm deep or more, attest-ing to a pattern of bashing nodules or tabular chunks of chert from the wall and trimming them on the spot before taking them out. A brief inspec-tion of the debris revealed no tools or retouched pieces, nor did Blatchley find any, although he does report seeing numerous fragments of char-coal not now present.

The only other chert source we visited was the Ice House near the Ballroom about 2200 feet beyond the Auger Hole. There is no evidence that it had ever been used by the Indians.

On our second trip into Wyandotte we also collected material for radiocarbon dating as follows:

Sample 1. Bark and sticks from the floor of a high, narrow cleft opening off the Animal Pit which underlies a part of Washington Ave. The sticks and bark seemed undisturbed but the floor of the cleft contained a good deal of bat guano and animal dung (possibly raccoon), so the context is not of the best, and this sample has a low priority.

Sample 2. Bark and wood from beneath small breakdown rocks on top of Rugged Mountain. This sample was run: A.D. 240 ± 80 (Table 31.2).

Sample 3. Bark from beneath breakdown rocks on the floor of Wyandotte Council Chamber. Also under these rocks were some cigarette butts and matches. This sample was not run.

Sample 4. Seemingly undisturbed bark and sticks from beneath the huge break-down boulder, Fallen Rock (or Falling Rock) in Washington Ave. This sample was run: 910 B.C. ± 60 (Table 31.2).

From the viewpoint of prehistoric human use patterns, Wyandotte differs in several respects from Salts and Mammoth Caves. We saw no clear evidence of mining, although, of course, the epso-mite could have been scraped off without leaving distinct traces. There is a considerable difference in the nature of presumed aboriginal debris littering the cave floor. Indians apparently penetrated only the Old Cave and that part of the New Cave (exclu-sive of the New Discovery passage dug out in the 1940s) south of the Auger Hole. In these areas the most conspicuous remains are hickory bark and—in lesser quantity—sticks, tie fragments, and pieces of wood (the latter of uncertain age but perhaps some of it prehistoric). Blackening of walls and ceiling is apparent in many places, but this—as in Mammoth Cave—could be at least partially the result of nineteenth-century candles and lanterns. I saw no indisputable torch smudges (perhaps they are not to be expected with bark torches rather than cane ones), no textile frag-ments, no squash or gourd fragments, no human paleofecal material. Although there were some hickory nuts and acorns in a few places, they were almost certainly brought in by pack rats. Finally, the rather intense past activity in the Washington-Avenue—Banditti-Hall area by four-footed animals of some sort (possibly raccoons) is unlike the Salts Cave and Mammoth Cave situations.

Part VI

PREHISTORIC MINERS AND HORTICULTURISTS OF THE MAMMOTH CAVE AREA

Chapter 30

Prehistoric Miners

PATTY JO WATSON

Washington University

Work carried out over the past three years has amplified and augmented the picture presented in *The Prehistory of Salts Cave, Kentucky* (Watson *et al*. 1969: 57–64), without significantly altering it. Our knowledge of specific passage complexes and kinds of passages used by the Indians has increased, especially for Lower Salts and Lower Mammoth (pages 65ff, 186ff, Figures 10.1, 23.2, and 23.3). Observations in these passages demonstrate fairly clearly what was suspected earlier from knowledge of only one such passage (Indian Avenue of Lower Salts), i.e., that the aborigines penetrated remote, lower-level passages to reconnoiter for minerals or simply to explore the cave.

Investigation of other caves in Mammoth Cave National Park and of Wyandotte in southern Indiana makes it clear that the Salts Cave mineral exploitation pattern was not an isolated instance of mining, but was characteristic of the region. Exploitation of the specialized natural resources offered by the large, dry caves was especially intense in Mammoth Cave and, to a somewhat lesser degree, in Salts Cave, with Bluff Cave, Wyandotte Cave, and Lee Cave showing slighter evidences of use. The general situation is summarized in Table 30.1.

The more general cultural–historical aspects of prehistoric mining in these caves have to do with the themes of local use and probable trade of the cave resources. There is very little evidence that is relevant to these subjects, but a few points can be discussed briefly. The first concerns the manner in which the mining was organized. We are fairly confident about our knowledge of aboriginal mining techniques, but are much less certain of the social organizational context. This question is discussed in Watson *et al.* (1969: 60 and 72) and is further considered in this volume by James Schoenwetter (pages 57–58). He suggests that the rather standardized and limited diet evidenced by constituents of the paleofecal remains is probably representative of the local population and not just an elitist group. That is, the people who went into the cave were probably not members of special work-groups, but simply individuals who wanted or needed cave minerals for personal or family use. This suggestion that cave visitation was by mixed and generalized groups fits various bits of independent evidence from Upper Salts: Unmistakably child-sized slippers have been reported from Salts Cave (Young 1910: 307; Nelson collection in the American Museum of Natural History,

TABLE 30.1 Summary of Prehistoric Caving Activity

Cave	Activity
Upper Salts	Mineral mining (gypsum, mirabilite, possibly epsomite) widespread and intensive; heavy traffic.
Middle Salts (cf. Blue Arrow Passage)	Mining and traffic less than Upper Salts
Lower Salts	Mineral mining sporadic and limited; light traffic.
Upper Mammoth	Mineral mining widespread; heavier traffic than Upper Salts.
Lower Mammoth	Mineral mining more restricted than Upper Salts but more intensive than Lower Salts; chert also mined. Traffic intensity like Middle Salts in many passages, a few (the Boiled Egg E survey, the northern part of the G survey) like Lower Salts.
Lee	Exploring, no clear evidence for mining, although removal of the magnesium and sodium sulfates would probably not leave permanent traces; traffic intensity less than Middle Salts but more than Lower Salts. Probably short-term use.
Bluff	Limited mineral mining; light to medium traffic.
Wyandotte[a]	Mining of chert and possibly of epsom salts and aragonite (the latter from a massive formation now known as the Pillar of the Constitution). Traffic probably heavy (comparable to Upper Salts), but the evidence is more difficult to disentangle from the remains of recent, historical activity than in any of the other caves.

[a]It should be noted that one of the radiocarbon determination for prehistoric material from this cave is the youngest in our entire series (A.D. 240 ± 80).

page 170 of this volume, item 20.0/5765); the body of a presumed gypsum-miner found in Mammoth Cave—Lost John—is that of an adult male, whereas the only known Salts Cave aboriginal body—Little Al—is that of a preadolescent boy;

the numerous hanks of raw fiber found in Salts Cave (Young 1910; and pages 171, 173 here) might be thought to pertain to women's work rather than men's; our experiments quickly convinced us that the torches used by the aborigines are an extremely effective, readily manufactured, and easily managed means of illumination (Watson et al. 1969: 33–36; Ehman 1966). Hence, on the basis of the present evidence, it appears that the more accessible portions of the cave interiors could have been and probably were visited by any member of the population who wished to do so. However, I think it very unlikely that exploration and work in the complex lower-level passages was undertaken by any but the most experienced and knowledgeable cavers, probably most of whom were adult men. Furthermore, such trips to relatively remote and inaccessible parts of the cave were probably undertaken by small groups of three to six persons, and must have necessitated at least a modicum of planning. Cane torches burn at a steady and predictable rate, but care would have had to be taken to ensure an adequate supply of fuel, quite apart from the question of food and water supplies. Thus, I suggest that the physical nature of this special environment necessitated some specific structuring of deep-cave trips. This would have been most efficiently accomplished if—as is done today—the person who knew the cave best was trip leader and the rest of the party agreed to accede to his judgment.

Possible uses of the minerals available in the caves—gypsum and mirabilite—are discussed in the Salts Cave report (Watson et al. 1969: 57–60). The only new information to be added is that epsomite has now been identified as definitely present at least in Lower Salts (page 69). We continue to be impressed with the medicinal potential of the sodium and magnesium sulfates (mirabilite and epsomite, respectively), and to be somewhat puzzled by the apparent intensity of effort to obtain calcium sulfate (gypsum) as well. It still seems likely—because of the large quantities removed—that some or all of these substances not only were used locally, but also were traded to areas outside the cave region.

Chapter 31

Prehistoric Horticulturists

PATTY JO WATSON

Washington University

It is clear from the kinds of constituents in the fecal material left inside the cave that visits were made there all year around (Yarnell 1969: 49–50; Schoenwetter, pages 55–56 of this volume; Marquardt, page 199 of this volume; Bryant, pages 208–209 of this volume). The pollen present in the samples so far analyzed by Schoenwetter and Bryant from Salts Cave and Mammoth Cave, respectively, indicates a rather high proportion of spring/summer deposits (13 of 25 specimens). Yet in all but two of these 13 specimens (Mammoth Cave Samples 11 and 14) there are also hickory nut shell fragments, chenopod seeds, sunflower seeds, or sumpweed seeds in various combinations.

Such spring/summer indicators as are available among the macrobotanical remains (presence of strawberry, *Rubus*, maygrass seeds in abundance, fruit and plant skin) support the suggestion that many fecal deposits were spring or summer ones. Then, because once again nearly all the spring and summer specimens also contain sunflower, sumpweed, chenopod, or hickory (or some combination of these), one can infer that these fall seeds and nuts were stored in considerable quantities and eaten throughout the year. The importance of these four species in the diet is amply demonstrated in all the analyses of macrobotanical constituents (Yarnell 1969 and in this volume; Marquardt, this volume). Yarnell's modified percentages for the series of 100 Salts Cave paleofecal specimens (Table 16.5 here) are 25% for sunflower, 25% for chenopod, 14% for sumpweed, and 16% for hickory nut. Stewart's data for the Mammoth Cave series give the following percentages by weight of plant food: sunflower 9%, sumpweed 2%, chenopod 30%, and hickory 31% (percentages calculated from weights in Table 24.1). These two sets of percentages are not directly comparable, however, because Stewart's are by weight (see discussion of quantification in the Appendix) and Yarnell's are systematized estimates of abundance.

Percentages of occurrence—simple presence/absence—can be compared more directly (Table 31.1). However, there is considerable uncertainty even in this comparison because Yarnell was assessing entire specimens, while Stewart was taking five very small samples (1 gm each) from each specimen. One point does stand out so strikingly in the comparison that it is perhaps significant: the difference in the sumpweed percentages. Percentage of occurrence of *Iva* in the Mammoth

TABLE 31.1   Percentages of Occurrence for the Four Main Plant Food Species in Salts Cave and Mammoth Cave Paleofeces

Mammoth Cave, Ganter Avenue[a] (see Table 24.1)		Salts Cave[b] (see Yarnell 1969: Table 8)
Sunflower	63%	90%
Sumpweed	44%	87%
Chenopod	67%	87%
Hickory	63%	78%

[a]Total of 27 specimens.
[b]Total of 100 specimens.

Cave series is only half what it is in the Salts Cave series. This could still be an accident of sampling in that all the Mammoth Cave specimens are from one localized part of Ganter Avenue in Lower Mammoth, whereas the 100 Salts specimens were collected from widely separated parts of Upper, Middle, and Lower Salts. The Mammoth Cave specimens are from what may then have been a latrine area used for a finite time period by a specific group or groups, whereas consideration of the Salts Cave series as a single data universe averages any seasonal or chronological variation that might exist similarly in discrete areas of that cave.

There are a number of difficulties in assessing prehistoric diet from paleofecal constituents (see the Appendix). But despite problems of detailed interpretation, it is obvious from the fecal data that the diet of the cavers was rather standardized and largely vegetarian, with considerable reliance on one kind of forest nut and a few kinds of seeds. Of the latter, sunflower and sumpweed were cultigens, and chenopod must have been at least an encouraged (harvested and stored) weed. Maygrass—although apparently not habitually stored—was also an important diet item when in season. The vegetarian emphasis demonstrated by the fecal constituents tends to be confirmed by the lack of evidence for a developed hunting pattern displayed in animal bone from the Vestibule. The nature of many of the animal remains in the feces (tiny rodents, a salamander, a snake, a frog, insects, a turkey foot) also suggest that animal protein was often not easily available.

Yarnell's study of charred plant materials in flotation samples from Salts Cave (pages 110–122) shows the same range of plant foods as in the fecal specimens, with a few minor additions (rhizome and tuber fragments, honey locust seeds, and hazel nut shell). Like the systematized estimates of plant foods in 100 Salts Cave paleofeces (Yarnell 1969 and Table 16.5 here), the flotation remains clearly indicate considerable reliance on the seeds of cultigens and of the weedy plants that would be expected to flourish in and around the gardens (Yarnell, page 122).

The general picture, then, is of a fairly steady plant food diet focused on hickory nuts, sunflower, sumpweed, and chenopod seeds with other seeds and occasional fruits in season. Squash and gourd were grown during the last millenium B.C. and may also have been eaten, but both were probably more important as containers than as foods (see Cutler's report in Watson et al. 1969: 51–52).

Deer, turkeys, and small mammals were also eaten, but probably not very often, as well as insects, amphibians, reptiles, and river mussels. The question of cannibalism is an open one, but the evidence is overwhelming that the Vestibule people were casual to the point of ruthlessness in their treatment of several, of the bodies represented in the excavated midden. As Robbins' account demonstrates, much of the human bone was handled like deer bone: broken, cut, burned, made into tools, discarded in the midden with other garbage. This treatment was accorded to the skeletal remains of children, adolescents, and adults. Moreover, the total quantity of human bone is nearly as great as that of all other animal bone combined. It is difficult to avoid the conclusion that the people who were responsible were either cannibals or habitual participants in the customs of systematic torture and cruelty characteristic of many protohistoric and early historic tribes in eastern North America (see Robbins' discussion, on pages 157–162).

The diet preserved in the caves is similar to that described by Asch, Ford, and Asch (1972: 26) for Woodland sites like Macoupin in the lower Illinois River Valley in contrast to the Archaic site of Koster, some three miles north of Macoupin. They utilize data from the Illinois sites together with Boserup's (1965) study and Binford's (1968) discussion of agricultural origins to build a generalized model of subsistence changes in the eastern woodlands. They hypothesize that subsistence changes occur as a result of pressure on the available food supply because of some such factor (or combination of factors) such as population expansion or environmental deterioration. They suggest that the Salts Cave dietary pattern indicates such a subsistence change—a trend to more intense seed use—in Early Woodland times, that then continued through the Middle Woodland period (Asch, Ford, and Asch 1972: 28). The most recent data from Salts Cave and Mammoth Cave can tentatively be viewed as supporting the general outlines of this reconstruction, as the following discussion makes clear.

It is necessary first to give some attention to the question of chronology of the Salts Vestibule occupation and of the local mining activity that inadvertently resulted in deposition of paleofecal matter in the cave interiors. All the presently available radiocarbon dates for Salts Cave, Mammoth Cave, and related sites are presented in Table 31.2 (see also Figure 31.1). There are five dates on paleofecal material from Salts Cave:

Three from Upper Salts:	290 B.C. $\pm$ 200	
	320 B.C. $\pm$ 140	
	620 B.C. $\pm$ 140	
Two from Lower Salts:	400 B.C. $\pm$ 140	
	710 B.C. $\pm$ 140	

These five specimens definitely seem to date the prehistoric caver diet to the Early Woodland period. However, dates on other materials from Salts Cave, Mammoth Cave, and Lee Cave indicate a much longer time span for activity in the caves. In particular, there is a determination of 1190 B.C. $\pm$ 150 for Lower Salts, a determination of 1125 B.C. $\pm$ 140 for Upper Salts, and three mid-second millenium B.C. dates for charcoal from the Vestibule middens. From Mammoth Cave there are two new dates to add to those already published in Watson *et al.* (1969: 70), and both are early: 1050 B.C. $\pm$ 70 from Lower Mammoth, Ganter Avenue, and 2170 B.C. $\pm$ 70 from Jessup Avenue in Lower Mammoth. The Lee Cave determination on cane fragments is the oldest of the present series: 2250 B.C. $\pm$ 65.

These relatively early dates from Salts, Mammoth, and Lee in combination with two new dates obtained by us from Green River shellmound Bt-5 (Carlston Annis) suggest that the caves were already being explored in Archaic times. The new Bt-5 dates are: 4250 B.P. $\pm$ 80 (UCLA 1845A) and 4049 B.P. $\pm$ 180 (UCLA 1845B). Both are uncorrected, Libby half-life (5568 $\pm$ 30) determinations (the dates are reported in a letter from Professor Rainer Berger, September 26, 1972; a description of the Washington University test excavation at Bt-5 during the spring of 1972 is provided by Marquardt 1972). Subtracting the 1950 base-date gives 2300 B.C. $\pm$ 80 and 2090 B.C. $\pm$ 180. The older of these dates is within the range of previous determinations on antler from Bt-5 (2950 B.C. $\pm$ 350, 2339 B.C. $\pm$ 300, 2383 B.C. $\pm$ 450), but other Bt-5 determinations (on shell) are older than either of the new dates (5424 B.C. $\pm$ 500 and 3199 B.C. $\pm$ 300). The shell and antler dates are reported in Arnold and Libby 1951 and Webb 1951.

Thus, it now appears that the big caves were probably entered as early as 3000 years ago [and it is interesting that some of the older dates are from lower-level passages remote from the entrance in both Salts—1190 B.C. for wood and bark from Indian Avenue, Lower Salts—and Mammoth (the Ganter and Jessup Avenue dates already referred to)]. This means that some of the paleo feces may reflect late Archaic, pre Early Woodland subsistence in the local area, as perhaps does the flotation material from the lower levels of the deepest Salts Vestibule pits. The results of Yarnell's analysis suggest to him that the levels below J IV 6 in the Vestibule midden deposits may represent a time prior to local cultivation of squash and gourd, when the prehistoric occupants were relying solely on indigenous North American species for plant food.

Three independent lines of evidence seem to suggest a change in the major vegetational pattern from closed to open oak–hickory woodland around Salts Sink during the second and first millenia B.C. First, the pollen spectra for J IV suggest to Schoenwetter an initial oak–hickory climax (levels 23 to 13) succeeded by a disclimax opening of the local forest canopy (levels 6 and 7 to 3), until, at the top of the sequence (level 2), the oak–hickory

TABLE 31.2   Summary of Available Radiocarbon Dates[a]

Provenience	Material	Date
Salts Cave Vestibule		
Test H, Fea. 2A	Charcoal	1540 B.C. ± 110 (GaK 2767)
Test E, Level 5	Charcoal	1410 B.C. ± 220 (GaK 2764)
Test G, Level 6	Charcoal	1460 B.C. ± 220 (GaK 2766)
Test E, Level 7b	Charcoal	710 B.C. ± 100 (GaK 2622)
Test E, Level 7b	Charcoal	990 B.C. ± 120 (GaK 2765)
Salts Cave Interior		
Upper Salts, P54[b]	Paleofecal Specimen containing squash seeds	290 B.C. ± 200 (M 1573)
Upper Salts, P38[b]	Paleofecal specimen	320 B.C. ± 140 (M 1777)
Upper Salts, P63–64[b]	Paleofecal specimen containing gourd seeds	620 B.C. ± 140 (M 1574)
Upper Salts, P54[b]	Soot	1125 B.C. ± 140 (I 256)
Upper Salts, Test A		
0–10 cm	Cane	560 B.C. ± 140 (M 1584)
30–40 cm	Cane	480 B.C. ± 140 (M 1585)
70–80 cm	Cane	890 B.C. ± 150 (M 1586)
140 cm	Wood	570 B.C. ± 140 (M 1587)
Middle Salts, Blue Arrow Passage, A60	Paleofecal specimen containing squash pollen	400 B.C. ± 140 (M 1577)
Middle Salts, Blue Arrow Passage, A42	Paleofecal specimen containing sunflower seeds	710 B.C. ± 140 (M 1770)
Lower Salts, Indian Avenue, 2 m east of I 76[b]	Wood	770 B.C. ± 140 (M 1588)
Lower Salts, Indian Avenue, 1 m southeast of I 67[b]	Wood and bark	1190 B.C. ± 150 (M 1589)
Little Al(ice)	Internal tissue from the Salts Cave mummy	A.D. 30 ± 160 (M 2259)
		10 B.C. ± 160 (M 2258)
Mammoth Cave Interior		
Upper Mammoth	Slipper	280 B.C. ± 40 (X 8)
Upper Mammoth	Cane	420 B.C. ± 60 (X 9)
Lower Mammoth, B10 Ganter Avenue	Wood	1050 B.C. ± 70 (UCLA 1730B)
Lower Mammoth, C7 Jessup Avenue	Twigs	2170 B.C. ± 70 (UCLA 1730A)
Lee Cave Interior		
Marshall Avenue, K83	Cane	2250 B.C. ± 65 (UCLA 1729A)
Marshall Avenue, J25	Fragments from a large log probably carried into the cave by floodwater before the first entry by humans	4100 B.C. ± 60 (UCLA 1729B)
Wyandotte Cave Interior:		
Washington Avenue, Fallen Rock	Bark and sticks	910 B.C. ± 60 (UCLA 1731B)
Rugged Mountain	Bark and wood	A.D. 240 ± 80 (UCLA 1731A)

[a]All dates calculated on the basis of the Libby half-life (5568 ± 30 years) and with 1950 base date; no corrections have been made for secular variations.

[b]Survey stations in Upper Salts and in Indian Avenue for Lower Salts are indicated on Figure 3 of Watson *et al.* 1969.

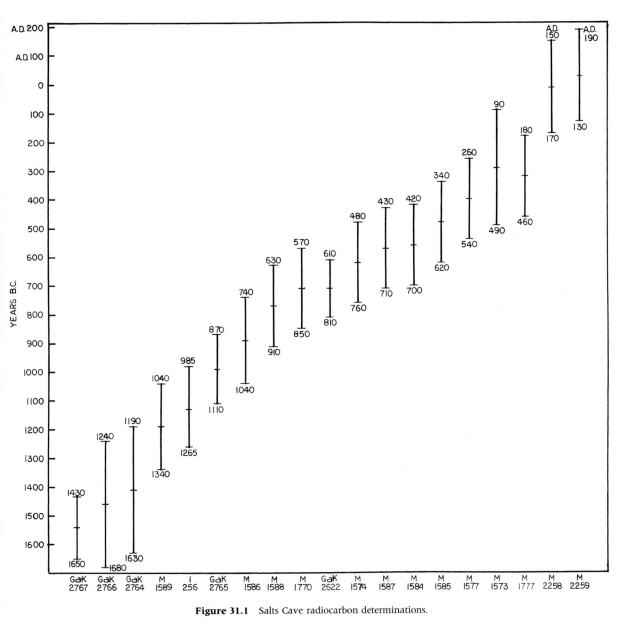

Figure 31.1 Salts Cave radiocarbon determinations.

woodland seems to be reestablishing itself (Figure 13.1 and pages 103–105). Second, in the flotation series from J IV levels 11 to 7, Yarnell has found small increases in the seeds of weedy annuals that imply relatively open or disturbed ground, fol- lowed by large increases of these plants in levels 4 to 6 (Figure 16.1–16.4, pages 117–118). Third, Duffield's ordering of the animal bone from all the trenches on the north side of the Vestibule by strati- graphic horizons suggests a sequence from use of dense deciduous woods, wood margins, grassland, and river to concentration on fauna of semiopen to open woods. (Table 17.1, page 131).

The possibility of a second to first millenium B.C. vegetation change is of considerable interest because the Salts Cave–Mammoth Cave paleofecal material dates from the same time range: late Archaic to Early Woodland. Like the flotation material, the paleofecal deposits show a very high proportion of seeds from weedy plants, the most abundant of which were cultivated or semicultivated species. As already noted, this dietary pattern contrasts with that of the earlier Archaic as exemplified at Koster in which nuts are overwhelmingly dominant and seeds are a very minor component. Because of a possible correlation between change in vegetation cover and change in subsistence pattern in the Mammoth Cave area, we need to know what might have caused a change to open woodland in order to understand the circumstances involved in the local appearance of increased seed use and of horticulture.

There are at least three different possible explanations for a change to open woodland. One hypothesis is that a regional climatic fluctutation caused the change. The second hypothesis is that the area surrounding Salts Sink was swept by a naturally occurring forest fire that destroyed much of the arboreal vegetation. The third hypothesis is that the data reflect a local change caused by the practice of some form of slash and burn horticulture in the area around Salts Sink.

It is obviously important to obtain further data that will help us decide among these hypotheses, for if the first were to be confirmed, one could go on to suggest that the climatic change that caused the open woodlands was possibly a partial underlying cause of the concurrent increased seed use and horticulture. That is, the trend to open woodlands caused by climatic change would decrease the nut harvest and also make the shift to increased seed use easier than it would be if (as the second and third hypotheses suggest) the woodlands had to be opened by the horticulturists themselves, or by a fortuitous accident of nature with only temporary influence (because of reforestation).

Each of these hypotheses proposes a necessary condition for increased seed use and horticulture in this area. However, no matter which hypothesis is confirmed, the demonstration of the mere presence of a major necessary condition is not adequate for explaining fully why the people did in fact increase their reliance on cultigens and other weedy annuals. That is, the presence of climatically caused open woodlands that were not very productive of edible nuts but were suitable for exploitation as garden areas would not explain their actual employment as garden areas. The question would remain as to why this was necessary or desirable. If the area around Salts Sink was made favorable for seed harvest and horticulture by a naturally occurring forest fire, once again, this would not explain why the local aboriginal population chose to exploit the fired area. Similarly, the demonstration of the occurrence of slash and burn horticulture around Salts Sink would not in itself explain why knowledge of this technique was applied here at this time.

In other words, once one answers the question of *how* the open woodland was caused— by a climatic change, by a naturally occurring fire, or by purposeful human behavior—the further question of *why* horticulture and seed harvest were increased in this open woodland remains.

Although the evidence for a change from closed to more open woodland is slim, it is strong in the sense that it is coherent and is suggested by three independent types of data. The evidence that there was a change to increased seed use and horticulture at that time in this area is quite strong. Thus, future work will be directed in part toward testing the alternative hypotheses about the causes of change to open woodland just described, and in part toward testing hypotheses about why the concurrent change to increased seed use and horticulture took place in the Mammoth Cave area.

Appendix # Theoretical and Methodological Difficulties Encountered in Dealing with Paleofecal Material[1]

PATTY JO WATSON

Washington University

Although prehistoric fecal material is an excellent source of dietary and other information (Heizer and Napton 1969), it is also very frustrating to work with, for a number of reasons. Difficulties encountered in paleofecal analyses have important consequences for the interpretations based on the results of those analyses, and therefore should be made as explicit as possible. The major difficulties inherent in all paleofecal analyses can be discussed with reference to two main issues: (1) the basic assumptions made by the analyst and interpreter of paleofecal material as regards human physiology and nutrition, and (2) the best or most useful ways of quantifying identified remains from such fecal material.

(1) As regards each fecal specimen: Do we take it to represent one meal, several (up to how many?) meals, food eaten during one day, or food eaten over a period of two or more days?

This is a complicated topic because there is a great deal of individual variation (even among healthy individuals) as well as an equally large amount of cultural variation with respect to timing and etiquette of elimination of bodily wastes. There is probably a tendency to regard one specimen as one meal, which would be simple and neat, but is almost certainly not correct.

About 75–150 gm minimally (Fry 1970 says as much as 300 gm) of fecal material are formed per 24 hours, but two-thirds of this is water. The rest is undigested cellulose fibers or other ingested, non-assimilable material plus mucus and digestive secretions, dead cells, and microorganisms of various kinds (bacteria, yeasts, fungi).

Swallowed food goes, of course, to the stomach but it does not remain there long. As Callen notes (1967: 263), the stomach empties in 2–4 hours. The rate of emptying depends on volume of gastric content as well as other factors such as temperature and salinity of the food, but Callen's estimate may be rather conservative. According to a study

---

[1] Much of the following discussion is based on Watson 1970.

quoted by Glass (1968), the stomach is virtually empty 100 minutes after the individual eats a full meal. After leaving the stomach, the food mass passes through the rest of the digestive tract in about 18–24 hours; hence, an estimate of 20–26 hours total transit time might be a fair approximation, and the end result might contain contributions from two to four meals.

Perhaps it can be agreed, then, that one specimen probably represents more than one meal but no more than four meals.

(2)   In the analysis of prehistoric fecal specimens, one of the primary points of interest is that of associations between and among various constituents. Associations occur because of mutual availability owing to: Seasonality, geographic and/or topographic distribution of the species in question vis-à-vis others, and storage (Is the species in question storable? Does the culture in question utilize appropriate storage techniques? Etc.), and menu preferences (these are, to some degree, dependent on all other above).

Even supposing we are interested in some or all of these points, why quantify the remains identified? Why not just record presence or absence? It is true that some information can be obtained using only presence/absence data, but one is considerably limited in defining and testing associations (see Chapter 24 by Marquardt). Recording simple presence/absence is a technique that does not take full advantage of the information potentially available. The question then arises, how precisely should we quantify and by what techniques? The answer, of course, depends on the problem, but the most basic question is how much of what different things were eaten, and with respect to that question some general points can be made.

There are three possible ways to quantify the remains isolated and identified in paleofecal material: counts, weights, and volume.

Counts are generally unsatisfactory in themselves. That is, one chenopod seed is not comparable to one hickory nutshell fragment nor to one piece of sunflower husk. Nor is one piece of sunflower husk necessarily comparable to all others, because achene sizes may vary considerably. In his study of the Salts Vestibule flotation

samples, Yarnell normalizes seed bulk for sunflower and sumpweed seeds (page 121).

Another consideration is that of relating the fragments found to the actual food item represented, which is a separate problem for each species. (How many nut shell fragments represent one nut meat? What is the minimum number of individual sunflower achenes represented by a masticated wad extracted from the fecal specimen?)

Still another problem is that of differential absorption of different foods in the human digestive tract, and of the effects of possible differential preparation before eating (roasting of some seeds and not others, for instance), as well as differential rates of progress for different substances passing through the digestive system.

Counts of individual items will usually have to be combined with other measurements (weight or volume), and in general are probably useful only for discrete seeds.

Observations similar to those made for counts can be made with respect to direct comparison of one species to another by means of weight or volume (one cubic centimeter or one gram of acorn shell is not the same as one cubic centimeter or one gram of hickory nutshell; see Yarnell page 119), and with respect to actual food consumed. (How many grams or how many cubic centimeters of hickory nutshell fragments equals one nut meat?) However, it would be possible to work out ratios or conversion factors for the latter (one could do this for counts, too, but the process would be much more complicated and not so reliable). One could utilize modern specimens of the same size and shape as the prehistoric seeds to work out weight equivalents of crushed or chewed and uncrushed or unchewed specimens. Then if crushed and chewed sunflower achene material is found, one can equate it at least approximately with the appropriate number and weight of uncrushed and unchewed specimens.

Finally, there are some categories of food remains identifiable but not really quantifiable. These include the meat debris and fleshy plant parts detectable if one uses the trisodium phosphate method (or some other wet method) of analysis. It also includes special cases such as the acorn remains in the Salts Cave feces. Because acorns are so much easier to shell than hickory nuts, they are almost certainly under-represented in the fecal material; this means we cannot assess their frequency with respect to hickory, and hence of total forest foods vis-à-vis cultivated plants, without extrapolating from nonfecal lines of evidence.

There is also a problem in quantifying animal remains in the feces. Identification of minimum numbers of individuals is difficult enough in a more or less normal lot of excavated faunal material, and extracting such information from fecal remains may be an extremely challenging task. Fish scales, feather, bits of insect chitin, and so on can probably be meaningfully recorded only by counts or weights.

The general conclusion is that food remains in paleofecal specimens represent a whole series of discrete universes, that meaningful quantification is a separate problem for almost every constituent, and that *direct* comparison of quantities of one category with those of another is only rarely possible. The problem of how to relate those quantities to the respective food items they represent is a complex but crucial one, the solution of which requires cooperation with nutritionists and biologists.

With respect to the general basic problem, however—what was eaten and how much—the fol-

lowing approach is suggested, using the Salts-Cave paleofecal constituents as examples:

(1) Count discrete seeds and then weigh them to establish a seed number/weight ratio. Once the ratio is established, only weights need be determined. This could be done for chenopod, sumpweed, maygrass, knotweed, etc.

(2) For sunflower, gourd and squash seeds, and hickory nutshell: establish number/weight ratios from whole to crushed and chewed fragments.

(3) These data can be converted to counts for all the major food species, enabling reasonably precise comparisons for one species from specimen to specimen. It should also be possible to define quite precisely the relationships among species by using these data.

(4) The last step would be to establish by experiment some equivalence between the fragments in the fecal matter and the food they represent for all the major species utilized.

Such a program is planned to aid the interpretation of the Salts Cave—Mammoth Cave paleofecal material.

REFERENCES

Adams, Benjamin
  1820 Account of a great and very extraordinary cave in Indiana. In a letter dated February 27, 1818, from the owner to a gentleman in Frankfort, Kentucky. Communicated to the President of the American Antiquarian Society, by John H. Farnham, Esq., of Frankfort, Ohio. *Transactions and Collections of the American Antiquarian Society* **1**: 434–436.

Altman, P. L., and D. S. Dittmer
  1968 *Metabolism.* Bethesda, Maryland: Federation of American Societies for Experimental Biology.

Arnold, J. R., and W. F. Libby
  1951 Radiocarbon dates. *Science* **113**: 111–120.

Asch, N. B., R. I. Ford, and D. L. Asch
  1972 Paleoethnobotany of the Koster site: The Archaic horizons. *Illinois State Museum, Reports of Investigation*, No. 24 (Research Papers No. 6, Illinois Valley Archaeological Project).

Baby, R. S.
  1954 Hopewell cremation practices. *Papers in Archaeology*, No. 1. Columbus: Ohio Historical Society.

Baerreis, D. A., and R. A. Bryson
  1965 Climatic episodes and the dating of the Mississippian cultures. *Wisconsin Archeologist* **46**: 203–220.

Barkley, F. A.
  1934 The statistical theory of pollen analysis. *Ecology* **15**: 283–289.

Bent, A., and H. E. Wright, Jr.
  1963 Pollen analyses of surface materials and lake sediments from the Chuska Mountains, New Mexico. *Geological Society of America, Bulletin* **74**: 491–500.

Binford, L. R.
  1963 An analysis of cremations from three Michigan sites. *Wisconsin Archeologist* **44**: 98–110.

  1968 Post-Pleistocene adaptations. In *New perspectives in archeology*, edited by S. R. Binford and L. R. Binford. Chicago: Aldine.

Black, M.
  1963 The distribution and archeological significance of the marsh-elder *Iva annua* L. *Papers of the Michigan Academy of Science, Arts, and Letters* **48**: 541–547.

Blatchley, W. S.
  1899 *Gleanings from nature.* Indianapolis: Nature.

Boserup, E.
  1965 *The conditions of agricultural growth: The economics of agrarian change under population pressure.* Chicago: Aldine.

Bohrer, V. L.
  1968 Paleoecology of an archeological site near Snowflake, Arizona. Unpublished doctoral dissertation, Univ. of Arizona, Tucson.

Boyd, L. T., and W. C. Boyd
  1939 Blood grouping reactions of preserved bone and muscle. *American Journal of Physical Anthropology* **25**: 421–434.

Bridge, J. F.
  1969 Introduction to Horace Hovey's article, "Brigham, the cave-dog," reprinted in *Journal of Spelean History* **2**: 88–91.

Brothwell, D. R.
  1963 *Digging up bones.* London: British Museum of Natural History.

Brucker, R. W.
n. d.   Search for the way down. Manuscript report submitted to P. J. Watson, Washington University, St. Louis.

Bryant, V. M., Jr.
1969   Late full-glacial and postglacial pollen analysis of Texas sediments. Unpublished doctoral dissertation, Univ. of Texas, Austin.

Bushnell, D. I., Jr.
1920   Native cemeteries and forms of burial east of the Mississippi. *Bureau of American Ethnology, Bulletin 71.*

Byers, D. S. (Editor)
1967   *Environment and subsistence.* Volume 1 of *The prehistory of the Tehuacan Valley.* Austin: Univ. of Texas Press.

Callen, E. O.
1963   Diet as revealed by coprolites. In *Science in archaeology,* edited by D. Brothwell and E. Higgs. New York: Basic Books.
1967   Analysis of the Tehuacan coprolites. In *Environment and subsistence* edited by D. S. Byers. Volume 1 of *The prehistory of the Tehuacan Valley.* Austin: Univ. of Texas Press.

Callen, E. O., and T. W. M. Cameron
1960   A prehistoric diet revealed in coprolites. *The New Scientist* **8**: 35–40.

Callen, E. O., and P. S. Martin
1969   Plant remains in some coprolites from Utah. *American Antiquity* **34**: 329–331.

Chaplin, R. E.
1971   *The study of animal bones from archaeological sites.* New York: Seminar Press.

Cleland, C.
1966   The prehistoric animal ecology and ethnozoology of the Upper Great Lakes Region. *Anthropological Papers, Museum of Anthropology, University of Michigan,* No. 29.

Collins, L.
1874   *History of Kentucky.* Second edition. Covington, Kentucky: Collins.

Cowan, W.
n. d.   Examination of flint waste materials from Salts Sink, Mammoth Cave National Park, Kentucky. Manuscript submitted to L. Duffield, University of Kentucky, Lexington.

Dick, H. W.
1965   Bat Cave. *School of American Research, Monograph,* No. 27.

Dunnell, R. C.
1966   1965 excavations in the Fish Trap Reservoir, Pike County, Kentucky. Department of Interior, National

Park Service, Southeastern Region, Richmond, Virginia.

Ehman, M. F.
1966   Cane torches as cave illumination. *NSS News* **24**: 34–36.

Erdtman, G.
1943   *An introduction to pollen analysis.* Waltham, Massachusettes: Chronica Botanica.

Faegri, K.
1956   Recent trends in palynology. *The Botanical Review* **22**: 639–664.

Faegri, K., and J. Iversen
1964   *Textbook of pollen analysis.* New York: Hafner.

Faust, E. C., P. F. Russell, and R. C. Jung
1970   *Craig and Faust's Clinical parasitology,* 8th ed. Philadelphia: Lea and Febiger.

Finkel, D.
1968   *Answer back.* New York: Atheneum.

Fish, S. K.
n.d.   Archaeological pollen analysis of the Powers Phase, southeastern Missouri. Manuscript report, Museum of Anthropology, Univ. of Michigan.

Flannery, K. V.
1970   Preliminary archaeological investigations in the Valley of Oaxaca, Mexico, 1966 through 1969. Report to the National Science Foundation and the Instituto Nacional de Antropologia e Historia.

Fowke, G.
1922   Archeological investigations. Part I. Cave explorations in the Ozark Region of central Missouri. Part II. Cave explorations in other states. *Bureau of American Ethnology, Bulletin 76.*

Fowler, M. L.
1971   The origin of plant cultivation in the central Mississippi Valley: A hypothesis. In *Prehistoric agriculture,* edited by Stuart Struever. New York: Natural History Press.

Freeman, J. P., G. L. Smith, T. L. Poulson, P. J. Watson, and W. B. White
1973   Lee Cave, Mammoth Cave National Park, Kentucky. *National Speleological Society Bulletin* 35:109–126.

Fry, G. F.
1970   Prehistoric human ecology in Utah: Based on the analysis of coprolites. *Univ. of Utah Anthropological Papers* (in press).

Fuller, R. G.
1915   Observations on a collection of crania from the prehistoric stone graves of Tennessee. Unpublished doctoral dissertation, Harvard Univ.

Funkhouser, W. D., and W. S. Webb.
1929   The so-called "ash caves" in Lee County, Kentucky. *The University of Kentucky Reports in Archaeology and*

Anthropology 1, No. 2.

1930 Rock shelters of Wolfe and Powell Counties, Kentucky. *University of Kentucky Reports in Archaeology and Anthropology*, 1, No. 4.

1931 The Duncan site on the Kentucky–Tennessee line. *University of Kentucky Reports in Archaeology and Anthropology* 1, No. 6.

Garn, S., and W. D. Block
1970 The limited nutritional value of cannibalism. *American Anthropologist* **72**: 106.

Geijvall, N.-G.
1963 Cremations. In *Science in archaeology*, edited by D. Brothwell and E. Higgs. New York: Basic Books.

Glass, G. B.
1968 *Introduction to gastrointestinal physiology*. Englewood Cliffs, New Jersey: Prentice-Hall.

Glemser, M. S.
1963 Paleoserology. In *Science in archaeology*, edicted by D. Brothwell and E. Higgs. New York Basic Books.

Greulich, W. W., and S. I. Pyle
1959 *Radiographic atlas of skeletal development of hand and wrist*, 2nd ed. Stanford, California: Stanford Univ. Press.

Hall, E. R.
1955 Handbook of mammals of Kansas. *Miscellaneous publication*, No. 7. Lawrence, Kansas: Univ. of Kansas.

Harlow, R., and M. DeFoor
1962 How to age white tailed deer. *Florida Wildlife*, December 1962: 18–21.

Harvey, E. B., H. E. Kaiser, and L. E. Rosenberg
1968 *An atlas of the domestic turkey* (Meleagris gallopavo): *Myology and osteology*. Washington 1123: United States Atomic Energy Commission.

Heiser, C. B., Jr.
1951 The sunflower among the North American Indians. *Proceedings of the American Philosophical Society* **95**: 432–448.

1955 The origin and development of the cultivated sunflower. *The American Biology Teacher* **17** (May): 161–167.

Heizer, R. F., and L. K. Napton
1969 Biological and cultural evidence from prehistoric human coprolites. *Science* **165**: 563–568.

Hoffmeister, D. F., and C. O. Mohr
1972 *Fieldbook of Illinois mammals*. New York: Dover.

Holmes, W. H.
1885 Prehistoric textile fabrics of the United States derived from impressions on pottery. *Bureau of American Ethnology* Third Annual Report: 393–425.

Hovey, H. C.
1897 Our saltpeter caves in time of war. *Scientific American*, May 8, 1897:291.

1912 *Mammoth Cave of Kentucky*. Louisville: John P. Morton and Co.

Jackson, G. F.
1953 *Wyandotte Cave*. Narberth, Pennsylvania: Livingston.

1969 The Russell Trall Neville expedition in Old Salts Cave, Kentucky. *Journal of Spelean History* **2**:45–50.

Johnston, F. E., and S. B. Jahina
1965 The contribution of the carpal bones to the assessment of skeletal age. *American Journal of Physical Anthropology* **23**: 349–354.

Jones, J.
1876 Explorations of the aboriginal remains of Tennessee. *Smithsonian Contribution to Knowledge*, No. 259.

Jones, V.
1936 The vegetal remains of Newt Kash Hollow shelter. In *Rock shelters in Menifee County, Kentucky* by W. S. Webb and W. D. Funkhouser. *University of Kentucky Reports in Archaeology and Anthropology* **3**, No. 4.

Kapp, R. O.
1969 *How to know pollen and spores*. Dubuque, Iowa: Brown.

Keller, J. E.
1970 The vertebrate faunal remains from two Mississippian sites in the Green River drainage of Kentucky. Unpublished master's thesis, Univ. of Kentucky.

Kelso, G. K.
1971 Hogup Cave, Utah: Comparative pollen analysis of human coprolites and cave fill. Unpublished master's thesis, Univ. of Arizona.

Knowles, N.
1940 The torture of captives by the Indians of eastern North America. *American Philosophical Society Proceedings* **82**, No. 2.

Krantz, G. S.
1968 A new method of counting mammal bones. *American Journal of Archaeology* **72**: 286–288.

Krogman, W. M.
1962 *The human skeleton in forensic medicine*. Springfield, Illinois: Charles C. Thomas.

Kurtz, E. B., Jr.
1948 Pollen grain characteristics of certain Cactaceae. *Bulletin of the Torrey Botanical Club* **75**: 516–522.

1963 Pollen morphology of the Cactaceae. *Grana Palynologica* **4**: 367–372.

Laudermilk, J. D., and R. A. Munz
1938 Plants in the dung of *Nothrotherium* from Rampart and Muave Caves, Arizona. *Carnegie Institution of Washington Publication* 487:271–281.

Leechman, D.
1951 Bone grease. *American Antiquity* **16**:355–356.

Lewis, T. M. N., and M. Kneberg
1958   *Tribes that slumber.* Knoxville: Univ. of Tennessee Press.

Lewis, T. M., and M. K. Lewis
1961   *Eva, an Archaic site.* Knoxville: Univ. of Tennessee Press.

McCance, R. A., and E. M. Widdowson
1940   *The chemical composition of foods.* New York: Chemical.

Marquardt, W. H.
1972   Recent Investigations in a western Kentucky shell mound. Research report presented to the 37th annual meeting of the Society for American Archaeology, May 4–6, 1972, Bal Harbour, Florida.

Martin, P. S.
1965   Pollen analysis of coprolites. In *A survey and excavation of caves in Hidalgo County, New Mexico,* by M. Lambert and R. Ambler, Santa Fe, School of American Research Publication.

Martin, P. S., B. E. Sabels, and D. Shutler, Jr.
1961   Rampart Cave coprolites and ecology of the Shasta ground sloth. *American Journal of Science* **259**: 102–127.

Martin, P. S., and J. Schoenwetter
1960   Arizona's oldest cornfield. *Science* **132**: 33–34.

Martin, P. S., and F. W. Sharrock
1964   Pollen analysis of prehistoric human feces: A new approach to ethnobotany. *American Antiquity* **30**: 168–180.

Meloy, H.
1971   *Mummies of Mammoth Cave.* Shelbyville, Indiana: Micron.

Meloy, H. and P. J. Watson
1969   Human remains: "Little Alice" of Salts Cave and other mummies. In The prehistory of Salts Cave, Kentucky, by P. J. Watson *et al. Illinois State Museum Reports of Investigations,* No. 16.

Merbs, C. F.
1967   Cremated human remains from Point of Pines, Arizona: A new approach. *American Antiquity* **32**: 498–506.

Meriam, E.
1844   "Mammoth Cave." *The New York Municipal Gazette* **1**, Feb. 21: 317ff.

Molnar, S.
1971   Human tooth wear, function and variability. *American Journal of Physical Anthropology* 34:27–42.

Morgan, M. C.
n.d.   Reminiscences of Mammoth Cave. A newspaper clipping from the *Glasgow Times* (no date); copies in the possession of Ellis Jones, Cave City, Kentucky, and Gordon Smith, Louisville, Kentucky.

Mosimann, J. E.
1965   Statistical methods of the pollen analyst: Multinomial and negative multinomial techniques. In *Handbook of paleontological techniques,* edited by B. Kummel and D. Raup. San Francisco: Freeman.

Napton, L. E., and G. Kelso
1969   Preliminary palynological analysis of coprolites from Lovelock Cave, Nevada. In *An archeological and paleobiological investigation in Lovelock Cave, Nevada,* edited by L. K. Napton. Kroeber Anthropological Society Special Publication, No. 2 Berkeley: Univ. of California press.

Nelson, N. C.
1917   Contributions to the archaeology of Mammoth Cave and vicinity, Kentucky. *Anthropological Papers, American Museum of Natural History* **22**, Part I.

Nelson, N. C.
1923   Kentucky; Mammoth Cave and vicinity. Manuscript on file at the American Museum of Natural History, New York City.

Neumann, G. K.
n.d.   Mammoth Cave "Lost John" notes, September 13, 1935. [A copy of the notes is in the possession of Louise M. Robbins.]
1938   The human remains from Mammoth Cave. *American Antiquity* **3**: 339–353.
1940   Evidence for the antiquity of scalping from central Illinois. *American Antiquity* **5**: 287–289.

Neville, R. T.
n.d.   Old Salts. Manuscript describing a 51-hour trip into Salts Cave in 1927. [A copy of the manuscript is on file with the Cave Research Foundation; a second copy is in the possession of Dr. William Halliday, Seattle, Washington.]

Nie, N. H., D. H. Bent, and C. H. Hull
1970   *Statistical package for the social sciences.* New York: McGraw-Hill.

Nie, N. H., and C. H. Hull
1971   *Statistical package for the social sciences: update manual.* Chicago: National Opinion Research Center, Univ. of Chicago.
1972   *Statistical package for the social sciences: update manual, revised edition.* Chicago: National Opinion Research Center, Univ. of Chicago.

Odum, E. P.
1959   *Fundamentals of ecology.* Philadelphia: Saunders.

O'Neale, L. M.
1948   Textiles of pre-Columbian Chihuahua. *Contributions to American Anthropology and History* **9**, No. 45. Carnegie Institution of Washington.

Orchard, W. C.
1920   Sandals and other fabrics from Kentucky caves.

Indian Notes and Monographs. New York: Museum of the American Indian, Heye Foundation.

Otten, C. M., and L. L. Flory

1964 Blood typing of Chilean mummy tissue: A new approach. *American Journal of Physical Anthropology* **21**: 283–285.

Parmalee, P.

1965 The food economy of Archaic and Woodland people at the Tick Creek Cave site, Missouri. *The Missouri Archaeologist* **27**: 1–34.

Parmalee, P. W., A. A. Paloumpis, and N. Wilson

1972 Animals utilized by Woodland peoples occupying the Apple Creek site, Illinois. *Illinois State Museum Reports of Investigations*, No. 23 (Illinois Valley Archaeological Program Research Papers, Vol. 5).

Pond, A. W.

1935 Report of preliminary survey of important archaeological discovery at Mammoth Cave, Kentucky. *Wisconsin Archeologist* **15**: 27–35.

1937 Lost John of Mummy Ledge. *Natural History* **39**: 176–184.

1938 Death posed a tableau. *University of Chicago Magazine*, June: 7–9, 24.

Powell, R. L.

1968 The geology and geomorphology of Wyandotte Cave, Crawford County, Indiana. *Proceedings of the Indiana Academy of Science for 1967* **77**: 236–244.

Putnam, F. W.

1875 Archaeological researches in Kentucky and Indiana. *Proceedings of the Boston Society of Natural History for 1874–1875* **17**: 314–332.

1876 List of additions to the Museum. In *8th annual report of the trustees of the Museum of American Archaeology and Ethnology* **1**, 1868–1876: 47–50.

Randall, M. E.

1971 Comment on "The limited nutritional value of cannibalism." *American Anthropologist* **73**: 269.

Redman, C. L.

1969 Context and stratigraphy: The need for observations. Unpublished Master's thesis, Univ. of Chicago.

Robbins, L. M.

1971 A Woodland "mummy" from Salts Cave, Kentucky. *American Antiquity* **36**: 200–206.

Schoenwetter, J.

1964 Pollen studies in southern Illinois. Manuscript report submitted to M. L. Fowler, Southern Illinois University.

Schoenwetter, J.

1966 Pollen studies in the Apple Creek area. Manuscript report submitted to Stuart Struever, Northwestern University (revised from 1964 manuscript).

1970 Archaeological pollen studies of the Colorado Plateau. *American Antiquity* **35**: 35–48.

in prep. Pollen analysis of sediments from the Koster site.

Schwartz, D. W.

1958a Sandals and textiles from Mammoth Cave National Park. Manuscript, Mammoth Cave National Park Library, Mammoth Cave, Kentucky.

1958b Archaeological report on materials in the John M. Nelson collection from Mammoth Cave National Park Library, Mammoth Cave, Kentucky.

1958c An archaeological report on physical remains from Mammoth Cave National Park. Manuscript, Mammoth Cave National Park Library, Mammoth Cave, Kentucky.

1958d Summary and evaluation of the 1916 American Museum archaeological work in Mammoth Cave National Park. Manuscript, Mammoth Cave National Park Library, Mammoth Cave, Kentucky.

1958e Description and analysis of museum materials from Mammoth Cave National Park. Manuscript, Mammoth Cave National Park Library, Mammoth Cave, Kentucky.

1958f Archaeological survey of Mammoth Cave National Park. Manuscript, Mammoth Cave National Park Library, Mammoth Cave, Kentucky.

1958g Report on two radiocarbon dates from Mammoth Cave National Park Library, Mammoth Cave, Kentucky.

1960 Prehistoric man in Mammoth Cave. *Scientific American* **203**: 130–140.

1965 Prehistoric man in Mammoth Cave. *Eastern National Park and Moment Association, Interpretative Series*, No. 2

Schwartz, D. W., and T. C. Sloan

1960 Archaeological base map and survey of Mammoth Cave National Park. Manuscript, Mammoth Cave National Park Library, Mammoth Cave, Kentucky.

Semenov, S. A.

1964 *Prehistoric technology: An experimental study of the oldest tools and artefacts from traces of manufacture and wear.* Translation and preface by M. W. Thompson. London: Cory, Adams, and Mackay. [Russian original, 1957.]

Sides, S. D.

1971 Early cave exploration in Flint Ridge, Kentucky: Colossal Cave and the Colossal Cavern Company. *Journal of Spelean History* **4**, No. 4:63–74.

Skinner, A. B.

1919 An ancient Algonkian fishing village at Cayuga, New York. *Indian Notes and Monographs* **2**: 43–57. New York: Museum of the American Indian, Heye Foundation.

Smith, D.
n.d.   Surface survey and test excavation of areas adjacent to Salts Cave Sink. Manuscript report submitted to P. J. Watson, Washington University, St. Louis.

Snow, C. E.
1948   Indian Knoll skeletons. *University of Kentucky Reports in Anthropology* **4**, No. 3: Part 2.

Stansbery, D. H.
1966   Utilization of naiads by prehistoric man in the Ohio Valley. *Annual Report for 1966 of the American Malacological Union*: 41–43.

Stelle, J. P.
1864   *The Wyandotte Cave of Crawford County, Indiana.* Cincinnati: Moore, Wilstach, and Baldwin.

Swift, G.
n.d.   Description and analysis of stone tools from excavations in Salts Cave Vestibule. Manuscript report submitted to P. J. Watson, Washington University, St. Louis.

Tsukada, M.
1964   Pollen morphology and identification. II: Cactaceae. *Pollen et Spores* **6**: 45–84.
1967   Chenopod and amaranth pollen: Electron-microscopic identification. *Science* **157**: 80–82.

Van Cleave, H. J., and J. A. Ross
1947   A method of reclaiming dried zoological specimens. *Science* **105**: 319.

Vayda, A. P.
1970   On the nutritional value of cannibalism. *American Anthropologist* **72**: 1462.

Veldman, D. J.
1967   *FORTRAN programming for the behavioral sciences.* New York: Holt.

Walens, S., and R. Wagner
1971   Pigs, proteins, and people-eaters. *American Anthropologist* **73**: 269–270.

Watson, E. H., and G. H. Lowery
1962   *Growth and development of children.* 4th ed. Year Book Medical Publishers.

Watson, P. J.
1969   Woven slippers and other fabrics. In The prehistory of Salts Cave, Kentucky, by P. J. Watson *et al.. Illinois State Museum Reports of Investigations*, No. 16.
1970   Paleofecal specimens from Salts Cave, Mammoth Cave National Park, Kentucky: Analyses and implications. Revised version of a paper presented at the 35th annual meeting of the Society for American Archaeology in Mexico City, April 30 to May 2, 1970.

Watson, P. J., *et al.*
1969   The prehistory of Salts Cave, Kentucky. *Illinois State Museum Reports of Investigations*, No. 16.

Watson, P. J., and R. A. Yarnell
1966   Archaeological and paleoethnobotanical investigations in Salts Cave, Mammoth Cave National Park, Kentucky. *American Antiquity* **31**: 842–849.

Watt, B. K., and A. L. Merrill
1963   *Composition of foods.* Agriculture Handbook, No. 18. Washington D. C.: United States Department of Agriculture.

Watts, W. A.
1971   Postglacial and interglacial vegetation history of southern Georgia and central Florida. *Ecology* **52**: 676–690.

Webb, T., III, and R. A. Bryson
1972   Late and postglacial climatic change in the northern Midwest, U.S.A.: Quantitative estimates derived from fossil pollen spectra by multivariate statistical analysis. *Quarternary Research* **2**: 70–115.

Webb, W. S.
1946   Indian Knoll, site Oh 2, Ohio County, Kentucky. *University of Kentucky Reports in Anthropology* **4**, No. 3: Part 1.
1950a The Carlson Annis Mound, site 5, Butler County, Kentucky. *University of Kentucky Reports in Anthropology* **7**, No. 4.
1950b The Read shell midden, site 10, Butler County, Kentucky. *University of Kentucky Reports in Anthropology* **7**, No. 5.
1951   Radiocarbon dating on samples from the Southeast. In *Radiocarbon Dating,* edited by F. Johnson. Washington, D. C.: Society for American Archaeology, Memoir 8.

Webb, W. S., and W. D. Funkhouser
1930   The Page site in Logan County, Kentucky. *University of Kentucky Reports in Archaeology and Anthropology* **1**, No. 3.
1932   Archaeological survey of Kentucky. *University of Kentucky Reports in Archaeology and Anthropology* **2**.
1936   Rock shelters in Menifee County, Kentucky. *University of Kentucky Reports in Archaeology and Anthropology* **3**, No. 4.

Webb, W. S., and W. S. Haag
1939   The Chiggerville site, site 1, Ohio County, Kentucky. *University of Kentucky Reports in Anthropology* **4**, No. 1.

Webb, W. S., and C. E. Snow
1945   The Adena people. *University of Kentucky Reports in Anthropology and Archaeology* **6**.

Wells, C.
1960   A study of cremation. *Antiquity* **34**: 29–37.
1964   *Bones, bodies, and disease.* New York: Praeger.

Whitaker, T. A., and H. C. Cutler
1971   Prehistoric cucurbits from the Valley of Oaxaca. *Economic Botany* **25**: 123–127.

White, T. E.
  1953   A method of calculating the dietary percentage of various food animals utilized by aboriginal peoples. *American Antiquity* **18**: 396–398.

Willoughby, C. C.
  1922   The Turner group of earthworks, Hamilton County, Ohio. *Papers of the Peabody Museum of American Archaeology and Ethnology* **8**, No. 3.

Wolpoff, M. H.
  1971   Metric trends in hominid dental evolution. *Case Western Reserve University Studies in Anthropology* No. 2.

Wright, H. E., Jr.
  1970   Late Quaternary vegetational history of North America. In *Late Cenozoic glacial ages*, edited by K. K. Turekian. New Haven, Connecticut: Yale Univ. Press.

Yarnell, R. A.
  1964   Aboriginal relationships between culture and plant life in the Upper Great Lakes region. *Anthropological Papers, Museum of Anthropology, University of Michigan* **23**.

Yarnell, R. A.
  1969   Contents of human paleofeces. In *The prehistory of Salts Cave, Kentucky*, by P. J. Watson *et al.* Illinois State Museum Reports of Investigations, No. 16.
  1972   *Iva annua* var. *macrocarpa:* Extinct American cultigen? *American Anthropologist* **74**: 335–341.

Young, Col. B. H.
  1897   "Rivals the Mammoth in Grandeur", *Louisville Courier-Journal*, Section 3, August 15, 1897: 1.
  1910   *The prehistoric men of Kentucky*. Filson Club Publications, No. 25. Louisville: John P. Morton.

Zimmerman, M. R.
  1972   Preservation of blood cells in a 2000 year old mummy. Paper presented at the national meeting of American Association of Physical Anthropologists, March, 1972, in Lawrence, Kansas.
  1973   Blood cells preserved in a mummy 2000 years old. *Science* 180:303–304.

Project Bibliography

Publications

1962 Benington, Frederick, Carl Melton, and Patty Jo Watson
Carbon dating prehistoric soot from Salts Cave, Kentucky. *American Antiquity* **28**: 238–241.

1966 Ehman, Michael F.
Cane torches as cave illumination. *NSS News* **24**: 34–36.

1966 Watson, Patty Jo
Preliminary report: archeological and paleoethno-botanical investigations in Salts Cave, Mammoth Cave National Park, Kentucky. *NSS News* **24**: 177.

1966 Watson, Patty Jo
Prehistoric miners of Salts Cave, Kentucky. *Archaeology* **19**: 237–243.

1966 Watson, Patty Jo, and Richard A. Yarnell
Archeological and paleoethnobotanical investigations in Salts Cave National Park, Kentucky. *American Antiquity* **31**: 842–849.

1967 Hall, Robert L.
Archaeology by lamplight: an exploration of Salts Cave, Kentucky. *The Living Museum* **28**: 84–85.

1968 Crane, H. R., and J. B. Griffin
University of Michigan radiocarbon dates XII. *Radiocarbon* **10**: 61–114.

1969 Watson, Patty Jo
Archeological investigations in Salts Cave, Mammoth Cave National Park, Kentucky. *Proceedings of the IVth International Congress of Speleology in Yugoslavia* (12–26 September 1965) **4–5**: 403–407.

1969 Watson, Patty Jo *et al.*
The prehistory of Salts Cave, Kentucky. *Illinois State Museum, Reports of Investigations* No. 16.

1969 Yarnell, Richard A.
Paleo-ethnobotany in America. In *Science and archaeology*, 2nd ed., edited by D. Brothwell and E. Higgs. London: Thames and Hudson.

1971 Robbins, Louise M.
A Woodland "mummy" from Salts Cave, Kentucky. *American Antiquity* **36**: 200–206.

1973 Zimmerman, Michael L.
Blood cells preserved in a mummy 2000 years old. *Science* **180**: 303–304.

1973 Freeman, J. P., G. L. Smith, T. L. Poulson, P. J. Watson, and W. B. White
Lee Cave, Mammoth Cave National Park, Kentucky. *National Speleological Society Bulletin* **35**: 109–126.

Papers Read at Professional Meetings

1965 Watson, Patty Jo, and Richard A. Yarnell
Archeological and paleoethnobotanical investigations in Salts Cave, Mammoth Cave National Park, Kentucky. Thirtieth Annual Meeting of the Society for American Archaeology in Urbana, Illinois, May 6–8, 1965.

1965 Watson, Patty Jo
Archeological Investigations in Salts Cave, Mammoth Cave National Park, Kentucky. Fourth International Congress of Speleology in Llubjana, Yugoslavia, 12–26 September, 1965.

1967   Yarnell, Richard A., and Patty Jo Watson
       The prehistoric utilization of Salts Cave, Kentucky.
       Thirty-second Annual Meeting of the Society for
       American Archaeology in Ann Arbor, Michigan,
       4—6 May, 1967.
1969   Freeman, John P., Gordon Smith, Thomas L.
       Poulson, Patty Jo Watson, and William B. White
       Lee Cave, Mammoth Cave National Park, Ken-
       tucky. Annual Meeting of the American Associa-
       tion for the Advancement of Science, 27 December,
       1969.
1970   Watson, Patty Jo, and Richard A. Yarnell
       Human paleofeces from Salts Cave, Kentucky.
       Paper contributed to a symposium on coprolite
       analysis organized by Eric Callen and Lewis
       Napton for the thirty-fifth Annual Meeting of the
       Society for American Archaeology in Mexico City,
       30 April—2 May, 1970.
1970   Robbins, Louise M.
         A woodland "mummy" from Salts Cave, Ken-
       tucky. Thirty-fifth Annual Meeting of the Society
       for American Archaeology in Mexico City, 30 April—
       2 May, 1970.
1971   Yarnell, Richard A.
       Flotation plant remains from Salts Cave, Kentucky.
       Seventieth Annual Meeting of the American Anthro-
       pological Association in New York, November, 1971.
1972   Zimmerman, Michael R.
       Preservation of blood cells in a 2000 year old
       mummy. National Meeting of the American Associa-
       tion of Physical Anthropologists in Lawrence,
       Kansas, March, 1972.
1972   Watson, Patty Jo
       Archeology of the Mammoth Cave Area. Thirty-
       seventh Annual Meeting of the Society for American
       Archaeology in Bal Harbour, Florida, 4—6 May,
       1972.

Other

1969   Redman, Charles L.
       Context and stratigraphy: the need for observa-
       tions. Master's thesis, University of Chicago.
1970   Watson, Patty Jo, ed.
       National Geographic Society—Cave Research
       Foundation Salts Cave Archeological Project,
       Mammoth Cave National Park. Interim Report,
       May, 1970.
1971   Watson, Patty Jo, ed.
       National Geographic Society—Cave Research
       Foundation Salts Cave Archeological Project,
       Mammoth Cave National Park. Interim Report,
       July, 1971.
n.d.   Brucker, Roger W.
       Search for the way down. Manuscript report sub-
       mitted to P. J. Watson, Washington University, St.
       Louis.
n.d.   Cowan, Wesley
       Examination of flint waste materials from Salts
       Sink, Mammoth Cave National Park, Kentucky.
       Manuscript submitted to Lathel Duffield, University
       of Kentucky, Lexington.
n.d.   Smith, David
       Surface survey and test excavation of areas adjacent
       to Salts Cave Sink. Manuscript report submitted to
       P. J. Watson, Washington University, St. Louis.
n.d.   Swift, Gregory
       Description and analysis of stone tools from ex-
       cavations in Salts Cave Vestibule. Manuscript report
       submitted to P. J. Watson, Washington University,
       St. Louis.

Subject Index